THE
COMPLETE
BOOK OF
SAILING

THE
COMPLETE
BOOK OF
SAILING

A
GUIDE TO BOATS,
EQUIPMENT, TIDES
& WEATHER,
BASIC, ADVANCED &
COMPETITION SAILING

BOB BOND, JONATHAN CLARK,
BRIAN GRANT, ADRIAN MORGAN,
DAVID PELLY

HAMLYN

First published in 1990 by
The Hamlyn Publishing Group Limited,
a division of the Octopus Publishing Group,
Michelin House, 81 Fulham Road,
London SW3 6RB

ISBN 0 600 56913 6

Produced by Mandarin Offset
Printed and bound in Hong Kong

FOREWORD

No single publication can hope to cover every aspect or specific interest of a sport as complex as sailing, so what we have done as writers, photographers, designers and editors is to put together a book that highlights the principal aspects of the sport as it exists today.

One of the great attractions of sailing is that the sailboat is a 'vehicle' to be used as the owner sees fit. One day it can be a racing machine, the next a platform for a family picnic, the next a way to whisk the occupants to a distant shore. It is this freedom and diversity of use that attracts so many people to boating in general and sailboating in particular.

The traditional pattern of first 'learning the ropes' in a small dinghy, and then graduating to a larger dayboat or cruiser racer, has been eroded in recent years by an influx into the sport of sailors in their twenties and thirties who want to learn from the outset in the type of their choice.

In Europe, a large number of sailing schools has grown up to meet this demand, whereas in the United States very few sailing schools cater for adults, largely because so many young people learn to sail through the many camps, college and sailing club summer programmes, and return to sailing in later years.

Throughout the complicated latticework of sailing skills you will encounter various views, theories and dogma. However, there is no specific 'one way' of doing anything connected with sailing, and what we have presented here are tried and tested methods, devised by experienced practitioners who appreciate that each sailor is unique and will develop his or her own peculiar methods of sailing and sailboat management.

Whatever your experience and skill level, I hope that you will find something in the book that will help you enjoy your sailing to the full.

BOB BOND

CONTENTS

EQUIPMENT

When you first start sailing you accept that the boat, its gear and its fittings are standardized. In fact, you are usually so busy learning to sail that you don't have much time to think about how the boat is laid out and whether there are alternatives to the multitude of ropes and fittings that you have to learn to use.

Later on, when you have more experience, or if you happen to visit a chandler's shop or look at a catalogue of sailboat equipment, you will begin to realize that many inventive minds have been applied to devising many alternatives for each piece of equipment. This section sets out the basics of each of the principal equipment groupings and gives just a few of the many alternatives.

Just a quick flip through the pages of any sailing publication will show that there are hundreds of different boat designs and thousands of marine businesses, each with its own specialist products, servicing the sailboat market.

Sailing clothing, for example, has been developed to the point where materials and designs are so good that manufacturers have moved into the 'designer' market to encourage colour-coordinated crews and the use of pastel shades for dinghy and inshore use. Offshore clothing now incorporates dayglow colours and reflective strips so that the wearer can be seen easily both day and night.

Unless you come into sailing by first building your own boat, you will not normally need to worry too much about the choice or construction of equipment until you have sufficient sailing experience and the mechanical and design skills to change the way your boat is rigged, or until you have to replace broken or worn equipment. It is at this point that you will appreciate the complexity of the sport and notice the paucity of impartial hard advice available.

Masts and booms are usually made of an aluminium alloy and come in a range of shapes. Recent developments include in-mast or in-boom mainsail furling systems to make sail handling simpler and safer without a dramatic loss of sailing performance. Sails for most applications are made of woven synthetics. It is only the racing sector which has moved into the exotic sheet and film products which give short-lived advantages.

Ropes have improved as synthetic fibres have been developed for specific applications. Characteristics such as stretch, wear, grip and feel are listed in manufacturers' catalogues to enable the rope purchaser to make a satisfactory choice when replacing or buying new. This readily-available information is especially important to the owners of racing dinghies, because many classes have opened up their class rules to permit a multiplicity of sail and rig controls.

On dinghies, the development of 'muscle boxes', which are essentially miniaturized versions of the multi-purchase tackles, have been matched on larger boats by the introduction of the self-tailing winch. The standard winch requires two people, the wincher and the tailer, to operate it, but the self-tailing winch is operated by one person and virtually eliminates the dreaded 'riding turn' which immobilizes the standard winch. In anchoring, the most significant developments have been the introduction of the one-piece Bruce anchor and the return to the vertical windlass, usually electric, to replace the mechanical anchor-chain handling systems.

Protecting a wooden boat requires the frequent application of a bewildering array of paints and varnishes, but plastic hulls may need to be repainted only every fifteen or twenty years, and only the antifouling and the wooden trim need to be attended to on an annual basis. Environmental concerns have led to the widespread banning of harmful tributyl tin derivatives as antifouling agents, and forced a return to the traditional copper-based products, but most boatowners have been pleased with the results.

It is a well-known fact that diesel engines thrive on hard work, but until the revolution in shipboard electronics most sailboat diesels died of neglect and lack of use. The increased requirements for electrical power to drive the extensive electrical and electronic systems of boats have made frequent engine use essential, to keep the batteries charged, and brought about the development of more efficient alternators and batteries. In addition, the engines themselves are smaller and lighter because of the developments that have taken place in the automotive industry.

The electronic instruments can do almost everything the human navigator can, and more in some cases, but the important thing to remember is that they are all merely aids to navigation and when it comes down to the wire it is the ability of skipper and crew that counts most.

Nowhere is the importance of this ability more evident than in the area of safety where, despite the increasing array of sophisticated equipment designed to rescue or save, it is still better not to abandon your boat until you can step *up* into the liferaft.

PARTS OF A BOAT

The language of the sea and seafarers is so intermingled with the English language that you will have no difficulty recognizing many of the terms used in sailing, but many others may be new to you.

In plan view, most boats have a pointed front end and a squared-off back end. A few have two pointed ends and others have two squared-off ends, but no matter what shape it is the front of any boat is called the *bow* and the back is the *stern*.

The sides of the boat are identified by facing the bow: The *port* side is to the left and the *starboard* side is to the right. When sailing, all objects appearing on the left side of the boat are described as being *to port*, those on the right *to starboard*.

Ahead, abeam and *astern* mean in front, to the side and behind the boat, and *fore* and *aft* mean at or toward the front and the rear respectively. The *beam* of a boat is its width, measured at its widest point, and its *length overall* is the length from the most forward part of the bow to the most rearward part of the stern.

The *hull* is the main body of a boat, and the dividing line between the part below the water and the part above it is the *waterline*. The hull above the line is the *topsides* and the vertical measurement from the waterline to the *gunwale* (or *gunnel*) where the sides join the deck is referred to as the *freeboard*; that below the line is the *underbody*. The bow and stern usually extend ahead of and behind the waterline, and this gives *bow and stern overhangs*.

Everything mounted on the deck to handle the sails or anchors is the *deck hardware*, and it includes the mast and boom that support the sails. On most boats the mast is held in place by wires called *standing rigging*. The ropes and wires used to hoist, lower and control the sails are called the *running rigging*.

At the stern of the boat the *rudder*, which helps to steer it, is controlled by a *tiller* or, on many cruisers, a *wheel*. Beneath the hull, there is a *centreboard*, a *daggerboard* or a *keel* to prevent the boat from drifting sideways when under sail.

The *forefoot* is the underwater angle of the bow as it curves back to the keel (or, on some boats, the keels). The back corner of the keel is the *heel* and the front is often referred to as the *foot* or *forefoot*. The front face is the *leading edge* and the back the *trailing edge*.

DINGHIES

The typical dinghy is a relatively small, open sailboat with a single mast. The smaller dinghies, such as the Laser and the Optimist, have unstayed (self-supporting) masts, but the larger boats have stayed masts held in place by wires (the shrouds and the forestay). A dinghy has no fixed keel, but uses an adjustable board — a pivoting centreboard or a sliding daggerboard — that functions as a keel to give lateral stability. There are some large, dinghy-like boats, such as the Flying Fifteen, that have keels instead of boards; these are called keelboats.

RIGGING

The ropes and wires used to raise, lower and control the sails are called the running rigging. This includes the halyards, which raise and lower the sails, and the sheets, which adjust and

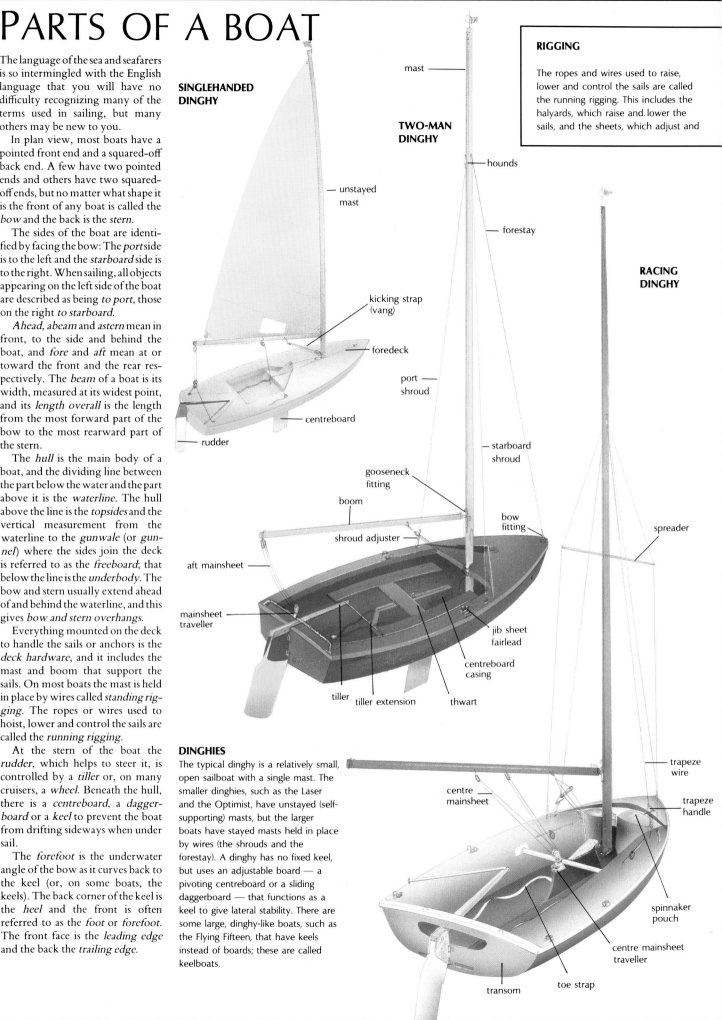

SINGLEHANDED DINGHY

— unstayed mast

kicking strap (vang)

foredeck

centreboard

rudder

TWO-MAN DINGHY

mast

hounds

forestay

port shroud

starboard shroud

gooseneck fitting

boom

bow fitting

shroud adjuster

aft mainsheet

mainsheet traveller

jib sheet fairlead

centreboard casing

tiller   tiller extension   thwart

RACING DINGHY

spreader

trapeze wire

trapeze handle

centre mainsheet

spinnaker pouch

centre mainsheet traveller

transom   toe strap

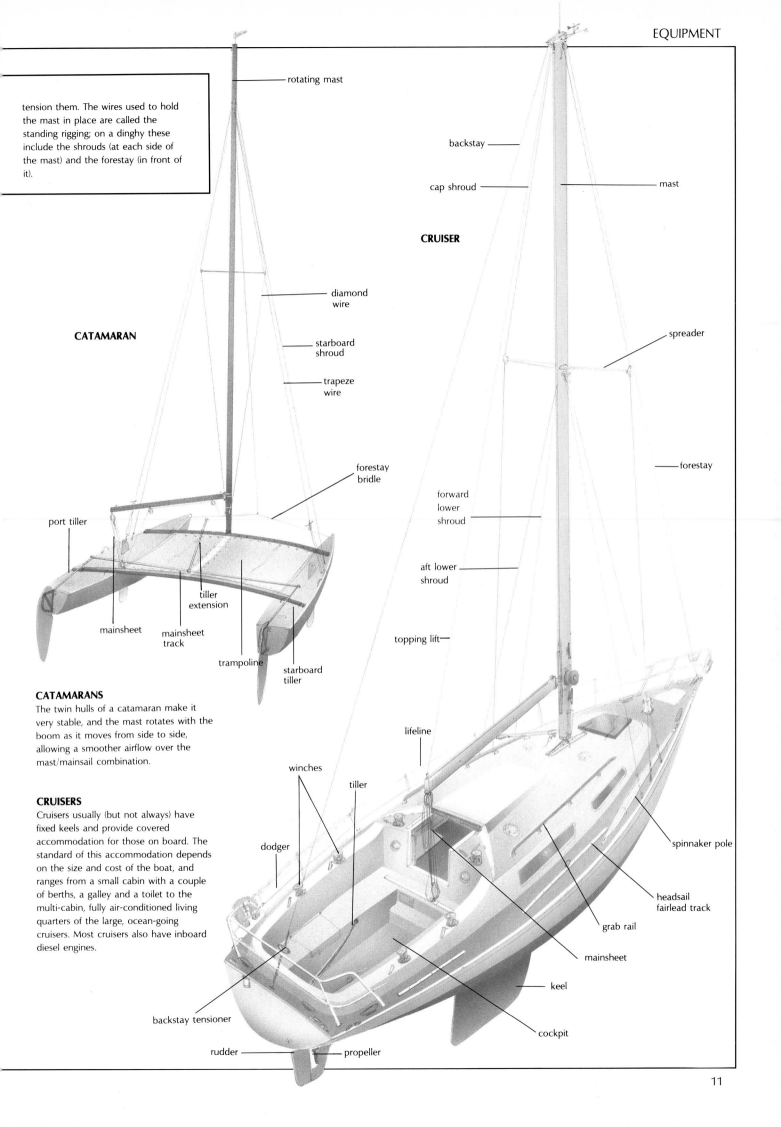

tension them. The wires used to hold the mast in place are called the standing rigging; on a dinghy these include the shrouds (at each side of the mast) and the forestay (in front of it).

rotating mast

backstay

cap shroud

mast

CRUISER

diamond wire

spreader

CATAMARAN

starboard shroud

trapeze wire

forestay

forestay bridle

forward lower shroud

port tiller

aft lower shroud

topping lift

tiller extension

mainsheet

mainsheet track

trampoline

starboard tiller

lifeline

CATAMARANS
The twin hulls of a catamaran make it very stable, and the mast rotates with the boom as it moves from side to side, allowing a smoother airflow over the mast/mainsail combination.

winches

tiller

CRUISERS
Cruisers usually (but not always) have fixed keels and provide covered accommodation for those on board. The standard of this accommodation depends on the size and cost of the boat, and ranges from a small cabin with a couple of berths, a galley and a toilet to the multi-cabin, fully air-conditioned living quarters of the large, ocean-going cruisers. Most cruisers also have inboard diesel engines.

dodger

spinnaker pole

headsail fairlead track

grab rail

mainsheet

keel

backstay tensioner

cockpit

rudder

propeller

11

SAILS

Sail design and cutting are now the province of the computer and laser, yet the end product, especially in the shape and distribution of the panels, is almost a work of art.

In the past, sails had to be constructed from whatever materials were to hand, such as skins, flax, cotton, bamboo, coconut fibre or jute. Whatever the material, all sails suffered from stretch and shrinkage and most let the air seep through, which adversely affected the sail's efficiency.

As racing became more popular, the older, heavier flax and canvas sails gave way to lighter, more closely-woven Egyptian cotton sails which, though prone to stretching and rot, nevertheless offered distinct advantages when new.

Because the huge gaff mainsails were woven in narrow panels, the sailmakers had, of necessity, to construct them with the panels running vertically. The seams then were, in effect, the supporting structure.

These vertical-cut headsails soon distorted, and it was found that the *mitre cut* helped to maintain the original design shape of the sail. Panels were arranged at right angles to the leech and foot, and met at a mitre line which ran from the clew to intersect the luff at an approximate right angle.

Because the strains in a sail come from every direction, all woven sailcloths suffer from excess stretch, especially on the bias at 45 degrees to the warp and the weft (or fill) of the cloth. You can see this for yourself when you pull on the opposite corners of a woven square of cloth. The creases run diagonally and create considerable distortion in the shape of the cloth.

In the quest for materials that would maintain their designed shape, synthetic yarns eventually replaced natural fibres. Dacron and Terylene were adopted for mainsails and headsails, nylon for spinnakers. The latest materials are non-woven sheets of plastic, for example Mylar with a woven backing of Kevlar to assist stability. Mylar and Kevlar are both every efficient but are short-lived, especially when used for racing.

It is the designer's job to create a sail for certain wind speeds and to arrange the panels in such a way that the final shape is as designed. This is achieved by arranging the cloths in the sail so that the air pressure loads act on the warp, the weft or the bias to produce the required shape in the windspeed for which the sail was designed.

After the designer has calculated the stresses and arranged the panels, most sail lofts (factories) use a computer-controlled laser cutter to shape the panels so that, when they are sewn together and placed on the mast and boom, they form an aerofoil shape which can be modified by sail controls to make it flatter for heavy winds and fuller for lighter winds.

The roach (curved area) of the leech has to be supported by stiffeners known as battens. The leech of the sail falls off (twists) between the clew and the head, and controlling the degree of leech twist is the function of the mainsheet and boom vang. Overtighten them and the leech will curve to windward, slowing the boat; ease them too far and the leech will sag off, destroying the sail's shape and depowering it. The luff is tightened by the halyard or Cunningham tackle, the foot by an outhaul or a flattening reef.

Luff tension in a headsail is controlled by a halyard tensioner on small boats and additionally by a backstay on keelboats. Foot and

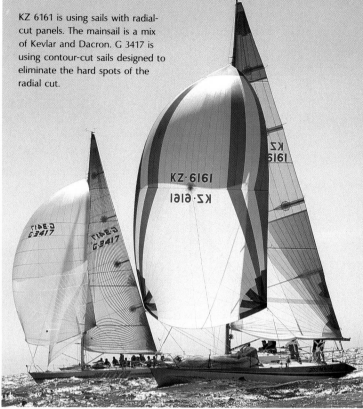

KZ 6161 is using sails with radial-cut panels. The mainsail is a mix of Kevlar and Dacron. G 3417 is using contour-cut sails designed to eliminate the hard spots of the radial cut.

leech tension are controlled by the sheet. Varying the sheeting position can tighten the foot and open the leech, apply equal tension to both foot and leech, or tension the leech to give a fuller sail.

The person who controls the shape of the sail on a boat is the *trimmer*. On dinghies this is the crew's job, and on larger boats there may be different trimmers for headsails, mainsail and spinnakers. Whatever the boat, it is the trimmer's job to adjust the shape of the sail to suit the windspeed and then to fine-tune it to the constant changes of angle and speed.

Spinnakers are usually made of rip-stop nylon, which has a natural tendency to stretch and recover. As with other sails, different weights of cloth (measured in ounces per measured yard) are used for different windspeeds. The lightest 'gossamer' cloths, of about half an ounce, are used in the lightest of winds, but for a 30-foot boat, cloths of $1\frac{1}{2}$ ounces will be suitable for most sailing conditions.

Spinnaker designers have produced a range of specialized sail types, each with different characteristics determined by the design of the cloth panels. The vertical (radial) cut produces a sail which lifts well but has a tendency to spread at the foot. The horizontal cut is used for light-weather sails which spread well, and the star cut produces a strong-wind reaching sail which remains very stable.

The tri-radial, which is a combination of all three cuts, is an all-round sail with good handling and power characteristics, while the radial head is a broad-shouldered, lighter-weather sail that can also be used for light-air reaching.

Mainsails have to operate in a wide range of wind speeds and need to be long-lived. For a 30-footer, a $5\frac{1}{2}$-ounce cloth would be the norm, with doubled panels for the uppermost section, and three sets of reef points will allow the sail to be used in winds of up to 35 or 40 knots.

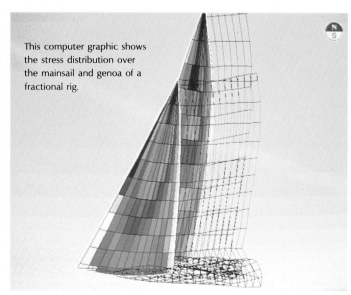

This computer graphic shows the stress distribution over the mainsail and genoa of a fractional rig.

This 3-panel, horizontal-cut Optimist sail sets perfectly on the hard-to-trim-spritsail rig.

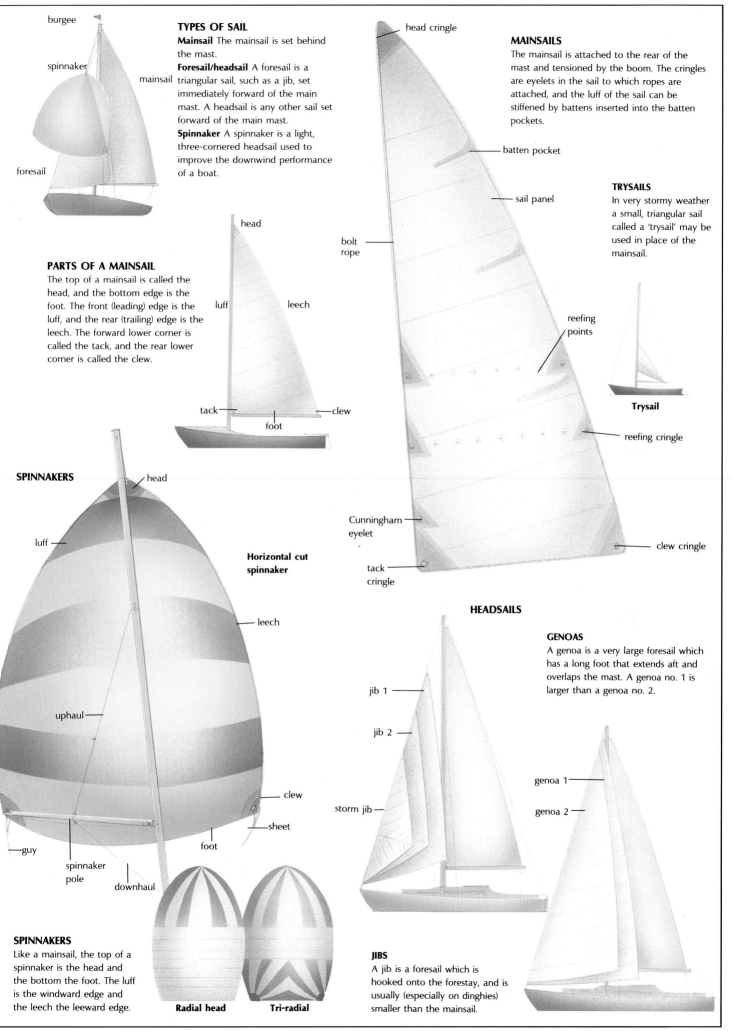

burgee

spinnaker

mainsail

foresail

TYPES OF SAIL
Mainsail The mainsail is set behind the mast.
Foresail/headsail A foresail is a triangular sail, such as a jib, set immediately forward of the main mast. A headsail is any other sail set forward of the main mast.
Spinnaker A spinnaker is a light, three-cornered headsail used to improve the downwind performance of a boat.

head cringle

MAINSAILS
The mainsail is attached to the rear of the mast and tensioned by the boom. The cringles are eyelets in the sail to which ropes are attached, and the luff of the sail can be stiffened by battens inserted into the batten pockets.

batten pocket

sail panel

TRYSAILS
In very stormy weather a small, triangular sail called a 'trysail' may be used in place of the mainsail.

bolt rope

head

PARTS OF A MAINSAIL
The top of a mainsail is called the head, and the bottom edge is the foot. The front (leading) edge is the luff, and the rear (trailing) edge is the leech. The forward lower corner is called the tack, and the rear lower corner is called the clew.

luff

leech

reefing points

tack

clew

foot

Trysail

reefing cringle

SPINNAKERS

head

Cunningham eyelet

tack cringle

clew cringle

luff

Horizontal cut spinnaker

HEADSAILS

leech

GENOAS
A genoa is a very large foresail which has a long foot that extends aft and overlaps the mast. A genoa no. 1 is larger than a genoa no. 2.

uphaul

jib 1

jib 2

clew

sheet

genoa 1

storm jib

genoa 2

foot

guy

spinnaker pole

downhaul

Radial head   **Tri-radial**

SPINNAKERS
Like a mainsail, the top of a spinnaker is the head and the bottom the foot. The luff is the windward edge and the leech the leeward edge.

JIBS
A jib is a foresail which is hooked onto the forestay, and is usually (especially on dinghies) smaller than the mainsail.

MASTS & BOOMS

A keel-stepped mast with deck seal and gaiter. Crash bars give protection to the crew, and the spinnaker pole is stowed on the mast.

The mast and boom form the supporting structure for most sails. Generally speaking, only the most exotic racing machines can exploit the state-of-the-art developments which have taken place. The majority of owners have to be content with the standard oversize (for safety) sections which can be produced in quantity. Wood, aluminium and carbonfibre are the most frequently used materials, aluminium being the normal choice, and the standard mast cross-section is elliptical, with an integral luff groove at its trailing edge.

The hollow spars (a collective term for masts, booms and other sail-supporting structures) are initially formed by extruding aluminium under immense pressure through a shaped die. Mast makers buy in a range of extruded sections, and then fabricate each mast to a set of precise design specifications. Where large spar sections cannot be extruded, they are fabricated from rolled panels which are glued, welded or riveted into the appropriate shape.

One of the first considerations of the mast designer is the bend characteristics of the finished spar. The bend of a mast is measured in the fore-and-aft plane, and can be quite considerable: up to three feet in some fractionally-rigged racing craft.

Pre-bend is the amount of bend placed in a mast when the main shrouds are tightened. This is achieved by angling the spreaders back and fixing them rigidly in position. Once the sails are rigged, the amount of draft (aerofoil shape) in the sail can be increased by straightening the mast to make the sails fuller, or decreased by bending the mast to make the sails flatter.

The rake of the mast forward or behind the vertical helps determine the amount of weather helm (tendency to turn into the wind) the boat carries. Foward rake, used when downwind sailing, decreases it, backward rake, used in upwind sailing, increases it. The backstay tensioner controls mast rake, and the mainsheet, boom vang and backstay all influence mast bend.

Athwartships (transverse) bend or sag of the mast is eliminated by the wires supporting it. In a typical cruiser there is a single spreader, about midway between the deck and the jib sheave (pulley), which carries the main shroud. The inboard end of the spreader is called the root, and any intermediate or lower shrouds are attached just below the spreader roots. Two shrouds on each side, led about two feet forward and aft of the mast, help support the bottom half of it. An inner forestay prevents the mast popping backward if the mast flexes 'out of column' in a seaway.

The multi-spreader rigs used on offshore racing boats use very thin mast sections which rely totally on an intricate web of supporting wires for their strength and stability.

When fabricating a spar, the mast maker carries out a series of standard operations and a limited number of custom options. Most dinghy spars have tapered top ends achieved by cutting a V-shaped section from the leading edge, and compressing the spar to be welded and then profiled with a grinder. Offshore racing boats and some cruiser/racers also have tapered spars.

Current practice is to attach all shrouds and stays internally, using specially-developed captive T-bars and in-mast terminals in an effort to cut down the considerable windage created by external tangs and toggles. The spinnaker pole track is mounted on the leading edge of the mast, and the gooseneck that holds the boom is on the trailing edge.

Halyards, control lines and electric and electronic instrument cables must all be carried inside the masts of larger boats. Conduits are provided within the mast to ensure that the halyards and electrics are kept apart. Special moulded alloy or fabricated stainless steel sheave boxes are incorporated into the masthead and halyard exit points. The masthead is also the mounting base for wind instruments, the tri-colour navigation light and the VHF aerial, and can become very cluttered, while the foot of the mast often resembles a mushroom farm because of the large number of pulley blocks used to disperse the halyards and controls to their destinations via turning blocks and rope stoppers.

Deck-stepped masts are usually mounted on an inverted T-shaped angle. Keel-stepped masts must be chocked tightly at deck level using wedges, and a neoprene gaiter covering the point where the mast passes through the deck prevents water finding its way below.

Booms perform a similar function to masts. They support the foot of the sail and, by use of the boom vang and mainsheet, can be used to control the draft of the sail and the degree of mast bend.

Booms usually have deep cross-sections to combat the excessive bending forces produced by the boom vang and mainsheet. As with masts, exotic racing machines sport booms with lightening holes, cutaway end sections and fabric covering to decrease weight without jeopardizing stiffness. The ordinary cruiser will have a standard oversize boom.

Slab reefing systems require specially fabricated end fittings. Inboard, the reefing lines run through quick-release stoppers, and outboard the reefing lines lead up from their appropriate places on the boom through the reef cringles to pulleys housed in the boom end.

Spinnaker poles are usually circular in section and equipped with specialized end fittings which vary from those of the permanently mast-mounted dipping pole, which has a different fitting at each end, to those of the end-for-end pole which

has identical fittings at each end.

The rapid development of in-mast and in-boom reefing systems has given mast makers the opportunity to produce specially-shaped sections which will accommodate the furled sail within the enlarged luff groove. The sails used with these systems must have hollow-cut leeches because battens cannot be fitted.

Racing multihulls often fit wing masts, which form an integral part of the overall aerofoil shape of the mast/sail combination. Laminated wood, aluminium and carbonfibre are the principal building materials used for these.

The masts and booms of small dinghies, such as the Laser, are generally very simple wooden or alloy structures. Singlehanded, single-sailed boats usually have unstayed masts, with no supporting shrouds or stays, but boats for two or more people, or those that carry more than one sail, have their masts supported by standing rigging comprising a shroud at each side and a forestay attached to the bow.

Above *This keel-stepped 505 rig features a boom with lightening holes, foredeck-mounted mast strut and boom-mounted pole stowage.*
Top right *By contrast the deck-mounted mast of a cruiser racer incorporates a slab-reefing winch, boom vang and halyard winches.*
Right *Another deck-mounted mast, with all halyards led aft via turning blocks at the base of the mast. The boom vang incorporates a spring-loaded strut.*

Above *The outboard end of this dinghy boom is cut away to save weight and incorporates a simple clew outhaul purchase.*
Left *A general view of a spar shop manufacturing a wide range of spars in a variety of sections and lengths.*

ROPES, CLEATS & SHACKLES

The choice of ropes, cleats and shackles facing the yachtsman or dinghy sailor is now wider than ever, but the most important factor to consider when you are buying one of these items is that it should be of the correct style and strength for its intended application. Safe working load figures for these products are available from your chandler or from their manufacturers, so if you know the working loads they will have to cope with, it is easy to choose the correct size when making a purchase. If in doubt, look at what size of rope or shackle is used for the same job on a boat of similar size to your own.

The commonest ropemaking materials are nylon, polyester and polypropylene, and the two principal forms of lay-up (rope structure) are 3-strand and 9-plait. Some ropes have an inner core made of a low-stretch polymer, such as Kevlar, Spectra or Dyneema, and such ropes are commonly used for spinnaker sheets and runner tails.

A basic 3-strand polypropylene rope will float and has good abrasion resistance, and so it is an ideal mooring rope. It is also highly resistant to degradation by sunlight, which enhances its longevity. 3-strand nylon can also be used for mooring ropes and again will float, and it usually has a hairy finish which helps it to knot well. Lightweight 3-strand nylon rope is sometimes used for halyard tails, but it will not withstand high loads.

The range of plaited ropes starts with plaited polypropylene, which is a soft and flexible floating rope that can be used for sheets in small yachts. Multiplait nylon is strong but it stretches, making it unsuitable for sheets. However, since it can readily absorb shock loads, this rope makes an ideal anchor warp.

For most yacht applications a multiplait polyester is the workhorse. There are two main types, one a pre-stretched rope and the other a hard-finish, close-knit braid ('hard finish' means that each strand has a lot of twist).

The pre-stretched type is a good choice for ropes under constant tension, particularly control lines and sheets, and its matt finish makes for ease of handling. The hard-finish braid is a good rope for sheets and halyards, where very low stretch and high strength are needed.

Finally, there are the 'exotics' of which the Kevlar-cored polyester was the first; these ropes have very low stretch but they are expensive. They are most commonly found on racing yachts, where expense is not necessarily a primary consideration,

and their applications include running rigging and control lines. The latest exotic, Dyneema, is specifically designed for high load applications where a rope of very low stretch must turn tight corners.

The function of a cleat is to hold a rope from slipping, and there are three principal designs: the two-armed deck cleat, the cam cleat and the clam cleat. Of these, the deck cleat is the most simple, having no moving parts and merely requiring a rope to be wrapped around it or clove hitched across it to function. This type of cleat is commonly used for securing genoa sheets, halyards and mooring ropes, and is usually made of acetal resin or high magnesium-content aluminium alloy.

The cam cleat has moving jaws that are controlled by a spring and which grip the rope to prevent it slipping. A wide variety of sizes and types of cam cleat are available, and they often have fairleads to aid handling. It is essential that a cam cleat be able to accept the size of rope chosen and that it should be capable of being released under pressure.

This type of cleat is typically used for those control lines which need frequent adjustment. A mainsheet system, for instance, will usually include a cam cleat incorporated into a suitable multiblock system. Cam cleats are also used to secure jib sheets on many yachts of 28 feet or below, as they can provide a quick-acting system.

Clam cleats have no moving parts, the ropes being held in a ribbed slot. These cleats are made of plastic or aluminium, and a variety of sizes is available to suit the rope diameters commonly in use. This type of cleat is ideally suited to securing halyards and control lines such as the kicking strap.

As well as cleats, rope clutches and sheet jammers may be used to secure ropes. Racing yachts commonly have a row of rope clutches on their coachroofs, and sheet jammers are used on genoa sheet turning blocks to allow sheets to be secured when changing sheets.

Shackles come in two main forms, the strip shackle and the polished steel forged shackle. Some shackles are available with captive pins, and these can be useful on main halyards. All shackles are designed to specific breaking loads, and other design points to consider when choosing a shackle are the pin diameter, the width of the shackle and the length. In general terms, strip shackles will be of less practical application on a yacht than will forged shackles, which will be more able to withstand high working loads.

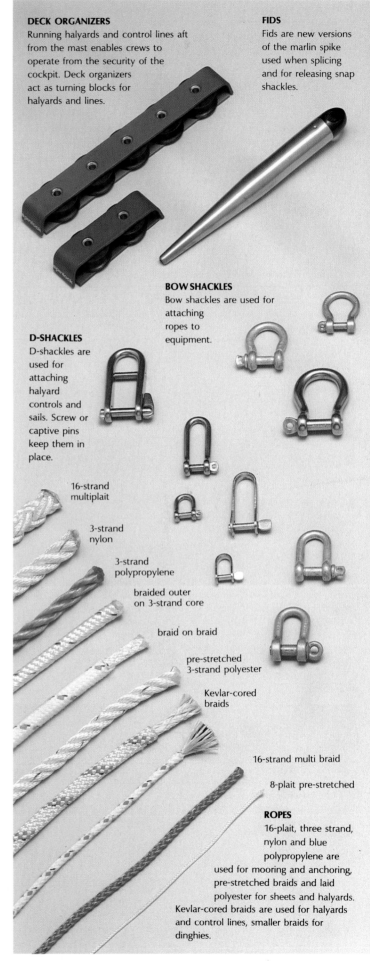

DECK ORGANIZERS
Running halyards and control lines aft from the mast enables crews to operate from the security of the cockpit. Deck organizers act as turning blocks for halyards and lines.

FIDS
Fids are new versions of the marlin spike used when splicing and for releasing snap shackles.

BOW SHACKLES
Bow shackles are used for attaching ropes to equipment.

D-SHACKLES
D-shackles are used for attaching halyard controls and sails. Screw or captive pins keep them in place.

16-strand multiplait

3-strand nylon

3-strand polypropylene

braided outer on 3-strand core

braid on braid

pre-stretched 3-strand polyester

Kevlar-cored braids

16-strand multi braid

8-plait pre-stretched

ROPES
16-plait, three strand, nylon and blue polypropylene are used for mooring and anchoring, pre-stretched braids and laid polyester for sheets and halyards. Kevlar-cored braids are used for halyards and control lines, smaller braids for dinghies.

TWISTED SHACKLE
Used where the fitting to be attached needs to be aligned with the shackle pin. Normally used with non-swivelling blocks.

CAM JAMMERS
When control lines and halyards are led back from the mast to the winches at the aft end of the coachroof, they are held in position by cam jammers. When the levers are lifted the ropes run freely; when they are lowered, the ropes are held in place.

FID-OPERATED SNAP SHACKLE
This shackle can endure the enormous loads imposed by spinnakers.

SNAPHOOK
Used on equipment that needs to be removed quickly, such as vangs.

LEVER-OPERATED CAM
The rope is held by a lever-operated cam.

CARBINE HOOKS
These heavy-duty self-locking hooks are used for non-permanent attachment of a rope or wire.

SAFETY SNAP SHACKLE
The only type of snap shackle to use with safety harness.

CLEATS
The horned cleat is the traditional fitting for securing a rope, which is wound in a figure-of-eight or clove hitches.

PISTON-RELEASE SNAP SHACKLES
These bronze or stainless steel shackles are for spinnaker work. The steel version shown here has a ring attached to the piston to make releasing under tension easier.

RING-PIN RELEASE
A short length of tape attached to the ring enables the crew to 'trip' a spinnaker prior to lowering it.

CORD-RELEASE SPINNAKER SHACKLE
The cord is attached to the internal cam release system, and kept short to avoid accidental tripping.

CAM CLEAT
The cam cleat or crab's claw is used where a sheet or control line is always led off in the same direction. The rope can be pulled in easily but can't return because the jaws close tightly under tension.

CAM CLEAT
This simple cleat has no moving parts. Its inward-slanting grooves ensure that a rope under tension forces itself into the cleat, making the grip even tighter.

WINCHES & BLOCKS

Marine winches, powered or manual, control the various ropes, wires and chains used in many of the activities involved in yacht sailing. Sails are hoisted, reefed and trimmed, crewmen are hoisted for rigging checks, parts of the rigging are tensioned, mooring lines are hauled, booms' angles are controlled, and anchors, dinghies, lifting keels and gangways are lowered or raised by winch or windlass.

The smallest and simplest design is the 'snubbing winch'. Like most bigger winches, it is designed to rotate in one direction and ratchet-lock in the other. A few turns of a loaded rope around the drum will sustain a high load through friction on the drum surface, provided that a light tension is maintained by hand on the loose 'tail' of the rope.

Pulling on the rope tail rotates the winch and gains rope from the loaded end, while easing the tension allows the turns to slip on the drum, so that the loaded rope is paid out under control but can be stopped again immediately (snubbed) by restoring the tail tension. Greater forces can be controlled by fitting a handle at the centre of the winch to provide leverage longer than the radius of the drum.

Further mechanical advantage is obtained by employing two or three levels of gearing between the handle and the drum. This is achieved extremely neatly on the majority of winches while still leaving the handle and the drum on the same rotational axis.

Most commonly, headsails are trimmed through ropes (sheets) running to two-speed winches. Turning the handle one way gives direct drive, and reversing it when the load increases gives a lower gearing, though the drum always rotates in the same direction. Once the sail is set, the tail of the rope is cleated fast. Alternatively, the loaded side is passed through a levered 'stopper' so that the rope can be released from the winch, leaving it available for other use. With an array of stoppers, one winch can serve many different ropes.

A 'self-tailing' winch has additional height to accommodate a circular groove into which the rope tail jams to provide the necessary tension, but can feed out as the drum rotates. This enables heavier loads to be managed singlehanded, though the action may be slightly slower than with two crewmen attending to the separate tasks of 'winding' and 'tailing'.

On larger yachts, three-speed winches are used. The third speed is selected by a button, which is

TWIN TURNING BLOCK
Turning blocks ensure a constant lead angle into winches for sheets and control lines, and can be mounted flat or on edge. Twin blocks usually have a lifting back section for easy loading.

BLOCKS
Blocks are pulley wheels that enable mechanical advantages to be gained by linking numbers of them together. The three below are a single with a fixed eye; a double with a swivel eye; and a triple with a swivel eye and a becket (loop), over the central sheave (wheel), to which the rope is attached.

FOOT BLOCK
The foot block serves the same purpose as a turning block. It is usually used on the deck where lines may need to be turned, or as part of a sail or track control system.

FIDDLE BLOCK WITH SNAP HOOK
This specialist block would be used to position the spinnaker guy and sheet on the toe rail.

SWIVEL FIDDLE WITH BECKET
Used on most mainsheets, this block produces a 4:1 purchase when used with a double block.

RING BLOCK
This unusual block has a rotating ball race to spread the sheet loads. The becket is a plastic saddle which enables the end of the rope to be attached through the centre of the block.

SNATCH BLOCKS
Snatch blocks are used where it is necessary to move ropes to different sheeting positions. The largest block shown here has a snap shackle to enable it to be repositioned on the toe rail, and is opened by pressing the 'snap' locking mechanism.

released automatically at the first change of handle rotation, leaving the winch set to engage the other two gears.

The crews of the largest racing yachts need to inject a large amount of manual energy into a single winch quickly and with maximum ergonomic efficiency. For this, one or more vertical pedestals with large double handles are linked to big winches a short distance away. This enables several crew to wind simultaneously, concentrating on putting all their musclepower into one winch while one man is entirely responsible for the tailing. Such an arrangement is known as a 'coffee grinder'.

Both in this case and in small boats with simple two-speed winches, the task of sheeting is the same. As a sail is tacked, the sheet is hauled rapidly and manually under light load, as with a snubbing winch. As the sail fills, the load increases with progressive winching and it becomes

WINCHES

The winch is a device for handling sheets, halyards and control lines. The winch on the right is a conventional two-speed winch with a 14:1 retrieve power ratio and a 42:1 tensioning power ratio. The winch on the left is self-tailing and so it can be used by one person. The self-tailing mechanism grips the rope and strips it off a bale arm similar to those on fishing reels.

TRACK EYE

The sliding track eye carries a sheet block. It fits onto a T-section deck track and is positioned by lifting its spring-loaded piston and sliding it along the track.

WINCH HANDLES

The length of a handle's arm determines its mechanical advantage. The two-handled version shown here is designed for serious racing and is fabricated from chromed bronze. Black anodized alloy is used for handles which are not severely stressed.

However, for the expensive superyachts a whole new range of powered 'captive' winches is emerging. These are placed below the decks where the sheets are led to large drum reels or first to a capstan drum and then onto separate drum stowage. This can result in very clear decks with all trimming under push-button control from the helmsman's station.

For yachts over 10 metres length overall, anchor handling is usually relieved by a powered windlass, which must either be reversible for raising or lowering anchors, or else have a lever-operated clutch to allow the cable to run out. It must also be capable of handling either chain or rope. The rope will pass over a smooth drum but the chain has to be gripped in a special wheel called a 'gypsy'.

The majority of traditional windlasses have two drums, one either side of the motor and gears and on a horizontal axis athwartships, and one side is used for rope and the other for chain.

There is a recent fashion on smaller craft for a vertical drum in the form of the ancient capstan. This is neat and unobstructive because the motor can be placed below deck, protected from seawater, leaving only the small profile of a winch that looks similar to a sheet winch. Its main difference is that the gypsy occupies the lower section below the rope drum. The power and direction of rotation is controlled by footpads set flush in the deck.

More recently, like many other devices, even yacht winches are seeing the influence of electronic control. Information can be provided on the instantaneous load in each line, so that within preset limits a drum can be stopped if a line goes slack, or eased if overloaded.

Blocks, casings containing one or more pulley wheels, are used extensively on all sailboats. Some, such as turning blocks and foot blocks, are used to change the directions of sheets and halyards, while others are arranged in combinations that provide *mechanical advantage*. The mechanical advantage of a pulley system is the ratio of its output force to the amount of force applied to it. For instance, if a mainsheet system has a mechanical advantage of 8:1, then pulling on the mainsheet with a force of 1 kg would result in a force of 8 kg being applied to the boom.

However, the price you pay for the mechanical advantage is that you have to pull the mainsheet farther than the distance the boom will be pulled by the system.

necessary to work down through the gears.

In winch design, the racing sailor has different requirements and criteria from the cruising sailor. For racing, the emphasis is on light weight, involving expensive materials like titanium and carbonfibre, and since only manual oper-ation is allowed, optimum gearing is essential to make the best of the crew manpower. For cruising, durability and low maintenance are more important, and in larger yachts electrical or hydraulic power reduces the dependence on multiple gears.

Reel winches are, as the name implies, those which (like a fishing reel) hold all the line that they wind in. On a simple drum, this technique is only suitable for thin line and was formerly used mainly for wire halyards which could not be tailed by hand. Since the advent of aramid fibres such as Kevlar for making ropes as strong as steel, wire halyards are decreasingly used.

ANCHORS

In spite of their apparent simplicity, anchors are probably the least understood of sailing paraphernalia. While everyone knows what they are intended to do, there is remarkably little scientific knowledge of how well they perform in all practical circumstances. This is because of the difficulty of watching them, especially when they are buried in the seabed, and because their behaviour depends primarily on the texture and strength of the seabed itself, factors which can vary greatly.

It is not the anchor that actually 'holds', but the shear strength of the ground that it tries to penetrate. Trials in artificial test tanks can be misleading, and only recently have anchors begun to be instrumented for study of their behaviour in detail. For these reasons it is impossible to say that this or that anchor is best overall.

There will often be a preference for a certain type of anchor in a particular locality, as a result of experience. Fashions come and go as experience tempers the claims of successive marketing promotions, and boats on extensive cruises often carry a variety of designs for use in different types of ground.

It is interesting that Classification Societies recommend weights of anchor in relation to size of boat, but avoid the controversy of specifying types. Indeed, plenty of weight and plenty of chain is an effective solution whatever the anchor, because the heavy chain itself absorbs much of the energy of a tossing boat before any disturbing force can reach the anchor. However, the desire is to save weight carried aboard, and many boats now carry nylon warp in preference to chain.

Although the nylon can absorb energy by its elasticity, it has little weight in water so averaged loads go direct to the anchor, putting more reliance on its ultimate holding performance. It is still essential

Anchors have developed from the basic four-pronged grapnel (**right**). The plough anchor (**top**) performs well in a wide variety of seabed conditions, while the Danforth (**far right**) works well in sand and mud but jams on small rocks. The Bruce anchor (**above**) has no moving parts and is designed to dig deep into the seabed.

The majority of cruising yachts stow their anchors lashed securely in bow rollers ready for immediate use (**left**).

PARTS OF AN ANCHOR

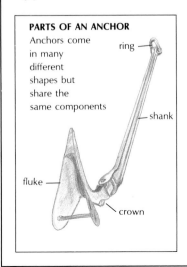

Anchors come in many different shapes but share the same components

ring

shank

fluke

crown

to have a few metres of chain (the leader) between the warp and the anchor to absorb the worst peaks of snatch loading.

Anchoring in light weather is no problem, and for this a kedge is used. A kedge is any anchor that is conveniently lighter than the bower (main) anchor. For serious anchoring in heavier wind and wave conditions, there is no substitute for as heavy an anchor as can be handled and carried. This is especially so for emergency anchoring where the all-important choice of holding ground and shelter is not available.

The most long-standing and universally-recognized type of anchor is the 'fisherman', still popular for many applications. Whichever way up it lands on the seabed, one of its flukes (points) will be in a downward position ready to penetrate the ground. A stock (crossbar) at the opposite end of the shank lies horizontally on the bed, keeping the flukes vertical.

Partly because most of the weight is felt at the tip of the fluke, this form is good on rock, weed and firm soils but is limited in soft ground by the small amount of fluke area available

to resist dragging. Moreover, the stock resists going deep to find firmer ground. The fisherman's attributes are its consistent performance in a wide variety of seabeds and its ability to reset quickly if dragged out.

In the same family is the grapnel, which has four flukes on cruciform arms and does not need a stock. Grapnel anchors are popular among fisherfolk in areas of hard sand and rock, but they are not easily stowed on yachts.

Most other forms are classed as 'high holding power' or 'stockless'.

They have relatively large fluke areas and are intended to bury themselves deeply. When they do, much higher performance is achieved but certain seabeds make them inconsistent in their holding power, which is the ratio of the force they can sustain compared to their weight.

Tumbling fluke anchors, typified by the Danforth or Meon, have a hinge which allows the flukes to 'tumble' either side of the shank, ready to point downward whichever side they land on on the bed. A significant attribute is that this form stows easily because it can lie flat on the deck ready for use. Although usable on rock, it is not ideal on hard ground but good in soft ground where its large flukes are effective.

Big ship anchors are similar in principle, and popular because they are stowed easily by drawing them directly into a hawse pipe. At the limit of their holding power these designs tend to roll out of the ground and may not reset if they have collected a stone between the shank and the fluke.

Plough anchors also have a large fluke area and are popular in spite of being cumbersome. The best known is the CQR, which has a strongly-forged hinge between the plough-shares and the shank. This assists the digging-in phase by causing the plough to 'screw' its way into the ground in an attitude which puts much weight on the fluke. These are good all-round performers, excelling in softer soils where they can penetrate deeply.

Recent design work, resulting from studying the point of break-out, promises a significant improvement in the optimum performance of plough anchors.

A radically different form is the Bruce, famous for its two curved horns which rotate the main fluke into the ground. It is good on softer ground but sometimes does not compete with other designs on harder ground if it cannot penetrate far. It has the advantage, on intermediate ground, that even if tending to roll out it usually retains some holding and has a fair chance of digging in again.

Some anchors, such as the mushroom and the rond, are not self-burying and are carefully placed in the ground for long-term use.

PAINTS & VARNISHES

Tree resins, natural tar, animal fats and vegetable oils were all used by the early boatbuilders to preserve the structure and ensure the water-tight integrity of wooden hulls, and the addition of pigments to these materials gave the colours which encouraged owners to decorate their vessels.

Today, there are three basic types of protective coatings: oil-based paints which dry by the evaporation of some of the oil; polyurethanes, which include varnishes and cure when in contact with the air; and two-part epoxies which cure by chemical reactions between the two parts.

Varnishes are produced without pigments and are used to bring out the natural colour of all wooden surfaces, including the on-deck varnished woodwork or 'brightwork'. On traditionally-decorated wooden boats the darker varnished mahogany of cabin sides, hatches and cockpit contrasts with the paler scrubbed teak decks and cockpit gratings.

Other teak structures, such as grabrails, are treated with teak oil which penetrates the wood and preserves its natural oiliness and gives it a slightly darker appearance.

The interiors of wooden boats were often finished with contrasting white planking and varnished beams and furniture. Matt finishes often gave a better contrast than the bright finishes which also showed up areas of wear.

The bilge area, often susceptible to rot, was usually treated with coal tar derivatives, or specially-mixed bilge paints containing fungicides, to prevent the onset of dry rot. The bilge is a particularly difficult area to keep clean, and is a repository for stagnant water and engine oil spillages.

The topsides of the boat were the obvious areas for the development of finishes which could be applied evenly and would dry to a perfect, hard gloss finish.

White has always been a favourite with owners but is one of the most difficult to apply because it shows up every blemish. This is particularly so now that older GRP hulls require painting to prevent the ingress of water into the laminate through a deteriorating gel coat.

The boot topping is the junction between sea and air on the hull and extends about three inches above the waterline. Boot top paints are a mixture of the harder topside paints and the softer, leaching antifoulings (paints that keep the hull clear of fouling, such as weed growth, by slowly releasing or 'leaching' their active ingredients). Most owners use a contrasting colour for boot tops.

The real battle between the hull and the elements takes place below the waterline, where the growth of weed and barnacles causes fouling resulting in a considerable loss of performance. In tropical waters, harmful marine borers penetrate wooden hulls and, once inside, chew away happily along the grain until the boat finally collapses.

Copper sheathing and copper and arsenic-impregnated antifouling paints were highly successful in combating growth and borers, but hulls still needed periodic scrubbing off during the sailing season.

The introduction of tributyl tin (TBT) in the 1970s revolutionized the protective coatings industry. TBT paints were excellent antifouling agents, but their harmful effects on shellfish populations and other marine life resulted in a complete ban on their use in the late 1980s and a return to the copper- and arsenic-based paints of previous decades.

Two grades of antifouling are produced. The hard racing finishes can be sanded smooth and leach slowly, while the softer cruising versions form a thicker protective coating which leaches quickly to prevent weed and barnacles from gaining a foothold.

The application of paint is one of the most skilled boat maintenance tasks and requires considerable time, patience and perfect working conditions. Successful finishes rely upon fastidious preparation of the surface to be protected or decorated, and unpainted wood and GRP surfaces must be filled and sanded so that all blemishes are removed.

The resulting surface will then have to be cleaned several times with degreasers and thinners, to ensure that the first phase of the paint system can key into the porous structure so that the whole finish does not flake off. Many layers of paint are applied, and throughout the application process each successive coat must be sanded down with wet-

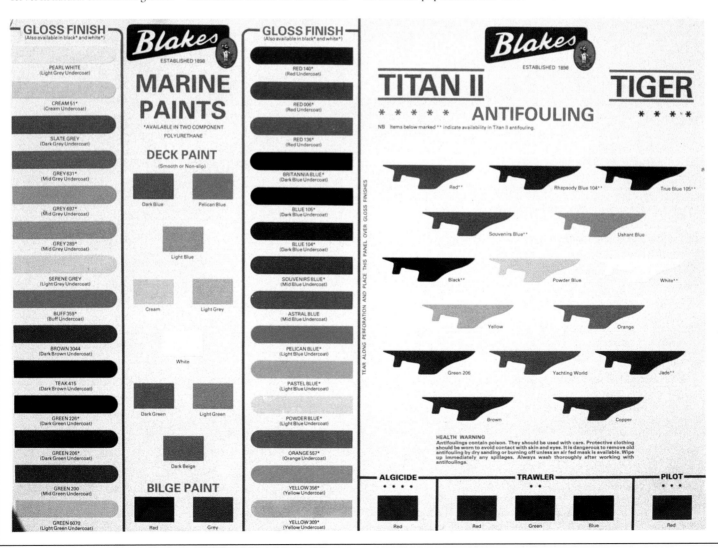

and-dry paper and cleaned with a 'tack rag' to remove all traces of dust.

Most systems start with a primer, which acts as a keying agent and filler. Sometimes the primer is combined with an undercoat, but if not, a specified number of undercoats is applied after the primer. After the priming and undercoating, a number of top coats are applied to give the sort of immaculate finish displayed on the side of the paint can. Brushes, rollers and mohair pads are all used to assist in producing the desired result.

Paint manufacturers have to bal-ance the quick-drying properties their products need to prevent runs, with the need to preserve a 'wet edge' that allows successive strips of painted boat to merge into one smooth skin free of brushmarks.

The treatment of GRP hulls is often best left to the professional spray shop. The aim is to use two-part epoxies to replace the original gel coat finish with an impervious coating, and so extend the life of the boat.

The treatment of the undersides of the hull to remove blistering caused by osmosis involves the removal of the entire gel coat by gritblasting or sanding. Osmosis is the slow seepage of water into the laminate, and it causes leaching of the resins which shows up as blisters.

The exposed laminate must be dried before a new epoxy barrier is built up and sanded to a perfect finish. Again, this is such an important process that it is best left to the professionals.

Steel and aluminium hulls also require treatment with appropriate paint systems. The first coat of primer is an inhibitor to prevent the formation of rust or corrosion. Thereafter, the paint systems are designed to build up an elastic pro-tective layer to prevent moisture getting near the metal.

As with all sophisticated pro-ducts, the wide variety of finishes available to the boat owner must be researched thoroughly before pur-chase. If you want a traditional but renewable finish, traditional paints and varnishes are the answer. Poly-urethanes tend to give quicker results but varnishes especially can peel off if moisture gets into the wood. Clear epoxy finishes may need a final protective coat of ultra-violet light stabilizer to prevent them going cloudy after prolonged exposure to sunlight.

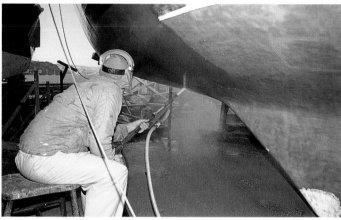

Good preparation is essential; steel hulls are sandblasted to bare metal.

Wooden hulls need many layers of paint and varnish for a proper finish.

Above *The contrast between varnish and light-coloured paint can be very effective.*
Left *A typical range of hull, deck and antifouling paint colours.*

NAVIGATION INSTRUMENTS

At all times the most important navigational instrument on board a boat is the skilled human navigator. That person is capable of plotting a dead reckoning (DR) position, using information entered in the ship's log relating to the course steered and the distance travelled through the water. All electronic navigation instruments, no matter how good their accuracy and reliability, must be regarded as *aids* to navigation, not as substitutes for good navigation practice, and should be used with caution.

For chartwork, the basis of marine navigation, you will need a decent chart table measuring at least 60 × 75 cm (24 × 30 inches), plus a small set of drawing instruments consisting of a parallel rule, a protractor or plotter, dividers, drawing compasses, pencils and an eraser. Your pencils should be soft-leaded (preferably 2B), and be hexagonal rather than round so that they don't keep rolling off the table.

You will also need a logbook, an up-to-date nautical almanac, and pilot books, charts and tide tables covering the area(s) in which you intend to sail.

The most usual design of parallel rule has two halves joined by a pair of pivoted arms, and can be 'walked' across the chart to transfer a line from one part of the chart to another without altering its angle. Protractors and plotters, like parallel rules, are usually made of clear plastic, and they are used for measur-

ing and marking angles.

There are several different types of plotter on the market, the most common being the square Douglas and Portland plotters, the Hurst plotter and the Breton plotter. The Hurst plotter is basically a square plotter incorporating a rotatable plastic circle, marked in degrees like a compass card, and a swinging plastic arm. The plastic circle and arm are used to read off courses and bearings, and the protractor can be set up to take account of magnetic variation, which saves you having to convert magnetic to true bearings or vice versa.

The Breton plotter is a rectangular plastic instrument which, like the Hurst plotter, has a rotatable plastic circle marked in compass degrees. The top and bottom edges of the Breton plotter are marked off in nautical miles, at scales of 1:25,000 and 1:50,000 along the top edge and 1:75,000 and 1:150,000 along the bottom.

To get the directional, distance and speed information you need for your chartwork, your boat should be fitted with at least one good-quality steering compass and a log. The steering compass, as its name implies, is used by the helmsman when steering the boat, and is usually either binnacle-mounted or bulkhead-mounted.

The binnacle compass, normally used on wheel-steered boats, is mounted on a pedestal which should be positioned so that the helmsman

TRADITIONAL INSTRUMENTS

The traditional plotting instruments are brass dividers, centre right, and the parallel rule, top centre. These have been joined by plastic plotters such as the Douglas square protractor, top centre, and the Breton plotter, bottom centre. The rotating card handbearing compass, bottom right, has a new electronic fluxgate rival complete with memory, bottom left. The sextant, top left, is still one of the most valuable of all navigational instruments.

can see the compass easily. Bulkhead compasses are mounted vertically on bulkheads and used on tiller-steered boats, which ideally should have one compass on each bulkhead so that the helmsman can see a compass clearly from either side of the boat.

Most steering compasses are of the traditional magnetic type, with the direction being shown by a circular, pivoted compass card marked in degrees around its circumference and carrying two or more small bar magnets or a ring magnet on its underside. The card is pivoted on a float, which sits on a mixture of alcohol and water that damps out any mechanical vibrations.

Electronic compasses, which have digital or analogue displays to show headings, are operated by sensors called *fluxgate magnetometers*. These work by detecting the direction of the lines of flux of the earth's magnetic field.

In addition to a steering compass, you should also have a handbearing (portable) compass to enable you to take the bearings of features such as buoys, landmarks or other vessels from the boat, plus a good pair of binoculars to help you identify the

features correctly. Like steering compasses, handbearing compasses may be either magnetic or electronic.

Logs measure the speed and distance travelled by the boat. The simplest types use an impeller, which is like a little propeller, either trailed in the water behind the boat or else permanently mounted below water level on the hull or transom. As the boat moves, the impeller is turned by the water stream and its rate of turn is proportional to the speed of the boat through the water. The motion of the impeller is transmitted mechanically or electronically to an inboard unit that computes and displays the speed and distance travelled.

Two other useful instruments are the depth sounder and the wind speed/direction indicator. Depth sounders work by sending an ultrasonic sound pulse down from a hull-mounted transducer (sensor), and measuring the time taken for an echo of the pulse to return to the transducer; the time taken is proportional to the depth of water beneath the hull.

The depth may be indicated by one or more of several types of

WIND INDICATORS

Because the wind plays such a vital role in sailing a boat well, very precise measuring instruments have been devised. Masthead sensors (**1**) detect the wind direction and speed. The information from the sensors is shown on instruments such as a wind direction indicator (**2**).

1

2

COMPASSES

The simplest type (**5**) is the traditional gimballed boats' grid compass. The most sophisticated is the electronic fluxgate compass with digital LCD readout (**6**). The 'porthole' spherical compass (**7** and **8**) features a card that can be edge- or top-read, and parallax wires that enable it to be read from the side of the boat. It may also (**7**) incorporate an angle of heel indicator.

3

ECHO SOUNDERS

Echo sounders have been available for longer than any other electronic navigation instrument. The display options available include a digital liquid crystal display readout with a keypad for selecting alarms and other functions (**3**), and a colour graphic display with keypad control (**4**).

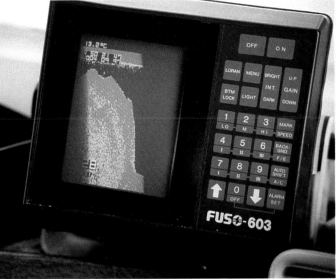

4

5

6

COMBINED SYSTEMS This custom navaid station is mounted directly in front of the steering wheel. It incorporates programmable depth, wind and log (speed and distance) instruments.

7

8

readout, ranging from a simple digital display showing the depth in feet, fathoms or metres, to full-colour video displays showing a profile of the seabed and any other underwater features present, such as shoals of fish.

Depth sounders are still one of the most important and reliable of shipboard instruments, but most yachtsmen fail to take full advantage of their usefulness. For instance, using a depth sounder to follow a seabed contour, especially in fog, can guide you into a safe anchorage or alert you to possible dangers. The addition of adjustable shallow- and deep-water alarms enables you to stay within a chosen depth 'cor-

ridor' when following a depth contour.

The wind speed/direction indicator shows the wind speed and direction by means of moving pointers or as digital readouts. The signals that drive it are generated by a masthead sensor unit consisting of a vane, which generates the wind direction signal, and a cup-type anemometer which generates the wind speed signal.

Electronic compasses, logs, depth sounders and wind speed/direction indicators can be used to provide information to integrated navigation systems, and all four may be incorporated into a single instrument. This instrument is connected

to the appropriate fluxgate, water speed, water depth and wind speed/-direction sensors, and the information is shown on a liquid crystal display (LCD) screen, the individual functions being selected by push-buttons.

One other navigation instrument, which has fallen out of favour since the introduction of electronic navigation systems, is the sextant. By using the sextant to find the angle of the sun (or the moon, or a specified star) above the horizon, and then referring to data tables, you can find your position with reasonable accuracy. If you make long journeys at sea, a sextant is a valuable backup to your electronics.

RADIO NAVIGATION AIDS

Radio aids to navigation are carried by most small craft venturing offshore, and they have proliferated since the advent of microcircuits. The electronic navigators use ground- and satellite-based transmissions to determine the latitude and longitude of the vessel, and use their computing power to derive other information, such as speed over the ground and the distance, bearing to, and time to reach a destination or *waypoint* (a chosen point on the route).

The latest position-finding technique is the Global Positioning System (GPS), based on a network of US satellites and already partially in use. By 1991, when all the satellites are in place, it will give worldwide coverage enabling position fixing anywhere on or above the earth's surface to within 50 metres or better, at any time and in all weather. Although the receivers currently cost from £2000 upwards, its high performance will make GPS the dominant marine navigation system within a few years.

Satnav, short for 'satellite navigation', has until now generally referred to an earlier system called Transit. It has been very popular for navigation on ocean voyages, but it is only accurate to within a few miles, and fixes can be a couple of hours apart, so it has limited value for inshore navigation. As GPS comes fully into service, the Transit satellites will no longer be maintained and the system will become defunct.

MF/RDF is Medium Frequency Radio Direction Finding. It was the earliest radio navigation aid and was used with low-cost receivers which also covered general broadcasting

stations. Consequently, it has been very widely used worldwide and is still a good standby, but it does not locate automatically. Bearings from two or more low-power radio beacons are taken by rotating a small antenna, and used to triangulate a position by chartwork.

The accuracy varies, particularly with range from the beacons, but the facility is excellent for homing onto a particular beacon in those areas where one happens to be conveniently located.

Dramatic price reduction in receivers over the last decade has revolutionized the use of Decca and Loran-C for inshore navigation, so that they are now found on the smallest of yachts and are available at prices down to £300. Both systems employ ground-based transmitters and give good positional accuracy, typically better than 300 metres where coverage is good.

Loran is most widely used in the United States, where it covers both coastal zones and is effective up to about 200 miles out, and where a new mid-Continental chain of stations is being established to cover the central areas of the country. Loran is also available in the North Atlantic, the Middle East and Japan, and there are plans to extend its cover to the northern and northwestern Pacific. Despite the introduction of GPS, Loran will continue in service well into the next century.

Decca has excellent coverage in UK waters and is currently the most practical aid in that area, but its transmitters have a shorter range than Loran's and its long-term future is in doubt. It is likely that after a decade with GPS in full operation, Loran will have expanded as a

back-up system but other radiolocation aids, including Decca, will diminish in importance or even disappear.

Small radars, like other navigation aids, have also benefited from the microelectronic revolution. Excellent performance can now be obtained at affordable prices on equipment which is no longer cumbersome. The signals are processed and 'cleaned' before presentation on video screens which can be viewed in daylight.

Apart from aiding collision avoidance with other vessels, the radar picture in inshore waters relates to charted features over a wide area and works in all conditions of visibility. The latest designs can superimpose waypoints and, for example, the vessel's Decca- or Loran-derived position, on the same screen, also adding digital information on range and bearing to chosen points, depth, speed and so on.

Typically, the range which fills the screen can be adjusted from one-eighth of a mile to thirty miles, but the radar works on line-of-sight and so is limited in detecting objects much beyond the horizon.

Radar detectors are available which simply show the presence and bearing of a transmitting radar. They can be confusing for use inshore among denser traffic, so have not found wide popularity except for shorthanded ocean passage making, where they are left on watch to warn of the rare encounter with large vessels.

Navtex is a system for receiving (but not transmitting) short printed telex messages transmitted by coastal stations and concerning weather,

gale and navigational warnings. There is wide international cooperation in its use, and all messages are in English. Some Navtex receivers produce a paper printout of the messages, while others store the messages electronically to be called up on a screen when needed. The advantage of the Navtex system is that essential recent information can be viewed at any time, and so there is no need to maintain a listening watch.

Weatherfax receivers are compact devices capable of slowly printing the pictorial synoptic forecast charts that are broadcast several times each day from the principal maritime countries. The reception is long range, reaching, for example, more than halfway across the Atlantic.

Even weather satellite signals can be received directly on some receivers, whose output shows the sea, land and cloud in colour-enhanced visible light or infrared images. The latter can, for example, accurately pinpoint the warm currents such as the Gulfstream which can add or subtract significantly to speed on long passages.

VHF (very high frequency) radiotelephony is now carried by the majority of vessels, primarily for short-range communication between vessels, for safety monitoring via the Coastguard and for normal international telephone calls via Coastal Stations. It has the advantage of being able to handle high volumes of radio traffic within a restricted area (20 to 60 miles across).

This is possible because, although there are many separate channels, the signals do not penetrate beyond the line of sight of the antennae.

This navaid and switch panel features a VHF radiotelephone (**left**) with separate speaker (to its **right**), a Philips navigation system (**top centre**), and below it a complete Brookes and Gatehouse Hercules system with wind speed/direction and boat speed/direction displays, which can be interfaced with Loran, Decca or satellite receivers. The instrument with the red cord is an electronic handbearing compass; at top right is a radio cassette unit, and below it are two fused switch panels.

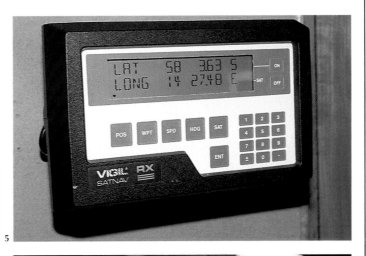

Picture **1** shows an antenna array housing radar reflector (**centre**), satellite navigation antenna (**left**), Decca Navigator antenna (**centre top**) and VHF aerial (**right**). The mobile handheld VHF transceiver (**2**) is gaining in popularity as reliability improves, and the shipboard VHF transceiver (**3**) is almost obligatory equipment in most countries. Picture **4** shows a powerful long-range high-frequency transceiver and a single sideband radio.

The satellite navigator (Picture **5**) can compute course and speed made good, distance and bearing to given waypoints and off-track errors. Picture **6** shows a Loran receiver and a shipboard fax receiver. The Loran system will remain operational when Decca and satnav are phased out in the 1990s.
Weatherfax, and Navtex (picture **7**) are receivers which print out weather or navigation information as required by the operator.

AUTOPILOTS & SELF-STEERING GEAR

Automatic steering is a boon for conserving crewpower, even on short passages, and for leaving shorthanded crew free for other tasks. Provided it is not abused, it can greatly contribute to safety by leaving the crew drier, warmer, more mobile and consequently more alert.

In recent years, electronic autopilots have largely superseded mechanical self-steering gears except on smaller yachts making long ocean passages. Even for these, the increasing reliability of autopilots and their small energy requirements (which can be supplemented by solar cells) combine with advantages of cost, compactness and performance so that self-steering gears are now rarely encountered.

The exception is for shorthanded ocean races, in which the smaller yachts use self-steering for upwind work but usually carry an electronic pilot as reserve and for downwind work in light weather. The larger yachts, and especially the fast multihulls, have to rely on the more adaptable control offered by electronics, and carry two or more units for reliability.

Early steering vane systems featured a large wooden or sailcloth vane, pivoted about its vertical axis and operating either its own small rudder well aft, or a trim tab on the main rudder. There were many designs and refinements, even employing windmills in place of single vanes, but the main weaknesses were loss of sensitivity as the boat heeled and loss of vane power when running downwind, due to the smaller relative windspeed.

The newer, more effective designs control the boat's rudder via the wheel or tiller. The windvane is counterbalanced about a near-horizontal axis, giving large changes of force on the vane for small changes of angle of incidence on either side of the wind. The windvane works through linkages to rotate an underwater blade, suspended on a pendulum mechanism, so that the waterflow strongly drives the pendulum to one side or the other.

This movement is transmitted through rope lines to the tiller or wheel. Thus the vane is sensitive to small course errors and does not have to provide the power to drive the rudder, because power is derived directly from the boatspeed rather than from the relatively small forces on the vane.

In use, self-steering is reliable and simple to operate. With the boat on the desired heading and the sails properly trimmed, the windvane is turned about its vertical axis so that

its leading edge is pointing into the apparent wind.

As long as the boat remains on course, the windvane stays upright and the pendulum blade is aligned amidships. If the boat deviates from the set course, the windvane is tilted over by the wind and it rotates the pendulum blade away from its amidships position. This causes the waterflow to push the blade to one side, and the rope lines attached to the pendulum pull on the tiller or wheel to steer the boat back onto the correct heading.

Electronic autopilots have various configurations, but they are all basically similar in principle. A direction sensor detects any difference between the ship's heading and the set course, and generates an electronic signal corresponding to the course error. The error signal is electronically processed to cause an actuator to move the rudder, so that the boat turns to cancel the error.

Modern autopilots have three main controls: rudder gain, autotrim, and seastate sensitivity. Rudder gain control sets how much rudder angle is applied for a fixed amount of course error, and autotrim is automatically applied as the fixed amount of rudder needed to maintain a straight course whenever there is a change of heel angle or propeller speed. This is necessary because certain lateral forces, generated by sails or propellers, mean that some compensating rudder is needed to keep the boat on a straight course even when there is no other disturbance.

Seastate control allows tight course-keeping in calm weather but some relaxation of response to the smaller course deviations as the sea grows rougher.

Use of microprocessors has enabled quite advanced intelligence to be built into even the smallest and cheapest autopilots. For example,

the seastate control can be made automatic by monitoring how hard the autopilot is working during a set period.

Frequent corrections imply rougher seas, so for economy of power, the boat is then allowed to yaw slightly within a limited sector before any rudder corrections are applied. As the sea flattens, and less work is done by the autopilot, this 'deadband' sector is reduced again to restore tighter course-keeping.

Although the basic intelligence and control features are similar in all autopilots, there is an increasing range of configurations and a trend to link into data provided by other yacht systems. For instance, magnetic field sensing is now usually by fluxgates, which give a more instantaneous signal than the conventional card compass and are more compatible with electronic circuits. Angular signals can also be obtained from small windvanes which are

Wheel steering systems can be driven by an autopilot linked to the rudder quadrant or, as in this example, the much more convenient demountable drive system. The sensing compass, at the front of the cockpit, activates the motor to turn the wheel via a toothed belt driving a hub-mounted drum.

Vane steering systems are designed to keep the boat on a course relative to the wind, not the compass. The pendulum type (**left**) activates a small servo rudder that turns the tiller to keep the boat on course. The vertical axis drive (**far left**) is linked via gears to an auxiliary rudder. The Navico **tiller-mounted autopilot** (**below centre**) can be programmed to cope with a wide variety of conditions. Its remote control (**below**) handles course changing, tack and waypoint programming.

feeding other yacht instruments.

For fast multihulls, signals can be processed to enable compass course settings to be slowly influenced by changes in wind vectors and boatspeed, and in high-performance craft, short-term reference can be made to inexpensive rate gyros.

Many autopilots can now be controlled directly from electronic navigators such as Decca, Loran, satnav and GPS. The navigator measures the distance of the vessel off a predetermined track between two waypoints. This measurement is passed to the autopilot which steers the boat back onto track.

Between the direction sensor and the rudder actuator lies the computer brain of the autopilot, which these days can be made quite complex for little hardware cost. This not only makes for good performance but also results in a system which is easy to instal and use.

The actuator is the muscle of the autopilot, and the maximum force it can provide, coupled with its speed of response in moving the rudder, generally determines the autopilot's limits of performance for a given size of boat. Most actuators are driven electrically but the more powerful are hydraulic.

The larger pilots have their actuators separate and 'plumbed in' to act directly on the rudder quadrant. They then need a remote-controlled clutch for engagement. Brookes & Gatehouse/Lewmar, Cetrek, Nautech and Robertson are leaders in the development of autopilots for larger pleasurecraft.

For average- to small-sized boats, popular autopilots come in a compact 'clip-on' form for owner installation. For wheelsteering, Nautech and Navico provide a belt drive to an auxiliary wheel clamped to the helm. Seafarer place their package between the wheel and its original spigot.

The compact tillerpilots have probably done most to popularize the use of autopilots in the smallest pleasurecraft. These are relatively inexpensive, self-contained units, simple to instal and with only a 12-volt power supply to connect. Nautech and Navico are the world's leading developers of such units, which now come with precise digital control and automatic responses.

The functions offered by Navico's HP 5000 handheld remote programmer typify the range of facilities which even tillerpilots can now provide: variable dodge manoeuvres to make a dogleg around an obstruction, remote steering, electronic navigator interface, preselected memorized courses, automatic tacking, off-course alarms and a 'man-overboard' aid displaying continual bearing and distance back to an alarm point.

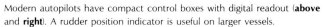

Modern autopilots have compact control boxes with digital readout (**above** and **right**). A rudder position indicator is useful on larger vessels.

ELECTRICAL SYSTEMS

The modern yacht is highly dependent on its electrical power supply, which provides power for both its luxury and its navigational equipment. While the electrical system of a small yacht needs to supply at least navigation and cabin lights, essential instruments and engine-starting capacity, the large yacht will have many additional luxury items including refrigeration, air conditioning and electrically-operated pumps and winches.

The basic source of power is the 12-volt lead-acid battery as used on motor vehicles. A yacht will carry at least two batteries which can be used together in parallel or separately. Although 12-volt supplies tend to predominate, some craft, especially in the United States, are equipped with 24-volt systems. The very large yachts, in addition to a bank of batteries, have independent motor-generators and provide power at several voltages including 230 and 110 volts ac for running standard appliances.

The principal source of battery charging is the standard alternator (and associated regulator) driven by the vessel's propulsion engine. The duty cycle of boat batteries is more demanding than that of automotive batteries. A car uses its battery for starting, then immediately takes its electrical power directly from the alternator, which also recharges the battery so that it remains fully charged and ready for the next start; overall, the battery spends little time supplying current on its own.

By contrast, the use of the navigation and other electrical equipment of a boat, particularly of a sailing yacht, may run down much of the battery's charge. Then, when it is needed to start an engine, its charge may be at its lowest. This 'deep cycling' is very hard on conventional batteries and limits their life, although the modern low-maintenance battery, which uses calcium in the lead instead of antimony, is much more tolerant. Nevertheless, most boats have some provision for battery charging from sources other than the engine-driven alternator.

In simple installations, it is common practice to reserve one battery for engine starting and use the other for services. Then, if the service (auxiliary) battery is depleted there is no worry about engine starting to recharge. The alternative school of thought is to keep both batteries balanced by using them together, but to monitor their state carefully, even using automatic alarms to avoid over-depletion. A useful standby is a 'torque battery' which

can hold its charge for many months and then, for engine start, can deliver typically 100 amps for about a minute.

In marinas, where running engines to charge batteries is unpopular or forbidden, shore power supplies are available for use with mains chargers. The shore power input should be controlled by earth-leakage circuit breakers ('earth-current trips'), which will break the circuit instantly should any dangerous stray currents arise.

If battery charging is to be unsupervised (for instance if the charger is left on between weekends of sailing), use only the more expensive chargers which take account of the charge state and reduce the supply accordingly. Cheap chargers can overcharge unless watched, and this causes gassing and will diminish battery life. Charge state can be indicated by a range of instruments, from complex indicators of percentage charge to simple voltmeters with an expanded scale covering the critical voltage range. Monitoring of current in and out is done by inserting a very low value resistor in the main cable and measuring the voltage drop across it with a remote meter.

Battery isolation and selector switches enable selection of one, two, none or both batteries, but a running alternator can be destroyed if disconnected from all batteries, even for an instant, so switches must be of high quality with built-in safeguards to prevent the alternator running open-circuited.

When batteries are connected

directly in parallel, a strong one will be bled by a weak one and the discharge can continue almost indefinitely. To counter this, large diodes should be connected between the batteries to prevent current flowing from one into the other.

Large yachts have built-in diesel motor-generator sets, which have watercooling and exhaust systems and are encased in acoustic silencing material. These can work when the main engines are off, and they use much less fuel.

Smaller yachts, on long ocean passages, cannot carry sufficient fuel to allow them to run the propulsion engine long enough to keep the batteries properly charged, so resort to several other charging methods. The most reliable reserve source of significant energy is a small, portable, aircooled petrol generator, which may be no bigger than a large briefcase and can be used on deck in fair weather.

Another option for sailing yachts on long passages is to use shaft generation. A large pulley on the propellor shaft (which is allowed to rotate in neutral gear while the boat is travelling under sail) drives a special alternator that can generate useful power at low revolutions. This can provide one amp per knot of sailing speed.

Wind generators are a good source of 'topping up' charging power on long-distance cruises, though they seldom provide for all the needs of a modern boat. One version, made by Ampair, allows the generator component to be driven either by windmill blades or

by a spinner towed in the water.

Solar panels, another source of topping-up power, are becoming more efficient and economic. In daylight they yield around 100 watts per square metre, and they typically cost about £1000 per square metre. A small panel with a 15-watt output will top-up between weekends, and several large panels on the wide deckspace of a multihull will provide most of the energy needed.

While much marine equipment is designed for 12- or 24-volt dc operation, it is also useful to have a modest level of ac supply at domestic voltages to allow on-board use of, for example, an electric drill or a video recorder. A solid-state inverter can provide this but will not stand heavy current loads.

For equipment which is used temporarily on deck, waterproof plugs and sockets are available. These are generally sealed with O-rings and successfully resist dangerous water ingress when in use, but the sockets must be capped with sealing covers when the plugs are removed.

Quite elaborate switch panels are now often provided to control the ever-increasing electrical circuits of yachts. These panels often have mimic lights indicating which circuits are energized, and there is a trend toward the use of small individual circuit-breakers in place of switches and fuses.

Water and electricity are a dangerous combination, so any electrical installation work on board a boat must be carried out to the highest standards to minimize the risk of shocks or fire.

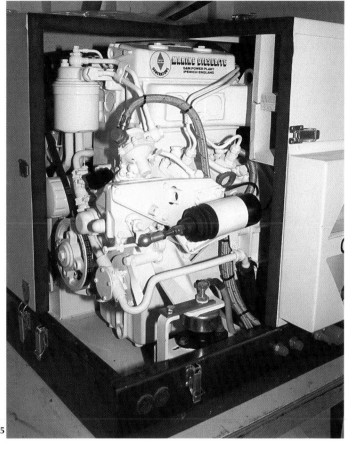

POWER SOURCES

In addition to the standard engine-mounted generator there is an increasing number of alternative power sources. The wind generators (**2** and **3**) and the solar panels (**4**) harness the freely-available natural power sources. Generally, they provide a trickle charge to keep batteries topped up, rather than powering equipment directly. Solar panels are robust and require a reasonably flat mounting surface, preferably away from areas of intense crew activity. As with all electrical generating systems, blocking or switching diodes are fitted to ensure that no discharge is possible when conditions are not suitable for generating electrical power. The self-contained gasoline or diesel generator (**5**) is a purpose-built generating station, usually mounted in an insulated housing to cut out noise and vibration. The Powerpack (**6**) is a rechargeable portable power source which can be taken on board to power a range of tools or appliances with a modest current requirement.

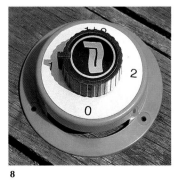

The well-designed marine switch panel (picture **1**) has separate controls for each electrical circuit on the boat, and meters to indicate battery state and charge. This example also incorporates fuel gauges, a clock and a heating and ventilation control. The marine alternator (**7**) is fitted with diodes which enables two batteries to be charged automatically, and the four-position isolation switch (**8**) allows manual switching between two batteries.

The gas detector (**9**) sounds an alarm if its bilge-mounted probe detects a buildup of explosive gas.

CRUISER FIXTURES & FITTINGS

The modern cruiser provides comfortable accommodation and is often as well-equipped as most homes, with hot and cold running water, full cooking facilities, central heating and air conditioning.

The most widely used method of central heating in boats of all sizes is ducted air warmed by a diesel oil burner. The oil is conveniently supplied from the engine fuel tank, with the draw pipe set higher in the tank than the engine supply pipe, for obvious reasons. The heater is started and controlled electrically and the airflow, which is fresh rather than recirculated, is forced through the ducting by a fan.

Older methods of heating include wood stoves (still to be found in classic boats, albeit often now made of stainless steel) and charcoal stoves. The latter are still quite common due to their safety, compactness and simplicity; a combusting layer works its way slowly up through a cylinder of charcoal, and the heat it produces is radiated and convected from the metal casing. Paraffin, petroleum spirit (SBP) and bottled gas are also used.

Where the combustion heats the cabin air directly, it has the disadvantage of producing water vapour equal to the weight of fuel, and so will only reduce humidity if there is good ventilation. For safety, gas and spirit heaters are preferably of catalytic form; the fuel is passed over a platinum gauze which glows hot, and there is no naked flame.

Air conditioning units, similar to those used in road vehicles, are used in motor vessels and the larger yachts. They generally consume electricity at a level only available by continuous engine running or the use of shore power. On smaller yachts, a sailcloth wind scoop can be effective for directing breeze down the forehatch. At sea, sailing yachts usually rely on natural ventilation through the familiar Tannoy vents or deck cowlings with Dorade boxes, boxes designed to pass air while intercepting water.

Cooking facilities vary from the simplest paraffin camping stoves to split-level cookers of the domestic type. Bottled gas appliances are the most commonly used because of their convenience and low fuel costs. They need careful handling because the gas is heavier than air, and leaking gas will accumulate in the bilge and form an explosive mixture. The danger of this is not as high as it once was, thanks to the introduction of 'flame-out' protection on stoves and gas bottle lockers that ventilate overboard. However, a reliable gas alarm should always

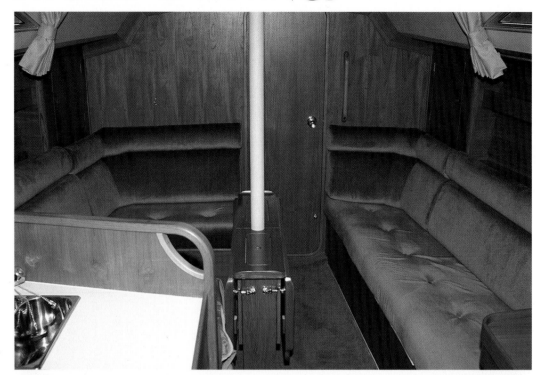

Top An attractive wooden interior with non-absorbent upholstery fabric. The fold-down table incorporates the mast support.
Above This well thought-out galley incorporates deep sinks, accessible storage and secure lockers.
Right Gimbals, a fiddle rail and a substantial crash bar ensure safe cooker operation in rough weather.

be fitted to warn you of any leaks.

The main alternative to gas cookers, for galleys that are going to be used at sea, is a paraffin pressure stove. These are very effective but a burner needs heating with methylated spirit for a minute each time it is started. Stoves using only methylated spirit are convenient and safe but the fuel is generally costly.

Large yachts whose generators produce kilowatts of power, or those spending most nights in a marina with accessible shore power, enjoy all the conveniences of domestic-style electric cooking. A

modern alternative to an electric cooker is the microwave oven, which is suitable for most types of vessel because its total power consumption is small. Even a small yacht can conveniently run its engine and alternator for the few minutes a microwave takes to complete each cooking operation.

Good marine cookers differ from those in the domestic or camping market in several important ways. The materials should not easily corrode, and the whole unit should be gimballed in the roll axis (only) of the vessel. With the movement of a

boat at sea, the utensils will slide or even jump off the stove unless constrained by special frames called 'fiddles'. These should be at least half the height of the utensils.

In good cooker designs, attention is also given to retention of grillpans and oven trays, whose contents can cause serious burns or scalds if spilled by the motion of the boat. The pressure cooker is a favourite utensil at sea because, being sealed shut during use, it does not spill its contents. It is also efficient in its use of fuel, and can keep several items of food piping hot so they don't need to be eaten

Above On large boats engine heat or electric power is used to convert seawater to fresh.
Left This 'heads' installation is unusual in that the bowl is mounted fore-and-aft, which might create problems for users when the boat is heeled.
Below A well-equipped 'heads' with hot and cold running water and a shower.

immediately after cooking.

Refrigerators for yachts include designs similar to camping and domestic units, and are operated by gas, thermoelectric or compression systems. The compression types have low electrical consumption, and one uniquely suited to any motorized boat has 'eutectic plates', inside the coolbox, through which Freon (or an ozone-friendly alternative) is pumped directly from a special compressor on the main engine. If the engine is run for at least 30 minutes each day, the thermal capacity of the plates will maintain normal refrigeration (including a small freezer compartment) for 24 hours.

Of the thermoelectric types, a compact and easily-fitted, solid state unit consisting of aircooled Peltier plates can maintain low (but not freezing) temperatures in a coolbox. The elements within the Peltier plates consist of layers of semiconductor material sandwiched between two sets of metallic strips. When an electric current is passed through the elements, heat is absorbed from the inner set of metallic strips (and thus from the coolbox) and emitted to the outside of the unit by the other set.

The heat is carried away from the unit by the aircooling of the plates. If the plates are watercooled, even lower temperatures can be maintained. However, Peltier plate refrigerators are not as popular as gas or compression types because they cannot produce really low temperatures.

Water storage tanks are made of metal, GRP or flexible fabric. There are generally few contamination problems with these if the original water supply is good and if light does not penetrate the tanks. An annual scouring with proprietary treatments based on chlorine is then sufficient precaution to ensure safe drinking water. The ideal source of the purest water is by desalination of seawater taken from well offshore. This desalination can be by evaporation, using the cooling water heat of large engines, or more commonly by a process called reverse osmosis.

INBOARD & OUTBOARD MOTORS

Sailing boats fitted with engines are sometimes described in advertisements as being 'auxiliary' or 'motor' sailers. The first description arose because the original engines fitted to boats designed to sail in all conditions were true auxiliaries; it was once common to fit, say, a 3-hp engine into a 40-foot boat which displaced 20 tons, to enable the owner to motor sedately in a flat calm, or to return to his mooring after a day's cruising.

The development of the 'motor sailer', based on workboat designs such as Scottish and Norwegian fishing vessels, gave the engine prominence as the principal propulsion unit with sails used for steadying purposes.

From a being a leisurely pastime for the few, sailing has become the weekend leisure activity of tens of thousands of ordinary people whose commitments require them to be back at work on Monday mornings. This hectic schedule has seen the engine size increase to enable cruising yachts to motor into a strong wind at 5 to 6 knots in order to get the owners home in time, and many cruising yachtsmen will switch on the engine if the wind drops and their sailing speed drops below 4 knots.

Early petrol or kerosene (paraffin) engines were slow-revving and prone to electrical contact prob-lems. The introduction of the larger, heavier marine diesel adapted from truck engines gave the yachtsman a motor ideally suited to the harsh marine environment, and the transition from the magneto to the alternator supplied a reliable source of electricity to power the increasing amount of electrical equipment installed by builders.

Only a few diesels are aircooled, as most utilize the freely-available lake, river or sea water as a cooling agent. The simplest system is the raw water cooling system, where sea water is pumped through a sea cock and strainer by an impeller pump. The water circulates through the coolant galleries of the engine and the heat exchanger which encloses the exhaust outlets from the cylinders.

The heated water is ejected into the exhaust pipe through a 'swan neck' pipe at a point below the exhaust manifold. The water then acts as an exhaust cooling agent as the exhaust gases and water pass through various water traps to emerge through the transom, where another swan neck prevents the ingress of external water into the exhaust system.

Engines are mounted on fore and aft bearers called 'beds'. Vibration is cut down by rubberized engine mounts which isolate the engine from the rigid structure of the boat. For convenience, most diesel engines are mounted under the cockpit below the companionway steps. This out-of-the-way position often makes access for servicing a difficult business unless the steps and side panels can be removed. Some engines are mounted in the saloon, with the engine box forming the base of the table, while a few racing boats fit small engines forward of the mast and use hydraulic drives to turn the propeller.

Engine compartments are acoustically insulted from the accommodation area by a sound-deadening sandwich of sheet lead and plastic foam with a non-porous skin. Air intakes and fan blowers ensure that fumes do not built up in the compartment and that the engine is supplied with sufficient quantities of air. It is prudent to mount an automatic fire extinguisher, triggered by a thermal sensor, in the engine compartment.

All modern diesels double as the generating plant for the electrical system (unless the boat has a separate generator set) and their alternators are connected to the batteries which are usually sited in, or close to, the engine compartment.

Reduction gearboxes incorporating forward, neutral and reverse gears transfer the engine power to the propeller shaft. The majority of gearboxes are watercooled, because their oil capacity is limited by their small size (which enables them to be fitted at the lowest point of the bilge).

The straight or in-line final drive has the propeller shaft in line with the final drive of the engine. This results in the engine having to be installed at the same angle as the propeller shaft. The down-angle gearbox delivers the drive at 7 degrees to the propshaft, permitting the engine to be mounted with less tilt aft. The V-drive takes the drive from the front of the engine, instead of the rear, and so the propeller shaft passes under the engine. Drive angles of up to 15 degrees are available in this configuration.

Where shaft alignment with the final drive is impossible, rubberized universal joints are used to keep the drive as smooth as possible. The propeller shaft is contained in a stern tube which has watertight seals, glands, or bearings at each end to prevent the ingress of water.

Propeller shafts are supported outside the craft by a P-bracket containing a bearing. Folding propellers snap shut when neutral is selected; feathering props stay open in neutral, but line up with the water flow. Variable pitch props can be adjusted from ahead to astern without touching the throttle setting.

Fixed-bladed props are common on cruising vessels, and their diam-

Outboards are used to power tenders and as auxiliaries on smaller yachts and multihulls. A tender's outboard can be stowed on a pushpit-mounted bracket (**above**). Note the safety lanyard. The engine on the right is mounted on a retractable bracket bolted to the transom of the central hull of a trimaran.

The Volvo Penta MD 31 is a mid-range diesel for use in yachts in excess of 35 feet. Note the flexible mounting blocks, and the down-angle of the final drive coupling.

The Volvo Saildrive combines the advantages of a diesel with the convenience of an out-drive leg. The glassfibre mount is shaped to fit the boat.

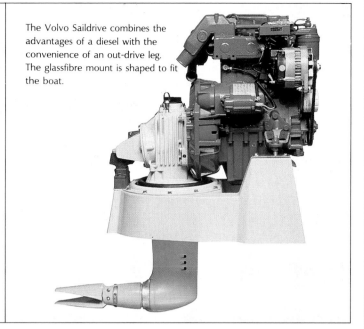

VOLVO PENTA MD31/MS4

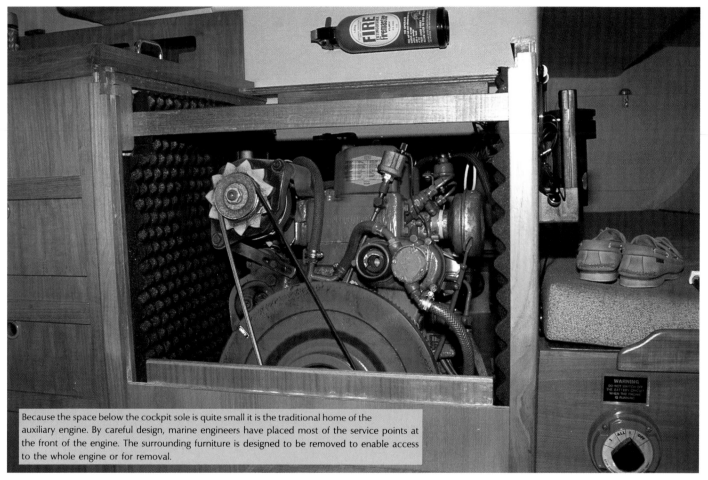

Because the space below the cockpit sole is quite small it is the traditional home of the auxiliary engine. By careful design, marine engineers have placed most of the service points at the front of the engine. The surrounding furniture is designed to be removed to enable access to the whole engine or for removal.

eter and pitch determine their driving power. The pitch of a prop is analogous to the thread of a screw, and is the theoretical distance the prop will drive the boat forward with each revolution. Fixed-bladed prop pitches are chosen to suit the engine of the boat: high-revving engines need fine-pitch props, slow-revving engines need coarse-pitch props.

The diameter and pitch of a propeller are expressed in inches, with the diameter given first. So a 15 × 8

inch prop is 15 inches in diameter and drives the boat forward 8 inches with each revolution.

One other drive system is via an outboard leg which protrudes through the bottom of the boat. The Volvo Saildrive is a good example of this type. The plastic housing for the drive leg has to be cut to fit the contours of the boat and sealed in place over a hole previously cut in the bottom of the boat.

A waterproof gasket seals the leg of the outdrive, which is shaped to

offer the least water resistance, and the propeller folds when not in use. The Saildrive combines the convenience of the outboard with the power of the diesel.

Outboard engines are self-contained units incorporating a petrol-driven two-stroke engine, ignition generator, drive shaft, gear train and final drive. Cooling water is drawn in by an impeller and discharged through the prop or a vent.

Outboards are commonly used on cruising and day boats of up to 23

feet, and are mounted on a transom bracket or inboard in the stern locker through a cutout. Small outboards are essential for dinghy work and are normally stored on the push-pit rail when not in use.

Their principal drawbacks are the need for stowage space for both engine and fuel, and the tendency of the propeller to jump out of the water in rough seas. Their advantages are their portability and the lack of a bulky engine installation in an already-cramped space.

CRUISER SAFETY EQUIPMENT

A quick look around a well-equipped yacht will reveal that uppermost in the minds of most sailors is the safety of the boat and its crew. Because a cruiser is both a working platform and a living space it has, of necessity, to incorporate safety systems for a wide variety of emergencies. Safety equipment is complex and expensive and seldom used in anger; but when it is, it must perform to specification.

On deck, the skipper's main safety concern is the protection of the crew from falling overboard. Wire lifelines supported by strong stanchions are attached to the tubular bow pulpit and stern pushpit.

When working on deck, crews should wear harnesses which are clipped to wire or webbing jackstays running down each side deck from bow to stern, and strong U-bolts sited at strategic points around the cockpit will enable crews emerging from below to clip on before they step on deck. At night, or in fog, crews should also wear lifejackets which can support their body-weight in the water. The folding, gas-operated versions are popular with racing crews.

During man-overboard recovery a dan buoy, equipped with a drogue to prevent drift and a flashing light to attract attention, is the first thing to be released. A line attached to the dan pulls a horseshoe buoy from its mounting outside the pushpit or guardrails. It may also have a drogue, a flashing light and a smoke canister.

Strobe lights have not gained universal acceptance by maritime agencies, but most skippers are prepared to use them to rescue a crew member, and to face the consequences later. Orange smoke canisters should be used by day to mark the approximate position.

If no dan is carried, two horseshoe buoys should be, one fitted with a drogue and light, the other attached to the boat with 100 metres of line so that the victim can be winched back once contact is established.

Stowing a raft presents considerable problems. If it is stowed on deck it has to withstand a breaking sea without being dislodged, and so it must be lashed firmly in its mounting chocks. However, it must also be capable of being released quickly by any member of the crew. If it is stored in a locker or below deck, it must be easily deployed and must be accessible if fire breaks out.

When a liferaft is deployed it *must* be tied to the parent craft and the painter must be pulled out rapidly to keep the raft alongside

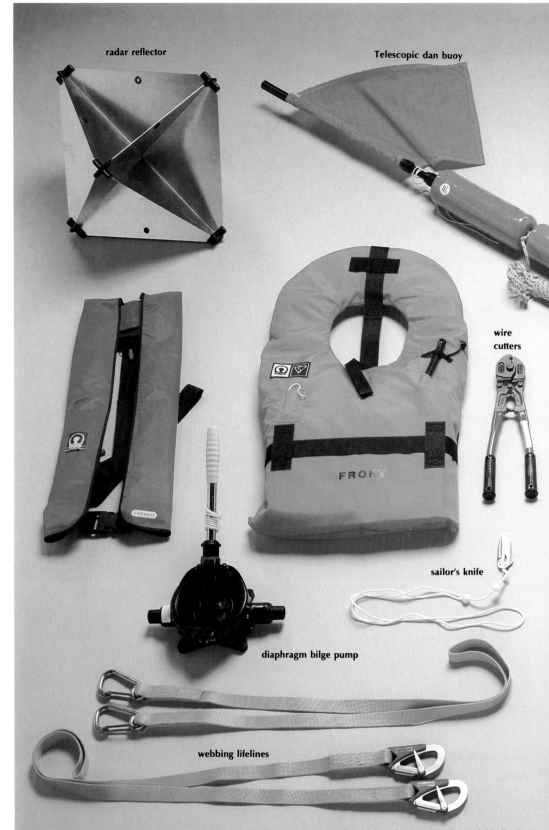

Radar reflectors are designed to reflect the incoming radar beam back to the sender. The example shown folds flat for stowage. Lifejackets should be chosen to suit their intended working environment, and the best option for offshore use is the CO_2-inflated jacket incorporating a safety harness. The foam-filled jacket is ideal for day sailing or for going ashore in the tender. Webbing lifelines clip to either a safety harness or to a specially-adapted lifejacket. When moving about the deck at night, or in rough weather, the wearer clips the snap clip to a jackstay running along the side deck or to strongpoints. The diaphragm bilge pump is a simple pump which enables large quantities of water to be pumped overboard. It is operated by rocking the handle to and fro. The sailor's knife usually incorporates a marlin spike for splicing ropes and a shackle key for tightening and loosening shackle pins.

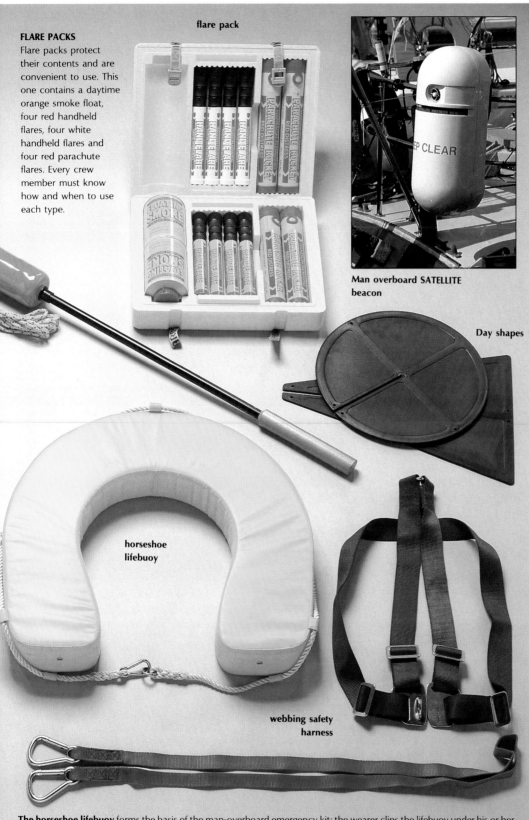

flare pack

FLARE PACKS
Flare packs protect their contents and are convenient to use. This one contains a daytime orange smoke float, four red handheld flares, four white handheld flares and four red parachute flares. Every crew member must know how and when to use each type.

Man overboard SATELLITE beacon

Day shapes

horseshoe lifebuoy

webbing safety harness

The horseshoe lifebuoy forms the basis of the man-overboard emergency kit; the wearer clips the lifebuoy under his or her arms for additional support. The **telescopic dan buoy** incorporates a flashing light which can be seen by the returning vessel. It is attached to the horseshoe lifebuoy and should have a drogue fitted to prevent undue drift in strong winds. The man-overboard/shipwreck **satellite beacon** is representative of electronic devices which when released pinpoint the position of the victim or vessel. Mechanical systems are designed to give the victim support and to enable the crew to winch him or her back to the boat. **Webbing safety harnesses** are designed to be worn over all protective clothing, but they are often difficult to get into unless properly adjusted beforehand. The front buckle is normally locked by inserting the snaphook of the lifeline. **Day shapes** are signals shown at the fore part of a vessel. A black ball denotes that the boat is anchored, while a black cone, apex down, shows that the boat is under power.

when it inflates. If you let the raft out to its farthest travel from a moving boat you may have great difficulty in pulling it back. For maximum protection the twin-tubed, double-floored rafts or the Givens buoy raft are difficult to better.

Keeping dry and warm is one of the secrets of survival at sea, and no-one should be permitted to swim to the raft unless circumstances dictate that course of action. Once inside, keeping warm and dry is the first priority, closely followed by seeking rescue.

Attracting attention sounds easy in theory, but even close inshore it may take some time for someone to recognize your distress signals and summon the rescue agencies. The VHF radio is the obvious choice for attracting attention because you can tell the agencies who you are and where, and what the problem is, and receive further questions, give answers and abandon ship knowing that someone is on their way to assist you.

The flare pack should be a plastic container with a secure top, which can be lifted out of its stowage and placed directly in the liferaft to augment the flares already there. The problem with flares is that you never know you've been seen until your rescuers arrive, and if you are far offshore you should ration your use of flares because your supply of them is limited.

Close inshore, though, you can usually afford to use flares or smoke of any colour at 3- to 5-minute intervals. If there are boats around, let off a white flare followed half a minute later by a red flare, then try again five minutes later.

Fires on boats can be lethal because of the toxic fumes given off by many of the fabrics, foams and resins used in building and furnishing them. Firefighting equipment is often confined to one or two dry powder, CO_2 or Halon extinguishers, which should be stowed in protected spaces because they get knocked over if stowed out in the open, but remember that you can extinguish many fires (except those involving fuel or electrical equipment) by dissipating the heat with buckets of seawater.

Fires in the engine compartment are rare, but can be stifled by inserting the extinguisher through a vent in the engine casing. Turn off the fuel at source but remember that the residual heat of the metal may flash up a fire again once the extinguisher has had its initial effect. Again, cooling with water is an alternative if it is safe to open up the compartment and if the fuel is turned off.

CLOTHING & FOOTWEAR

Splash proof thermal jacket

Splash proof thermal long-john

padded waistcoat

polo neck sweater

towel scarf

rugby shirt

thermal socks

boot liners

cotton trousers

thermal underwear

If you are dinghy sailing where the weather and water are warm, or cruising on a warm, dry day, your choice of clothing depends basically on your personal preferences and perhaps on the current fashions. Most large chandlers sell a good range of casual clothing – such as shirts, sweaters and caps – designed specifically for the leisure cruising market, but they also stock the more practical clothing you will need for serious sailing in cold weather and rough seas.

Sailing clothing has two principal roles to perform: to keep you dry and to keep you at the right temperature, neither too hot nor too cold. Sailing footwear also has a dual purpose, in that it should enable you to remain securely on your feet as you walk about the boat, and be capable of providing some form of weatherproof protection for your feet. If your clothing (and footwear) looks good, then all the better, but it must be capable of doing its job.

Neoprene wetsuits are popular with many dinghy sailors, but for coastal cruising or offshore sailing the three-layer system of sailing clothing is now becoming the market standard. This system begins with a

The use of non-absorbent materials for clothing worn under waterproofs has revolutionized the way sailors dress. The thin, non-absorbent **thermal undergarments** wick the moisture away from the skin and prevent moving air from cooling the body. Being very thin and light they permit freedom of movement. They are used when the air temperature falls below 10°C (50°F). The intermediate-layer clothing has a thin, lightweight outer shell which is water-repellent but still permits body water vapour to pass through. The inner lining of 'fluffy' non-absorbent material creates a thick layer of trapped air which insulates the wearer from the elements. Available in high-waist or **long-john trousers**, with waistcoat and long-sleeved jacket, this style of clothing is very popular with cruising and racing crews for a wide range of weather conditions. It can be worn under the heavier waterproof protective clothing. **Thermal socks** and **boot liners** ensure that the feet and lower legs remain warm, while a **towelling scarf** will prevent water dribbling down one's neck. Casual sailing clothing has replaced the more traditional sailing jerseys and **cotton/canvas trousers. Rugby shirts** and loose cotton trousers combine warmth and protection with style, as do tracksuits made of thicker materials.

layer of lightweight underwear next to the body, designed to draw perspiration rapidly away from the body while providing some warmth and comfort.

Over this foundation goes a 'bodywarmer' layer, consisting of manmade fabric garments, which provides genuine warmth by trapping air beneath it. This layer may also provide a limited amount of waterproofing. Finally, an outer layer of foul-weather gear is applied to keep the weather at bay.

In modern sailing clothing systems, manmade fibres rule the roost as there is little or no place for natural fibres, such as wool and cotton, which have poor thermal qualities when damp. For the foundation layer, the most popular fabric – used

by nearly all the major manufacturers – is Merkalon. This polypropylene fibre has a very low thermal conductivity as well as being ideally suited for the job of carrying moisture away from the surface of the skin.

Your choice of garment style for the foundation layer will be between an all-in-one suit and separates consisting of long-john pants and a crewneck or polo-neck top. In summer, this foundation layer can provide you with adequate warmth when worn under a single waterproof outer layer.

If conditions are not warm, you will need a bodywarmer layer. For this, a variety of options exist ranging from the 'furry bear' suit, which is the classic polar garment, to suits

made of the more modern fabrics such as Terrida and acrylic polyester. The majority of polyester fabrics used for this middle layer are no longer prone to 'pill' and have very low water absorption. The ability to dry quickly is a further asset of these materials.

Many middle-layer garments currently produced have a lightweight outer skin of waterproof fabric. This feature can be a major asset on those days which do not merit full oilskins, as you can get some water protection from your middle-layer clothes without the added (and perhaps unwanted) warmth of an outer oilskin layer.

For middle-layer garments a number of options exist, but the current trend is toward a one-piece, sleeveless top/trousers combination plus a jacket, as this offers the greatest flexibility in controlling body temperature.

The one-piece garment keeps your legs and body warm, and when the weather isn't too cold you can wear it, without the jacket, under your oilskins. As the temperature drops, the jacket can be added to give more warmth to your body and arms.

With a well-designed clothing system, you can combine the various garments in a number of different ways, to give you just the right amount of warmth and waterproofing for the prevailing conditions. There is as little point in getting too hot as there is in getting too cold, and this is where well-chosen clothing will play its part.

For your outer, foul-weather layer of clothing there is a very wide range to choose from, and one of the most important factors to take into account when making your choice is the type of sailing you intend to wear it for. An expensive set of deep-ocean racing oilskins, for example, would be pointless for leisurely estuary cruising, while oilskins suitable for mainly inshore sailing will struggle to keep the water out on a long and windy day of sailing offshore.

No oilskins will keep out the elements unless they fit you properly. It is worth checking that, for instance, the trousers are long enough even when you are in a crouched position, and good wrist seals and neck protection are essential if you are not to suffer a continuing deluge of water within your clothing.

Outer clothing is made from a wide range of fabrics, including PVC and woven nylons which will have an inner proofing to prevent water ingress. Since all fabrics are sewn together it is important to ensure that the seams of any chosen garment are adequately and securely taped.

External features to consider are handwarmer pockets, a hood to keep your head dry, and attachment points for a lifejacket and a safety harness. Many oilskins also incorporate additional safety features such as whistles and reflective safety strips.

When you're choosing your clothing, don't forget that you will also need protection for your head and hands. A large proportion of the heat loss from your body is through your head, so on a chilly day a polypropylene hat or balaclava will provide much extra comfort. For your hands, a good set of leather gloves will provide not only warmth but also protection against cuts and blisters, and are a valuable investment.

It is also worth remembering that even on apparently overcast days at sea it is possible to get sunburnt, so a proprietary cream and lip salve are useful additions to the kitbag of any sailor with sensitive skin.

There are three principal types of footwear for sailing: rubber boots, leather deckshoes and the sailing version of running shoes. Of these, the leather deckshoes are perhaps the most popular and least practical, as they provide little water resistance and need constant attention to prevent drying-out and cracking.

The running-shoe type have specially-designed soles of soft rubber to provide good grip on wet decks. Like the leather deckshoes they have no real water resistance, but they are very comfortable on summer days when the wind is blowing at 15 knots or less.

For anyone planning a long time at sea, a good pair of rubber sailing boots is essential. A non-slip sole is vital and a tie around the top of the boot will help keep water out. There are many types and styles to choose from, and a useful feature to consider is a removable liner/insole which will enable the boot to be dried easily. To complete the kit, a good set of wool/nylon or acrylic deck socks will cushion your feet and keep them dry and warm.

A harsh sailing environment often necessitates the wearing of a totally waterproof outer layer of clothing that stands up to heavy abrasion. The majority of materials used for this type of clothing are designed to prevent water passing through and are often lined with permeable layer so that body vapor condenses on the inside of the outer shell material and runs off it.

High-fit pants are kept up with elasticated suspenders, and a Velcro adjuster permits the bottoms to be fitted snugly to deck boots. Hooded jackets totally protect the upper body and are the key to an efficient waterproofing system. With its built-in safety harness and reflective strips, the jacket shown here is intended for serious offshore use.

Deck boots are designed to protect and to give a good grip, while thick socks or thermal liners keep the feet warm. Gloves and a wool hat complete the protection of the offshore sailor. Deck shoes and a yachting cap can be worn on sunny days or when going ashore.

TIDES & WEATHER

Together, the individual and combined natural forces of the tides and the weather still preoccupy the thinking of all those who sail on the sea. For all but a small band of dedicated racing and long-distance cruising crews, the decision to set sail is primarily dependent upon the forecast wind and wave conditions.

Once under way, the destination of a sailboat is often determined by any improvement or deterioration in the existing conditions. All the time, the skipper is weighing up the seaworthiness of the boat, the welfare of the crew (usually the family), and his or her ability to second-guess the mass of readily available broadcast weather information.

Sailing, especially out of sight of land, presents one of the few frontier challenges left to modern man, but there is a marked contrast between today's sailors, with their banks of electronic equipment, weather printouts and instant radio contact, and their seafaring ancestors whose survival depended on their ability to interpret sea, sky and seabed. Yet each generation shares the common elements of seamanship and decision-making, and experience in dealing with the unexpected is still an important attribute.

There *are* sailing areas, such as Southern California and the Mediterranean, where 'ideal' sailing conditions can be found for much of the year. However, most of the world's sailors, living in the northern latitudes of Europe and North America, have to learn to live with the changeable weather dished out by the prevailing westerly airstream and with the changes in the height of the surface of the sea caused by the twice-daily tides.

Unlike the difficult business of predicting the weather, it is possible to predict the times and heights of each day's tides a long time in advance and with a great deal of accuracy. These predictions are published as tide tables and are available on a national and local basis in most popular sailing areas.

The force that generates the tides is the strong gravitational pull of the moon, which is relatively close to the earth, combined with the weaker gravitational pull of the more distant sun.

The predictability of tides is due to the regular movement of the moon around the earth once every 24 hours and 50 minutes. This regular movement, combined with the relative position of the sun, gives us our two-week cycles of spring and neap tides.

We talk about weather systems because there is a semblance of order about weather patterns, and in predicting the weather the barometer has long maintained its importance as an essential indicator of approaching weather systems. Its function is to display the pressure of the atmosphere at the earth's surface, this pressure being measured in inches (of mercury) or in millibars.

The original standard measuring instrument, invented in the 17th century by Italian physicist Evangelista Torricelli, was a column of mercury contained in a 32-inch test tube upended in a dish of mercury. Pressure fluctuations are only about 20 percent of the column, seldom exceeding a low of 25.5 inches (863.5 millibars) or a high of 31.5 inches (1066.7 millibars).

The invention of the less accurate (but more convenient) aneroid barometer, by Lucius Vidi in 1843, was a welcome advance. Pressure is shown on a clock-like display by a pointer, activated by a mechanical linkage attached to a thin-walled, partially-evacuated metal container that expands and contracts as pressure decreases and increases.

A second pointer can be moved by hand to record existing pressure, thereafter becoming a reference point that shows clearly whether the air pressure is rising or falling.

A refinement of the aneroid barometer is the barograph, which makes a continuous record of pressure changes by marking them on a paper chart wrapped around a slowly-revolving drum. This delicate instrument can be taken to sea if suitably damped (insulated from shocks) and gives a comprehensive record of pressure patterns.

Sailors need to know the trends of pressure changes because these are closely related to well-documented weather patterns associated with large masses of high- and low-pressure air.

Most barometers are marked up to show the general conditions to expect when pressure is rising or falling, but these markings (such as 'fair' and 'rain') are only an approximate guide and should not be relied upon.

Excesses of pressure differences, especially in areas of extremely low-pressure air originating in the tropics or at the interface of polar and tropical air, combine to produce intense and sometimes extensive storms. These storms — typhoons, hurricanes and localized tornadoes — cause considerable damage and loss of life and are bad news for the unwary sailor.

The combination of wind-induced waves, rapid changes in pressure and the movement of surface water can produce awesome sea conditions. Hurricane-force winds produce short, unstable waves that can exceed 40 feet from trough to crest and will easily overwhelm small craft.

Given that seafarers need a lot of help to ensure their safety, it is not surprising that weather forecasts are of special importance. These are available from a wide variety of agencies including TV, radio, coastguard stations and newspapers.

Specialist marine or 'shipping' forecasts give stylized predictions for designated sea areas, as well as giving reports from weather stations enabling experienced sailors to draw their own weather charts. In addition, many craft carry weatherfax equipment that prints out weather charts at regular intervals to give a visual update of prevailing conditions.

TIDES

As the moon orbits the earth, its gravitational pull causes two tidal 'waves', on opposite sides of the world, to follow its progress. These waves do not rush around the oceans causing havoc, but rather they are bulges causing up to fifty feet of change in sea level between high and low water.

A tidal bulge becomes most noticeable when it approaches the shallows of the continents and is translated into the lateral movement of water—the incoming flood tides, and the outgoing ebb tides.

When the sun and the moon are both in line with the earth — at new moon and full moon — their gravitational pulls combine to produce the highest high tides (the spring high tides) and the greatest movement of water.

At the neap tides, the sun and moon are at 90° to each other relative to the earth — the first and last quarters of the moon — and so their gravitational pulls work against each other, producing the lowest high tides and the least amount of movement of water.

Fortunately, the predictability of the relative positions of the sun and moon enables hydrographers to produce tide tables years in advance of the event. These are published as nautical almanacs covering numerous ports or tidal stations, or as localized tide tables, and are available from chandlers or fishing tackle shops.

Since the moon orbits the earth once every 24 hours and 50 minutes, the two tidal waves representing high water occur approximately every 12 hours and 25 minutes.

Low water occurs between 5 and 6½ hours after high water, depending on the location of the tidal station.

As with most simple concepts there is a plethora of names to describe the various phenomena related to tides. For instance, the *chart datum* is the level from which measurements are made to determine the heights of tides. It is normally the level of low water at the time of the *lowest astronomical tide* (LAT). Everything above this line is shown on charts (maps of the coast and seabed) as *drying heights*. Everything below this line is shown as *charted depths* in metres.

Tide tables give the times of high and low water together with the height of high water (above chart datum) and the height of low water (above chart datum). Subtracting low water from high water heights gives the *range* of the tide which is the depth of the moon's tidal wave.

Sooner or later, most sailors have to sail over areas of the seabed which dry out at low water. The first essential for this is to know how much water there is at a given point at a given time to enable your boat to sail over it without striking the seabed or an obstruction.

A very rough guide, but one which is better than a blind guess, is the *rule of twelfths*. This is based on observations that show that in the six hours between low and high water, the hourly depth changes related to the range (difference in tidal heights) are:

- first hour — 1/12 range
- second hour — 2/12 range
- third hour — 3/12 range
- fourth hour — 3/12 range
- fifth hour — 2/12 range
- sixth hour — 1/12 range

These twelfths of the tidal range can be memorized easily, as they are simply 1, 2, 3 and then 3, 2, 1, over the six-hour period.

On a falling (ebb) tide you cannot afford to make a mistake, for once aground you will stay there until the moon drags the next tidal wave to your rescue. A more accurate method is to use the published tidal curves to calculate the depth.

The rhythmic cycle of the tide creates accompanying periodic river-like movements of water, especially where the oceans shallow along coastlines. The effect is greatest around headlands and in restricted shallow waters.

These horizontal movements of water are known in the United States as currents, and in Britain as tidal streams. To the English, currents are the non-periodic horizontal movements of water caused by the major wind systems of the world. These non-periodic movements include the Gulf Stream, originating in the Caribbean and flowing to the Newfoundland Banks, and the North Atlantic Drift, sustained by the prevailing westerly winds and carrying water from the North American coast to well within the Arctic Circle.

Because of their predictability, sailors can learn to use tidal streams to their advantage by sailing with them whenever possible and by gauging the depths of water so that they can traverse shallows at high water.

On the downside, when the wind and a tidal stream are in opposition they can create life-threatening rips and tidal races in narrows and off prominent headlands.

You should also remember that, when you are sailing against the tide, if the stream is running faster than your boat can sail you will find yourself going backward, even though your sails are full and you

Above *Slipways make it easy to launch dinghies at low tide.*
Right *When anchoring, allow for the rise and fall of the tide.*

seem to be making good speed over the water. If you are approaching the shore under these conditions, the stream will carry you farther out to sea; if you are heading out to sea, it can wash you back to the shore, and possibly aground or onto rocks.

Most of the tidal stream atlases that are published contain 13 charts showing tidal streams at hourly intervals from 6 hours before high water to 6 hours after it at a designated Standard Port.

Before delving into tidal stream atlases, though, it's important to appreciate that tidal flow can be observed and that this is always the best guide to its direction, especially in estuaries.

A pole, buoy, moored boat or a rock will all show a wake streaming out in the direction that the water is moving. It's almost as if they are moving through stationary water and, if the stream is strong, they will have a bow wave on the upstream side. Moored boats will point into the tide if the wind is light.

If you are afloat and uncertain of the direction of the stream, let the boat drift and observe the relative positions of a shoreline feature and a feature somewhere behind it. Imagine that the front mark is stationary. Any apparent movement of the back marker will be in the same direction as that of the tidal stream.

In estuaries, the strongest stream is in the deepest channel and, should you find yourself battling against an adverse stream, back eddies and weaker streams are to be found at the edge — but watch the depth of water beneath you!

ESTIMATING DIRECTION OF TIDAL FLOW

A pole, buoy, moored boat or a rock will show a wake streaming in the direction that the water is moving

flow →

USING A TRANSIT TO GAUGE TIDAL FLOW

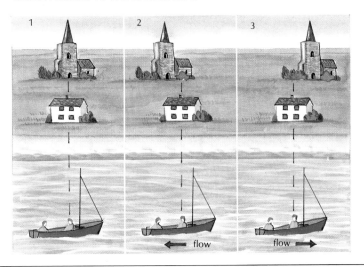

1   2   3

← flow   flow →

1 To find the direction of a tidal stream or current, let your boat drift and observe the positions of shoreline features. When two are in line with each other, as seen from the boat, the imaginary line joining them is a 'line of transit'.
2 and 3 Any apparent movement of the back marker (here a church tower) relative to the front marker (the house) will be in the same direction as the tidal stream or current is flowing.

ESTIMATING TIDE RISE

You can use your tide tables and the 'rule of twelfths' to estimate the depth of the water at a particular time and place. The rule of twelfths is based on the amount the tide rises and falls during each successive hour from low to high tide and vice versa.

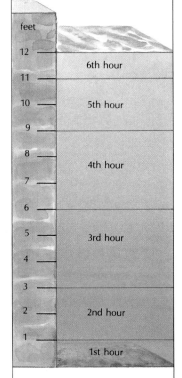

feet	
12	6th hour
11	
10	5th hour
9	
8	4th hour
7	
6	
5	3rd hour
4	
3	2nd hour
2	
1	1st hour

The approximate hourly rise of a twelve-foot tide from low to high water. The actual time from low to high water is only 6 hours approximately.

AIR MASSES & CLOUDS

Left *Clouds are a useful indicator of what is happening with the weather.*

The weather is the result of the nature, motion and interaction of low-pressure and high-pressure air masses. To find out where these large areas of low and high pressure air originate we have to look at what drives the weather — the heat from the sun.

When the sun shines on the earth's surface it heats it, and as a result the air above it heats up, expands and rises. This rising warmed air creates a partial vacuum — an area of low pressure — and as it rises, surrounding higher-pressure air flows in to replace it.

When the sun doesn't shine — at night, or during polar winters — the earth's surface cools, contracts and sinks. This denser, heavier high-pressure air flows outward, displacing the surrounding lighter low-pressure air.

Because the sun's effects are greater in the tropics than at the poles, there are semipermanent bands of high- and low-pressure air masses around the earth at different latitudes. There is a region of high pressure at each pole, and a band of low pressure around the equator.

Warmed air rising from the equatorial regions spreads to the north and the south, and as it does so it cools and sinks again over the Horse Latitudes, forming bands of high-pressure air masses (the subtropical highs) at about 30°N and 30°S. Between these bands of high pressure and the polar high pressure regions are further bands of low pressure, at about 60°N and 60°S. Each pressure band is sustained by the global and local heating effects of the sun.

Air returning to the equatorial zone from the adjacent high pressure bands is deflected to the west by the Coriolis Effect — a result of the earth's rotation — to become the Northeast Trades in the Northern Hemisphere and the Southeast Trades in the Southern.

Air flowing to higher latitudes from these high pressure bands becomes the Prevailing Westerlies of the Northern and Southern Hemispheres, while the outward flow from the areas of cold, dense air at the poles is deflected to the west by the rotation of the earth to create the Polar Easterlies.

There are four categories of air mass, each with its own characteristics and classified according to where it originated. These are Continental Polar air (cold and dry, originating over land near the poles), Continental Tropical (warm and dry, originating over land in the tropics), Maritime Polar (cold and wet, formed over seas near the poles) and Maritime Tropical (warm and wet, formed over tropical seas).

An air mass may thus be warm or cold, and wet or dry, but once formed, it tends to retain those characteristics even when in contact with different air masses. Different air masses do not readily mix and it is this characteristic which creates the weather systems, especially at the interface or *front line* of converging masses of air.

In the Northern Hemisphere, air flowing out of the high pressure zones is diverted to the right by the Coriolis effect. This results in slow-moving high-pressure air masses (anticyclones) that rotate slowly in a clockwise direction. In the Southern Hemisphere, the flow of high pressure air is deflected to the left, and so the southern anticyclones rotate in a counterclockwise direction. Anticyclones usually bring clear, settled weather.

Sea-based low pressure areas are established in northern and southern latitudes over water which is warmer than the adjacent polar ice-caps. Air flowing into these low pressure areas is deflected by the Coriolis effect, producing a vortex spiral (counterclockwise in the Northern Hemisphere, clockwise in the Southern) which is seen at its most extreme in hurricanes and typhoons. Low pressure is characterized by mostly unsettled, moist and windy conditions.

The opposite rotation of pockets of warm and cold air enables them to intermesh like a giant system of cogs in a global gearbox. It is only at the junctions between high- and low-pressure air masses that conflict occurs, and the battle intensifies as the air masses intermingle and either gradually lose their identity or combine to produce destructive forces.

For most of the time, warm, moist, low-pressure air rises, cools, deposits its excess moisture and descends without a great deal of fuss, but it can sometimes act as a catalyst to produce violent weather conditions.

A depression forms when the convex leading edge of an approaching cold, high-pressure air mass slides under the concave edge of the lighter, warm air of a low-pressure air mass, forcing it to rise. The line of interface between the two, with its attendant high, white cloud, slopes away from the observer. This is the often-volatile *cold front*, with its attendant thunderstorms and strong, veering winds.

Warm moist air overtaking cool denser air climbs up and over the convex slope, creating clouds as it rises and cools. The line of interface and its cloud formations slope toward the observer, and the first indication of this approaching *warm front* is the high cloud of the already-mixing air. This is followed

POLAR AND TROPICAL AIR MASSES

This map shows the average movement of the world's major Maritime Polar (MP), Maritime Tropical (MT), Continental Polar (CP) and Continental Tropical (CT) air masses.

→ MP
→ MT
→ CP
→ CT
----- Equator

Average movement of Polar and Tropical air masses

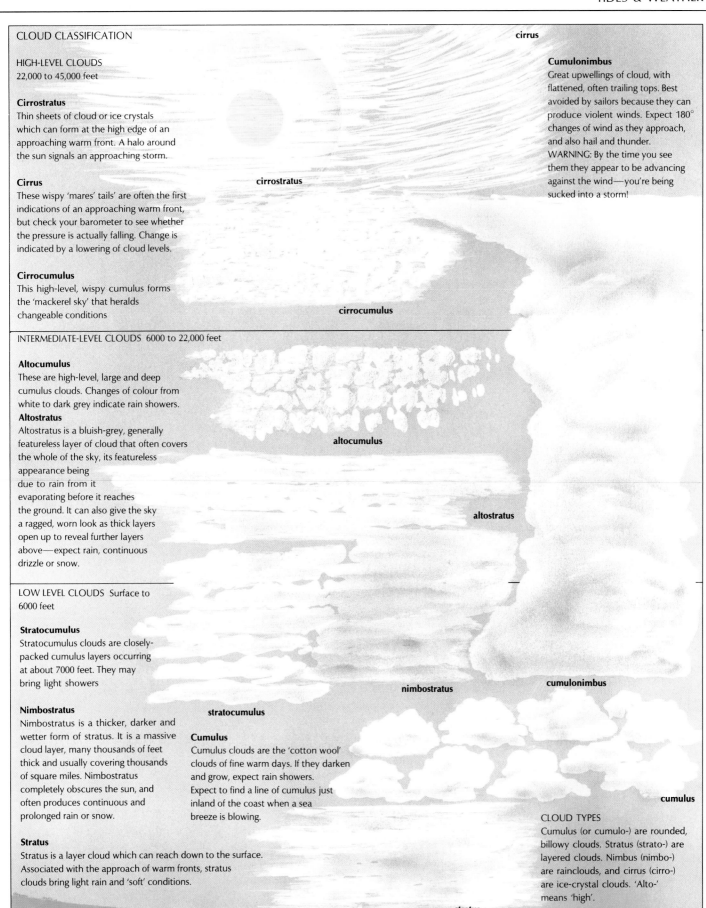

CLOUD CLASSIFICATION

HIGH-LEVEL CLOUDS
22,000 to 45,000 feet

Cirrostratus
Thin sheets of cloud or ice crystals which can form at the high edge of an approaching warm front. A halo around the sun signals an approaching storm.

Cirrus
These wispy 'mares' tails' are often the first indications of an approaching warm front, but check your barometer to see whether the pressure is actually falling. Change is indicated by a lowering of cloud levels.

Cirrocumulus
This high-level, wispy cumulus forms the 'mackerel sky' that heralds changeable conditions

INTERMEDIATE-LEVEL CLOUDS 6000 to 22,000 feet

Altocumulus
These are high-level, large and deep cumulus clouds. Changes of colour from white to dark grey indicate rain showers.

Altostratus
Altostratus is a bluish-grey, generally featureless layer of cloud that often covers the whole of the sky, its featureless appearance being due to rain from it evaporating before it reaches the ground. It can also give the sky a ragged, worn look as thick layers open up to reveal further layers above—expect rain, continuous drizzle or snow.

LOW LEVEL CLOUDS Surface to 6000 feet

Stratocumulus
Stratocumulus clouds are closely-packed cumulus layers occurring at about 7000 feet. They may bring light showers

Nimbostratus
Nimbostratus is a thicker, darker and wetter form of stratus. It is a massive cloud layer, many thousands of feet thick and usually covering thousands of square miles. Nimbostratus completely obscures the sun, and often produces continuous and prolonged rain or snow.

Stratus
Stratus is a layer cloud which can reach down to the surface. Associated with the approach of warm fronts, stratus clouds bring light rain and 'soft' conditions.

Cumulus
Cumulus clouds are the 'cotton wool' clouds of fine warm days. If they darken and grow, expect rain showers. Expect to find a line of cumulus just inland of the coast when a sea breeze is blowing.

Cumulonimbus
Great upwellings of cloud, with flattened, often trailing tops. Best avoided by sailors because they can produce violent winds. Expect 180° changes of wind as they approach, and also hail and thunder.
WARNING: By the time you see them they appear to be advancing against the wind—you're being sucked into a storm!

CLOUD TYPES
Cumulus (or cumulo-) are rounded, billowy clouds. Stratus (strato-) are layered clouds. Nimbus (nimbo-) are rainclouds, and cirrus (cirro-) are ice-crystal clouds. 'Alto-' means 'high'.

by a period of rain and poor visibility until the arrival of the next air mass.

An *occluded front* occurs when one wedge of cold air catches up with a preceding one, and the warm air that was separating them is squeezed upwards en masse. This gives rise to strong winds and rain if the cold and warm air masses differ considerably in temperature and humidity.

Clouds, which are classified according to their shape, colour and height, are useful indicators of approaching weather systems. Because each family of clouds is created by specific circumstances of temperature, humidity and height, clouds tell the experienced observer what is happening with the weather and what is to come, hence their importance to navigators world-wide.

WINDS & STORMS

Sailboats are designed to derive most of their power from the effect of the wind on the sails, yet many recreational sailors choose to sail in only a very small range of the winds available to them.

20 knots of wind is a fresh breeze, and will have many family cruisers scurrying for shelter. 30 kts is a yachtsman's gale. Beyond 30 kts those who choose to leave harbour must have the experience and the type of craft to cope with extreme conditions. 40 knots of wind means the air is moving at 46 mph — try keeping your arm extended out of the window of a car moving at that speed and you will begin to appreciate the power of strong winds.

The main reason for the general dislike of fresh to strong winds is not the wind itself, but the choppy seas it generates in a relatively short time, especially when the wind is blowing against the tide.

Inexperienced family crews or friends out for the day quickly succumb to the large angles of heel, the cold spray and seasickness. The wise, experienced skipper will pay careful attention to the forecasts and choose the days which best suit his or her chosen style and crew.

Winds are caused by air moving from an area of high atmospheric pressure to one of lower pressure. These areas of differing pressure may be air masses such as anticyclones and depressions, or they may be of more local origin. For instance, air cooling and sinking over a cold expanse of water will cause a localized increase in pressure, while air being heated and rising over adjacent warm land will cause a localized drop in pressure.

Whatever their origin, the closer the centres of high and low pressure are to each other, and the

greater the pressure difference between them, the stronger the wind will be.

Some of the most violent and destructive winds are associated with some of the smallest weather systems. The principal culprits are cumulonimbus clouds; because of their vertical development and unstable air, these create vortexes and whirlpools of air that, at their worst, result in tornados or waterspouts.

The rapidly-rising air associated with cumulonimbus clouds sucks in surrounding air with a rotary motion. The centre of rotation can develop into an intense area of low pressure which reaches down to the earth's surface and, like a huge vacuum cleaner, sucks up solid objects and explodes buildings.

At sea, waterspouts are created in thundery conditions associated with an extremely cold front breaking up hot, humid weather.

Tornados and waterspouts experienced in Britain are usually weak compared with those of the central states of the USA. However, infrequent but violent line squalls are a feature of UK weather, especially along the south coast of England. Again, they are associated with the approach of a cold front following a period of settled weather, or the rapid development of massive cumulus clouds on a hot day.

If, when you are sailing, the wind suddenly changes direction by 180°, look at the sky in the downwind direction — the direction in which the new wind is travelling. If the sky there is dark grey, or black, or greenish purple, and the sun becomes progressively obscured, prepare yourself, your crew and your boat for a violent squall, or seek immediate (within 15 minutes) shelter. On open water you will see an

intense white line at the junction of sea and sky. This bright line is the rain hitting the sea; don't ask any more questions — act!

The squall, usually another 180° change of wind, will be preceded by violent rain falling out of the front of massively-developed thunder heads. In such conditions, winds of up to 70 knots have been recorded on what were previously hot summer days.

The term 'depression' — formerly used to denote interactions between cold and warm air masses— is now also used to describe larger, well-developed areas

Above *Even experienced racing crews can have problems in very strong winds.*

of strong to hurricane-force winds.

The classic ingredients of a depression are fairly large masses of well-developed cold polar air and warm moist tropical air thrown together over a warm land mass or, better still, over a warm sea.

The stirring motion that mixes the depression is supplied by the natural cogwheel-like interaction between the different air masses, and it is the rotation of the low-pressure warm air that drags in, and down from the upper atmosphere, the

---

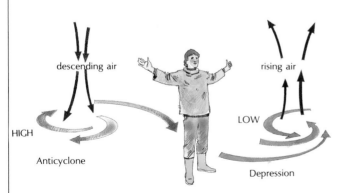

AIR MOVEMENT
Winds are caused by air flowing out of an area of high pressure into adjacent areas of low pressure

descending air

rising air

HIGH

LOW

Anticyclone

Depression

BUYS BALLOT'S LAW In the Northern Hemisphere, if you stand with your back to the wind you will have low pressure to your left (in the Southern Hemisphere it will be to your right)

THE PREVAILING WINDS
This is the basic pattern of prevailing winds around the world.
In practice, this pattern is distorted by the land masses and the passage of weather systems.

LAND AND SEA BREEZES
These breezes are the result of differences in temperature between the air over the land and that over the sea.

60°
Westerlies
30°
NE Trade Winds
SE Trade Winds
30°
Westerlies
60°

Sea breeze

Land breeze

THE BEAUFORT WIND SCALE

SCALE	DESCRIPTION	WIND SPEED km/hour	knots	VISIBLE SIGNS	SAILING CRITERIA
0	Calm	<1	<1	Flat, calm sea. On land, smoke rises vertically, leaves are still.	Dinghies should be heeled to reduce wetted area and allow the sails to form aerofoil shape. Cruisers need to use engines to make steerage way.
1	Light air	1–5	1–3	Slight rippling of the sea. Smoke drifts, wind vanes unaffected.	Dinghies can make gentle forward motion with flattened sails, and balanced to be slightly bow-down and heeled to leeward. Cruisers need engine power.
2	Light breeze	6–11	4–6	Small wavelets develop. Leaves rustle, flags and weather vanes stir. The wind can be felt on the face.	Dinghies can sail upright at a reasonable speed and with full sails. With 6 knots of wind, a good cruiser racer may make 3 to 4 kts; other cruisers need engine power.
3	Gentle breeze	12–19	7–10	Wave crests begin to break. Leaves move continuously, light flags are extended.	Ideal conditions for dinghies because there is sufficient wind and the waves are still quite small. Cruisers can make steady progress under sail.
4	Moderate breeze	20–28	11–16	Wave lengths increase, with frequent white horses. Most flags extended, light branches move and dust may be raised.	Good for experienced dinghy sailors but learners should go ashore. Most cruisers can reach hull speed; some need reefed mainsails and part-furled headsails.
5	Fresh breeze	29–38	17–21	Many breaking wave crests. Small, leafy trees begin to sway, tops of all trees move.	Excellent for experienced dinghy crews; the less experienced may be capsized. Ideal for cruisers, but light boats need to use smaller sails to reduce heeling.
6	Strong breeze	39–49	22–27	Large waves develop, with foamy crests and spray. Large tree branches move, wind whistles in telephone and electricity lines.	Most dinghy crews at their limit; many will be overpowered. Most cruisers will head for shelter, with mainsails double-reefed and crews wearing harness.
7	Near gale	50–61	28–33	Waves heap and foam is blown downwind. Whole trees sway, and walking against the wind becomes tiresome.	Dinghies should stay on shore. Most cruiser crews will find it hard to cope and should seek shelter or, if gales are forecast, heave to and ride out the storm.
8	Gale	62–74	34–40	Waves become large with deep troughs and much blown foam. Twigs break off trees, and walking is difficult.	Dinghies should be securely tied down. Cruisers should have deeply reefed main and small headsails; all except essential crew should be safely below deck.
9	Strong gale	75–88	41–47	High foam-streaked waves with breaking crests. On land, roofs, chimneys and fences may be damaged.	Cruisers in danger of knockdown. Even the most experienced of crews will have problems, and most will need to lower the sails and lash the tiller.
10	Storm	89–102	48–55	Waves very high with breaking crests and large, frothy patches of foam. Trees are uprooted; much structural damage.	Wave heights of 20 to 35 feet can capsize large cruiser racers lying a-hull. Breaking crests can pitchpole a large yacht running with or across them.
11	Violent storm	103–117	56–63	Waves become extremely high, and sea surface obscured by driving foam. Severe structural damage on land.	Extreme danger, especially when close to a shelving coast. Capsize and 90° knockdowns possible. Keep well away from coastline if at all possible.
12	Hurricane	>117	>63	Huge waves. The sea becomes completely white and visibility is seriously affected by driving foam.	The worst possible danger. Survival is the most you can hope for, and your only priority.

The Beaufort Scale of wind speeds was devised by the English admiral Sir Francis Beaufort in the 19th century.
The scale is not linear; the range of wind speeds for each number of the scale increases progressively up the scale.

cold air that disperses the original pocket of warm air.

An interesting feature of a depression is that the cold air drawn into it is induced to change its flow from clockwise to counter-clockwise rotation (in the Northern Hemisphere; it's from counter-clockwise to clockwise in the Sou-thern) and that the direction of tra-vel of the depression is governed by the winds in the warm air. Particu-larly destructive depressions shoot down the corridors formed by older, more static depressions, using them to change direction and increase their speed.

Superimposed on the global pat-tern of heating and cooling, and the air masses and winds that it pro-duces, is the daily cycle produced by the sun. In many coastal and inland areas, local winds override the gradient winds (those created by anticyclones and depressions) to give more predictable patterns to sail by. These local winds include sea breezes and land breezes.

Sea breezes are onshore winds caused by the replacement of rising, heated inland air by cooler air from off the coast. Land breezes are off-shore winds which occur mostly at night, when the cooling land-based air sinks and flows out to the now-warmer sea.

FOG & MIST

Over the last decade or so, the miniaturization (and the easy availability) of electronic navigation equipment has changed the attitude of long-time sailors and is taken for granted by newcomers to the sport.

The great differences between the newcomers and the small-boat sailors who sailed before the electronic revolution is that the latter can quickly revert to using their old, well-practised skills when necessary, for instance in fog, but those who rely implicitly on their little black boxes will risk being well and truly lost unless they learn the traditional back-up navigational skills.

To the car driver, fog can be a daunting experience, and many drivers pull off the road to avoid having to drive in it. The sailor does not usually have any option but to sail on when he encounters fog, and unless he is sailing close inshore or in an estuary, anchoring will not be a viable alternative.

In fog, not being able to see more than a few few feet, and not being able to focus properly on a fixed point of reference, can cause spatial disorientation. So the use of sensible boat-handling strategies is essential if the safe navigation of the craft and the safety of its crew are to be ensured.

The various types of fog are essentially clouds which form at the earth's surface, and are products of temperature differences and moisture in the air.

The amount of moisture a given amount of air can contain, in the form of invisible water vapour, depends on its temperature: warm air can hold more water vapour than cold air can. The ratio of the *actual* amount of water vapour in the air, at a particular temperature, to the maximum amount of water vapour that it *could* hold at that temperature, is called the *relative humidity*.

The relative humidity is expressed as a percentage; air containing the maximum amount of water possible at a given temperature has a relative humidity of 100 percent, and is said to be *saturated*.

As warm, moisture-laden air cools, its relative humidity increases, and if it is cooled sufficiently it will reach saturation. The temperature at which this happens is called the *dewpoint temperature*, because at that point the moisture will begin to condense out of the air and form water droplets, creating dew, clouds or fog.

Radiation fog may form when the sun sets and the earth begins to radiate its heat. If the sky is cloudy, it acts in the same way as roof insulation and traps a warm layer of air between the clouds and the earth's surface.

If there is no cloud, though, the heat radiates out into the atmosphere and the surface air cools rapidly as the earth's surface cools. Strong winds will remove this layer of cooled air, but a gentle breeze will simply stir it up into a deeper layer that continues to cool.

Under these conditions, if the ground is damp or the humidity already high, continued cooling to and beyond the dewpoint causes condensation in the form of dew and mist. Further cooling produces dense fog in layers extending to hundreds of feet above the ground. In valleys, mist and fog roll down the hillsides forming cold 'lakes' of air containing mist and fog and capped by warmer air. In winter, hoar frost forms when the dewpoint is below 0°C (32°F).

Seasonal differences are marked. In summer, the rising sun soon burns the fog off or causes it to rise as dispersing stratus cloud. In spring and autumn, there is additional moisture in the air and the weaker, later-rising sun takes time to disperse the fog.

In winter — especially in settled conditions of high pressure — radiation fog, fuelled by vehicle exhaust gases and industrial pollution, may persist for days.

Sailors moored or anchored in sheltered estuaries may experience this type of reduced visibility, but offshore the only noticeable effect of these conditions will be that they inhibit the formation of sea breezes in settled spring and autumn weather.

Advection fog is the product of moving air. Humid air blowing over a cold surface capable of

cooling it below its dewpoint will produce fog. This occurs especially in spring, when the sea is cold and the returning sun is warming the often-saturated winter land to produce saturated air. When this air is blown over the cold sea, advection fog may form. Maritime tropical air, with its high moisture content, is also liable to produce thick banks of advection fog as it reaches the cooler waters of higher latitudes.

Sailors can expect advection sea fog to be accompanied by winds of up to 12 knots and exceptionally of 20 knots if the incoming air is already at or near dewpoint.

Onshore winds meeting cliffs or mountains often lift the fog a little for up to a mile offshore, creating a corridor of visibility along the shore. Use your VHF radio to contact any yachts or fishermen who may already be in the clear zone.

Warm sector mists may form in the area of warm moist air trapped between two colder fronts in a depression. The compressed warm air becomes increasingly saturated as occlusion takes place, so that only a small drop in temperature by contact with a cold sea, or air in the

As soon as you see mist or fog developing, establish your position as precisely as you can.

EQUIPMENT USEFUL IN FOG

Echo sounder

An efficient, frequently-used echo sounder will give you a known dimension: the depth of water under your boat. If it has shallow and deep alarms you can set them to enable you to traverse a seabed contour that will lead you safely to the shore.

Radar

Radar is the 'eye' which penetrates the surrounding gloom and which in experienced hands, can be used in conjunction with the echo sounder to guide you to your destination and to avoid collision with other vessels.

Radar reflection

Being visible to radar is essential. Make sure your reflector has been proven to work and is not filled with junk. Hoist it high to increase the distance from which it can be detected.

VHF radio

If caught out in the shipping lanes, especially in heavy traffic, go with the traffic flow and cross behind passing ships as the opportunity arises.

Speak to surrounding craft, even using a Securite message if you think you have not been detected on their radar. You must know your vessel's approximate position before sending a Securite warning.

Position indicator

Decca, LORAN and satnavs, when properly used and calibrated, are excellent navigation aids; but note that fog banks can distort the incoming signals. Known waypoints which have been achieved time and again should be used when closing a familiar coast.

---

cold sector, is needed to produce fog.

One further type of fog, sometimes seen in the United States in very hard winters but not often met in the UK, is arctic sea smoke. Super-cooled continental polar air, blowing over yet-to-be-frozen sea water, produces lanes of fog. These seldom rise above 10 to 15 feet.

Most sailors rely on professional forecasters to warn them of impending foggy conditions, but you can predict them yourself with some degree of success if you have a humidity meter on your craft. If it reaches 90 to 95 percent, and the sea water temperature is 5°C to 10°C, there's a good chance of fog.

A more accurate way to determine the likelihood of fog is to use a hygrometer to find the dewpoint temperature of the air.

A typical hygrometer, called a psychrometer, consists of two thermometers — one wet bulb, one dry bulb — that are used to determine the relative humidity of the air. When you know the air's relative humidity, you can find its dewpoint temperature by referring to tables. If the dewpoint temperature is just a few °C below the actual air temperature, expect fog as night approaches. If your boat doesn't have a hygrometer, you should listen carefully to broadcast weather forecasts, especially during settled conditions of high pressure and in spring and autumn.

At the onset of mist or fog, establish your position as exactly as you can; knowing where you are, or cannot possibly be, is the key to safe conduct in reduced visibility. Thereafter, update your estimated position (EP) at half-hourly intervals or when major changes of direction are made, and pay particular attention to tidal streams as these will still be operating as they would on a sunny day. Double-check all EPs and fixes, and verify them by using the echo sounder.

When approaching land or a chosen harbour, *always* estimate your time of arrival, consult the tidal stream atlas, and initially aim for a point some miles upstream of your actual destination.

This permits you to close the shoreline, choose a seabed contour to follow, correct for the height of the tide, and then change direction toward your chosen destination with some degree of confidence.

Whenever possible, during fog everyone should be on deck, or ready to come up at a moment's notice. Considerable danger of collision exists in busy shipping lanes, at the entrance to busy harbours and on fishing grounds, so lookouts should be given two white flares and posted bow and amidships to look and listen for approaching ships. The fog signal should be sounded as appropriate for sailing or motoring to warn other vessels of your presence.

WEATHER FORECASTS

Having the luxury of being able to blame someone else for getting the forecast radically wrong is not necessarily 'enjoyed' by the sailor who has been on the receiving end of a particularly unpleasant experience at the hand of the weather.

Forecasting is always going to be an inexact science in areas of complex pressure and temperature changes. Most of the time, professional forecasting agencies and government departments get it right, and that saves each of us a lot of time watching the sky, bar-

ometer and bits of seaweed for signs of a change in the weather.

What is needed of today's sailors is the ability to look at a chart representing the weather at a given point in the past, or near future, recognize the important features and trends, and compare the outlook forecast to what is actually happening to the barometric pressure, visibility, sea and sky in their locality.

Weather maps are drawn, in the form of 'contour maps', from thousands of simultaneous observations taken at land and seaborne weather

stations around the world. Observers measure temperature, humidity, barometric pressure, sunshine, precipitation, windspeed, wind direction, cloud type, cloud cover, visibility and, where applicable, sea state.

This information is then telexed or sent via satellite to hundreds of central plotting stations as the raw material for the production of weather charts by computer, or sometimes manually by experienced forecasters.

Large agencies such as the US

National Weather Service and the UK Meteorological Office have sophisticated computers — among the most powerful in the world — that construct predictive models based on the information supplied, augmented by information derived from records of previous similar weather patterns.

In the UK, special forecasts for Port Areas can be obtained by telephoning one of the thirteen Regional Met Office forecasting centres. These Met Offices will also give reports of present weather,

which can be extremely valuable if you are planning to sail in their area.

Another useful source of weather information is ITV's ORACLE teletext service. As well as useful weather charts and satellite pictures, this service provides a special marine forecast on page 162.

In the United States, special VHF weather radios equipped with severe weather alarms are used to receive a continuous flow of updated local weather information. Most local airfields and some coastguard stations contribute

to this information service.

The US National Weather Service broadcasts it on 162.40 MHz, 162.475 MHz and 162.55 MHz. All shipborne VHF radios are able to receive one or more of these Wx channels devoted solely to continuous weather broadcasts.

In the UK, sailors have to consult lists of the times of weather bulletins on a wide variety of frequencies, ranging from the shipping forecasts on 200 kHz (1500 m) AM long wave to VHF forecasts broadcast by Coast Radio Stations. How-

ever, since 1989, HM Coastguard has advised those wishing to obtain a forecast to telephone for one, and the use of VHF for weather forecasts will be increasingly discouraged by them.

In addition, because of frequent changes to broadcast weather forecast services in the UK, you should consult the 'weather' sections of up-to-date nautical almanacs for all information relating to the frequencies and times of all Coast Radio and BBC forecasts.

Official British Met Office forecasts are broadcast by the BBC on their long wave transmitters at 0033 hrs, 0555 hrs, 1355 hrs and 1750 hrs. The standardized format and speed of delivery is intended to permit the skilled listener to record the details in meteorological 'shorthand' for use in compiling a personal weather chart. Experience dictates that a pocket tape recorder is very useful for this.

These forecasts are based on specific sea areas extending from Iceland to northern Spain, and they can be received in all the sea areas that they cover. Books of charts of these sea areas, with spaces to record the forecasts, are available from the Royal Yachting Association and the Met Office.

Each broadcast begins with a list of gale warnings. This is followed by a general synopsis giving the position and movement of pressure systems, fronts and depressions in the next 24 hours. Forecasts for the next 24 hours are given for each sea area, commencing with Viking, Forties and Cromarty and continuing in a generally clockwise direction, finishing with South East Iceland.

Details given include wind direction and Beaufort speed with expected changes and weather and visibility. This is followed by reports from coastal stations giving wind force and direction, weather, visibility, barometric pressure and barometric change.

Constructing your own chart from the broadcast information takes some practice, but with some outside help and reference to professional maps you can soon grasp the basics, especially if you have the forecast chart from your previous day's newspaper to refer to.

The Coastal Station Reports give you the basic data you need, such as pressure and wind speed, and you should enter these on your chart at the appropriate station.

Pressure is shown in millibars, and wind as an arrow blowing *away* from the observed direction. The wind's force is represented by oblique lines on the tail of the arrow,

the force being numerically equal to twice the number of lines. For example, a wind of force 4 is represented by two lines, and one of force 7 by three and a half lines.

The general synopsis part of the broadcast will have given you the centres of pressure areas and the positions of fronts. Pencil these in at the correct positions, writing 'H' for high and 'L' for low.

Isobars are the lines on a weather chart joining areas of equal pressure. You now have to draw in isobars at 2-millibar intervals relative to the pressure reading that you've already written against each coastal station on the chart. For example, if a station reported a pressure of 1021 mb, then the 1020 mb and 1022 mb lines go either side of that station.

Wind speeds are a guide to the spacing of the isobars. The *geostrophic scales* printed at the top of the chart show the spacing to use for given wind speeds (this spacing is labelled 'Beaufort force' on the scales).

The forecast information for sea areas concerns the 24-hour period following the time your chart relates to. You can now enter this forecast information to show the pattern of change over the next 24 hours.

Of course, if fiddling about with shipping forecasts late at night or early in the morning does not appeal to you, you can always invest in a weatherfax machine. This will happily print out a range of accurate weather charts for you to ponder over, but as with most electronic equipment it is essential that you get proper training in its use if you are to get the best out of it.

BOATS

There surely could not be a greater contrast between the tiny Optimist, a first-time training dinghy for children, and the USS *Eagle*, an 1800-ton square-rigged ship. What they share, of course, is that both are dependent on the wind, that infuriatingly fickle source of motive power that has been making life so difficult for sailors for thousands of years.

It is this variety in boats that makes them so fascinating and in the following pages you will find sporty ones, sturdy ones, ones that you need the agility of an acrobat to stay aboard and ones that are complete floating homes ready to carry you all over the oceans of the world.

Sailing was once the sport of the rich but nowadays virtually everyone who wants to can get afloat in something. There are even boats specially designed for the disabled and a ship they can go aboard in a wheelchair. Smaller and cheaper boats have put the sport of sailing within the reach of most people and, as a result, it is now one of the most popular of all leisure activities.

This popularity is reflected by the huge increase in the ownership of cruising yachts, whose owners demand ever-increasing standards of reliability and comfort, plus easy handling. Reliability means a sturdy hull and rig, well fitted-out with strong but simple gear that is easy to handle and will not let you down in an emergency. In addition, virtually every cruising yacht is now fitted with a diesel engine to reduce dependency on favourable wind conditions, make the boat easier to manoeuvre in marinas or other confined spaces, charge the batteries and in many cases to provide hot water as well.

To be able to live comfortably aboard a boat for more than a few days calls for roomy accommodation, with a degree of privacy if possible, and plenty of stowage space for clothing and personal gear. The galley must be capable of producing full cooked meals, not just snacks, and have room to store sufficient food to last for weeks at a time; most people consider a fridge or freezer virtually essential today. A chart table with room for a small library of books and guides is also essential, as is sufficient room for navigational instruments and radios.

Racing crews tolerate spartan conditions, sleeping (if at all) in their clothes and staggering ashore to the club shower-room to get cleaned up after the race.

The cruising sailor, however, expects to be able to live as normally as possible when on board and this calls for a decent washroom (with a hot shower if possible) and space to keep towels and washing gear. Above all, the modern cruising yacht must have a pleasant, welcoming ambience with room for those aboard to sit down and relax in comfort when not on deck. The idea, after all, is to make sailing a pleasure rather than an ordeal.

When you're choosing a boat, think carefully about what you want from it and take full account of what owning it will involve, in terms of finance, time, convenience and your own (and your potential crew's) ability to handle it.

For instance, small dinghies are cheaper to buy and easier to care for than larger boats and can be launched and recovered by one or two people, whereas most cruisers must be craned or launched by professionals at boatyards or marinas, and you then have to foot the bill for the berthing or mooring of the boat when you're not sailing it.

Once afloat, however, the dinghy is far more responsive and tippy to sail than a cruiser, and will capsize easily given the right conditions, whereas most cruisers, especially the newer ones, are very stable and relatively easy to handle, and sail well.

Basically, though, the decision to buy a particular type of boat – such as a dinghy which is kept ashore, or a trailer sailer which is kept at home and trailed to various sailing venues, or a cruising boat which is kept on a mooring or in a marina – is usually governed by the potential owner's financial status.

All boats, even secondhand ones, tend to be expensive and it is therefore essential that prospective owners who know nothing about sailing should seek the help of a qualified marine surveyor once they have chosen the boat most likely to suit their purposes. When buying a used boat, as when buying any secondhand vehicle, the buyer should beware.

The boats that appear on the following pages have been carefully chosen to show a little bit of every type of sailing and are among the best-known internationally. Yet this survey only scratches the surface of a vast fleet with literally thousands of different designs, and every year there are more, as designers and builders strive to squeeze just a little bit more into their latest models.

CHOOSING A BOAT

If you are already a sailor, you will have some idea of what type of boats you like to sail and the type of boat that would suit your particular circumstances. If you are new to sailing, but are determined to be a boat owner before you know how to sail – don't get a big one!

In most cases, the purchase will be influenced by the availability of finance, and as with the purchase of other expensive items there will be many agencies only too willing to lend you the money and charge you interest on it. Remortgaging your home is a worthwhile option unless interest rates look to be moving against you.

Before setting foot in a broker's office you should have worked out a maximum outlay figure, bearing in mind that the annual upkeep of a boat is about 10 percent of its purchase price and that mooring and marina fees can treble that if you live in a popular sailing area.

Make a realistic appraisal of your

The Cadet is one of the many classes of dinghy intended specifically for young people to sail.

The 505 is a large, fast two-man dinghy, exciting to sail but not a boat for the inexperienced sailor.

family and their enthusiasm for sailing. Do you regularly go out together? Do you take holidays or go camping together? Do they have any interest in your project? If the answer is no on all counts, buy a singlehander. Alternatively, ask your friends if they are interested and whether they are keen enough to share the purchase price.

Before you set out to buy, decide whether you want a dinghy, a dayboat, a cruiser or a racer. Bear in mind not just your current interest in sailing but how your interest might develop in the future, and that while dinghies and small keelboats can be trailed behind the family car and launched and recovered by the crew, cruisers need specialist handling equipment and cradles and have to be 'shipped'.

The nature of your home port will decide whether your boat is kept afloat or ashore. If you want a cruiser, can you have a fin keeler or must it have bilge or lifting keels because the mudflats dry out? Do you have to row out to it or is there a launch service? Is the boat's berth accessible at all states of the tide?

If you want a cruiser, scan the 'for sale' ads in the many yachting magazines to get a feel of the price of used craft compared with that of new ones, remembering that new boats need to be equipped with all safety gear, clothing, warps, anchors, dinghies, instruments and so on and that you will need to add 20 to 25 percent to the advertised price to

ensure that you have everything needed to go to sea.

If you don't know anything about boats you will not recognize an O'Day from a Westerly and therefore you would be wise to visit a broker's display lot and choose a few boats to look over. Don't be afraid to let the appearance of a boat influence your choice. Ugly boats *are* ugly: they don't look right and they don't sail right, so if the shape doesn't appeal to you leave it for someone else.

If you buy a new yacht you will be getting a known product at a reasonably competitive price. There are a lot of add-ons, but the dealer can be persuaded to make a considerable discount for the gear in order to secure the sale of the boat. You should haggle, and if the dealer won't bargain then try the guy down the road with similar products.

When you decide to order a new boat which has yet to be built, beware! You will need to consult your lawyer to ensure that your deposit and stage payments are safeguarded should the company fold. It is usually better to make the agreement with the dealer rather than the builder, because the dealer has to supply you with alternative merchandise if the builder goes under.

There is a commissioning period for any new boat, during which you should thoroughly test all systems and make a list of defects to be corrected. Should you decide to follow

the used-boat route, on the basis that you will get more for your money, you would be wise to bear in mind that the 'more' could include trouble.

Alone, or with a friend, visit the brokers' lots and the locally-advertised boats to get a feel of what is available in the category of boat you want. Choose two or three as a final shortlist and go over them with a fine-toothed comb making a list of good and bad points.

Choose your boat from the shortlist and determine, by haggling, what is the lowest price the vendor will accept. Make an offer *subject to survey* but don't part with any money yet. Engage the services of a certified Marine Surveyor, who will carry out a detailed inspection and submit a written inspection report pointing out work and repairs needed, the overall condition of the yacht and its approximate value as it stands. If you still want the boat, pay the offer price subject to all defects being put right by a boatyard to the satisfaction of the surveyor. Otherwise, offer a reduced price to take account of survey defects.

Once the offer is accepted a deal is struck and you will have problems backing out of it, so be sure that you really want to buy before you commit yourself to the purchase. In addition, get your lawyer to ascertain that the vendor does actually own the vessel which, in turn, is free from all debts and writs.

Above left *Catamarans are fast and relatively stable.*
Above right *A small cruiser is simple to rig and handle, and a good choice for the beginner.*
Right *When you buy a cruiser, have it surveyed to make sure it's seaworthy.*

Experienced sailors, who may already own or have owned a boat, can fall into the trap of thinking that they know enough about general defects and the condition of used boats to dispense with the services of a surveyor. However, wood, steel, aluminium and GRP hulls all need inspection by a specialist who is skilled in interpreting certain features as pointers to serious structural defects.

Newcomers would be wise to start with a small boat which is simple to rig, easy to manoeuvre and which will withstand the inevitable knocks experienced in the first season of ownership. Get an expert opinion of the type of rig and how it should be reefed, and steer clear of one-off and experimental rigs. Go for a used production boat that has retained its original specification, and not been heavily modified.

The size of boat you buy will depend on how many people you expect to go sailing in it at any one time, but as a rough guide, if it's a dinghy you want go for a 14- to 16-footer. If it's a cruiser, go for one of 25 to 30 feet, and select the boat which has got the best equipment if all else is reasonably equal.

TYPES OF RIG

When we think of rigs, we tend to think of the development of triangular sails from the square sails that predominated until the early 20th century. This ignores the quite separate development of a wide variety of rigs, such as the junk, lateen and crab's claw, which have been in use for thousands of years.

The junk rig, as used in eastern Asia, is a refined, multipurpose trading rig which, while not being close-winded, is very efficient off the wind. There have been attempts to popularize the rig in the West, and 'Blondie' Hasler, one of the originators of the singlehanded transatlantic races, used such a rig on the now-legendary *Jester*, a wooden folkboat which was a regular entrant in these races.

One of the attractions of the rig is the ease with which it can be set and reefed, operating on the same principle as horizontal-slatted window shades. The original junk sail was made up of closely-spaced split bamboo or vegetable fibres, and therefore lent itself to quick reefing, and the modern sail has full-length battens, usually made of bamboo, which self-stow when lowered.

The control of the twist and set of the sail is achieved by control lines led from the helmsman to a complex single, solid wood block which has lines leading to the end of each batten. Other control lines are used for hoisting and for determining the fore-and-aft position of the sail on the unstayed mast. Large ocean-going junks can have up to four masts, but two or three is the norm.

Most junk masts are raked forward, and a similar forward rake is used by the traders and fishermen of the Arabian seas to support the weight of the lateen rigs of their fast and powerful dhows. The dhow's mast is short but the yard supporting the sail is both long and heavy. The triangular sail is efficient because it has such a long leading edge and can be sheeted close to the wind.

The feluccas of the Nile have a similar rig, carried higher to catch the wind above the river banks. Again it is a trading rig which developed over thousands of years, and was used in every type of boat on the Nile until engine-powered boats arrived. The popular Sunfish dinghy, like the dhow and the felucca, has a lateen rig.

Out on its own is the crab's claw rig, which is similar to a lateen sail in basic shape except that it has a spar on each of the two longer edges. In use, the sail is set point-down with both spars angled upward. Recent research with this rig shows that it may have the potential to produce

Above *A gaff rig, efficient but difficult to hoist and control.*
Left *The sprit-rigged Optimist.*

more power than any other sail type on all but a close-hauled course.

The square sail is a great downwind rig because it can be wider than it is high, thus keeping its centre of effort (the capsizing factor) low, but it is not possible to use it closer than about 60 degress to the wind.

In its original form, the square sail had a spar at its upper edge that was controlled by lines to set it, and the sail, to the desired angle to the wind.

Square sails set in this fashion developed in complexity and size to power vessels such as the 19th-century tea clipper *Cutty Sark* (named after the witch in Robert Burns' poem *Tam O'Shanter*, who wore only a short skirt or 'cutty sark').

The use of square sails on small

TYPES OF RIG

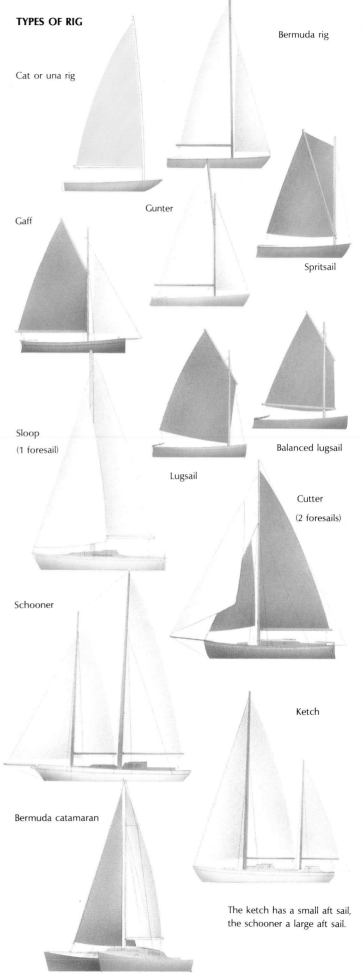

Cat or una rig

Bermuda rig

Gaff

Gunter

Spritsail

Sloop
(1 foresail)

Balanced lugsail

Lugsail

Cutter
(2 foresails)

Schooner

Ketch

Bermuda catamaran

The ketch has a small aft sail,
the schooner a large aft sail.

inshore boats led to the development of the sprit and lugsail versions. The lugsail has its tack set at the mast, which results in the yard being cocked up at an angle or, more commonly, led forward to the windward gunwale where it is attached to a tack hook. When changing tacks, the yard was lowered on its mast traveller so that it could be dipped around the mast to be hoisted and set on the leeward side. Meantime, the tack was moved to the windward tack hook.

The sprit rig is still used on the Optimist dinghy and the Thames Sailing Barges. Its configuration lent itself ideally to converting the inefficient square sail into a good upwind rig. It is an extremely rewarding sail to tune to get the best out of it.

The popularity of the gaff rig, with or without a boom, arose because it was a rig which created the power needed by fishermen, pilots and coasting trading vessels. It is a fairly complicated rig and requires considerable effort to hoist and control. Once up and drawing, though, especially from a close reach to a run, it is very efficient at harnessing the wind's power.

Splitting the rig up into smaller sails gave rise to the classic two-masted gaff ketch and schooner rigs. The schooner differs from the ketch in that the main mast is taller than the foremast. This rig was developed to perfection on the fishing schooners of the Grand Banks.

Above *The very popular Bermuda rig requires additional sails for downwind work.*

For the inshore fisherman, the small mizzen and larger main of the ketch gave the correct degree of balance when trawling, especially with the addition of a large and powerful overlapping tow foresail.

The gunter rig developed the four-cornered sail into something resembling the now familiar Bermuda rig. The gaff was designed to be hoisted almost parallel to the mast to give the sail height. In dinghies, it ensured that the spars were short enough to stow in the boat.

The Bermuda rig, with its triangular sails, is reputed to have come from the sails used on the islands' dinghies which, in turn, were developed from ships' boats. The transition from the two spars of the gunter rig to the single Bermuda spar would have been a natural development, and as triangular sails were used for the headsails of most square-riggers, their efficiency was well known. The familiar triangular-sailed rigs of today have been developed for upwind work and require additional special sails for downwind work.

Single-sailed Bermuda-rigged boats, or those designed without headsails, are described as being cat-rigged or una-rigged; multiple-masted versions are cat-rigged ketches or cat-rigged schooners.

OPTIMIST, SABOT & SUNFISH

In sailing, as in most sports, the lucky ones are those who start young, when learning is easy and fun. It used to be thought that the only way to learn to sail was to go out in a boat with someone more experienced, but in recent years there has been a swing in opinion toward letting quite young children, of 10 years old or less, start off in small, singlehanded dinghies. With the right kind of supervision, the learning rate is quite amazing. For such young children, the boat needs to be as small and light as possible so that the helmsman's lack of body-weight and strength is not a disadvantage. It also helps to have a trainer that is virtually impossible for an adult to sail, as this shows the young skipper that the boat really is his or hers and fosters a great pride in ownership. Of course, there are plenty of adults who want to learn to sail too, and for them a slightly larger boat is needed as a basic trainer.

INTERNATIONAL OPTIMIST

Florida boatbuilder Clark Mills set out to produce the most basic little 'matchbox' boat possible, for use by the children of his local club, and the result (designed in 1947) was the Optimist.

Little did he know that, over forty years later, this ultra-simple but clever little boat would become the most popular children's trainer in the world, with thousands and thousands in use in virtually every country where sailing goes on. Equally surprising is the fact that it has become a very important racing class, with young people up to the age of sixteen competing with tremendous enthusiasm.

An important part of the formula was to keep the boat as simple and therefore as cheap as possible. For that reason there is no standing rigging and the mast stands in a hole in the forward thwart. The almost-square sail is extended by a 'sprit', a lightweight pole extending form the top corner of the sail to a strop on the mast, while the centreboard is a simple 'dagger' that slides up and down inside a box. Mainsheet and sprit adjustment are virtually the only fittings on the boat.

In spite of this very basic design, the Optimist sails amazingly well and is a really sporty performer in a brisk breeze. It is also surprisingly seaworthy for its size and quite difficult to capsize, thanks to the beamy hull and very low rig. The young sailor who loses his or her nerve can simply let go of everything, and the ultra-forgiving 'Oppie' will then stop and await the next instruction.

One problem that the class has faced in recent years is that due to the pressure of international racing, the construction of the boat has become more sophisticated and hence expensive. This doesn't often affect the beginner, who is likely to get the most basic model or a second-hand boat, but parents of children who want to race do face increasing costs.

SABOT

The 'Naples' Sabot, designed by R McCulloch, serves a similar purpose to the Optimist but, although as many as 10,000 have been built, it is almost unknown outside the United States and is popular mainly in California. Unlike the better-known Oppie, the Sabot was not designed initially as a children's boat but instead developed from the kind of small pram dinghy used as a yacht's tender.

To this was added a simple rig and, most unusually, leeboards. The idea of these is that it is not necessary to cut a hole in the bottom of the boat and mount a waterproof box on it as required for a centreboard or daggerboard. Also, the leeboard will swing up without damage if it hits the ground, whereas an Optimist will come to a juddering stop—with possible damage to the daggerboard—if it goes aground.

The rig is quite conventional, with a single Bermudan sail laced to an unstayed mast, and the mainsheet is taken down to the centrethwart so that is doesn't drop over the rudder when gybing. A sturdy little boat, the Sabot can just about carry an adult and so parents can have a go too.

SUNFISH

It is a surprise to many to find that the humble Sunfish is—or has been—one of the most popular small boats in the world, with over 200,000 sold. Not designed primarily as a youth boat, the Sunfish has given countless

OPTIMIST

OPTIMIST
Designed over forty years ago, the Optimist is a simple and inexpensive dinghy for young sailors. There are over 200,000 in use worldwide.

adults an informal opportunity to try a new sport.

This is partly because it filled the role of ultra-simple, splashy funboat in the era before the sailboard was invented. It used to be the boat almost universally favoured by waterside hotels and beach hire operators and because of this, thousands of people have had their first sailing experience on a Sunfish.

The shallow hull is almost flat-bottomed and the cockpit is very shallow—in fact, the Sunfish belongs to a class of boat that was known as a 'sailing surfboard' before the first windsurfer came along. The lateen rig is a bit of a monstrosity and because the whole sail is set on one side of the short pole mast, the Sunfish sails to windward badly on one tack and very badly on the other.

However, it does plane very readily and is at its best swishing along on a reach—preferably in a nice warm place where the fact that you are virtually sitting in the water doesn't matter much.

Considering that it was originally intended purely as a funboat, it is perhaps surprising that, at the height of its popularity, the Sunfish was a popular racing class. It also made possible the idea of running championships at attractive holiday venues, with all the equipment provided so that, as a competitor, all you had to bring was yourself and a swimsuit. This was a very nice idea that has since been copied by others such as the Laser and several sailboard classes.

SUNFISH

SABOT

SUNFISH
Rivalling the Optimist in terms of numbers produced, the Sunfish is an ideal funboat for beginners of all ages.

SABOT
The Sabot is unusual in that it gets its lateral stability from leeboards instead of from a centreboard or a daggerboard.

NAME	LENGTH OVERALL	BEAM	WEIGHT	SAIL AREA	SPINNAKER	FEATURES
International Optimist	2.3 m (7.5 ft)	1.3 m (4.3 ft)	35 kg (77 lb)	3.5 m² (38 ft²)		Safe, enjoyable boat for children
Sabot	2.4 m (7.9 ft)	1.2 m (3.9 ft)	45 kg (99 lb)	3.5 m² (38 ft²)		Leeboards instead of centreboard
Sunfish	4.2 m (13.8 ft)	1 m (3.3 ft)	57 kg (126 lb)	8 m² (86 ft²)		Very simple and fun to sail

TOPPER, MOTH & EUROPE

After progressing from a training dinghy, the young sailor can decide whether to go into partnership in a two-handed dinghy or stay with a singlehander. There are plenty of arguments for both, but the key argument for a singlehander is that you don't have to depend on anyone else: if you want to go sailing, you can just pick up your gear and go. To carry this argument to its logical conclusion, the singlehanded sailor should really choose a boat that he or she can rig and launch without help. Furthermore, it should be one that suits his or her body-weight and style of sailing. There are plenty of singlehanders around, each with a slightly different character, and here we look at three of the light ones.

The modern International Moth is quite extraordinarily fast for its size and a very lively, tricky boat to sail. By no means a knockabout like the Topper, it calls for careful handling and is a specialized racing boat for those with a strong interest in design.

INTERNATIONAL EUROPE

Designed in 1960 by Alois Roland, the Europe is a class that has stepped into the limelight, after years of relative obscurity, as a result of being chosen as the women's singlehanded dinghy class for the 1992 Olympics.

Originally a part of the Moth family, it is now a one-design class with only a small amount of variation of layout and equipment permitted. Though nowhere near as light or fragile as an International Moth, it is still a lively, lightweight dinghy that is well suited to a helmsman weighing 45 to 75 kg.

TOPPER

Designed by Ian Proctor in 1976, the Topper was designed to take advantage of what was then a new manufacturing process: injection-moulding in polypropylene. Polypropylene is a fantastically tough form of plastic and, unlike glassfibre, which is basically a laminate covered with a thin waterproof skin, it is the same all the way through and so minor scratches and dents really don't matter much.

Proctor saw the Topper as a fun singlehander rather than a serious racing boat and, as the name implies, one that would be particularly suitable for car-topping. But because it has such a sporty performance it has developed into a popular racing class, and because it's so tough, it has become a favourite for training, too.

The rig is as simple as can be, with a single sleeve sail that fits over the mast, and all the other fittings are simple and sturdy. The hull is very shallow and the bow rounded rather than sharp, so the Topper sailor gets a wet, bouncy, exciting ride, especially in a strong breeze. Many thousands of Toppers have been sold all over the world and provide a great deal of fun for not-too-serious sailors.

INTERNATIONAL MOTH

The Moth was originally conceived as a light, singlehanded development class with fairly open rules, and over the years this family of boats has given birth to various offspring, such as the Europe and the British Moth, which are one-designs with the basic Moth dimensions.

The International Moth is one of the very few classes with no minimum weight requirement, and as a result, extremely light hulls weighing around 25 kg are built using very thin stressed plywood.

A few years ago there were two distinct types of design—the European narrow dinghy, and the Australian beamy scow which had more power in strong winds. But then John Claridge combined the advantages of each type, producing a narrow skiff with wide tubular metal 'wings' to give extra sitting-out power, and this is used universally now. Any design of rig is allowed within a maximum area.

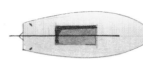

TOPPER
The Topper is a robust boat with a tough polypropylene hull, which makes it popular as a training dinghy. It is also widely used for racing.

TOPPER

Any boat used in the Olympics inevitably becomes increasingly specialized and costly as a result of the pressure of competition, and the Europe is no exception. But being so much smaller and lighter than the Finn, the men's singlehander, it should be possible to keep costs within bounds.

What seems certain is that as the hull is fairly narrow and there is no trapeze or other sitting-out aid, the successful girl helmsman will be of above-average height for her weight and able to react quickly to the demands of this sporty little boat.

EUROPE

MOTH

EUROPE
The Europe has been chosen as the Olympic women's singlehanded dinghy class.

MOTH
The International Moth is a fast, lively boat with tubular metal 'wing' decks.

NAME	LENGTH OVERALL	BEAM	WEIGHT	SAIL AREA	SPINNAKER	FEATURES
Topper	3.4 m (11.2 ft)	1.17 m (3.8 ft)	52.2 kg (115 lb)	5.2 m² (56 ft²)		Fun singlehander
International Moth	3.35 m (11 ft)	2.24 m (7.4 ft) (maximum)	unrestricted	8 m² (86 ft²)		Fast and lively for its size
International Europe	3.35 m (11 ft)	1.4 m (4.6 ft)	63 kg (139 lb)	7.43 m² (80 ft²)		Well suited to lightweight crews

LASER, OK & FINN

If you are keen to race and want to stay with a singlehander, then several courses of action are open to you and three of them are illustrated here. The Laser is by far the most popular singlehanded racing dinghy in the world, but it is a simple boat with the minimum of equipment and so its appeal is not technical in nature. At the opposite end of the spectrum, the Finn is a heavy dinghy for one person and has a rig that calls for a good deal of experience and tuning skill. The Laser can be treated purely as a fun boat, while the Finn calls for a lot of dedication and training. The OK comes between the two, being a lightweight dinghy with a Finn-type rig.

INTERNATIONAL FINN
Although designed over forty years ago, the Finn is still the Olympic singlehanded dinghy. Because the boat is heavy and slow, strength and tactical skills are needed when racing it.

OK

OK
Designed as a trainer for the larger Finn, the OK is strictly a singlehanded dinghy.

OK

Designed in 1957 by Knud Olsen, the OK is a considerably older design than the Laser. It has undoubtedly suffered from the latter's phenomenal success, but it is a dinghy with its own character and appeal and it has a loyal if fairly small following. The OK was conceived as a trainer for the Olympic Finn; lighter and cheaper but with the same type of bendy, unstayed mast. The small cockpit is perfectly logical for a one-man racing boat but does mean that it is impossible to take anyone else for a sail.

At its best in a good breeze, the OK is a bit more demanding and specialized than the Laser and the owner is allowed some degree of freedom in the layout of the interior and its controls. The class originated in Scandinavia, which is still its stronghold, and there are smaller groups in other parts of Europe.

INTERNATIONAL FINN

Most yachtsmen would agree that the Finn, designed in 1949 by Rickard Sarby, is something of an anachronism. And yet, time after time, it has been voted in as the chosen singlehanded dinghy for Olympic competition. The reason is that the Finn is so demanding, both physically and mentally, that it produces a true champion.

Brutally heavy for a single-hander, the Finn slugs its way to windward and the helmsman has to fight for every metre gained. Because it is relatively slow, any tactical mistake is liable to be disastrous as there is so little opportunity to recover by superior speed. Sailing down-wind calls for a highly-developed technique in order to extract every bit of benefit from helpful waves while remaining just on the right side of the rules.

Racing a Finn at top level is a tough, lonely business that calls for both physical and mental strength. Few would claim that it was a bundle of fun, but there is always that gleam of gold on the far horizon.

LASER

Some years ago, Canadian boat designer Bruce Kirby had the perception to see that dinghy sailing was losing its popularity because too much time was being spent on maintenance, preparation, measuring, rigging, tuning and so on compared with the time spent actually afloat. He therefore designed the Laser (in 1970) to be as simple as possible consistent with a really sparkling performance.

He also conceived the idea of a 'manufacturer's class' in which as much as possible of the administrative hassle of racing was taken care of as a kind of 'after-sales service'. When you buy a Laser, you get a boat that is guaranteed ready to race in every respect, and which comes with the assurance that an extensive racing programme is out there waiting for you.

This idea for giving people

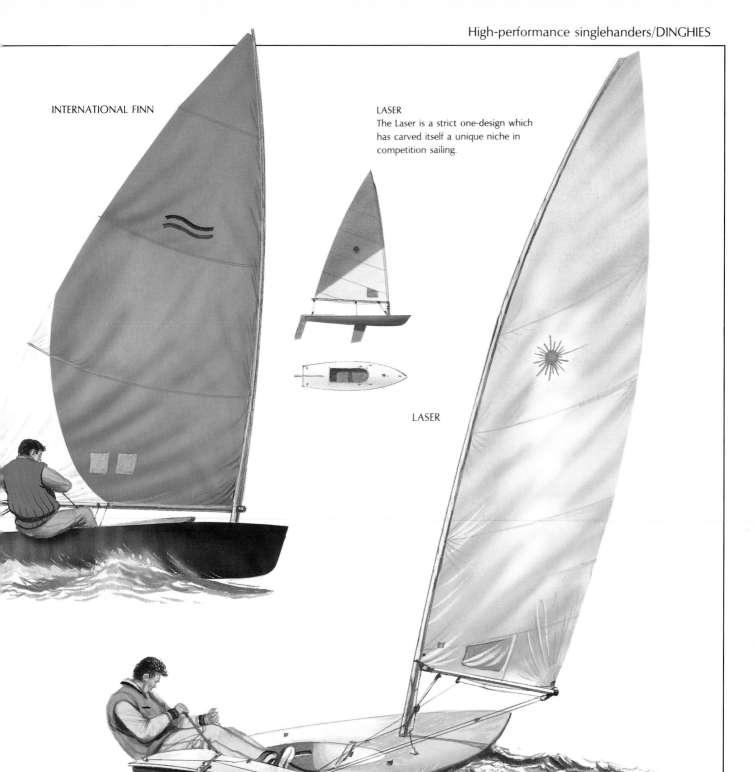

INTERNATIONAL FINN

LASER
The Laser is a strict one-design which
has carved itself a unique niche in
competition sailing.

LASER

NAME	LENGTH OVERALL	BEAM	WEIGHT	SAIL AREA	SPINNAKER	FEATURES
OK	4 m (13 ft)	1.5 m (4.9 ft)	72 kg (159 lb)	8.5 m² (92 ft²)		At its best in a good breeze
International Finn	4.5 m (14.8 ft)	1.5 m (4.9 ft)	145 kg (319 lb)	10 m² (107 ft²)		Very demanding boat to sail
Laser	4.23 m (13.9 ft)	1.37 m (4.5 ft)	59 kg (130 lb)	7.06 m² (76 ft²)		Fast and highly competitive

more fun for their money has
been brilliantly successful, and
the Laser is by far the most numerous and widely-distributed
racing dinghy, with over
136,000 sold in 85 countries.

But it would never have
worked unless the boat itself was

outstanding, and here again
Kirby was spot-on with a
dinghy that looked and was
tremendous fun as well as being
brilliantly simple. There is no
rigging, and the sail has a sleeve
luff that fits over the two-part
mast. There are just a few, low-

tech fittings in the boat and there
is very little to go wrong.

The tremendous popularity
of the Laser means that there is
keen racing almost anywhere
you go. National, regional and
World Championships are
tremendously hard-fought and

the boat has been used for a
number of years for the IYRU
World Youth Championships.
All this makes the Laser so much
more than just a boat—it is virtually a complete sports movement.

CADET, MIRROR & 420

Although many young sailors start their training in singlehanded boats such as the Optimist, there is much to be said for a two-person dinghy and, in fact, it was once thought that this was the only way to learn to sail. The Cadet and Mirror are very often sailed by a teenaged helmsman with a younger crew, who may be a beginner and can often learn a lot from the more-experienced helmsman. Teamwork is called for and each of the boats described here has a spinnaker to add to the fun of off-wind sailing.

INTERNATIONAL CADET

In 1947 Teddy Haylock, the then editor of the British magazine *Yachting World*, saw the need for a cheap children's trainer that could be built by amateurs, and commissioned the outstanding London boat-builder Jack Holt to design one. Holt used the new technique of glued and screwed waterproof plywood to produce a boat that looked a bit crude and boxy, but sailed well and could easily be built in any school workshop.

The guiding idea behind the Cadet was that it should be a complete miniature racing yacht that was deliberately too small for adults to fit into. The spinnaker is tiny, but that makes it all the more important to use it well.

Nowadays there are plenty of other trainers around, but for something like twenty years the Cadet was *the* children's racing boat and was built all over the world. Untold numbers of champions, including several Olympic winners, began their racing careers in a Cadet and the annual championship at Burnham-on-Crouch has always been a hotly-contested affair.

In spite of its dated design and quaint appearance, it is still difficult to better the Cadet as a race trainer and the concept is just as valid today as ever.

MIRROR

In 1963, the DIY expert Barry Bucknell had an idea for a dinghy made from precut ply panels 'sewn' together with copper wire, with the joints made strong and waterproof by covering them with glassfibre tape. He offered this idea for a cheap, lightweight dinghy to the *Daily Mirror* newspaper, which sensibly called in Jack Holt to reshape and strengthen the prototype. The resulting

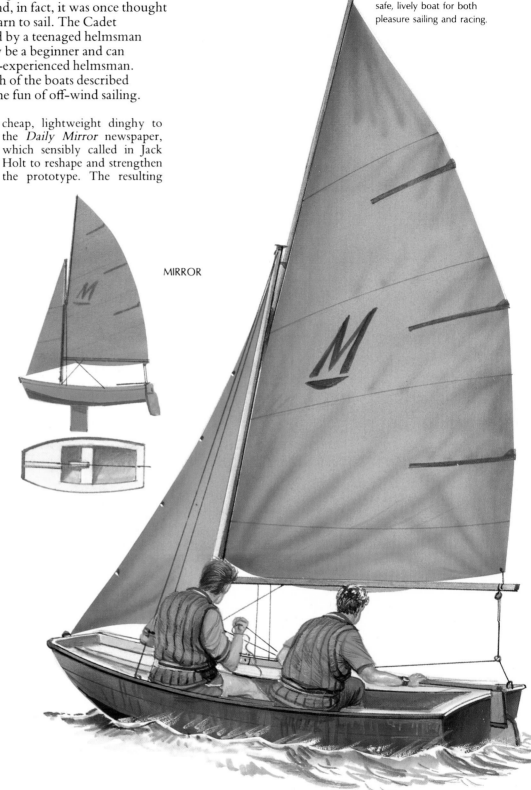

MIRROR
Designed to be owner-built from a kit, the red-sailed Mirror is a safe, lively boat for both pleasure sailing and racing.

MIRROR

NAME	LENGTH OVERALL	BEAM	WEIGHT	SAIL AREA	SPINNAKER	FEATURES
International Cadet	3.22 m (10.6 ft)	1.27 m (4.2 ft)	54 kg (120 lb)	5.2 m² (55.5 ft²)	4.65 m² (50 ft²)	Excellent children's racing trainer
Mirror	3.3 m (10.8 ft)	1.4 m (4.6 ft)	68 kg (150 lb)	6.41 m² (69 ft²)	6.08 m² (65.5 ft²)	Fine all-rounder
International 420	4.2 m (13.75 ft)	1.71 m (5.6 ft)	100 kg (221 lb)	10.25 m² (110 ft²)	8.01 m² (97 ft²)	Widely used trainer/racer

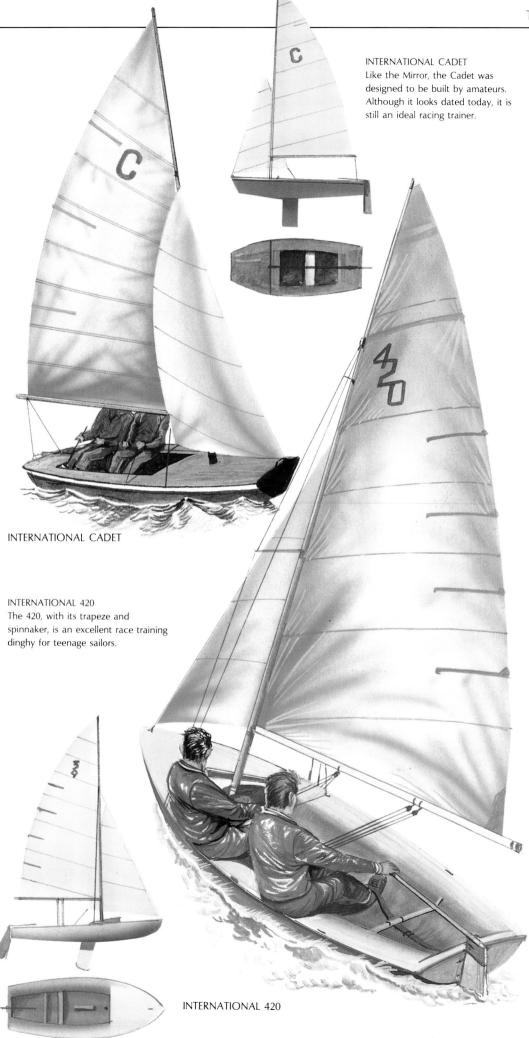

INTERNATIONAL CADET
Like the Mirror, the Cadet was designed to be built by amateurs. Although it looks dated today, it is still an ideal racing trainer.

INTERNATIONAL CADET

INTERNATIONAL 420
The 420, with its trapeze and spinnaker, is an excellent race training dinghy for teenage sailors.

INTERNATIONAL 420

'people's dinghy' is one of the most successful dinghies ever, with more than 100,000 built worldwide.

Apart from its simplicity and low cost, the appeal of the Mirror lies in the fact that it is a brilliant all-rounder that can be used either as a racer or a knock-about by both children and adults. The unusual gunter rig, first used by Holt for the Heron dinghy, means that the spars fit inside the length of the boat so that it can easily be carried upside-down on a car roof-rack. The construction incorporates large buoyancy tanks, making the Mirror particularly safe.

With more sail area than the Cadet, the Mirror makes a lively racing boat either for two children or an adult skipper and young crew, and in Britian there are not many sailing clubs where you will not see fleets of these jaunty little dinghies.

INTERNATIONAL 420

Designed in 1960 by Christian Maury, and a larger and more serious racing dinghy than either the Cadet or Mirror, the 420 is still regarded as a trainer and is often used as the youth class for international racing events. It is also the only one of the trio to be designed from the outset for glassfibre construction, and thus has a rounded hull rather than the 'chines' which are characteristic of plywood boats.

The sail area is greater than that of the Cadet or Mirror, and there is a trapeze to enable the crew to stand out from the gunwale and make much greater use of his or her weight.

Many people who have not tried it imagine that trapezing is difficult, but in fact, once the technique has been learned, it proves not only easy but much more comfortable than 'hanging out' over the side. It is also much to be recommended for a boat of this character because it enables relatively lightweight crews, and especially boy/girl pairs, to compete on equal terms.

Being from an earlier generation of glassfibre dinghies, it has to be said that the 420 is a bit of a soap-dish to look at and with its relatively small rig is no great performer in a light wind. On the other hand, it comes into its own in a strong breeze, when a well-sailed 420 can be a very hard boat to get past, With 'all the strings' of a grown-up racing dinghy but on a modest scale, the 420 is an excellent dinghy for teenagers.

ENTERPRISE, WAYFARER & LASER 16

The racing dinghies that maintain their popularity for decades are the sound designs that can be adapted for many purposes: racing or family sailing, inland or coastal sailing. A good boat is a good boat, and a sure sign of one is that owners find all sorts of uses for it that the designer never envisaged. For example, it is certain that Ian Proctor never imagined that his Wayfarer design would be used for passages of several hundred miles in the open sea, but that is exactly what has happened on a number of occasions. A comparison between the Wayfarer and the Laser 16 is particularly interesting as the latter is clearly an attempt to improve on the older boat by using modern materials.

ENTERPRISE

Designed in 1965 by Jack Holt, the blue-sailed Enterprise was designed primarily as a dinghy for inland waters and for that reason it was built fairly lightly and given a generous sail area. Jack Holt also gave it a double-chine plywood hull that was a little harder to build than a simple shape like the Cadet or GP 14, but faster and more sensitive to sail. The Enterprise became virtually the standard boat for inland clubs but, thanks to the perversity of human nature, it is widely used for coastal racing as well.

In its original form, the Enterprise had a reputation for being a tricky boat to handle in a strong wind, having a mast that was hard to keep in the right curvature and a marked tendency to 'death roll' on a square run. With maturity, the Enterprise has grown out of these childish tantrums, thanks mostly to modern spars and sails. Perhaps surprisingly, it has never had a spinnaker or trapeze, thanks to its original concept as a budget cruiser-racer.

In strong winds, and especially in waves, the Enterprise can still be a handful, but its high power-to-weight ratio still makes it an ideal boat for smoother waters. More than 20,000 have been built and a large proportion are used for pleasure and family sailing rather than competition.

WAYFARER

Ian Proctor has two claims to fame—as an outstanding small-boat designer and as one of the pioneers of metal masts. But he could not have a more enduring achievement than the Wayfarer, the sturdy dinghy that seems ready to take on virtually any task given to it.

Designed in 1957 and built originally in marine ply, the beamy, sturdy hull has large watertight compartments at bow and stern that can also be used for dry storage. The mast is stepped on a below-deck tabernacle that makes it simple to raise and lower.

There is room in the cockpit for four, or even five, crew and there are raised floorboards so you don't get your feet wet as soon as there is a cupful of water in the bottom. Newer, glassfibre versions are made self-draining, in other words with a raised floor so the water simply runs out through scuppers.

Perhaps the most important quality is that the Wayfarer sails really well and is an exciting boat to race, especially in coastal waters. It is exceptionally strong, and over the years has become almost the standard boat for sailing schools which send an instructor out with three or four pupils on board.

A capacious picnic boat, the Wayfarer has often been used for quite ambitious coastal cruises while one particular enthusiast, Frank Dye, has made some amazing long-distance passages lasting several days in Wayfarers. This is a boat that is very hard to better as an all-rounder.

LASER 16

Designed in 1985 by Bruce Kirby, the Laser 16 is a bold attempt to produce a completely modern general-purpose boat, having nearly all the advantages of a boat such as the Wayfarer plus some extra ones of its own. For a start she is completely buoyant and self-draining. This is not only a very worthwhile safety feature when sailing, it also means the boat can be left unattended on moorings with no need to 'pump out' after rain or bad weather.

Hardly any dinghies have satisfactory reefing arrangements—basically, you are expected to be able to handle full sail or to stay ashore. Yet there are plenty of occasions, such as when you encounter a sudden increase in wind when out sailing with a novice crew, when a reduction in sail is the prudent way. The Laser 16 solves this with a roller furling system for the jib and a simplified version of the 'slab' mainsail reefing that the vast majority of racing yachts use.

The mast is deck-stepped, leaving clear access to a large watertight hatch into the forward locker which has ample room for gear, clothing and stores. There is also an aft locker big enough to take a small outboard motor which fits onto a bracket on the stern.

The folding swim ladder is also a safety feature as it is surprisingly difficult to climb back on board a boat from the water—even onto a relatively small one such as the Laser 16.

ENTERPRISE

ENTERPRISE
Although designed for use primarily on inland waters, the Enterprise has proved successful in coastal racing as well.

WAYFARER

LASER 16

The mast breaks into two for easy stowage and there is a tailor-made trailer with a winch for easy launching and recovery.

On top of all these good, practical features, the Laser 16 sails well—in fact, it has been said that she is the type of boat that you could learn in and still find challenging years later.

WAYFARER
The Wayfarer is a fine all-round family dinghy with room aboard for up to five people.

LASER 16
The Laser 16, which is fully buoyant, is a very practical family dinghy and sails well.

NAME	LENGTH OVERALL	BEAM	WEIGHT	SAIL AREA	SPINNAKER	FEATURES
Enterprise	4.04 m (13.25 ft)	1.6 m (5.25 ft)	94 kg (207 lb)	10.5 m^2 (113 ft^2)		Roomy and stable
Wayfarer	4.82 m (15.8 ft)	1.85 m (6.1 ft)	169 kg (372 lb)	13.1 m^2 (141 ft^2) (main + genoa)	13.5 m^2 (145 ft^2)	Sturdy family dinghy
Laser 16	5.19 m (17 ft)	2.06 m (6.8 ft)	250 kg (550 lb)	14 m^2 (151 ft^2)	11.54 m^2 (124 ft^2)	Good general-purpose boat

SNIPE, GP 14 & ALBACORE

The term 'general-purpose' can mean different things to different people, but most would agree that a general-purpose dinghy should be sturdy, durable and adaptable to either cruising or racing. As this type of boat is frequently used for family sailing and picnicking, safety is important and the ability to carry a small outboard motor is desirable. But its performance under sail must still be good because nobody enjoys sailing a dull boat.

SNIPE

Designed in 1931 by William F Crosby, the Snipe was one of the first (if not *the* first) dinghies specifically intended for amateur construction. Waterproof plywood had not yet arrived so the Snipe was planked, but it had 'hard chines' (sharp angles between bottom and sides) which made it quite easy to build.

It was cleverly promoted in the United States by *Rudder* magazine, of which Crosby was editor. With a nice eye for a publicity gimmick, Crosby had the prototype built by a 14-year-old schoolboy. As well as being a pioneering design, the Snipe led the way in showing how valuable the backing of a magazine or newspaper could be in getting it widely known. Plans were sold through the magazine and there were articles to collect on how to build it.

The Snipe was an immediate success and soon became the most popular small boat in the United States, a position it was to hold for many years. It also gained a considerable foothold in Europe, especially in Spain and Portugal, but has recently declined as more modern designs have appeared.

Nowadays the Snipe is built in glassfibre, but it is still very heavy compared with most dinghies and this, together with its relatively modest sail area, makes its performance stately rather than sparkling. However, it is important to remember that speed does not necessarily make for good racing because it tends to spread a fleet out, whereas boats that all tend to sail at around the same speed result in close, tactically exciting racing.

GP 14

Designed in 1949 by Jack Holt as one of a series of 'Build Her Yourself' dinghies promoted by *Yachting World* magazine, the GP 14's name proclaims that she was intended as a 'General Purpose 14-footer'. A kit of parts was produced by Bell Woodworking of Leicester, hence the bell logo on the sail, and it was not long before adult education workshops, garages and even bedrooms were full of partly-built GPs.

Jack Holts's design was a model of what this type of boat should be: sturdy, roomy, safe, equally at home under sail or outboard and yet with a satisfying sailing performance. Though never conceived as a racing craft, the GP soon built up a large number of enthusiasts, especially at coastal and estuary clubs where rough conditions and hard knocks were an inevitable part of sailing.

Although technically a one-design, the GP is also a good example of what can be done to keep the appeal fresh by sensible modernization. The changeover from plywood to glassfibre construction is the most obvious improvement, but a substantial increase in sail area (including a good-sized spinnaker) and

GP 14

GP 14
The GP 14 was designed in 1949, but has been much updated over the years and remains popular for training and pleasure sailing as well as for racing.

SNIPE
The Snipe, designed in 1931, is one of the oldest classes of racing dinghy and is still raced in over sixty countries.

improvements to the layout, with built-in buoyancy rather than airbags, have been almost as important. The result is a boat that is still fulfilling its role admirably after forty years and which has a large and faithful following.

ALBACORE

Designed in 1959 by Uffa Fox, the Albacore (known to its friends as the 'Applecore') was one of a series of sporty dinghies designed by him for Fairey and named after aircraft built by that company. All Fox's designs employed hot-moulded wood construction in which thin strips of wood were laid up on a male mould with thermosetting glue between layers. Then the whole boat was cured under heat and pressure in an autoclave.

This was a wonderful method of boat construction that produced light, strong, stiff, smooth, goodlooking hulls, and it is a great shame that high costs led to its abandonment.

The 12-foot Firefly was the first of the line, followed by the 15-foot Swordfish, the Albacore and the Jollyboat. The Albacore was given extra freeboard to make it a drier boat than the racy Swordfish while still retaining good performance. Like all the 'Uffa' dinghies, it has a full, chesty entry that lifts the whole

forward end of the boat up when there is enough wind for planing.

As well as being successful in their native England, Albacores were well received in Canada and the United States where they are still raced and cruised. For some years, the hulls have been built in glassfibre but there are still plenty of the original wooden Albacores around, many of them looking just as good as they did when they were built.

SNIPE

ALBACORE
Like the Snipe and the GP 14, the Albacore was originally a wooden-hulled boat but is now made in glassfibre.

ALBACORE

NAME	LENGTH OVERALL	BEAM	WEIGHT	SAIL AREA	SPINNAKER	FEATURES
Snipe	4.72 m (15.5 ft)	1.52 m (5 ft)	174.6 kg (385 lb)	11.89 m² (128 ft²)		Heavy, rather slow
GP 14	4.27 m (14 ft)	1.52 m (5 ft)	132.9 kg (293 lb)	10.5 m² (113 ft²) (main + genoa)	8.4 m² (90.5 ft²)	Safe general-purpose dinghy
Albacore	4.57 m (15 ft)	1.52 m (5 ft)	109 kg (240 lb)	11.61 m² (125 ft²)		Good racing/general-purpose dinghy

FIREBALL, 470 & LASER II REGATTA

For those of us who still think in Imperial measure, 16-foot seems to be the magic size for a serious racing dinghy with trapeze and spinnaker—unless you go in for one of the superdinghies such as the 505 or Flying Dutchman. A 16-footer seems to have a lot going for it; it is big enough for two grown men to race but not too large for two teenagers or a couple. It is seaworthy enough for open sea racing but still light enough for easy trailing or cartopping and fits into a standard-sized garage. None of these three dinghies claims to be a 'general purpose' design; they are all purely racing dinghies—in one case an Olympic class.

INTERNATIONAL LASER II REGATTA

The guiding Laser philosophy—of producing a highly standardized boat without expensive extras—is harder to sustain in the cause of a two-person racing dinghy with spinnaker and trapeze because in this type of racing, setting the boat up just the way you want it is part of the game. On the other hand, there are plenty of people who would like a boat that is ready to race 'straight out of the box' and the Laser II, designed by Frank Braithwaite, is the boat for them.

Smaller than the other two dinghies here, the Laser II also has less sail and the spinnaker in particular is fairly modest, perhaps in the belief that it is better not to frighten the paying customers to death.

Very Laser-ish in hull shape, but with more freeboard and a bigger cockpit, the Laser II shares the same sparkling performance, especially off the wind. It also has some of the very simple control systems such as the sliding-rope mainsheet traveller. This is cheap and needs no maintenance, but is a bit basic for a serious racing boat.

INTERNATIONAL 470

Designed in 1963 by Andre Cornu. 'Not just an Olympic Class' is one of the slogans of this class, which has suffered from the fact that ordinary club sailors tend to shy away from what they see as the premium prices and excessive pressure of anything to do with the Olympics. And this is a shame because the 470 is really an ideal club racer, being a

practical boat in every way and particularly suited to the lighter weight of a typical mixed crew.

The 470 was selected as an Olympic class because the exist-

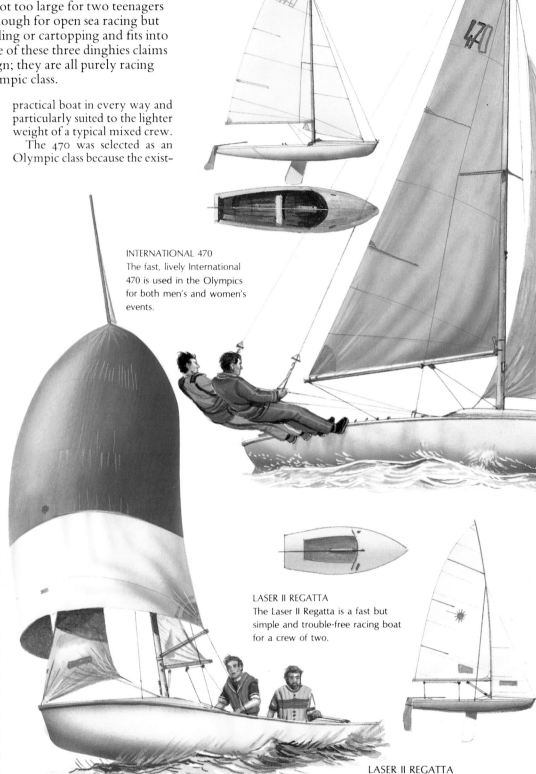

INTERNATIONAL 470

INTERNATIONAL 470
The fast, lively International 470 is used in the Olympics for both men's and women's events.

LASER II REGATTA
The Laser II Regatta is a fast but simple and trouble-free racing boat for a crew of two.

LASER II REGATTA

NAME	LENGTH OVERALL	BEAM	WEIGHT	SAIL AREA	SPINNAKER	FEATURES
International Laser II Regatta	4.39 m (14.4 ft)	1.42 m (4.67 ft)	79 kg (174 lb)	11.52 m² (124 ft²)	10.2 m² (110 ft²)	Two-man racer with trapeze
International 470	4.7 m (15.4 ft)	1.68 m (5.5 ft)	120 kg (265 lb)	12.7 m² (137 ft²)	13 m² (140 ft²)	Olympic class two-man dinghy
International Fireball	4.93 m (16.17 ft)	1.35 m (4.5 ft)	79.4 kg (175 lb)	11.43 m² (123 ft²)	13 m² (140 ft²)	Two-man racer with trapeze

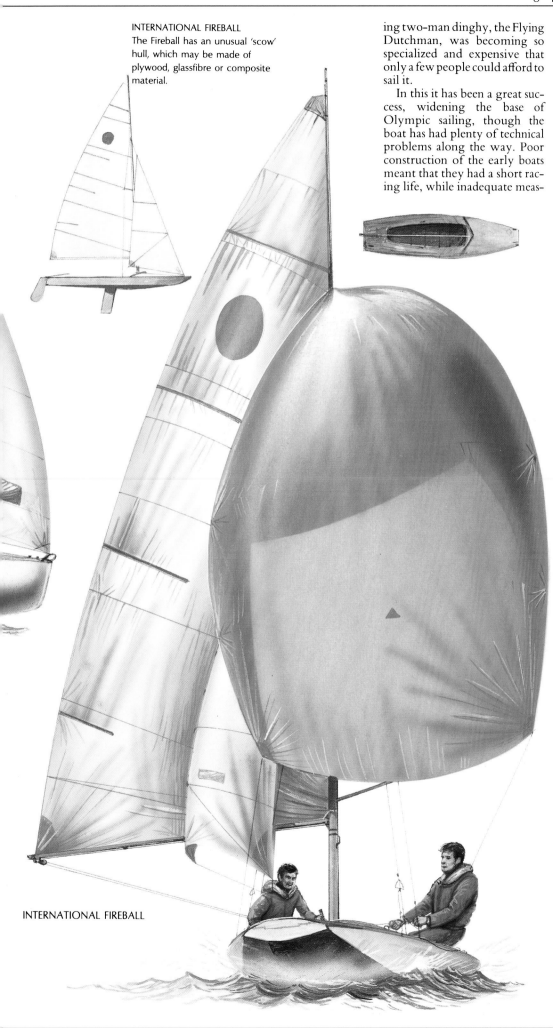

INTERNATIONAL FIREBALL
The Fireball has an unusual 'scow' hull, which may be made of plywood, glassfibre or composite material.

INTERNATIONAL FIREBALL

ing two-man dinghy, the Flying Dutchman, was becoming so specialized and expensive that only a few people could afford to sail it.

In this it has been a great success, widening the base of Olympic sailing, though the boat has had plenty of technical problems along the way. Poor construction of the early boats meant that they had a short racing life, while inadequate meas-

urement rules allowed unscrupulous builders to 'tweak' the hull shape. Hopefully, these problems are now in the past.

The fast, lively performance of the 470 is best suited to an agile, lightweight crew and this has led to its important role in women's sailing. In 1988 there was a women's sailing class in the Olympics for the first time—sailed in 470s.

The 470 is a strict one-design with a limited freedom of interior layout and controls, though thanks to the ingenuity of top competitors, small changes can be made to have a big influence on performance. With troublesome teething problems in the past, the 470 should really occupy a key position in the dinghy racing world.

INTERNATIONAL FIREBALL

Designed in 1962 by Peter Milne, the unusual scow hullform of the Fireball means that it is particularly suitable for plywood construction, and this is one class where this material is still favourite although glassfibre is permitted.

The designer's intention was to create a really fast racing dinghy that could be built at home, and although this still holds true, most of today's top Fireballs are made by professional builders using carefully set-up moulds and jigs to take the best advantages of measurement tolerances. These give a limited freedom of layout and, in theory, a one-design hull shape. On the other hand there is a lot of free choice in rig control systems and there is always lots of development going on in this area.

When it first appeared, the Fireball had no trapeze and must have been quite a dull boat, for it only really comes to life when the crew gets his weight over the side. Rather insensitive to windward because of the flat bottom, the Fireball is at its best on a spinnaker reach. Then, few boats can match its power and speed.

With careful tuning of the rig, it is possible to be successful in the Fireball with a wide variety of crew weights and there have been some interesting pairings with, for instance, a girl at the helm and a man on the wire.

At one time there was a suggestion that the Fireball should be an Olympic class, but after the 470 took this slot it resumed its role as an owner-controlled high-performance racing boat.

INTERNATIONAL 14, FLYING DUTCHMAN & 505

During the 1950s there was a competition to find a new high-performance racing dinghy for the Olympics. The Flying Dutchman won this, and has been in the Olympics ever since, but there were plenty who felt that the 505 should have been the winner and have stayed faithful to it ever since. The International 14, another boat with a faithful following, will always have a place in history as the class that really started the trend toward lightweight planing dinghies. A trendsetter in the 1920s, it still is today.

INTERNATIONAL 14

The story of the International 14-foot Dinghy goes right back to 1922, when in England the Small Boat Association combined the rules, of three popular dinghy classes to form a new 'National 14-ft Class' that could be raced anywhere in the country on equal terms—a novel idea at the time. It quickly became popular, and when the then Prince of Wales presented a cup for the annual championship race, the 'Fourteen' was established as the racing dinghy in England.

The International 14 also pioneered the idea of a 'restricted development' class, in which any design can be used within certain limits of length, beam, weight, sail area and so on. This led to healthy competition between designers, and in 1928 two boats—*Avenger*, designed by Uffa Fox, and *Pintail*, designed by Tom Thornycroft—changed the whole course of dinghy design by demonstrating planing for the first time.

Before this, only fast motorboats had been able to get up and skim across the water surface, but by using a veed bow and broad, flattish stern, Fox showed that a sailing dinghy could do it too. In 57 races during 1928, *Avenger* had 52 firsts, two seconds and three thirds.

After this great surge of innovation, the class became more conservative and it banned the trapeze when Peter Scott first tried it in 1938.

For many years after the Second World War, the International 14s had a kind of 'vintage sports car' appeal, being beautifully-built boats with a slightly dated appearance, but this changed in the 1980s when fundamental rule changes allowed much lighter boats to be built with both helmsman and crew on trapezes and a more modern rig. The result is that the Fourteen is now back at the forefront of development.

With such a large sail area (including a huge, asymmetric spinnaker) on a hull of modest length, the International 14 is a very fast and demanding boat to sail, and like the Flying Dutchman and the 505 is certainly not a boat for beginners.

INTERNATIONAL FLYING DUTCHMAN

Designed by U van Essen in 1951 to meet the need for a high-performance dinghy in the Olympic Games, the Flying Dutchman has filled this position with distinction since 1960. A big, beamy, stable boat, it has a rig that now looks a little old-fashioned, with a relatively small mainsail and a large overlapping genoa. The hull shape is one-design but construction and interior layout are free, which results in the boat being very expensive as every one is individually built and fitted-out.

Highly sensitive to tuning, the Flying Dutchman is an

INTERNATIONAL 505

INTERNATIONAL 14

INTERNATIONAL 14
With its large sail area, double trapeze and high speed, the 470 is for experts.

extremely technical boat to sail and invariably fitted with a large number of complex controls. For instance, a very large adjustment of mast rake is considered necessary and to achieve this, jib halyard, shrouds and jib sheeting positions must all move in unison. Many familiar items of equipment, such as the continu-

INTERNATIONAL 505
The International 505 is a fast, powerful two-man dinghy. Its slim hull has distinctively flared topsides.

ous trapeze system and the fly-away spinnaker pole, were developed in this class.

Because of its size, the FD is best suited to big men and the

crews in particular are normally of exceptional height. They are also called upon to wear weight jackets to further increase the power of the boat, though recently limits have been placed on the amount of weight that may be carried. Not by any means a popular boat, due to its cost and specialized nature, the FD is nevertheless a 'leading edge' class which others look to for technical expertise.

INTERNATIONAL 505

John Westell designed a dinghy for the Olympic trials, named the Coronet, that was runner-up to the Flying Dutchman. The Caneton Association in France wanted a new boat and asked Westell to adapt the Coronet slightly to their requirements. The result, in 1953, was the 505, a somewhat smaller but more lively dinghy than the FD with a

very strong character of its own. Westell's secret was to give the boat a slim, slippery hull surmounted by flared topsides and a wide deck to give additional power.

Fast, powerful and demanding, the 'Five-O' has been one of the top racing classes for thirty years and has a strong international following. More closely-controlled than either the FD or the International 14, the 505 cannot be built in costly composite plastics and this helps to keep the cost of ownership down, although the gear and sails are certainly not cheap.

INTERNATIONAL FLYING DUTCHMAN
The Olympic-class Flying Dutchman is a fast but complex boat to sail.

INTERNATIONAL FLYING DUTCHMAN

NAME	LENGTH OVERALL	BEAM	WEIGHT	SAIL AREA	SPINNAKER	FEATURES
International 14	4.27 m (14 ft)	1.68 m (5.5 ft)	91 kg (200 lb)	17.64 m² (190 ft²)	18.6 m² (200 ft²)	For experienced sailors only
International Flying Dutchman	6.05 m (19.9 ft)	1.68 m (5.5 ft)	125 kg (275 lb)	18.6 m² (200 ft²) (main + genoa)	17.6 m² (190 ft²)	Olympic class two-man dinghy
International 505	5.05 m (16.5 ft)	1.94 m (6.33 ft)	127 kg (280 lb)	16.3 m² (175 ft²)	23.22 m² (250 ft²)	Two-man racer with trapeze

HOBIE 14, NEW CAT F1 & CATAPULT

The intoxicating speed of the catamaran, combined with the relative ease of handling, is one of the great thrills of small-boat sailing. But as many people have found out, owning and sailing a 'cat' is not always that simple. A number of designers and builders have tried to tackle this problem of the 'unapproachability' of catamarans, and here we look at three attempts to offer cats that are as basic and simple as possible.

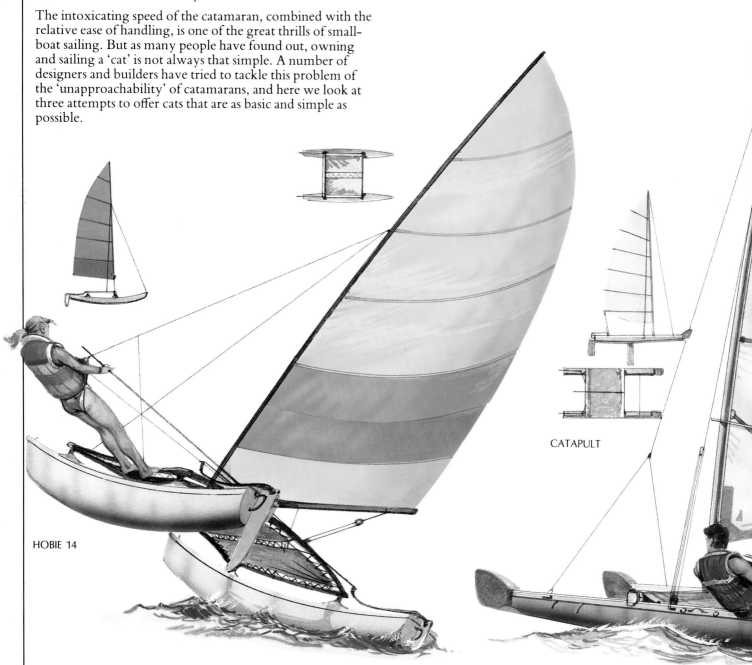

HOBIE 14

CATAPULT

HOBIE 14

In 1969, the Californian designer Hobie Alter created a catamaran that was simple to sail, cheap to build and could be operated off a beach—the Hobie 14.

In order to eliminate the need for a centreboard, he gave the Hobie 14 deeply-curved 'banana' hulls that have sufficient grip on the water without boards. This shape made the centre of the hulls very low in the water, so he put the crew platform, the 'trampoline', on a raised tubular metal frame that also forms the connection between the hulls. Finally, he designed a special rudder that kicks up out of the way when it hits a solid object.

With its short length and single sail, the Hobie 14 gives a very sporty ride for one person but is often sailed with two on board. The fact that it can be sailed straight onto a sandy beach means that it is a favourite boat for hotels, holiday hire and the like, and it is easily the most popular catamaran worldwide.

In strong winds and rough seas the small Hobie can also be something of a bucking bronco, with the interesting ability to capsize in any direction—sideways, forwards, backwards or diagonally. More to the point, though, in any normal weather you don't need to be an expert to sail one and it can be terrific fun.

NEW CAT F1

There is more than one way to design a catamaran without centreboards, and the Hobie's deeply-curved hulls certainly have some drawbacks. Another solution, adopted by the French-made New Cat and others, is to have a rather deep hull with a kind of shallow keel moulded onto the underside. This allows straighter, easier-running hulls and a lighter crossbeam.

In addition, the New Cat hulls are one-piece mouldings in heavy-duty polyethylene and filled with plastic foam, making them unsinkable and exceptionally tough yet easy to repair. The rig is quite sophisticated with a high-aspect-ratio, fully-battened mainsail and a small jib.

The F1 was designed to be a singlehanded racer or a two-person fun boat, and the deep hulls are reasonably tolerant of extra weight. A number of sailing schools have adopted either the F1 or other models in the New Cat range and have been very impressed by its seeming indestructibility. Although it is certainly no way to treat a boat, people have been known to sail F1s straight onto concrete ramps with hardly any ill-effects. For someone wanting the thrills and excitement of a catamaran, but with the minimum of trouble, the New Cat would seem a very practical answer.

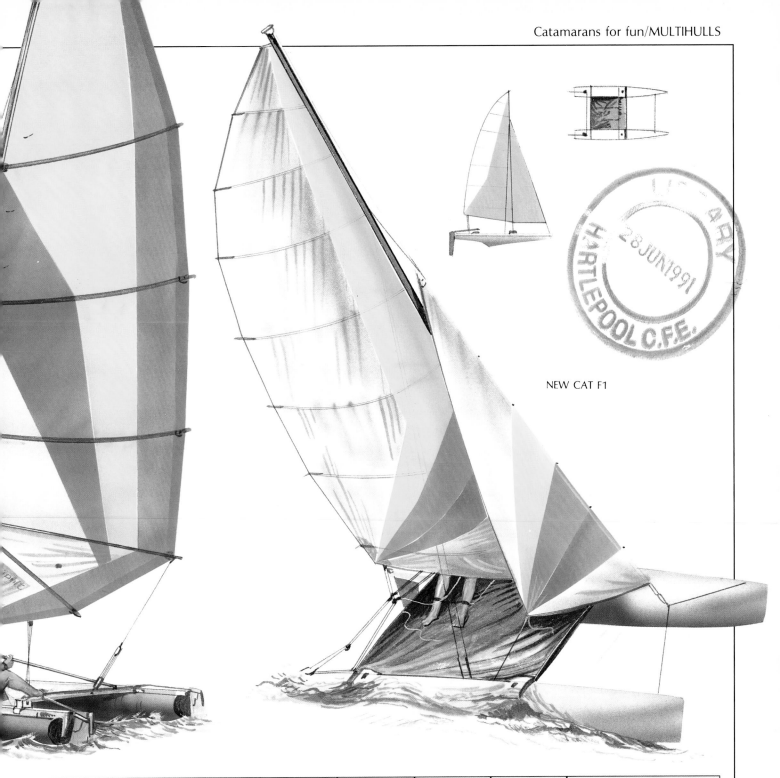

NEW CAT F1

NAME	LENGTH OVERALL	BEAM	WEIGHT	SAIL AREA	SPINNAKER	FEATURES
Hobie 14	4.27 m (14 ft)	2.34 m (7.7 ft)	108.8 kg (240 lb)	10.96 m² (118 ft²)		Very simple and fun to sail
New Cat F1	4.2 m (13.8 ft)	2.2 m (7.2 ft)	105 kg (231 lb)	12.5 m² (134.6 ft²)		Tough, enjoyable and very practical
Catapult	5 m (16.4 ft)	2.24 m (7.35 ft)	81.2 kg (180 lb)	10 m² (107 ft²)		Inflatable hulls with rigid bows

CATAPULT

Human ingenuity being what it is, almost any type of boat can be built, but who would have thought of an inflatable catamaran? And more to the point, why?

The perfectly logical thinking behind the Catapult, designed in 1981 by Jon Montgomery, is that many people do not have the room to store a rigid 5-metre catamaran and might find it a nuisance to transport. To solve this problem, the Catapult's hulls can be deflated and rolled up while the framework, ingeniously made in tubular aluminium, dismantles into a collection of short, straight pieces. The whole thing can be stored indoors or tidily folded away in a garage, and it can easily be transported by car.

The difficult part was to design an inflatable hull that sailed well and would not suddenly fold up under heavy strain. It took Montgomery several years to perfect the technology, which basically consists of two separate tubes within an outer cover. A moulded plastic bowpiece protects the tubes, in case of impact or hitting the ground.

As part of the testing procedure for this design, Montgomery more than once entered it for the famous annual speed-sailing competition at Portland Harbour, Dorset, where he achieved the remarkable speed of 17 knots, which is highly satisfactory for any small catamaran.

The Catapult is a thoroughly entertaining little craft, and for those people with any kind of boat storage problem it could represent a very practical solution.

HOBIE 16, PRINDLE 16 & DART 18

All three boats here are medium-sized and fairly serious racing machines and were designed to give the full excitement of catamaran racing at reasonable cost. The most effective way of doing this is to have what is called a 'strict one-design', which means that you have to race the boat just as it is supplied by the manufacturer, without modification. The aim of this is not only to make the racing more equal, but also to protect owners against an unrestricted 'arms race' in equipment. There's no doubt that the best performance in a multihull is achieved when the hull has a semicircular underwater shape and daggerboards to give lateral resistance. But daggerboards cost money, weaken the hull and make the risk of damage on going aground much greater. The designers of all three of these boats have found ways of getting along without daggerboards.

HOBIE 16

Although it looks as if it is just a scaled-up version of the smaller Hobie 14, the 16 is a far more impressive sailing machine in every way. Designed by Hobie Alter in 1972, it has the same sort of deeply-rockered hulls and raised platform as the smaller boat, but there the similarity ends. The big, high-aspect-ratio sloop rig, with fully-battened mainsail and rotating mast, gives a great deal of power and to harness this power, both helmsman and crew use trapezes.

As catamarans go, the Hobie is heavy and its deep hulls are not particularly efficient but, rather like many American cars, it overcomes the weight penalty by having plenty of power. It makes a good racing boat because it tacks faster than most cats and is very sensitive to fore-and-aft trim. It does not point up to windward especially well, but is genuinely fast and spectacular on a reach.

Many Hobie 16s are bought

DART 18

DART 18
The cleverly-designed mainsail of the Dart, with its angled mainsheet, has no boom, which reduces both the weight and the cost of the boat.

without any thought of racing, and although not really suitable for beginners they make fast and enjoyable funboats. As with the smaller boat, they can be sailed straight onto a sandy beach without damage. When the wind is light and the sun is hot, the raised trampoline makes a very agreeable sunbathing platform.

Hobies are found nearly everywhere in the world and there are racing fleets in a number of countries, particularly in the boat's native United States.

PRINDLE 16

Ranging from 15 to 18 feet in length, the Prindle range of catamarans is one of the best known, especially in the United States. The original boat was the 16, which is an excellent racing or leisure boat for two people with a combined weight of under 140 kg, making it ideal for a couple.

In this case, the need for daggerboards has been eliminated by using asymmetric hulls which are nearly flat on their outer sides and rounded on their inner sides. The flat sides are supposed to dig into the water to stop the boat going sideways while, if the crew 'fly a hull', the one left in the water tends to act as a foil that develops lift to windward. With kick-up rudders as a standard fitting, this is another boat that can be sailed onto or off the beach without problems.

To get the trampoline a reasonable distance above the water, the hull freeboard is generous and the foredeck rounded, giving an added reserve of buoyancy and protection against burying. The cross-beams are directly connected to the hulls to keep the structure light and rigid. An efficient sloop rig with fully-battened mainsail makes the Prindle a very lively performer.

Other members of the Prindle family, especially the 18, are rather more race-oriented, but the 16 is a fine all-rounder and being a popular boat there is plenty of class racing, especially in the United States.

DART 18

Having previously designed the Tornado, the ultra-high-performance catamaran used in the Olympics, Rodney March turned his thoughts to a production boat. He and the builders spent a lot of time working out the engineering in order to achieve a structure that was light and stiff and could be assembled in a matter of minutes without special tools.

There are two major design innovations in the Dart, which was designed in 1976. In order to eliminate daggerboards without compromising hull shape, March gave each Dart hull a downward extension or blade, rather like the keel of a yacht but without any ballast in it.

The hulls themselves are symmetrical, and very slim so that they cut through the water as easily as knife blades. A clever design of mainsail with an angled mainsheet made it possible to eliminate the boom, at the same time reducing cost, weight and the risk of being hit on the head.

A strict one-design, the Dart is more of a dedicated racer than the other two boats shown here and is normally handled by two people, the crew having a trapeze. However, one of the class rules is that the boat can also be raced singlehanded with the jib removed, in level competition with the two-handed boats.

Light, lively and sensitive, the Dart is a most exciting boat to sail and in a good breeze is one of the fastest boats around. There are good racing fleets in many parts of Europe and especially in England, but the Dart is not well known in the United States.

Thanks to its simplicity, the Dart 18 and the other two boats in the family are perfectly practical funboats. In moderate weather they are well-mannered and docile boats though the adrenaline level tends to go up with the wind strength.

PRINDLE 16
The Prindle 16, with its asymmetric hulls and light but rigid structure, is an excellent two-person craft for racing or leisure sailing.

PRINDLE 16

HOBIE 16

HOBIE 16
To make best use of the power available from its big sloop rig, the Hobie 16 has trapezes for both skipper and crew.

NAME	LENGTH OVERALL	BEAM	WEIGHT	SAIL AREA	SPINNAKER	FEATURES
Hobie 16	5.11 m (16.8 ft)	2.4 m (7.9 ft)	154 kg (340 lb)	20.25 m² (218 ft²)		Fast pleasure/racing boat
Prindle 16	4.87 m (16 ft)	2.4 m (7.9 ft)	136 kg (300 lb)	17.57 m² (189 ft²)		Fast all-rounder
Dart 18	5.49 m (18 ft)	2.29 m (7.5 ft)	134 kg (295 lb)	16.08 m² (173 ft²)		Powerful but stable

UNICORN, HOBIE 18 & TORNADO

A boat salesman might tell you that the product he is trying to persuade you to buy is perfect for everything from taking granny for a sail to winning the Olympics, but the truth is that every boat has its own particular place in the scheme of things. There is no doubt where the three boats shown here belong: they are all out-and-out racers though with very different characters.

HOBIE 18

HOBIE 18
The Hobie 18, designed specifically as a racing boat, has a sail area of almost 24 square metres.

UNICORN

During the mid-Sixties, it was intended to have two catamarans in the Olympics, a two-man B Class cat and a singlehanded A Class. The two-man boat made it, in the shape of the Tornado, but the singlehander never did.

Following various trials there were two candidates for the Olympic A Class, the Australian *Australis* and the British *Unicorn*. The Australian boat never became popular, but the Unicorn, designed in 1967 by John Mazotti, is widely raced throughout Europe where it is the first choice as a dedicated one-man racing catamaran.

The hull lines are extremely fine and so the hulls have extra freeboard forward of the main beam, in order to give additional buoyancy. This is needed because of the strong tendency of catamarans to bury the lee bow when driven hard on a reach.

If you decide to race within A Class, you can use any kind of rig you like, within the maximum area, and there have been lots of experiments with rigid aerofoils, but the Unicorn Class uses a normal cloth sail on a tall, bendy mast.

The idea of this very limber mast is that it can be set up for different crew weights and wind strengths, but obviously you need to know what you are doing. Another indication that this is a pure racing boat is that it has a foil section daggerboard in each hull; these are highly efficient and a darned nuisance when beaching.

The Unicorn is sailed by one person on a trapeze and he or she certainly has plenty to do, what with operating the tiller, sheet, daggerboards and rig control, not to mention deciding on racing tactics. The performance is absolutely electrifying, and in fact there is probably no faster singlehander.

HOBIE 18

Following the great success of his 14- and 16-foot cats, which were always intended as general-purpose fun-and-racing boats, Hobie Alter decided to go for a pure racer and in 1978, together with Phil Edwards, he designed the Hobie 18. To get the extra performance of a thoroughbred, he knew that he would have to give away the convenience of a beachable boat and straighten out his famous 'banana' hulls.

Being a production boat in glassfibre and polyester, the Hobie 18 is quite heavy—heavier, for instance, than the larger Tornado—but to make up for this it has the really massive sail area of just under 24 square metres. Most cats have tall, high-aspect-ratio mainsails and small jibs because this tends to be the most efficient arrangement, but the Hobie 18 has a sizeable genoa which gives added punch in light weather and helps to keep the height of the rig within bounds.

To harness the power of all this sail, both crew members use

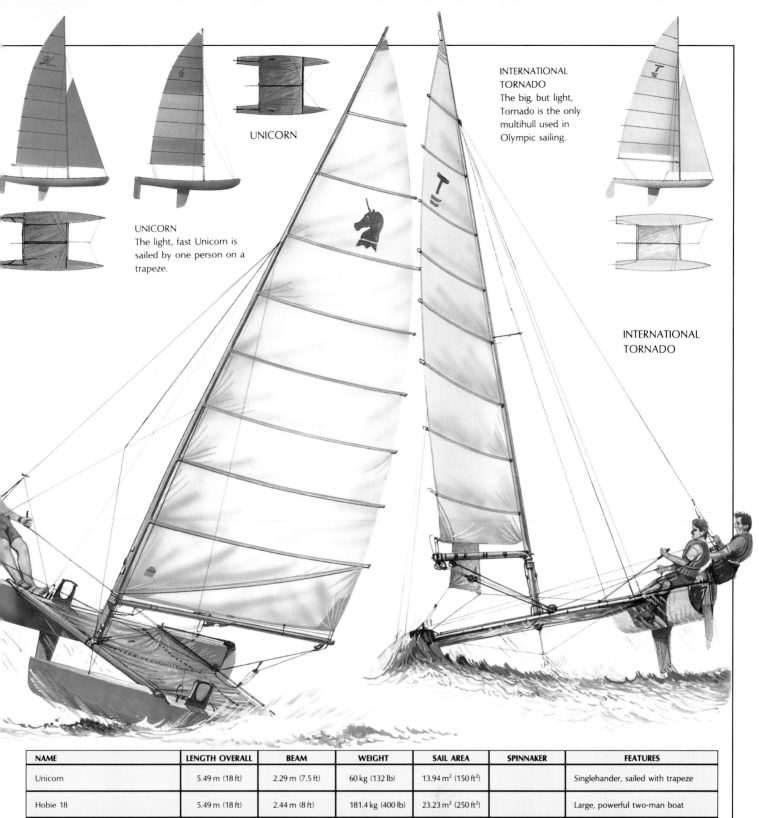

UNICORN

INTERNATIONAL
TORNADO
The big, but light,
Tornado is the only
multihull used in
Olympic sailing.

UNICORN
The light, fast Unicorn is
sailed by one person on a
trapeze.

INTERNATIONAL
TORNADO

NAME	LENGTH OVERALL	BEAM	WEIGHT	SAIL AREA	SPINNAKER	FEATURES
Unicorn	5.49 m (18 ft)	2.29 m (7.5 ft)	60 kg (132 lb)	13.94 m² (150 ft²)		Singlehander, sailed with trapeze
Hobie 18	5.49 m (18 ft)	2.44 m (8 ft)	181.4 kg (400 lb)	23.23 m² (250 ft²)		Large, powerful two-man boat
International Tornado	6.1 m (20 ft)	3.05 m (10 ft)	127 kg (280 lb)	21.83 m² (235 ft²)		Olympic class catamaran

trapezes and the taller and heavier they are the better. Strong arms to handle the sheets are also a distinct advantage. There are centreboards in the hulls but they are the tipping kind so that hitting the ground should not normally result in damage.

Being a production boat, the Hobie is not a delicate dancer like the Unicorn. Instead, its character is something more like a Trans Am sports car— big, beefy with bags of power.

INTERNATIONAL TORNADO

The only multihull used in Olympic competition, the Tornado is naturally something of a flag-bearer for all racing catamarans, and a very worthy one it is, too. Designed in 1966, the big, light, powerful and demanding Tornado is a real expert's boat but also rewarding to sail at lower levels of competition.

If aircraft were developed in the way that the Tornado was, very few test pilots would sur-

vive. The designer, Rodney March, and the builder, Reg White, deliberately made every part of the boat as light as they could and then, if anything broke, made it slightly stronger. That way they ended up with a boat that was very light, and just strong enough.

The original hulls were made from stressed plywood, but nowadays glassfibre with some kind of foam core is universally used. The shape is one-design but the construction is free, so a

lot of effort goes into making hulls as stiff as possible without increasing the weight.

The Tornado rig is an almost direct copy of the best C Class boat of the time—*Emma Hamilton*—with a streamlined, rotating mast, full-battened, high-aspect-ratio mainsail and small jib. This very powerful power unit has since been copied by virtually all production catamarans, and although the technology is now dated it still works very well.

FLYING FIFTEEN, SQUIB & ETCHELLS 22

A few years back, it looked as if day-sailing keelboats were in danger of dying out. For those ready to move on from dinghies, the first choice always seemed to be some kind of cruiser while the day keelboat, one of the oldest forms of racing yacht, was being missed out. Thankfully, that has now changed and fleets of Flying Fifteens, Squibs, Etchells, Dragons and all the others are now recovering, though for no particularly clear reason.

INTERNATIONAL FLYING FIFTEEN

When Uffa Fox, designer of so many famous planing dinghies, felt he was getting too broad in the beam for sailing such frisky boats, he turned his thoughts to a planing keelboat, a revolutionary idea at the time. He wanted a boat that was fast and lively but had sufficient ballast to make it impossible to capsize, and the result, designed in 1947, was the Flying Fifteen. The hull is one of his best, with an attractive, raking bow.

In place of a centreboard, a very slim keel swells out into a cast-iron bulb of ballast. Though elegant-looking, this keel is one of the boat's eccentricities as there is no doubt that it would sail much better to windward with a more conventional-looking fin keel.

The original idea was that you could take the keel off, put it in the back of the car and carry the hull inverted on the roof, but Uffa himself was one of the few people who ever tried this; nowadays, Flying Fifteens are moved around on trailers with the keel in place.

A more successful idea was the rudder assembly, which forms a box which can be lifted out of its slot in the stern. This enables it to be kept clean if the boat is left on moorings. Since Uffa's day, the rig has been modernized and now has a good-sized spinnaker which puts a real zip into the boat's offwind performance. There is no trapeze, so energetic sitting-out is required by both helmsman and crew.

The Flying Fifteen has now been around for over forty years and has a very loyal following in Britain, Ireland, Australia, New Zealand and Hong Kong.

SQUIB

Instantly recognizable by its tan sails, the Squib was designed by Oliver Lee in 1967 with the specific intention of filling the need for a modern, easily sailed and maintained 'club' keelboat. This need arose from the fact that many local designs of keelboat were getting old and expensive to maintain. Furthermore, there was a clear advantage in replacing the multiplicity of local classes with one that could be raced anywhere in the country.

In practice, however, people are fanatically loyal to the boats they have known and loved for years, and are reluctant to make a change, so the growth of the Squib Class has been a lot slower than many expected. But with around 800 in use they are more numerous than any other British keelboat and get very good fleets of around eighty boats for their annual championship.

Designed as a sit-in keelboat for a crew of two, the Squib is quite capable of carrying four or five people when not racing. With built-in buoyancy, wide side-decks and a small cuddy forward, the Squib is a very safe boat that is quite capable of taking coastal and estuary conditions in its stride but is still small enough to be used on rivers, lakes and reservoirs.

The typical weekend sailor does not want to spend all his spare time maintaining the boat, so the Squib is all glassfibre with a small amount of teak trim that needs only occasional attention. It is normally kept on moorings but is simple to 'dry sail' if a club has a suitable jetty and cranes.

The sail area is fairly modest, but the hull shape is a sweet one and in a strong wind the Squib is quite capable of planing. None of the gear is heavy and this makes the boat one that can be raced with equal success by men and women.

Not the most spectacular of racing boats, Squibs are nevertheless good fun to race and as strict one-design they are normally very even in performance.

ETCHELLS 22

The requirement for a new keelboat to replace the Dragon in the Olympics led to rush of new designs in the mid-Sixties. The Soling was the winner but the

INTERNATIONAL FLYING FIFTEEN

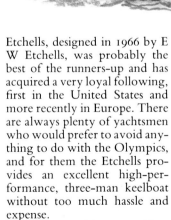

Etchells, designed in 1966 by E W Etchells, was probably the best of the runners-up and has acquired a very loyal following, first in the United States and more recently in Europe. There are always plenty of yachtsmen who would prefer to avoid anything to do with the Olympics, and for them the Etchells provides an excellent high-performance, three-man keelboat without too much hassle and expense.

In order to achieve a considerably better performance than the Dragon's, 'Skip' Etchells gave the E22 a longer waterline and dramatically less weight, with about the same basic sail area and a larger spinnaker. As a result, the E22 has a much better power-to-weight ratio than the Dragon and is indeed a lively performer.

The deep hull gives good protection to the crew and the whole boat seems to be very much on top of the water rather than ploughing through it. An excellent all-round performer, the Etchells planes readily in a fresh breeze.

The drawback to a boat such as the Etchells is that is needs a deepwater mooring and not all clubs are able to provide this. It is also fairly big for a dayboat and needs space to stretch its sealegs. Big, semi-sheltered sailing

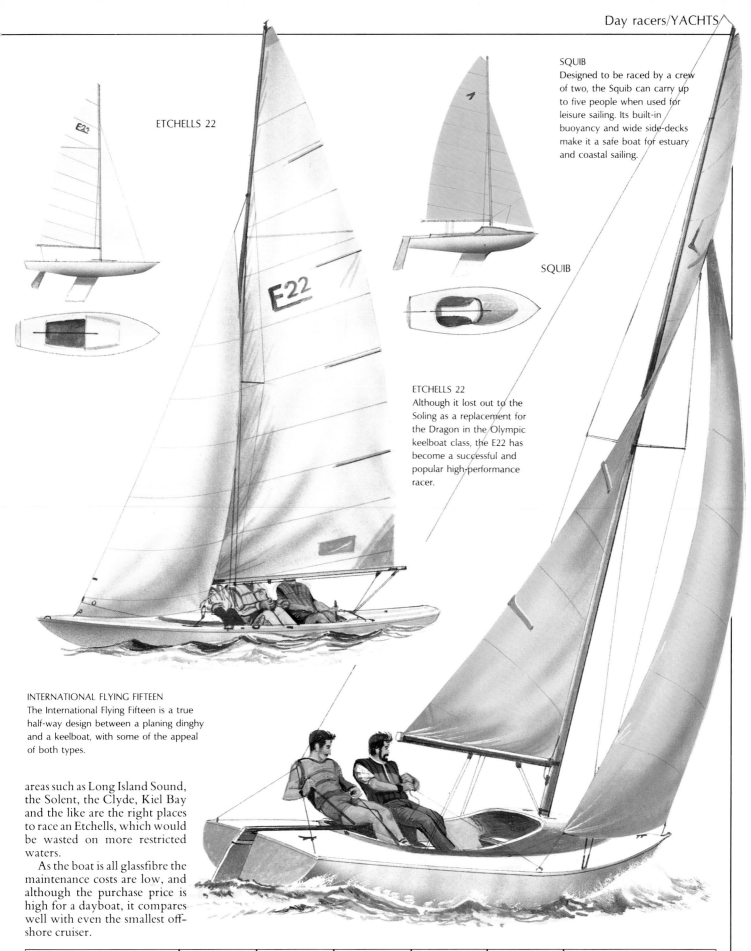

ETCHELLS 22

SQUIB
Designed to be raced by a crew
of two, the Squib can carry up
to five people when used for
leisure sailing. Its built-in
buoyancy and wide side-decks
make it a safe boat for estuary
and coastal sailing.

SQUIB

ETCHELLS 22
Although it lost out to the
Soling as a replacement for
the Dragon in the Olympic
keelboat class, the E22 has
become a successful and
popular high-performance
racer.

INTERNATIONAL FLYING FIFTEEN
The International Flying Fifteen is a true
half-way design between a planing dinghy
and a keelboat, with some of the appeal
of both types.

areas such as Long Island Sound,
the Solent, the Clyde, Kiel Bay
and the like are the right places
to race an Etchells, which would
be wasted on more restricted
waters.

As the boat is all glassfibre the
maintenance costs are low, and
although the purchase price is
high for a dayboat, it compares
well with even the smallest offshore cruiser.

NAME	LENGTH OVERALL	BEAM	WEIGHT	SAIL AREA	SPINNAKER	FEATURES
International Flying Fifteen	6.1 m (20 ft)	1.52 m (5 ft)	328.9 kg (725 lb)	13.94 m² (150 ft²)	13.94 m² (150 ft²)	Planing keelboat
Squib	5.79 m (19 ft)	1.88 m (6.2 ft)	680.4 kg (1500 lb)	16.07 m² (173 ft²)	13.94 m² (150 ft²)	Safe, stable all-rounder
Etchells 22	9.3 m (30.5 ft)	2.13 m (7 ft)	1564 kg (3450 lb)	27 m² (281 ft²)	37 m² (400 ft²)	Fast, three-man keelboat

DRAGON, STAR & SOLING

Here we have two Olympic keelboats and one ex-Olympic keelboat, three racing boats with very different characters but all raced at the highest level in a number of countries and internationally. Although it was a trauma for the Dragon Class at the time, being dropped from the Olympic fleet was not really a reflection on its merits, as the policy at the time was to replace at least one class during each Olympiad.

INTERNATIONAL DRAGON

With its classic Scandinavian good looks the Dragon, designed in 1926 by Johan Anker, has a timeless elegance which positively demands the highest standards of construc-

tion and finish. Although the vast majority of modern boats are glassfibre, 40-year-old mahogany boats still win races because they were so superbly made in the first place.

Heavy, and with an old-fashioned long keel, the Dragon is not as nippy and manoeuvrable as more modern designs but still gets around the racing course at a very respectable rate.

More to the point, most well-kept and properly-equipped Dragons sail at about the same speed so that racing tends to be very close even after hours of sailing.

The rig has been steadily modernized over the years and is now virtually identical to the one used on the majority of off-shore yachts.

Sailing a Dragon calls for good teamwork from the three crew, especially at mark roundings when a lot of strings have to be pulled in the right order at

just the right moment. This makes getting it right very satisfying and is one reason that the Dragon Class tends to be very social, with a strong sense of camaraderie.

Recently, the Dragon has been making a strong comeback in Europe and Australia where it is once again one of the premier racing classes, but unfortunately it has all but died out in the United States and Canada.

INTERNATIONAL DRAGON

INTERNATIONAL STAR

INTERNATIONAL DRAGON
The three-man International Dragon, designed in 1926, lost its role as the Olympic keelboat to the Soling, which made its first Olympic appearance in 1972.

INTERNATIONAL STAR
The International Star, one of the first true one-design classes, made its first Olympic appearance in 1932.

INTERNATIONAL STAR

One of the real marvels of the sailing world, the Star was designed by William Gardner in 1911 and first used in the Olympics in 1932, and apart from a single hiccup, it has been an Olympic boat ever since. A victim of the rolling modernization programme in 1976, it was reinstated in 1980 after its replacement, the Tempest, failed to achieve a wide following.

Gardner had designed a small boat—the Bug—as an ultra-cheap sailing scow, and in 1911 he made a larger and smarter version of it—the Star—for sailing on Long Island Sound. It was made like an elongated box, and the keel was a flat metal plate with a lump of iron bolted onto the bottom.

To the surprise of all, it sailed really well and soon attracted a large following in the United States and subsequently all over the world. As one of the first properly-regulated one-design classes, the Star has had a lot to teach others about organization and many classes have copied its system of national, regional and world championships.

Modernized several times, the present-day Star has an enormous mainsail set on a very thin, bendy mast with a lot of adjustments. The boom is extremely low and the crew have to duck down into the narrow cockpit to get under it when tacking or gybing. There is no spinnaker and the jib is small, but the key point about the Star is that it is very sensitive and responsive to the smallest changes of trim.

INTERNATIONAL SOLING

When the Dragon dropped out of the Olympics, the Soling dropped in. It was designed by the Norwegian, Jan Linge, in 1966, for just that purpose and won a competition against the Etchells, the Trias and others. It is a fast, exciting three-man keelboat with a one-design hull, and produces remarkably close and exciting racing.

Being designed from the outset for glassfibre construction, it is a strong and relatively trouble-free boat that lasts well in competition. It is a modern design with a deep, narrow fin keel and a separate spade rudder, which means that it has very quick, accurate steering—more like a dinghy than a keelboat—and tacks extremely quickly compared with, say, a Dragon.

The development of the Soling is an illustration of what intense competition can do to a boat. As originally designed, the Soling had a deep cockpit that the crew could sit inside, but this put the crew at a disadvantage when racing against boats whose crews could use their weight more effectively, and so the design had to be modified.

The first step was to raise the floor so that the crew could sit on the deck more easily. Next, toestraps were fitted to enable the crew to sit right on the deck edge, and these were followed by ankle hobbles which enable them to get right over the side. These padded ankle cuffs are attached to a wire in the centre of the floor and mean that the crew of the Soling can virtually hurl themselves overboard after a tack and end up sitting on the outside of the hull.

The jib is a small, efficient blade which can be made self-tacking. It flops across to the new tack on its own, rather like the jib on a model yacht, and this is one reason the boat tacks so quickly.

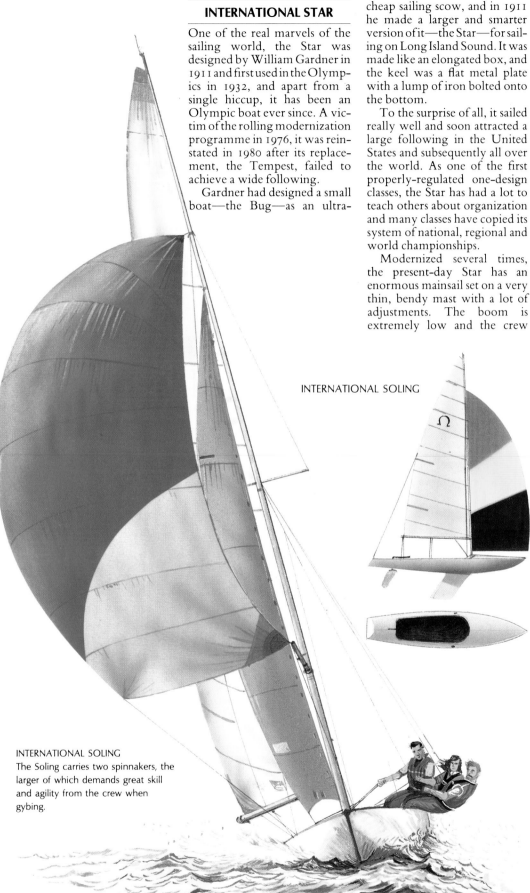

INTERNATIONAL SOLING

INTERNATIONAL SOLING
The Soling carries two spinnakers, the larger of which demands great skill and agility from the crew when gybing.

NAME	LENGTH OVERALL	BEAM	WEIGHT	SAIL AREA	SPINNAKER	FEATURES
International Dragon	8.92 m (29.3 ft)	1.91 m (6.3 ft)	1700 kg (3750 lb)	27.4 m² (295 ft²)	30.66 m² (330 ft²)	Former Olympic class keelboat
International Star	6.92 m (22.7 ft)	1.73 m (5.7 ft)	671 kg (1480 lb)	26.94 m² (290 ft²)		Olympic class keelboat
International Soling	8.2 m (27 ft)	1.9 m (6.2 ft)	1035 kg (2282 lb)	21.7 m² (234 ft²)	33 m² (355 ft²)	Olympic class keelboat

J22, SONATA & O'DAY 22

Just as with the smaller dayboats, the variety of boats with cabins and capable of sailing on the sea is enormous. They range from the smallest coastal racing and cruising boats up to mighty ocean racers and sail training ships.

These three nippy little boats are each used for both racing and cruising. The J22 is the most race-bred of the three, and has very basic accommodation, while the other two are for those who value comfort a little more highly. These three boats are also 'offshore one-design' craft.

J22

The smallest member of the well-known 'J' family, the 22 was designed by Rod Johnstone specifically to be a one-design racing class with strictly-controlled hull, rig and fittings. At the same time, owners who do not want to sail in a one-design fleet can convert the boat into a 2-berth weekender. Small enough to be trailed behind a normal car, the J22 is nevertheless seaworthy enough for coastal conditions.

The sail area is quite generous for a boat of this size, with a lot of the power in the mainsail in order to avoid the need for a big genoa. Instead, the headsail just overlaps the mast and this makes the boat quick to tack and gather way. In many ways, the J22 is like a big dinghy with a fixed keel, and has both the advantages and the drawbacks that the concept implies. Performance is very lively and particularly exciting downwind, but the boat must be kept light and cannot be treated as a real 'offshore' boat that will look after its crew in all conditions.

Unlike the larger J24, the 22 is mainly confined to its native United States where it sails both in one-design fleets and also in handicap events such as those organized by the Miniature Offshore Racing Club (MORC).

SONATA

One of the first of the modern offshore one-designs, the Sonata is different in concept from the 'J' family in that it does not make a complete break from the style of design that belongs to handicap racing. Indeed, designer David Thomas's aim was to give owners the choice of racing in one-design fleets or of having their boat rated by the IOR formula. As a result, the Sonata had to conform with the minimum requirements for stability and accommodation that the IOR calls for.

What this means in practice is that the Sonata is rather more of a tiny yacht and less of a large dinghy than a 'J' is. For instance, there is perfectly adequate accommodation for four people, including a galley and toilet, but the penalty for that is rather less cockpit space. In sailing terms, the Sonata is more of an all-rounder but without the same flat-out planing characteristics of the J22. It is also drier, more seaworthy and reassuring in bad weather.

A great success in Britain, the Sonata has also been exported to many European countries but is hardly known in the United States. It has spawned a number of versions such as a bilge-keeler and a centreboarder and one with additional equipment intended more for cruising than racing. Many yachtsmen who were not especially keen on racing welcomed the Sonata as a tiny cruising boat that sails really well. Although intended for coastal use, plenty of Sonatas have cruised far and wide.

O'DAY 22

When the little O'Day 22 appeared in the early 1970s she was quite a revelation: a trailer-sailer that was seaworthy, shoal draught, could sleep four and was a lively sailor – all in 22 feet.

The real secret of the design – by Ray Hunt & Associates – was the long, shallow keel that made the boat self-righting with a very modest draught of only two feet. This made it possible to launch and recover the boat off a normal ramp without the need to use a crane or boat lift. This ability to keep the boat at home on a trailer and simply drive it down to the water when required is an enormous help in keeping down the cost of sailing. In addition to being self-righting, the O'Day 22 has built-in foam buoyancy and a self-draining cockpit, another relatively unusual feature at the time, making her a thoroughly safe little boat.

In order to make the boat self-righting without a deep keel, the mast was kept fairly short and she was given a masthead rig with a small mainsail and big, overlapping genoa. Nowadays, this is regarded as a rather dated arrangement, as a taller mast with a bigger mainsail turns out to be more flexible in use.

Below, a bulkhead separated the cabin into two and gave privacy to the WC, which was fitted below the twin forward bunks. The main part of the cabin had two separate bunks and a tiny galley with a two-burner cooker.

An awful lot of O'Day 22s were built and most of them are still around, making it a very well-known boat in North America. Many of its features could be improved today, but when designed it was a very modern and sensible little basic cruiser with a fair turn of speed.

J22

J22
The little J22, smallest of the 'J' family, is raced both in handicap events and in one-design fleets.

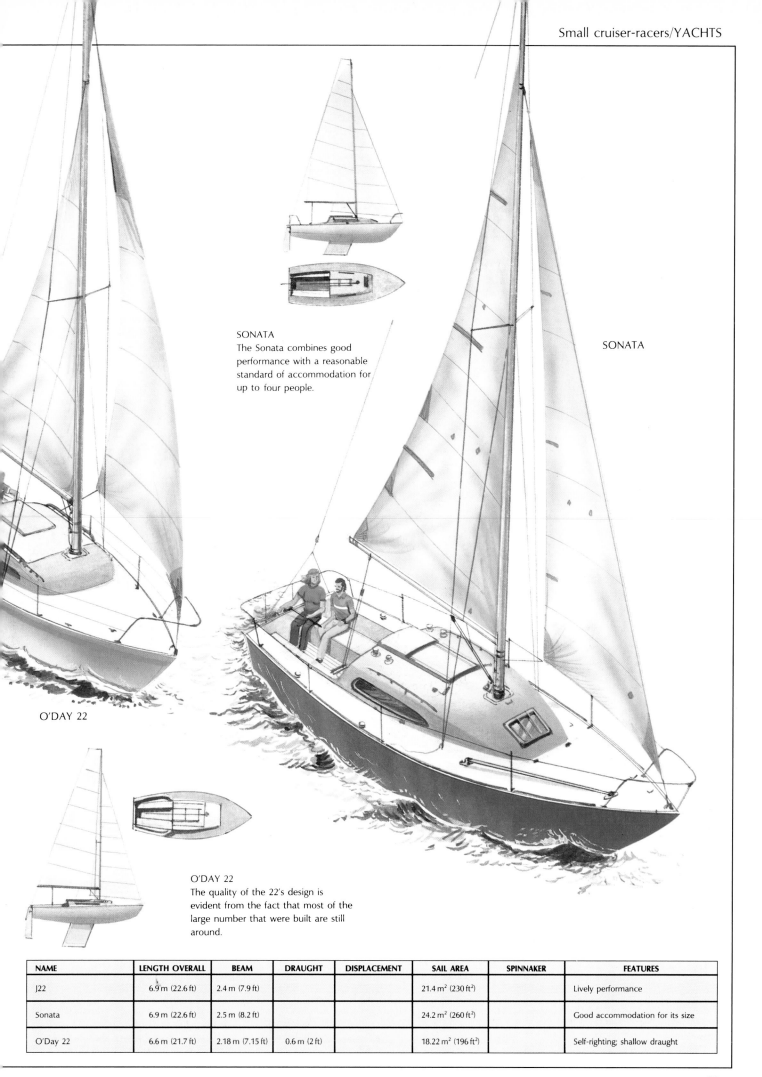

SONATA
The Sonata combines good
performance with a reasonable
standard of accommodation for
up to four people.

SONATA

O'DAY 22

O'DAY 22
The quality of the 22's design is
evident from the fact that most of the
large number that were built are still
around.

NAME	LENGTH OVERALL	BEAM	DRAUGHT	DISPLACEMENT	SAIL AREA	SPINNAKER	FEATURES
J22	6.9 m (22.6 ft)	2.4 m (7.9 ft)			21.4 m² (230 ft²)		Lively performance
Sonata	6.9 m (22.6 ft)	2.5 m (8.2 ft)			24.2 m² (260 ft²)		Good accommodation for its size
O'Day 22	6.6 m (21.7 ft)	2.18 m (7.15 ft)	0.6 m (2 ft)		18.22 m² (196 ft²)		Self-righting; shallow draught

J24, FORMULA 28 & SIGMA 33

Each of these three boats are one-design offshore racing boats, though each has a different emphasis. The J24 was a real breakaway boat which owed its success to the fact that the designer, Rod Johnstone, understood that people were bored with handicap racing and wanted something much more like regular one-design dinghy racing. The Formula 28 and Sigma 33 are both dual-purpose designs in that they are intended to race (either as one-designs or in handicap events) as well as to be used as family cruising yachts.

J24

The great popular success of the J24 has made it one of the best-known boats in the world – a kind of grown-up Laser, one might say. Like the Laser, the J24 was conceived as a boat that would be fast but simple, without needing a lot of complex and expensive equipment. The hull lines are particularly clean and undistorted with a long, straight run to the stern that enables the boat to plane readily in a strong wind.

Light in weight, the J24 relies a good deal on crew weight for its stability. It is possible to capsize a J24, and for this reason it is worth pointing out that it is intended as a lively racing boat rather than an offshore cruiser.

Normally raced with a crew of five, the J24 appeals particularly to those with a background of dinghy sailing who appreciate its very quick responses. Like a dinghy, it needs to be trimmed constantly and sailed with great concentration in order to maintain full speed. All J24 sailors speak with enthusiasm, bordering on awe, of its downwind performance in a strong wind when it is capable of flying past much larger boats.

FORMULA 28

The Formula 28 was the result of Hunter Boats deciding to prove that it was possible to build a real 'gung-ho' buoy racer on a production-line basis. She was not intended to be a one-design like the Sigma or the J24 but instead was designed to blitz the handicap fleet at a reasonable cost, or at least for very much less than the cost of a one-off racer.

Designer Stephen Jones gave her a typically IOR-influenced light, beamy, flat-floored hull shape with a massive three-quarter rig set on a tall, bendy mast. As usual with this type of rig, running backstays are needed to control the mast and this is one of the features that makes a boat like the Formula 28

rather unsuitable for inexperienced or 'family' crews.

In keeping with her racing parentage, the Formula 28 has a very long but shallow cockpit and a minimal cabin top, which is made as narrow as possible in order to leave as much space as possible on the side-decks for genoa sheet tracks and all other sail controls. The big difference between this and a cruising yacht is that absolutely everything is adjustable and a veritable forest of small lines leads back from the mast to a 'control panel' of rope clutches on the cabin top just forward of the hatch.

SIGMA 33

One of the most popular production sailing yachts on the European market, the Sigma 33 owes its success to its remarkable versatility. Designed in the first

instance as a one-design racing yacht, it competes almost as successfully in handicap fleets whether under the IOR or IMS rules, and in a large number of cases doubles as a family cruiser as well.

As with the J24, the concept was for a yacht that would give good racing but avoid the costly arms race of the IOR fleet. But unlike the J24, the Sigma is a careful compromise design, being a good all-round performer and rating reasonably well under the IOR system. Furthermore, the IOR rating authorities accept the Sigma as a standard design, and so a rating can be obtained relatively cheaply.

The real skill of the designer (David Thomas) was in producing a class in which there is remarkably little difference in performance throughout the fleet. This places all the emphasis on the skill of the crew in getting the best out of the boat, and makes for very close racing. In

events such as Cowes Week, one can see 50 or more Sigmas racing together and enjoying the sort of really close competition usually reserved for the dinghy fleets.

Yet this is not a stripped-out racer. The Sigma 33 has seven berths in two separate cabins, an enclosed washroom, a full galley and chart table and an 18-shp Volvo Penta 2002 diesel auxiliary. Its simple rig can be handled by a small crew, and so cruising with a family crew presents no problems. There are two versions: the Sigma 33 OOD offshore one-design, for which there are strict class rules aimed at keeping the boats as similar as possible; and the Sigma 33 MH performance cruiser, which has a simpler masthead rig.

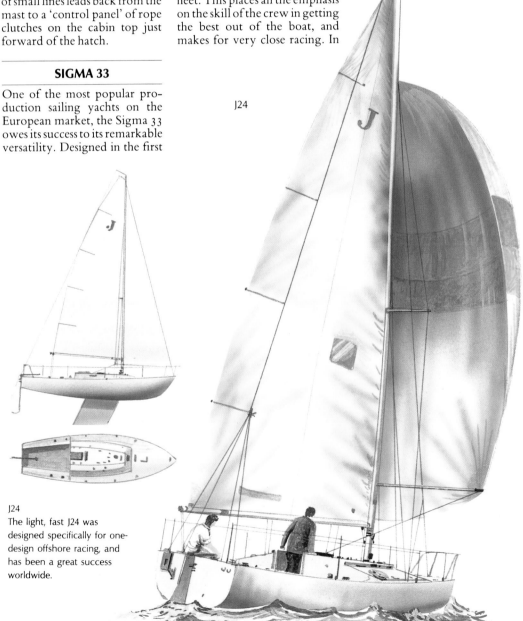

J24

J24
The light, fast J24 was designed specifically for one-design offshore racing, and has been a great success worldwide.

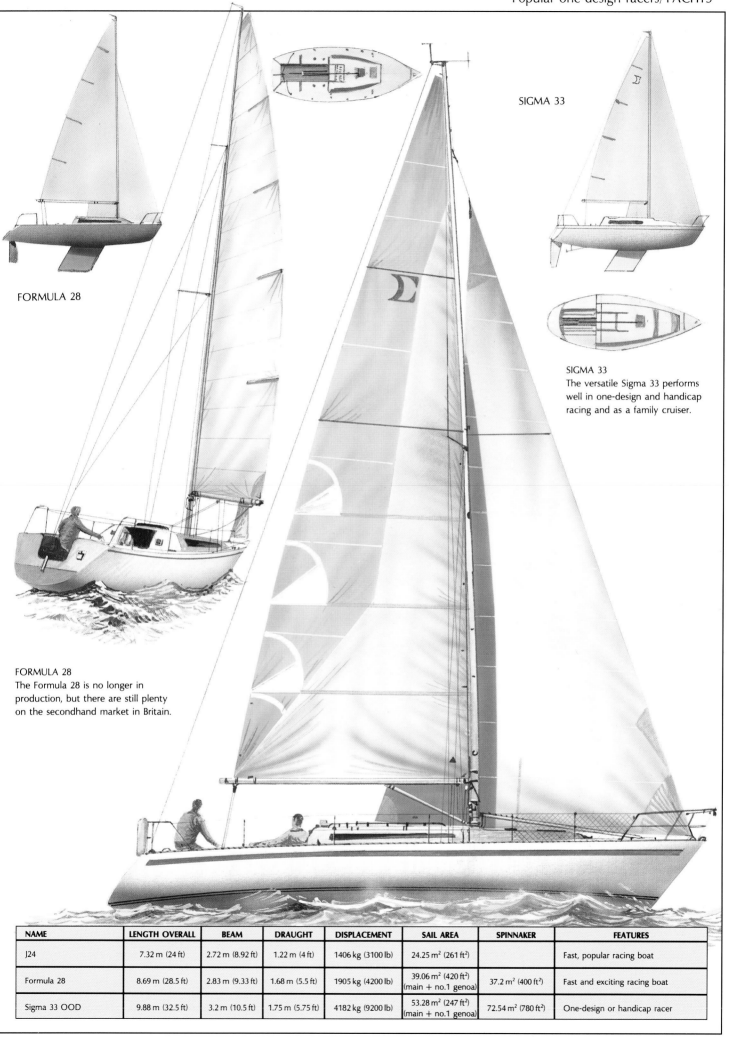

FORMULA 28

SIGMA 33

SIGMA 33
The versatile Sigma 33 performs
well in one-design and handicap
racing and as a family cruiser.

FORMULA 28
The Formula 28 is no longer in
production, but there are still plenty
on the secondhand market in Britain.

NAME	LENGTH OVERALL	BEAM	DRAUGHT	DISPLACEMENT	SAIL AREA	SPINNAKER	FEATURES
J24	7.32 m (24 ft)	2.72 m (8.92 ft)	1.22 m (4 ft)	1406 kg (3100 lb)	24.25 m² (261 ft²)		Fast, popular racing boat
Formula 28	8.69 m (28.5 ft)	2.83 m (9.33 ft)	1.68 m (5.5 ft)	1905 kg (4200 lb)	39.06 m² (420 ft²) (main + no.1 genoa)	37.2 m² (400 ft²)	Fast and exciting racing boat
Sigma 33 OOD	9.88 m (32.5 ft)	3.2 m (10.5 ft)	1.75 m (5.75 ft)	4182 kg (9200 lb)	53.28 m² (247 ft²) (main + no.1 genoa)	72.54 m² (780 ft²)	One-design or handicap racer

DUETTE 23, O'DAY 23 & SADLER 26

A high proportion of yachtsmen and women have no great interest in racing, but this does not mean that they will be satisfied with a slow yacht. There is no doubt that slow boats are boring, and even the most died-in-the-wool cruising enthusiast is proud to tell you how easily his or her boat slips along. These three boats are trailerable cruisers with a very good turn of speed, and there is nothing to prevent them from racing in club events.

DUETTE 23

Planned as an 'entry-level' cruising yacht, the David Thomas-designed Hunter Duette 23 is aimed at keeping the costs within bounds while still providing a reasonable level of comfort and performance. The purchase price is reasonable, and the simple but good-quality hardware on deck and the minimum of outside woodwork help to keep maintenance costs low.

In addition, a swinging mooring will probably be a lot cheaper than a marina berth, especially if it is in a place where the boat goes aground at low water, and this is where the Duette's twin keels come into use. With a draught of just 94 centimetres (3 ft 1 in), she can sail up virtually any creek and take the ground between tides without lying over at an angle.

The argument against twin keels in the past has been that they led to poor performance, but this was mainly due to clumsy design. The Duette's two neat little ballasted fins are nearly as efficient as a normal fin keel, and give the very useful ballast ratio of 55 percent so that the boat stands up to her sail well and feels reassuring.

Down below, the open layout keeps things simple but by providing a pilot berth on one side of the saloon, five berths have been fitted in. Basic cooking and washing facilities are provided and a self-contained toilet fits under one of the forward bunks. An interior like this lacks the stowage space for really serious cruising with a full crew, but as a weekender she is completely practical.

As a final cost-saver, the Duette can be completed from a kit, and it is hard to imagine a more sensible boat for the price.

O'DAY 23

American sailors have always liked centreboards because they have plenty of bays and estuaries with relatively shallow water to sail in. The trick that Ray Hunt & Associates used with the O'Day 23 was to combine a centreboard with a fixed iron ballast keel that has sufficient weight to make the boat self-righting, even with the centreboard raised. This means that she can be launched off a normal ramp and sailed into shallow water without risk. Once in deeper water, the board can be lowered fully to give a much better grip on the water and hence good windward performance.

One drawback to this kind of keel, as plenty of yachtsmen have found out for themselves, is that if you let the boat go aground on a muddy or pebbly bottom, material gets jammed into the centreboard slot so that the thing will not lower next time you want it. On the other hand, it is fine if you normally launch the boat off a trailer straight into deep water. Another problem with a stub keel is that if the rudder is deeper than the keel, it must be either hinged or removable. O'Day used to offer a short, wide fixed keel as standard and a deeper one as an optional extra for racing.

SADLER 26

People mean different things when they talk about 'cruising'. Many do not go far from their regular mooring, or only take occasional weekends away. For others, the term means nothing less than going away for a full-length holiday. The Sadler 26 is planned for the second type of owner – she is a compact and

reasonably-priced boat but has the features and equipment needed for real deep-sea sailing.

In the modest overall length of just under 26 feet, Sadlers have managed to pack in an amazing amount of accommodation. Six berths, separate WC compartment, galley, chart table, dining table and, perhaps

most surprising, standing headroom. There is an inboard 10-bhp diesel engine with an alternator and full electrical system, which means that really useful electrically-driven extras such as a tillerpilot can be fitted without worries.

On deck, there is a sturdy masthead rig with a permanent

DUETTE 23

NAME	LENGTH OVERALL	BEAM	DRAUGHT	DISPLACEMENT	SAIL AREA	SPINNAKER	FEATURES
Duette 23	6.89 m (22.6 ft)	2.59 m (8.5 ft)	0.94 m (3.1 ft) (twin keel)	1206 kg (2660 lb)	23.7 m² (255 ft²)		Fast and very stable
O'Day 23	7.01 m (23 ft)	2.41 m (7.9 ft)	0.6 to 1.64 m (2 to 5.4 ft)		22.78 m² (245 ft²)		
Sadler 26	7.85 m (25.75 ft)	2.74 m (9.4 ft)	varies with keel option	2177 kg (4800 lb)	34.78 m² (374 ft²) (main + no.1 genoa)	50.9 m² (548 ft²)	Unsinkable hull

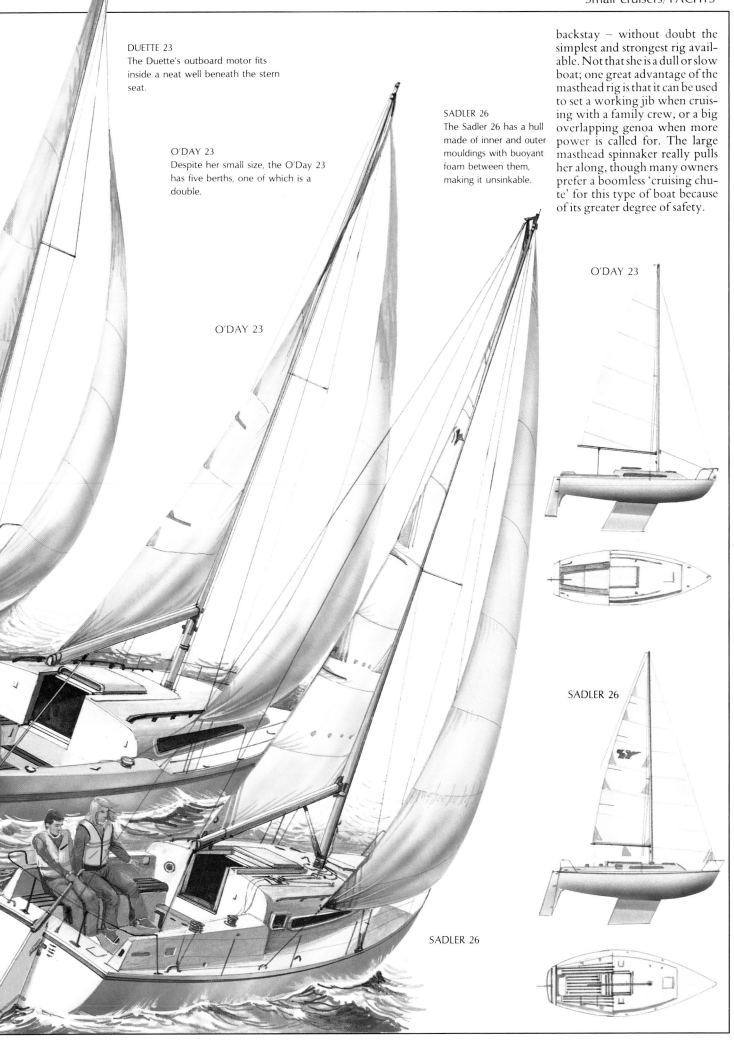

DUETTE 23
The Duette's outboard motor fits inside a neat well beneath the stern seat.

O'DAY 23
Despite her small size, the O'Day 23 has five berths, one of which is a double.

SADLER 26
The Sadler 26 has a hull made of inner and outer mouldings with buoyant foam between them, making it unsinkable.

backstay – without doubt the simplest and strongest rig available. Not that she is a dull or slow boat; one great advantage of the masthead rig is that it can be used to set a working jib when cruising with a family crew, or a big overlapping genoa when more power is called for. The large masthead spinnaker really pulls her along, though many owners prefer a boomless 'cruising chute' for this type of boat because of its greater degree of safety.

O'DAY 23

O'DAY 23

SADLER 26

SADLER 26

VANCOUVER 36, WESTERLY 33 & MOODY 33

A pure cruising yacht calls for qualities that are very different from those of a racing boat. What most people actually mean by a cruising yacht is one that they can live aboard during a holiday, but there are also many thousands of people who set off on extended cruises that may last for months and cross wide oceans. In either case, what they need from their yacht is reliability and comfortable accommodation.

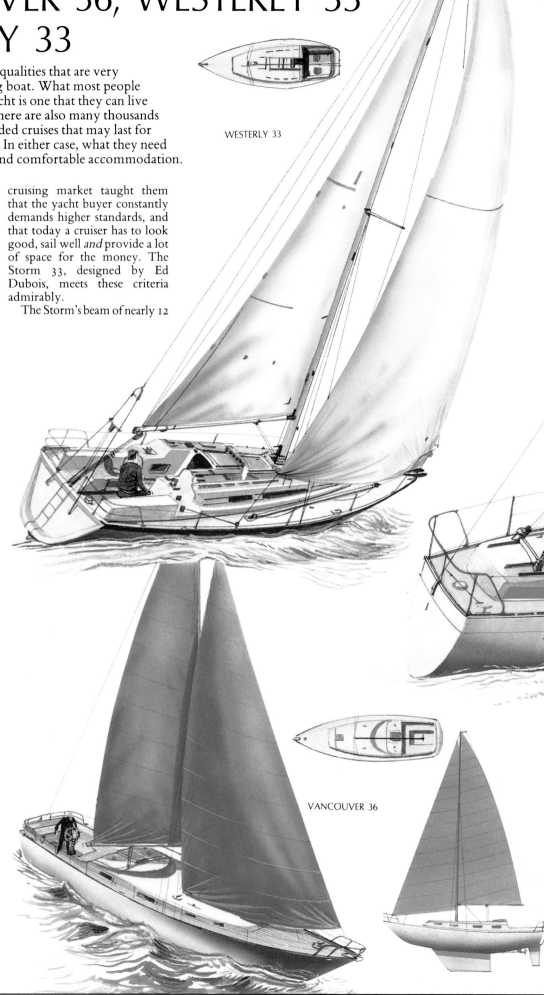

WESTERLY 33

VANCOUVER 36

The well-known Vancouver 28 and 32 cruising yachts were designed, by the Canadian naval architect Robert Harris, on strictly traditional lines with long, continuous keels and heavy-displacement hulls. The Vancouver 36, designed by Tony Taylor, is more of a compromise because although the keel is long and deep by modern standards, she does have a separate rudder set aft on a substantial skeg. Although long keels are something of an article of faith with dyed-in-the-wool cruising types, there is really no doubt that a properly-designed fin and skeg hull peforms better and steers more easily.

The Vancouver has two genuinely private double cabins, one forward and the other right aft on the starboard side. In addition there is a permanent pilot-berth on the starboard side of the saloon and one extra canvas 'root berth' that can be rigged above the dinette if required.

The saloon is not huge, but is cosy and comfortable with a U-shaped settee around the dining table and another settee opposite. At the foot of the companionway steps there is a large galley to port and a chart table with its own seat opposite.

On deck, the sturdy cutter rig is very much in keeping with the Vancouver tradition with a big 'Yankee' jib that will in virtually every case be fitted on a roller for ease of handling, plus a much smaller, 'bullet-proof' staysail that should hardly ever need to come down.

WESTERLY STORM 33

Westerly have always been the experts at giving the maximum amount of accommodation for a given amount of money. In the past some of their models were, frankly speaking, a bit tubby, but their long experience of the cruising market taught them that the yacht buyer constantly demands higher standards, and that today a cruiser has to look good, sail well *and* provide a lot of space for the money. The Storm 33, designed by Ed Dubois, meets these criteria admirably.

The Storm's beam of nearly 12

VANCOUVER 36

WESTERLY 33

WESTERLY STORM 33
The Storm 33 is a powerful racing yacht that also offers comfortable accommodation.

VANCOUVER 36
Though not cheap, the Vancouver 36 is a pleasant, comfortable cruising yacht that is safe in most weather conditions.

MOODY 33

MOODY 33
The 33 is no longer in production, but as a pointer to the way yacht design was going it was absolutely correct.

feet provides plenty of internal space, and none of it is wasted. For instance, although the boat has an overall length of only 33 feet there is a luxurious three-cabin layout with a total of seven berths and a maximum head-room of 6 feet 2 inches. The saloon is very big for a boat of this size.

The simple sloop rig consists of a slab-reefing mainsail of moderate size, with a jib or a large genoa. For ease of sail handling, there are twin luff groove systems and twin headsail tracks, and all the halyards are led aft to quick-release jammers. When it comes on to blow hard, even a small, family crew can get themselves out of trouble by rolling away the jib and continuing quite safely under mainsail only. The engine is an 18-hp diesel.

MOODY 33

Back in 1973, Moody and Sons were builders of top-quality 'bespoke' gentlemen's yachts, each one individually designed and built by hand for its owner. But they had the foresight to see that the future lay not in building, but in marketing production boats that would appeal to a far wider buying public. They therefore engaged Angus Primrose to design, and Marine Products of Plymouth to build, a cruising yacht for everyman and called it the Moody 33.

No raving beauty, the Moody 33 was beamy, bulbous and basic but packed a quite astonishing amount of accommodation into a modest length – no fewer than seven berths in three separate cabins. Primrose used the device of a 'centre' cockpit, positioned above the engine, with a small double cabin aft and a fairly conventional two-cabin layout forward. The cockpit is deep, well-protected and very reassuring while the sloop rig on a short, single-spreader mast is about as simple as it could be, especially if the jib is set on a roller-furler which most owners specify.

Many traditionalists thought the Moody 33 was hideous, and said so, but they really missed the point, which was that the boat offered tremendous value as a family cruiser.

NAME	LENGTH OVERALL	BEAM	DRAUGHT	DISPLACEMENT	SAIL AREA	SPINNAKER	FEATURES
Vancouver 36	10.97 m (36 ft)	3.66 m (12 ft)	1.7 m (5.6 ft)	9296 kg (20,495 lb)	60.75 m² (654 ft²) (main + no.1 genoa)		Comfortable and well designed
Westerly Storm 33	10.11 m (33.17 ft)	3.52 m (11.6 ft)	1.68 m (5.5 ft) (fin keel)	5130 kg (11,310 lb)	62.89 m² (677 ft²) (main + no.1 genoa)	97.2 m² (1045 ft²)	Powerful racing yacht
Moody 33	10.06 m (33 ft)	3.51 m (11.5 ft)	1.35 m (4.43 ft)		53.9 m² (580 ft²)		Safe, practical and comfortable

FORMULA 40, HALF-TONNER & 50-FOOTER

In the rarified world of *grand prix* yacht racing, there is no single top competition but a whole series of different ones, involving different boats and different types of race. For instance, many of the big transocean events are for huge, lightweight multihulls which do not have to conform to any governing formula at all, whereas the various 'ton cups' are very strictly controlled.

A common theme running through all forms of yacht racing is that people get bored with handicap racing, in which you never know who has won until someone has worked out a lot of complex sums. It is a lot more fun to race boat-for-boat – first over the line is the winner – and sailors tend to be attracted to this kind of racing, which includes Formula 40, half-tonner and fifty-footer racing.

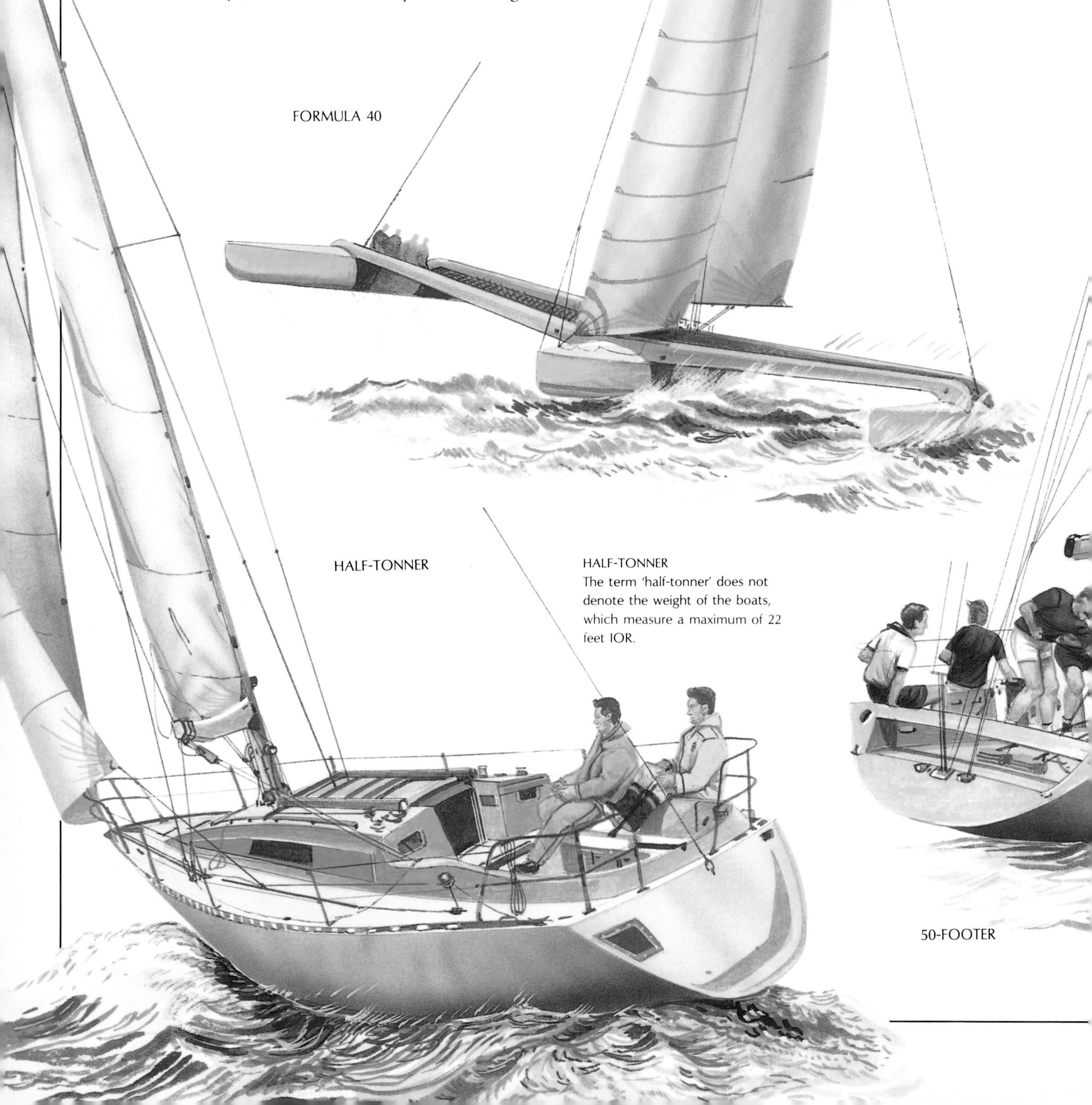

FORMULA 40
The Formula 40 class of boats consists of catamarans and trimarans built within maximum dimensions of 40 feet long and 40 feet wide (12.2 × 12.2 metres).

FORMULA 40

HALF-TONNER

HALF-TONNER
The term 'half-tonner' does not denote the weight of the boats, which measure a maximum of 22 feet IOR.

50-FOOTER

50-FOOTER The 50-foot class boats have undergone considerable development and provide some of the most exciting offshore racing.

FORMULA 40

French professional yachtsmen created the fleet of big, ocean-going multihulls that compete in various high-profile ocean races, but then realized that there were severe drawbacks to this concept, especially the exceptionally high cost of the boats and the fact that they are out of sight of the spectators for most of the time.

A group of these sailors therefore proposed a new class of racing multihull that they called 'Formula 40' because it is based on maximum dimensions of 40 feet long and 40 feet wide. There are various other limits, but the idea is to allow absolutely any design within those limits. A great deal of design development has gone on as a result, with a constant battle between catamarans and trimarans and also very rapid development of sails and spars.

Virtually all the boats are sponsored and professionally sailed, and the racing is organized as a 'circuit' of meetings in various parts of Europe. The idea is to have short, highly visible races in places that can either be watched from the shore or covered by TV cameras. The whole thing is an attempt to make yacht racing faster, more spectacular and more interesting to the general public.

HALF-TONNER

Back in 1964, Jean Peytel of the Cercle de la Voile de Paris had the very clever idea of a series of races to be sailed without handicap by offshore yachts using a fixed maximum rating. What this meant was that yachts of various different designs could be raced on level terms. To get the competition going, the club re-presented one of its most prestigious old trophies, the 'One-Ton Cup', though the term 'one-ton' has absolutely no relevance to the yachts that take part in the competition today.

The success of the idea was such that it was soon extended to cover both larger and smaller offshore yachts and these new competitions were given names which were a play on the original – thus Quarter-Ton, Half-Ton, Threequarter-Ton and even Two-Ton – though as before these names have no real bearing on the size of the yachts. In 1964, offshore racing adopted the IOR system of racing and the Half-Ton Cup is for yachts measuring a maximum of 22 feet IOR.

Nowadays, a half-tonner is a highly developed racing machine of around 10 metres overall length, which sails with a crew of seven. There are absolutely no creature-comforts on board, beyond the very basic minimum of bunks, cooker and toilet required by the rules. Indeed, even in offshore racing, the crew are expected to remain on deck all the time because their weight forms an important part of the yacht's ballast.

A typical half-tonner has a very tall, bendy mast with lots of complex rigging to keep it under control and a very high sail area/displacement ratio. They are very fast but difficult to sail well and call for experienced and highly-trained crew. The hull will certainly be built from exotic composite plastics, at great cost, and will probably be considered out of date within one or two seasons. They require a large wardrobe of very expensive sails.

50-FOOTER

Although the letters 'IOR' stand for 'International Offshore Rule', the 50-foot class is a clear case of owners deciding to drop the word 'offshore'. Like the ton cups, the 50-foot class is a sub-group formed at a particular rating in order to give exciting racing on a boat-for-boat basis, but it is also a kind of breakaway group of owners for whom the idea of huddling on the rail of an offshore racer for days and nights at a time holds absolutely no appeal.

Instead, the 50-footer owners have created their own circus of events consisting of a relatively small number of regattas held in glamorous parts of the world such as Hawaii and Sardinia. The races themselves are purely daytime coastal affairs over shortish courses with windward and leeward legs only. This is because it is seldom possible to overtake on a reach, in this type of boat, whereas both beats and runs give the opportunity to get away from the other boats and make tactical gains.

The boats themselves are like one-tonners only more so. The hulls are made from the most advanced composite plastics, with carbon and Kevlar skins over lightweight core materials, such as Nomex or Divinycell, laminated with epoxy resins. The actual shell, without the keel or any equipment, is astonishingly light and stiff and, needless to say, extremely costly.

SWAN 44, NICHOLSON 58 & PEARSON 385

In the world of big, luxury cruising yachts there is never any question of whether a particular feature is good value for money: owners of this class of yacht demand the best, regardless of the cost. Features like teak-laid decks, which are beautiful to look at, are the best-possible nonslip surface and cost a fortune, can be regarded as commonplace. So can private cabins with *en suite* bathrooms, beautiful hand-made interiors and the very best equipment.

hull moulding, an almost infinite variety of arrangements is possible.

There are three choices of

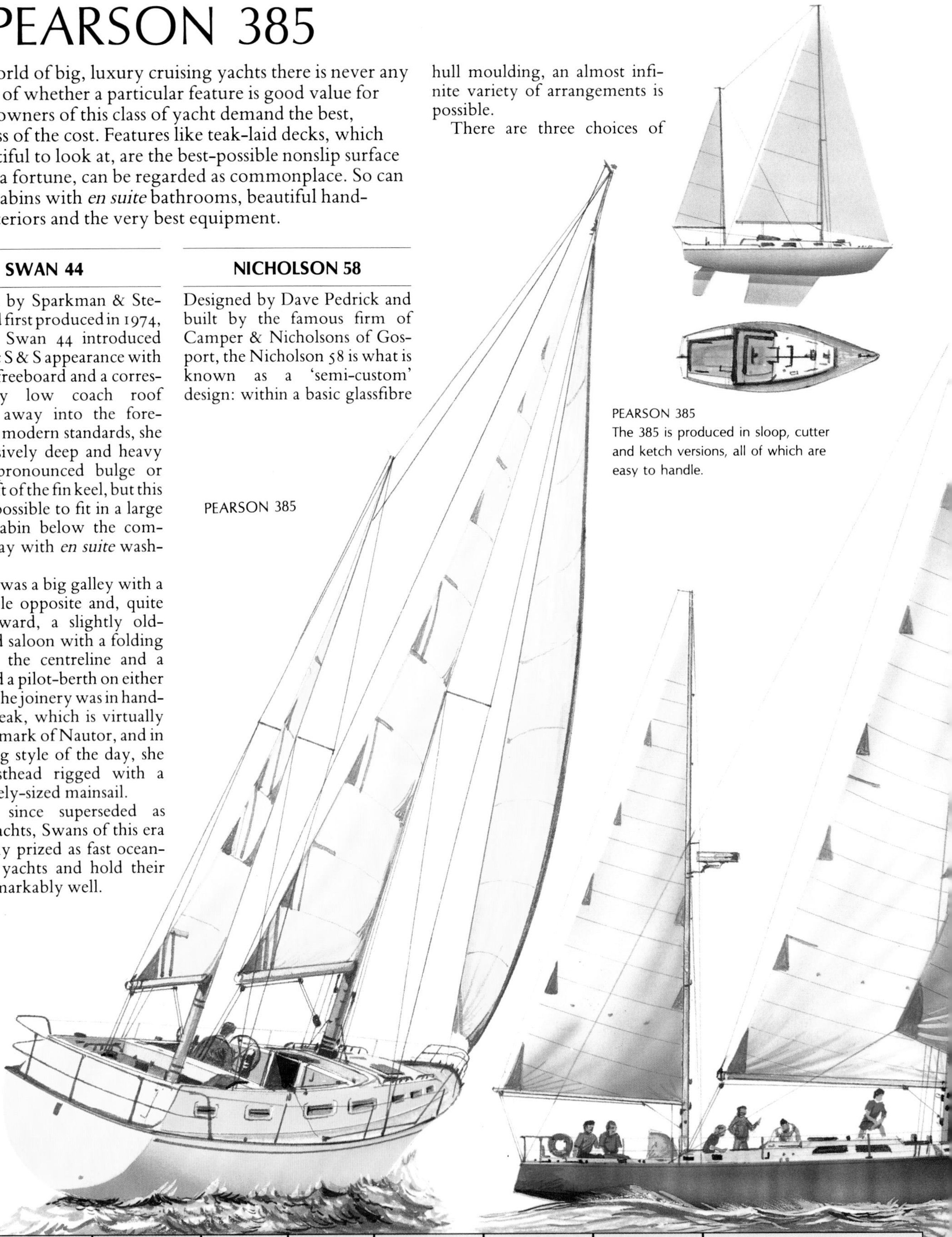

SWAN 44

Designed by Sparkman & Stephens and first produced in 1974, Nautor's Swan 44 introduced the classic S & S appearance with the high freeboard and a correspondingly low coach roof tapering away into the foredeck. By modern standards, she was massively deep and heavy with a pronounced bulge or 'bustle' aft of the fin keel, but this made it possible to fit in a large double cabin below the companionway with *en suite* washroom.

There was a big galley with a chart table opposite and, quite well forward, a slightly old-fashioned saloon with a folding table on the centreline and a settee and a pilot-berth on either side. All the joinery was in hand-rubbed teak, which is virtually the trademark of Nautor, and in the racing style of the day, she was masthead rigged with a moderately-sized mainsail.

Long since superseded as racing yachts, Swans of this era are highly prized as fast ocean-cruising yachts and hold their value remarkably well.

NICHOLSON 58

Designed by Dave Pedrick and built by the famous firm of Camper & Nicholsons of Gosport, the Nicholson 58 is what is known as a 'semi-custom' design: within a basic glassfibre

PEARSON 385

PEARSON 385
The 385 is produced in sloop, cutter and ketch versions, all of which are easy to handle.

NAME	LENGTH OVERALL	BEAM	DRAUGHT	DISPLACEMENT	SAIL AREA	SPINNAKER	FEATURES
Swan 44	13.41 m (44 ft)	10.74 m (35.2 ft)	2.19 m (7.2 ft)	10,800 kg (23,810 lb)	81.4 m² (876 ft²)		Classic Sparkman & Stephens design
Nicholson 58	17.55 m (57.6 ft) or 18.28 m (60 ft)	4.75 m (15.6 ft)	varies with keel option	various	various		Wide range of design options
Pearson 385	11.67 m (38.3 ft)	3.52 m (11.6 ft)	1.67 m (5.5 ft)	8670 kg (19,114 lb)	56.91 m² (613 ft²)		Big and roomy; sails well

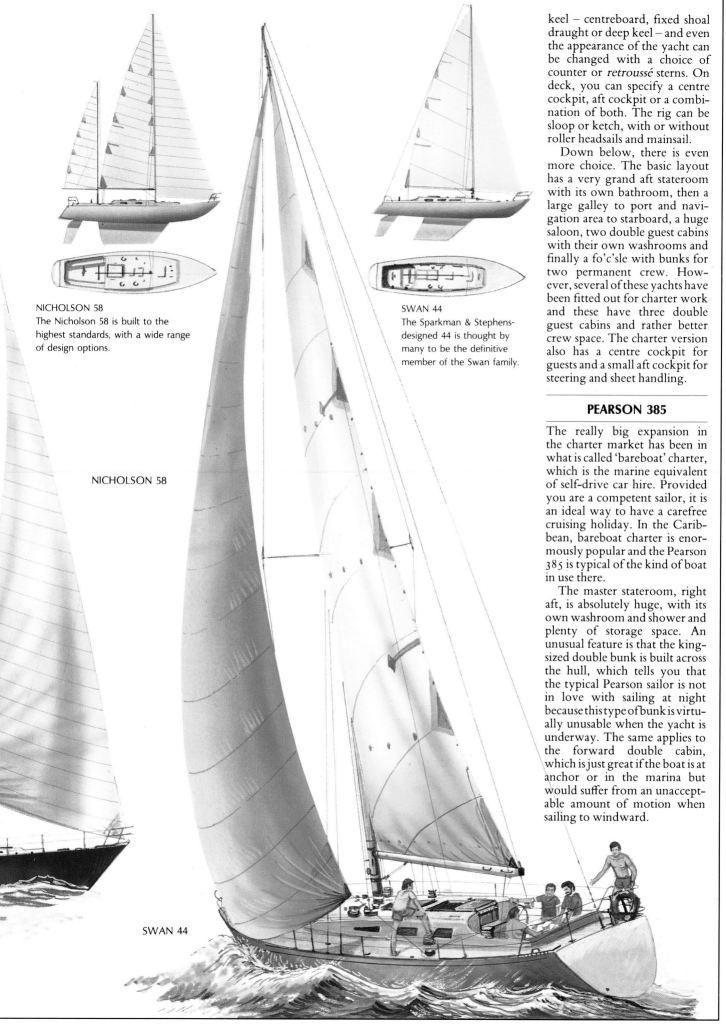

NICHOLSON 58
The Nicholson 58 is built to the highest standards, with a wide range of design options.

NICHOLSON 58

SWAN 44
The Sparkman & Stephens-designed 44 is thought by many to be the definitive member of the Swan family.

SWAN 44

keel – centreboard, fixed shoal draught or deep keel – and even the appearance of the yacht can be changed with a choice of counter or *retroussé* sterns. On deck, you can specify a centre cockpit, aft cockpit or a combination of both. The rig can be sloop or ketch, with or without roller headsails and mainsail.

Down below, there is even more choice. The basic layout has a very grand aft stateroom with its own bathroom, then a large galley to port and navigation area to starboard, a huge saloon, two double guest cabins with their own washrooms and finally a fo'c'sle with bunks for two permanent crew. However, several of these yachts have been fitted out for charter work and these have three double guest cabins and rather better crew space. The charter version also has a centre cockpit for guests and a small aft cockpit for steering and sheet handling.

PEARSON 385

The really big expansion in the charter market has been in what is called 'bareboat' charter, which is the marine equivalent of self-drive car hire. Provided you are a competent sailor, it is an ideal way to have a carefree cruising holiday. In the Caribbean, bareboat charter is enormously popular and the Pearson 385 is typical of the kind of boat in use there.

The master stateroom, right aft, is absolutely huge, with its own washroom and shower and plenty of storage space. An unusual feature is that the king-sized double bunk is built across the hull, which tells you that the typical Pearson sailor is not in love with sailing at night because this type of bunk is virtually unusable when the yacht is underway. The same applies to the forward double cabin, which is just great if the boat is at anchor or in the marina but would suffer from an unacceptable amount of motion when sailing to windward.

TALL SHIPS

After cargo-carrying under sail finally became uneconomic, in the years between the two World Wars, it looked as if the 'tall ships' of the world were destined to rot quietly away until they were no more. What prevented this was the use of sailing ships as training vessels. Now, far from dying out, the number of big sailing ships is increasing as more and more countries and institutions realize the value of sail training.

It is not the actual practice of handling sheets and sails that is so important, nor the physical toughness that it develops, but the ability to live with the sea in all its moods and to understand and to respect its latent power. There is also a certain quality of confidence and self-reliance that is hard to define but which sail training is exceptionally good at bringing out.

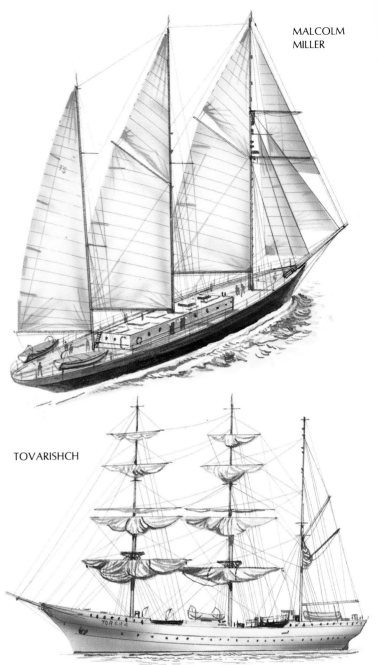

MALCOLM MILLER

TOVARISHCH

MALCOLM MILLER

Neither the British Royal Navy nor the Merchant Navy are convinced of the need to maintain sail training vessels, and so in Britain this task is left to various charitable organizations, such as the Sail Training Association (STA) which owns two schooners, the *Sir Winston Churchill* and the *Malcolm Miller*. They are kept in commission for nine months of the year and carry a crew of about forty trainees plus permanent officers and crew.

The STA schooners (which were built of steel in 1966 and 1967) are a compromise design, being based on plans for a pre-war yacht by Camper & Nicholsons, whereas most training ships are more traditional for the very good reason that it gives cadets more to do. For short training cruises, carrying young people with no previous experience of sailing, it was felt to be essential to have ships that could be handled in complete safety by the permanent crew. As a result the two ships, which are virtually identical, are rigged as topsail schooners with one Bermudan-rigged and two gaff-rigged masts.

When they have gained a little confidence and knowledge, the trainees can be sent aloft to set or furl the topsails, but these are a fair-weather extra rather than an essential part of the rig. Both boys and girls can sail on the schooners and many return to serve as watch leaders to pass on the essential elements of seamanship that they have learned.

TOVARISHCH

Originally named *Gorch Fock*, the *Tovarishch* was the first of a series of six near-sister ships built by Blohm and Voss during the 1930s, and was built as a naval school-ship. She carried 240 officers and men, of whom 108 were cadets. Right at the end of the Second World War she was sunk in the Baltic, but the Russians decided to raise her and take her over.

After a complete refit, she was recommissioned in 1951 and renamed *Tovarishch*, and began a new career training cadets for both the Soviet Navy and merchant marine. Based in the Black Sea, she continued in service for a further twenty years until she was replaced by another, larger, sail training ship.

In the meantime the Federal Republic of Germany which lost its entire fleet of sailing ships after the Second World War, built a new *Gorch Fock* which was launched in 1958. Designed and built, like the original, by Blohm and Voss of Hamburg, she is an enlarged and modernized version of the original but very similar in concept.

Both are three-masted barques, with relatively short masts so that they can fit under the bridges of the Kiel Canal, but even so, scaling the rigging is certainly not a task for the faint-hearted. They were designed as proper square-rigged sailing ships in the old style, and as such are a kind of living museum for the skills of sailing such ships.

EAGLE

Another former German school-ship, *Eagle* was built in 1936 as the *Horst Wessel*. She is similar in design to the present-day *Gorch Fock* and also to the Portuguese training ship *Sagres*. During the Second World War she was used as a depot ship in the Baltic, but managed to avoid serious damage. Afterwards,

MALCOLM MILLER
The 'Malcolm Miller' is one of the two schooners operated by the Sail Training Association.

TOVARISHCH
The Soviet barque 'Tovarishch' is a rebuild of the original 'Gorch Fock', built in Germany.

however, she was confiscated by the US Government, which allocated her to the Coast Guard.

Renamed *Eagle*, the old ship has been the flagship of the US Coast Guard fleet ever since. In the United States, the Coast Guard has a much wider responsibility than in most countries and is a large and highly professional service which maintains a considerable fleet of cutters and smaller boats. Every trainee spends time aboard the *Eagle*, which generally carries around 180 crew on courses lasting up to three months.

It is fascinating to find that the most advanced nation on earth still regards sail training as highly valuable, if not actually essential. In fact, due to the relatively easy life led by most young Americans, the toughness and self-reliance created by sail training could be said to grow even more important as years go by. *Eagle* is now a very elderly sailing ship and it will be most interesting to see if the US Coast Guard decides to commission a new sailing ship to replace her.

EAGLE
The 'Eagle' is the sail training ship of
the US Coast Guard. Built in Germany
in 1936 as the 'Horst Wessel', she was
confiscated by the US government
after the Second World War.

EAGLE

TECHNIQUES

Choosing or finding a suitable boat may be difficult enough in itself, but learning to sail from scratch without the benefit of professional instruction can be a nightmare unless the new owner makes adequate preparations and has some idea of what to expect.

Whatever your choice of boat, this section on techniques is a simple guide to some of the more common methods of rigging, handling ashore and afloat and what to do in emergencies.

The actual business of going sailing is relatively simple. The skill levels needed to be reasonably competent are not excessive and you often have sufficient space to make your mistakes without endangering yourself or others.

There is, however, one area which should be avoided (as far as it can be) in the early stages of learning to sail, and that is sailing language and terminology. Complicated technical language can easily confuse the newcomer at a time when he or she is having enough problems learning to sail without the additional burden of learning a new language.

To begin with, try to keep to simple everyday descriptions like 'back' and 'front', 'left' and 'right', 'push' and 'pull'; you can learn the proper nautical terms for the various pieces of string and parts of the boat and its rigging as and when you need to.

Even so, some parts of the boat – such as the boom, mast, mainsail and jib – have names which must be used from the start because they have no everyday alternatives, and you will need to spend some time identifying these and working out how they are used.

Rigging an unfamiliar boat can be difficult. Always try to get the vendor to show you where the bits go, especially if it is an unusual craft. Take photographs or make drawings, and mark assembled items with coloured tape to ensure that you can put them together unaided when the time comes.

Choose your first sailing venue with care and try to get an experienced sailor to 'show you the ropes' and teach you the basics. This will get you through the most difficult phase.

By far the best policy is to invest in a suitable sailing course at a reputable sailing school. Once you have sufficient experience to sail in a variety of wind and sea conditions, the next stage is to learn about those official organizations such as the Coastguard or the rescue services and the requirements they place on you: just as there are rules for driving on the roads, there are 'rules of the road' for seafarers. There is also a comprehensive international system of buoyage for marking obstructions and denoting channels, and a set procedure for sending emergency signals.

Finding your way is dependent upon precise navigation, using either traditional methods of dead reckoning or the very latest satellite navigation aids which can plot your latitude and longitude with great accuracy. However, even if your boat has the very latest and best in electronic navigation systems, you should learn how to navigate without it otherwise a power failure could leave you hopelessly lost.

As a casual sailor, especially of dinghies, you need only learn the basics of boat handling and to keep out of the way of anything really big. But if you are the owner of a cruising boat the book work and learning should be a continuous process, perhaps involving attendance at night schools or special navigation and seamanship seminars.

The topics covered in this section are essentially first steps: the basic information is designed to be developed by the reader and to form a solid foundation for further learning. Don't forget, though, that sailing is intended to be a pleasurable way to spend your time, and if you become sufficiently skilful you will have the courage to use your boat to its maximum, and so get the maximum pleasure from it.

HOW A BOAT SAILS

It is true that there is an incredible amount of aerodynamic and hydrodynamic theory involved in how a boat sails, but many sailors have learned about it by a process of trial and error and a rudimentary understanding of the concepts.

All sailboats are equipped with foils: *aerofoils*, which are above the water, and *hydrofoils*, which are below the water. Those above the water – the sails – are used to create power to drive the boat forward; those below the water – the daggerboard, centreboard or keel, and the rudder – are used to prevent the boat sliding sideways or, in the case of the rudder, to change its direction.

The wings of birds and aircraft and the sails of boats rely on a simple principle to enable them to operate. The top surface of a wing, when viewed from the side, is convex, and therefore longer from front to rear than the flat bottom surface is. As a result, air flowing over the top surface has to speed up to reach the rear of the wings at the same time as air flowing over the bottom surface.

The faster an airstream flows across a surface, the lower the pressure it exerts on that surface. So the air pressure on the top surface of a wing is lower than that on the bottom surface, and this lower pressure creates the *lift* that keeps birds and aircraft aloft.

The sail of a dinghy or yacht acts like a vertical wing, with the lee-ward side of the sail acting like the curved upper surface of a wing and generating the 'lift' that gives sailboats their driving force. This lift force is augmented by the pressure of the wind on the windward side of the sail.

The sail is angled in the airstream so that the lift it generates drives the boat forward, and for the boat to sail efficiently the sail must be set at the correct *angle of attack* to the wind. As an aid to setting the sail at the correct angle, pairs of tell-tales are attached at regular intervals to both sides of the forward part of it to indicate the airflow over the sail.

Tell-tales can be made from coloured wool sewn through the sails, knotted on either side of the cloth to prevent them slipping through. Red and green are used as contrasting port and starboard indicators, and you can see the tell-tales on the leeward side of the sail because sailcloth is semi-transparent when under tension. About three sets on main and jib will help you set the sails correctly most of the time.

At the optimum angle of attack the sail is creating its maximum lift. At this point the tell-tales on both sides of the sail assume the same slightly upward angle throughout most of the forward edge of the sail.

If the sail is pulled in too much, the leeward tell-tale begins to flutter and rotate. This tells you that the sail

TELL-TALES

These are fine strands of tape or wool which fly free on each side of a sail – red on port, green on starboard.
1 Jib tell-tales parallel: the sail is set correctly.
2 Tell-tales fluttering on leeward side: let out sail or push tiller to leeward.
3 Tell-tales fluttering on windward side: pull in sail or pull tiller to windward.

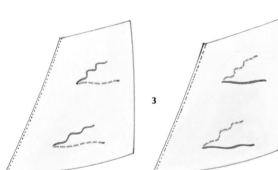

The windward side is normally the one facing the wind, and the leeward side is the one facing away from the wind. With the wind directly behind the boat, however, the side on which the boom is set is designated the lee side.

HOW SAILS WORK

On a boat with two sails it is important that they act together as a single aerofoil.
1 Jib sheeted in too far, causing an interrupted or turbulent airflow.
2 Sails trimmed correctly, giving a smooth flow of air over both sails with no turbulence.

AEROFOIL EFFECT

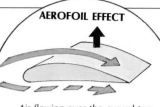

Air flowing over the curved top of an aerofoil has to speed up, creating low pressure, and thus lift, on the upper surface

SAIL SHAPE

The mainsail should be set to suit the wind and the course sailed. **1** The stronger the wind, the flatter the sail should be. A flat sail is also used when on a close-hauled course.

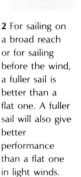

2 For sailing on a broad reach or for sailing before the wind, a fuller sail is better than a flat one. A fuller sail will also give better performance than a flat one in light winds.

EFFECTS OF INDIVIDUAL SAILS

WIND

1 Sails set behind the mast tend to turn the bow into the wind.
2 Sails set in front of the mast tend to turn the bow away from the wind.

Each individual sail has a particular effect on the directional stability of the boat.

When balanced together, the turning effects of the sails cancel each other out.

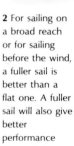

mainsail only

jib only

EFFECT OF CENTREBOARD

Wind pressure on the sails pushes the boat sideways as well as forward. The centreboard (or daggerboard) is used to counter this, although as it cannot be stopped completely, sideways motion (called 'leeway') is always present to some extent.

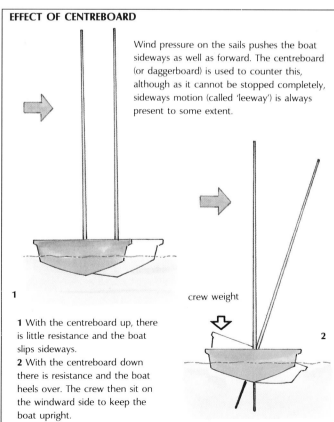

crew weight

1 With the centreboard up, there is little resistance and the boat slips sideways.
2 With the centreboard down there is resistance and the boat heels over. The crew then sit on the windward side to keep the boat upright.

The slot between the jib and the mainsail acts to speed up the flow of air over the mainsail, which improves its performance.

is now at too great an angle of attack and the airflow around the back (leeward) side has broken down into turbulence instead of flowing smoothly.

At this stage, with turbulent airflow over the upper surface of its wings, a bird or aircraft would stall and fall out of the sky. Fortunately, the sailor only loses forward drive, which can be regained by either letting the sail out (toward the fluttering tell-tale) or by pushing the tiller toward the same side as the fluttering tell-tale. When the tell-tales on each side of the sail are flying together, the sail is again creating its maximum drive.

If you let the sail out too much, the windward tell-tale will rotate. This means that the angle of attack is too small and turbulence is occurring on the bottom of the sail. To correct the situation, pull the sail in or pull the tiller toward the same side as the fluttering tell-tale. Again, when the tell-tales on both sides fly together the sail is working correctly.

Single-sailed boats, such as the Optimist and Finn, require sails designed to operate efficiently alone. Boats with two or more sails require each sail to be shaped so as to interact correctly with the others.

For example, the jib of a two-sail boat influences the airflow over the mainsail, and together, especially when the boat is sailing close to the wind, they should act in effect as a single aerofoil. In these circumstances, the front part of the mainsail may not set correctly, and flutter, but this is acceptable because the majority of the sail will be working at maximum efficiency as part of the combined aerofoil.

This efficient working of the mainsail is due to the effect of the slot formed by the gap between the overlapping parts of the jib and the mainsail. This slot constricts the air flowing through it, creating a pressure difference between the air at the windward end of the slot and the air at its leeward end. Because of this pressure difference, the airflow through the slot accelerates.

This means that the airflow over the convex leeward side of the mainsail is faster than it would be if the jib were not there. The air pressure on that side of the sail is correspondingly lower, and so the lift it generates is increased.

So the effect of the slot between two sails is to improve the overall efficiency of the sail behind the slot,

such as a mainsail. This is especially so in sailboats with masthead rigs, where the jib or genoa reaches to the top of the mast and the relatively small mainsail is inefficient by itself.

As well as generating driving forces, individual sails have a marked effect on the directional stability of the boat. Sails in front of the mast turn the bow away from the wind, and sails behind the mast turn the bow toward the wind. When properly balanced, the sails cancel out these turning movements to produce forward drive.

The combination and interaction of sails, keels, centreboards and rudders determine the sailing characteristics of all boats. When considering the overall efficiency of your own boat, it is important to appreciate that the sails act as a single unit and so they must be tuned together on every point of sailing. The keels and rudder also act as a single unit and must be tuned together, although except in the case of a lifting keel or centreboard only the rudder angle can be changed to tune them.

The keel(s) or centreboard and the rudder(s) act as hydrofoils, which means that the water flow acts on them in the same way as the airflow acts on the sails, creating 'lift' on them if they move through the water at an angle to the forward motion of the boat.

The primary function of keels and centreboards is to reduce the tendency of the boat to move sideways as well as forward when under sail. This sideways motion or *leeway* can never be totally eliminated, but the resistance of the keel or centreboard to being pushed sideways through the water reduces it to a minimum. However, one side effect of this resistance is that it causes the boat to heel over, which is why dinghy sailors often have to use their weight to keep their craft upright.

In the case of fixed keels the most you can do in the way of tuning is to ensure that the finished surface is as smooth as you can get it so that it creates the minimum of drag. Centreboards may not be the perfect hydrofoil section, but they do enable you to adjust the amount of board that is exposed beneath the boat. This is especially important because each point of sailing requires just sufficient centreboard to combat the sideways force generated by the sails.

When sailing as close to the wind as possible you need all the centreboard down, but when sailing downwind you need none at all, or maybe just a little to give some lateral stability.

BASIC SAILING MANOEUVRES

If you can drive a car you may remember how, when you were learning, operating all the controls in the right order was often difficult. As an experienced driver, however, you seldom have to think about what you are doing because your experience has built up what amount to automatic reflex actions.

Sailing a dinghy presents you with similar sequences of operations which, at the outset, will often appear confusing but which soon slot together into reflex actions.

Awareness of the wind direction is the key to successful sailing, and so the first essential is to develop such an awareness. Smoke and flags will give you an indication of wind direction, as will surface waves and wavelets, although these are more subtle. A masthead flag or 'windex' is another useful, and accurate, indicator. However, being able to sense the wind's direction by the feel of it blowing on your face or ears is a useful skill, and one which is essential in competitive sailing.

Getting the boat sailing, and controlling its speed, is the function of the set of the sails. The optimum set of the sails is the one that allows them to work at their maximum efficiency, and so drive the boat at maximum speed.

It follows that to vary the speed from maximum it is necessary to adjust the sails away from their optimum position to give the exact amount of drive you want. This is especially important when manoeuvring to pick up a mooring, to come alongside another boat or to approach a landing place.

Basically, to slow down you let the sails out, and/or turn the boat toward the wind without adjusting the sails. To get the boat moving faster, either pull the sails in to the position that gives you the speed you want, or turn away from the wind.

The principal points of sailing – angles to the wind at which a boat can sail – are *reach*, *close reach*, *close-hauled*, *broad reach* and *run*.

For beginners, the reach (or beam reach) is the key to all manoeuvres, and to the experts it is one of the most exciting points of sail. During the reach, the boat is sailing across the wind, and so the wind is blowing at right angles to the boat and directly onto the skipper's back. (The skipper of the boat is the person holding the tiller and mainsheet, and he or she should *always* sit on the windward side of the boat, facing the sail.) The centreboard should be half down, and the sails pulled in far enough to set them.

As with all vehicles, it is essential to know how to stop your boat. Boats do not have brakes, and only stop completely when they are aground, anchored or moored. In the basic *hove-to* position, though, the boat is almost at a standstill and that is the best that can be achieved once afloat. In this position, the sails are let out so that they no longer convert the wind into a driving force but flap like flags.

To heave-to on a reach, let the sails out to their fullest extent, so that the boom is against the leeward shroud and the jib is almost at right angles to the centreline of the boat. The windex or masthead flag will show the wind at 90° to the centreline, and the boat will virtually stop. When you are learning to sail, one of the useful features of the reach is that it is the point of sailing that offers the greatest safety when the

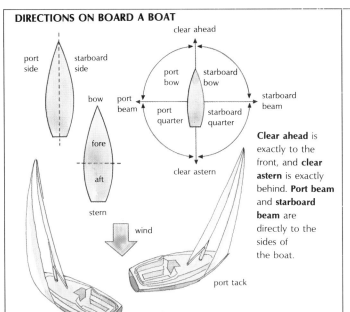

DIRECTIONS ON BOARD A BOAT

port side · starboard side

bow · fore · aft · stern

clear ahead · port bow · starboard bow · port beam · starboard beam · port quarter · starboard quarter · clear astern

wind

port tack

starboard tack

Clear ahead is exactly to the front, and **clear astern** is exactly behind. **Port beam** and **starboard beam** are directly to the sides of the boat.

TACKS With the wind over the starboard side (boom on port side) the boat is on a starboard tack. With the wind over the port side (boom on starboard side) the boat is on a port tack.

HEAVING-TO

wind

To heave-to, the jib is backed on the windward side and the mainsail eased. The tiller is pushed to leeward to counter the effect of the jib, and the centreboard is set to threequarters down.

In the hove-to position, the boat is almost stationary.

sails are let out.

Experienced sailors also use the reach to heave-to, but with the jib aback (pulled to the windward side) and the tiller pushed away. As the boat *forereaches* – moves forward under its own momentum without any power from the sails – the rudder turns it into the wind while the jib turns it away again. This results in the boat moving in a series of scallops toward and away from the wind.

Another way of stopping or slowing down is to turn the boat toward and into the wind without changing the set of the sails. The boat then slows to the point where it is all but stopped. In an emergency, when things are going wrong or if you have to avoid a collision, turn toward the wind to slow and stop.

To sail on a close reach, begin by sailing on a reach and then push the tiller gently, to turn the boat toward the wind, until the sails just begin to flap. When the boat has turned onto the new course, pull the sails in to set correctly, and move the centreboard from half-down to three-quarters-down to combat sideways drift.

If you turn the boat even farther toward the wind, you will reach a point where the sails – even when they are pulled right in and the centreboard is fully down – will not set and the windward tell-tale will rotate. When this happens, pull the tiller gently until both fully-tensioned sails set correctly. This is the close-hauled point of sailing, which is as close to the wind as the boat will sail.

The boat heels most on this point of sail, and so in stronger winds the crew's weight must be placed as far outboard as possible. To assist in safe sitting-out, toestraps (hiking straps) are fitted at each side of the centreboard casing. These can be adjusted so that the crew can sit right out with his or her backside close to the outer side of the hull. An alternative is to use a trapeze wire.

To sail on a broad reach, start again on the reach and then pull the tiller to turn the boat away from the wind by about 45° and steer a straight course. The sails will appear to be set, but the tell-tales will show that the leeward airflow has broken down. Let the sails out until the tell-tales show that they are set correctly, and raise the centreboard to the quarter-down position.

In strong winds with big seas, the broad reach is the fastest point of sailing, causing the boat to *plane* – to skim over the surface of the water rather than plough through it.

The run is the point of sail when the wind is directly behind the boat. The jib loses most of its drive and should be set on the windward side of the boat (sailing like this, before the wind with the mainsail on one side and the jib on the other, is called *goosewinging*). About six inches of the centreboard should be exposed beneath the boat to give some lateral stability.

Sailing dead downwind can be tricky in strong or gusty winds. If the boat starts to gyrate wildly, the golden rule is to steer it to follow the top of the mast: as the boat rolls to the right, steer right, and as it rolls to the left, steer left.

Remember that any turn *toward* the wind requires the sails to be pulled in and the centreboard to be lowered, and any turn away from the wind requires the sails to be let out and the centreboard raised.

POINTS OF SAILING

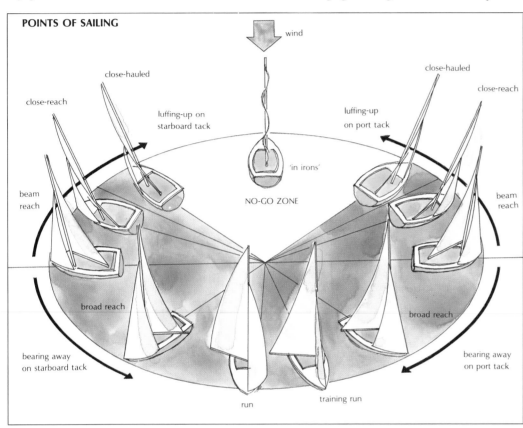

wind

close-hauled
close-reach
luffing-up on starboard tack
beam reach
broad reach
bearing away on starboard tack
run

'in irons'
NO-GO ZONE

close-hauled
close-reach
luffing-up on port tack
beam reach
broad reach
bearing away on port tack
training run

DIRECTIONS WHEN CHANGING COURSE

LUFFING-UP is when the boat turns toward the wind.

1 Any turn toward the wind requires the sails to be sheeted in and the centreboard lowered.

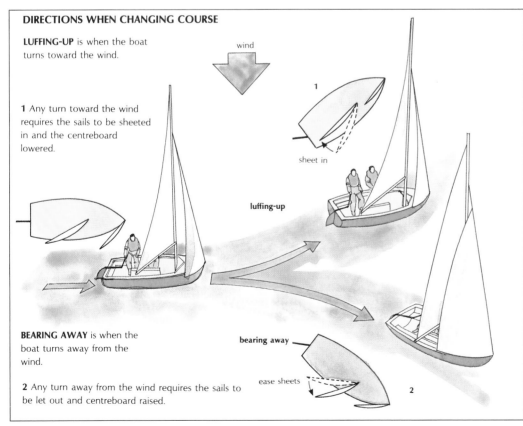

wind

sheet in

1

luffing-up

BEARING AWAY is when the boat turns away from the wind.

2 Any turn away from the wind requires the sails to be let out and centreboard raised.

ease sheets

bearing away

2

CAR TOPPING & TRAILING

One advantage of a small sailing craft is that it is relatively easy to transport on, or behind, a small vehicle. This enables you to keep the craft at home or, if you sail from a club base, to transport it to other sailing venues.

The simplest method is to carry the craft inverted on the vehicle roof, on two bars fitted securely to the existing guttering or into the special roof tracks provided on cars without gutters.

Larger or heavier craft must be trailed on a purpose-built road trailer. To do this, you will need to have your car fitted with a suitable towbar and a connecting socket for the trailer's lighting system. As a general rule, if four reasonably fit

adults cannot lift a boat onto a roof rack, it should be trailed.

Roof racks designed specially to enable you to carry a wide range of summer and winter sports equipment are now widely available. Before you buy any type of roof rack, though, it is essential that you check out the vehicle's handbook to discover the manufacturer's maximum recommended roof loadings. These take into account the aerodynamic loads imposed by bulky objects.

Webbing straps with self-locking, easily-adjusted buckles must be used to secure the load to the vehicle. For added stability, attach a line from the front and back of the load to the respective bumpers (but only

if these offer secure anchoring points for the line).

Loading a dinghy such as a Laser, which has a hull weight of nearly 60 kg (130 pounds), needs careful organization if you have no helpers.

One method is to stand the boat on its transom with its bottom leaning against a wall, and secure it to prevent it falling. Back the vehicle to within about 2 metres (6 feet) of the boat, then gently lower the boat until it makes contact with the rear of the roof rack. Lift the back of the boat and slide it forward onto the rack and beyond its point of balance to its correctly-loaded position. Normally, a boat is correctly loaded when there is an equal amount of overhang beyond the front and rear

roof bars.

If you have a team of helpers, place the boat alongside the vehicle with equal numbers of helpers standing at each side of the boat. To invert it, first lift up one side while pressing down on the other to get it standing vertically on one side. Then push it beyond the vertical with everyone helping to lower the high side to the ground.

With a concerted lift from equal numbers of helpers on each side, get the boat to shoulder height and locate the back of the boat onto the rearmost roof rack bar. Reposition some of the helpers to assist with swinging the front end across onto the rack, and position the craft correctly before securing it.

TYPES OF TRAILER

Right A simple two-wheeled trailer carrying a single dinghy. The boat is lashed to the trailer with ropes at each side as well as at the front.

Below left A four-wheel trailer carrying a small cruiser. The boat is sitting on its keels, and is securely lashed to the trailer at the bow and the stern.

Below right A trailer carrying two dinghies, one inverted above the other. Each of the dinghies seen here has its own launch trailer attached to it, so that it can be launched easily without the road trailer having to go into the water.

Spars, and sometimes sails, may also be carried on roof racks. By far the neatest way is to use a large-diameter, thin-gauge plastic tube which is tailored to accept short spars and rolled-up sails. The tube should be securely attached to the roof bars and have removable end caps, each with a securing lanyard to prevent loss. If you do not use tubes, you must ensure that the spars are securely attached to the racks.

You can lash the boat to the rack with two webbing straps, either one to each roof bar, or criss-crossed over the upturned hull to help stabilize the load. Lash the spars together on the extremities of the bars.

If you prefer to use rope to secure the load, you must use padding (such as sponge rubber or pieces of old carpet) beneath it to protect the hull from abrasion by the rope. The highwayman's or truck driver's hitch is a useful way of tightening down the ropes.

Boats which are too heavy to carry on the roof rack must be trailed behind the vehicle. Again, consult the vehicle's handbook to find the maximum towing weight for it. When calculating towing weights, always add the weight of the boat and all its equipment to the weight of the trailer and then add about 10 percent to allow for extra personal gear.

Each country has specific laws relating to the construction, braking and lighting of trailers, and the display of information on the trailer and the towed vehicle. Check with your local police department or with the supplier of the trailer to ensure that yours conforms to the rules.

The mast of a trailed boat may often be too long to be carried legally on a roof rack, but an adjustable mast support fitted to the front of the trailer will enable the mast to be carried at an angle to clear the roof of the towing vehicle, with the inboard end of the mast located in a specially shaped and padded fitting near the inside of the transom.

Most dinghies require a launching trolley as well as a road trailer, so it's worth investing in one that is designed to load and lock onto the road trailer in one easy movement. This arrangement ensures that the wheel bearings of the road trailers are never immersed (but remember that whether they are immersed or not, they need regular maintenance and lubrication to ensure their reliability).

Protecting a trailed boat is of great importance because road debris, silt-laden rainwater and oil all harm the highly-polished surfaces. Custom top and bottom covers should be used to enclose the boat and its gear completely. If you keep your boat outside, the top cover should be made from a plasticized cloth which keeps rainwater out.

1

2

3

4

TOPPING AND TRAILING

This sequence of pictures shows a small dinghy being put onto the roof rack of a car, and a trailer carrying a larger boat being hooked to the car's towbar. First, the small dinghy is taken from its launch trolley and placed, inverted, on the roof rack (**1**), and then securely lashed in place with webbing straps (**2** and **3**). Next, the trailer is prepared for towing; here, a board carrying lights, reflectors and the car's registration number is fixed to the stern of the boat (**4**). The rules for marking a trailer in this way vary from one country to another, so check with the relevant authorities if you are planning to take your boat abroad on a trailer. Finally, the small dinghy's launch trolley has been secured on top of it, and the trailer is hooked to the towbar (**5**).

5

RIGGING A DINGHY

Rigging a dinghy entails fitting the mast, attaching its supporting wires (if fitted) and the boom, and fitting the ropes or wires that haul up the sails and the ropes that control them.

Singlehanded (one-person) boats usually have a single sail, fitted onto an unstayed (unsupported) mast housed in a substantial tube or mast support at the front of the boat. The Optimist, Laser, Sunfish and Topper dinghies are examples boats using this type of mast. In the case of the Laser, the mast is made up of two pieces which slot together like a fishing rod.

Two-person boats, and those which have two or more sails, usually have a mast which is supported (stayed) by three wires. The bottom of the mast (mast foot) is either housed on the deck (deck-stepped) or inside the boat (keel-stepped).

A fixed mast foot has a tenon which fits snugly into a mortice cut into a wooden pad. An adjustable mast foot fits into a track with adjustable pins.

The U-shaped type of adjustable track is drilled at regular intervals to accept the two pins that are inserted to prevent the mast foot slipping forward or back once the position has been chosen. Another type, the inverted T-bar, accepts a grooved mast foot and uses a single pin to locate the mast once it has been positioned.

The mast may be a simple tube (as on the Optimist, Laser, Sunfish and Topper), or a complicated tapered aluminium extrusion with an integral groove to accept the front (luff) of the mainsail.

The foot of the mainsail fits into a groove running along the top of the main boom. The main boom is the horizontal spar, made of aluminium or wood, attached to the aft side of the mast by a fitting called the gooseneck. This may be fixed in a permanent position, or be a sliding fitting that can be adjusted up or down to alter the boom height.

The tack of the mainsail is locked into position by a fitting at the foward end of the boom, and the clew is secured by a line called the clew outhaul. This is lashed to a fitting at the aft end of the boom and used to tension the foot of the sail.

The sail is tensioned overall by a fitting called the kicking strap, kicker or boom vang, which is attached to the underside of the boom, about a quarter of the way from the mast, and to a shackle at the base of the mast. It tensions the sail by pulling down on the boom.

Most tube masts (those of the Optimist and Sunfish are exceptions) fit into a pocket or sleeve at the front of the mainsail, and you should fit the sail to the mast before putting the mast into the hull of the boat. Once the mast is in place, the sail will catch the wind and so the front of the boat should *always* be pointed *into*

the wind while rigging.

Stayed masts are normally supported by three wires, one at each side and one at the front. The two side wires are called shrouds, and the wire to the front (bow) of the boat is the forestay.

The wires are usually attached to a mast fitting called the hounds, which is about threequarters of the way up the mast, by strip shackles or clevis pins. Alternatively, the wires may be swaged into T-bar fittings that slot into holes in the mast wall. Catamaran wires are usually taken to a single large shackle attached to the front edge of the mast.

At their bottom ends, shrouds are attached to the shroud plates by lanyards, adjustable bottle screws or rigging plates. Simple shrouds finish in an eye that is reinforced against wear by a stainless steel thimble.

The forestay, which on modern dinghies is there to keep the mast up when the jib is not rigged, is often kept in place by a simple lanyard lashing. Older boats have bottle screws, especially if the jib is attached to the forestay with metal hanks.

Tensioning the shrouds beyond

Above *Once the mast has been stepped, the supporting forestay and shrouds are tensioned.*
Right *The rudder and tiller should be fitted after the mast and sails have been rigged.*

the normal supporting role causes the mast to bend forward in the middle, while adjusting the forestay determines the amount of rake (forward or backward slope) of the mast. Different wind conditions require different settings of the mast.

In addition to the three supporting wires, the mast will be fitted with wire or rope halyards that are used to raise and lower the sail. These are usually inside the mast and exit at the bottom through pulley blocks contained in a multiple sheave box. This is usually an alloy casting that also incorporates the mast foot.

The jib halyard sheave is at the front of the mast just below the forestay fitting, and the spinnaker halyard sheave is above the forestay. The halyards may be led down to small swivel blocks or fixed rings. The mainsail halyard sheave is often incorporated into the mast head fit-

MASTS AND STANDING RIGGING

UNSTAYED MAST

Small dinghies usually have unstayed masts, which have no supporting rigging.

STAYED MAST

Larger dinghies usually have stayed masts, which are supported by three wires — one at each side and one in front.

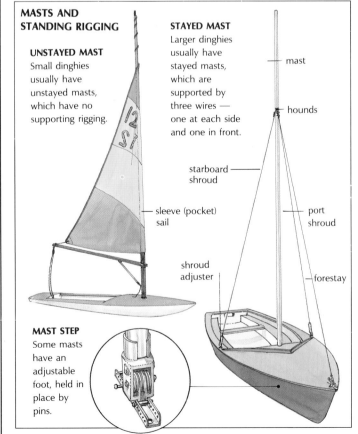

mast

hounds

starboard shroud

sleeve (pocket) sail

port shroud

shroud adjuster

forestay

MAST STEP

Some masts have an adjustable foot, held in place by pins.

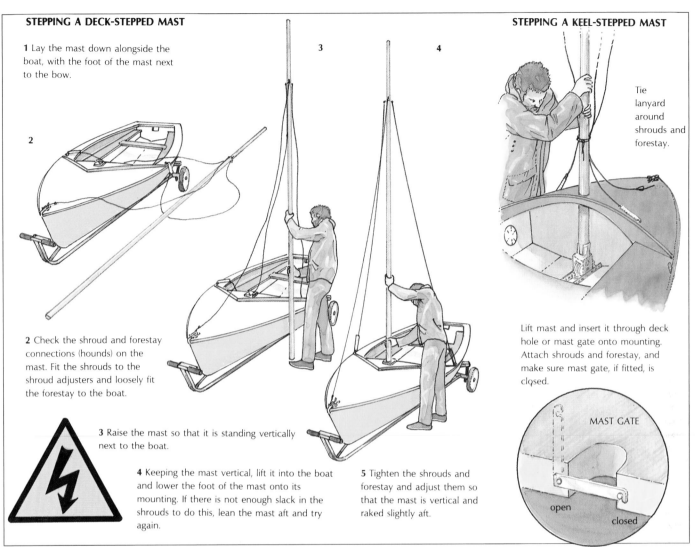

STEPPING A DECK-STEPPED MAST

1 Lay the mast down alongside the boat, with the foot of the mast next to the bow.

2 Check the shroud and forestay connections (hounds) on the mast. Fit the shrouds to the shroud adjusters and loosely fit the forestay to the boat.

3 Raise the mast so that it is standing vertically next to the boat.

4 Keeping the mast vertical, lift it into the boat and lower the foot of the mast onto its mounting. If there is not enough slack in the shrouds to do this, lean the mast aft and try again.

5 Tighten the shrouds and forestay and adjust them so that the mast is vertical and raked slightly aft.

STEPPING A KEEL-STEPPED MAST

Tie lanyard around shrouds and forestay.

Lift mast and insert it through deck hole or mast gate onto mounting. Attach shrouds and forestay, and make sure mast gate, if fitted, is closed.

MAST GATE

open

closed

ting and is at the back of the mast inside the sail track.

Older or very simple rigs may have external halyards that run through pulley blocks in the appropriate position for main, jib and spinnaker.

To ensure trouble-free identifi-

cation and ease of rigging, always lash or tape halyards to the mast before unstepping it to ensure that they will not get in the way when you next come to step the mast.

To rig a deck-stepped mast, first check that the boat is stable, preferably attached to its trolley or trailer,

or on tyres. Lay the mast alongside the boat, with the foot next to the bow. Attach the shrouds to the boat, then fasten the forestay loosely so that when you start to raise the mast it will support it.

Raise the mast to a vertical position and lift it, against the pull of the

forestay, onto its deck mounting. Adjust the shrouds and the forestay so that the mast is raked slightly aft (sloping to the rear).

To ensure that the mast doesn't lean to one side, use the main halyard as a gauge to equal up the shrouds. Apply sufficient tension to the shrouds to produce a 'twang' when you pluck them.

Keel-stepped masts may have to be fed through a hole in the deck, or located in a mast gate. Whichever you have, you need to be inside the boat to place the vertical mast into position. It is advisable to use helpers to steady the mast with the wires, or to pass it to you.

When the mast is in place, lead the halyards to their respective control positions at the front, centre or rear of the boat, and then fit the boom and sails.

Before stepping any mast, it is essential to check that you are well clear of any overhead power lines. Also ensure that you can wheel the boat to the water without the mast touching or even coming close to the power lines.

SAIL RIGGING & REEFING

Sails are extremely sophisticated aerofoils constructed from carefully-shaped panels of closely-woven synthetic sailcloth. Masts and booms are carefully matched to the cut of the sails to give a wide range of sail shapes to suit changing wind and sea conditions, and sails are controlled by ropes which are termed *running rigging* to differentiate them from the *standing rigging* supporting the mast.

To understand the different shapes required of a single sail, we can compare them to the shapes and sections of birds' wings. High speed birds, such as swifts and hawks, have narrow, curved wings which are very thin (flat) in cross-section.

Similarly, a flat sail is needed in strong winds. This is achieved by tightening the boom vang (kicking strap) to tension the sail. This bends the top of the mast toward the stern, and the middle of the mast is bowed forward. The front edge of the sail – the luff – is stretched tight by the halyard and Cunningham tackle, and in section the sail is flat.

In light winds, the sail controls are eased to produce a straight mast and a full-section sail similar to the thick wing of a soaring bird such as an eagle or a buzzard.

Sails come in a variety of shapes and can be triangular or trapezoidal (with four sides). It helps to remember that the tack of a sail faces forward in the boat and the clew is aft. The foot of the sail is always at the bottom.

The foot of the mainsail can be attached to the boom loose-footed, with a lashing at the tack and clew, or it 'can be laced along its length with rope. More commonly, the clew is fed into a groove in the top of the boom and hauled out to the boom end, the tack being kept in place with a tack pin. The clew is often attached to a rope or wire outhaul to enable the foot to be tensioned.

Halyards are used to haul the sails up the mast or forestay. The simplest rope halyards are tied to the head of the sails either by passing the rope through and tying a double thumb knot, or by the traditional halyard hitch. The usual way, though, is to use a shackle, preferably the type with a captive pin. At their bottom ends, halyards are secured to simple cleats or the wire part is tensioned by a Highfield lever or muscle box.

The jib is either set on its own internal wire stay, or attached to the forestay with plastic or metal clips called hanks. The jib tack attaches to the stem headfitting, which secures the forestay to the bow.

Before hoisting the jib you must attach the jib sheets, either by a shackle (which is dangerous) or by tying a bowline to the clew or, if you wish to use one piece of rope, by tying double overhand knots each side of the clew.

The jib is controlled by ropes led down either side of the mast to fairleads. These can be simple solid bullseyes, or sophisticated ratchet blocks which help to take the strain out of holding the ropes, which are called sheets. Alternatively, the rope can be jammed into a crab's-claw jamming block or a serrated cleat while sailing.

Small jibs normally sheet inside the shrouds, but large genoas sheet outside; spinnaker sheets are rigged outside everything, including the forestay. The spinnaker is usually housed in a bag or pouch adjacent to the mast, and its halyard is led outside the jib and under the jib sheets. When the spinnaker pole is placed on the mast, the windward jib sheet must be on top of the pole.

Numerous devices are used to vary the sheeting position of the spinnaker sheets while sailing. The most common is the Barber hauler, situated just forward of the shrouds and consisting of a ring or pulley.

The various sail controls on a boat are designed to change the shape of the sails to cope with a wide variety of wind conditions. Halyards, for example, control luff tension, and the stronger the wind the greater the tension needed.

Another method of tensioning the luff of a sail is to use a Cunningham tackle, a tensioning line which runs through the Cunningham eyelet, a hole in the sail a little way above the tack. The Cunningham tackle is adjusted so that, when the boat is sailing, the luff has a smooth curve. The luff is too slack if it develops scallops or horizontal creases, and too tight if it has vertical creases.

The boom vang or kicker is attached to the bottom of the boom and runs from there to the foot of the mast, or to the kingpost if the mast is deck-stepped. The vang is usually a multipart purchase with a mechanical advantage ranging from 4:1 to 32:1, and its purpose is to pull the boom forward and down so as to control mast bend, leech shape and sail cross-section.

The mainsheet is usually a 4:1 system used to position the boom at the optimum angle to the wind. It can

This boat is aft-sheeted, the mainsheet being led from the end of the boom to the transom.

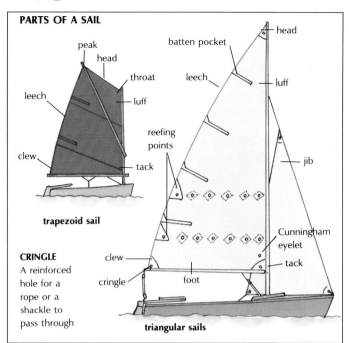

PARTS OF A SAIL

peak
head
head
throat
leech
luff
leech
batten pocket
leech
head
luff
reefing points
clew
tack
jib
trapezoid sail

CRINGLE
A reinforced hole for a rope or a shackle to pass through

clew
cringle
Cunningham eyelet
tack
foot

triangular sails

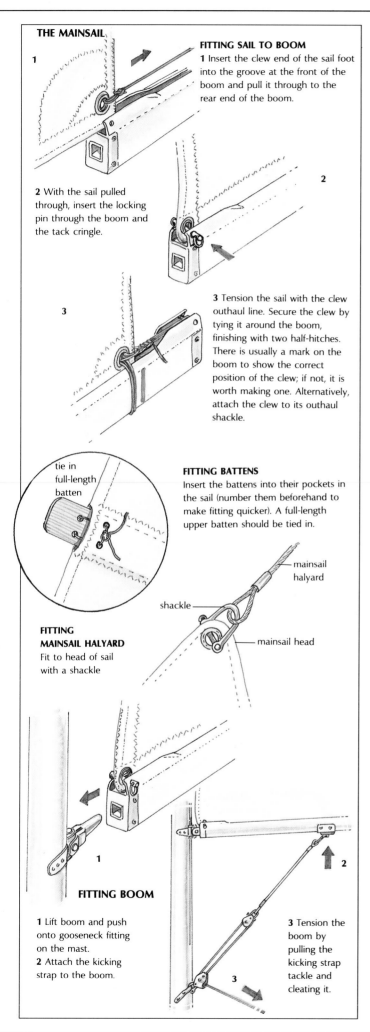

THE MAINSAIL

1

FITTING SAIL TO BOOM

1 Insert the clew end of the sail foot into the groove at the front of the boom and pull it through to the rear end of the boom.

2

2 With the sail pulled through, insert the locking pin through the boom and the tack cringle.

3

3 Tension the sail with the clew outhaul line. Secure the clew by tying it around the boom, finishing with two half-hitches. There is usually a mark on the boom to show the correct position of the clew; if not, it is worth making one. Alternatively, attach the clew to its outhaul shackle.

tie in full-length batten

FITTING BATTENS

Insert the battens into their pockets in the sail (number them beforehand to make fitting quicker). A full-length upper batten should be tied in.

mainsail halyard

shackle

mainsail head

FITTING MAINSAIL HALYARD

Fit to head of sail with a shackle

FITTING BOOM

1 Lift boom and push onto gooseneck fitting on the mast.
2 Attach the kicking strap to the boom.

1

2

3 Tension the boom by pulling the kicking strap tackle and cleating it.

3

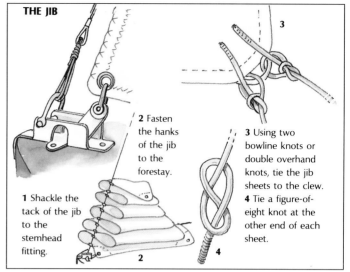

THE JIB

2 Fasten the hanks of the jib to the forestay.

1 Shackle the tack of the jib to the stemhead fitting.

2

3

3 Using two bowline knots or double overhand knots, tie the jib sheets to the clew.
4 Tie a figure-of-eight knot at the other end of each sheet.

4

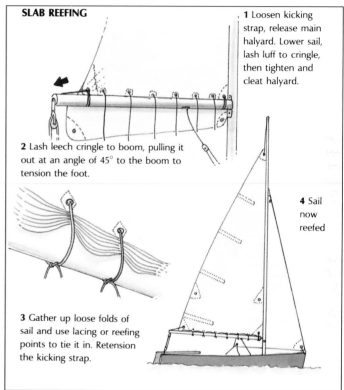

SLAB REEFING

1 Loosen kicking strap, release main halyard. Lower sail, lash luff to cringle, then tighten and cleat halyard.

2 Lash leech cringle to boom, pulling it out at an angle of 45° to the boom to tension the foot.

3 Gather up loose folds of sail and use lacing or reefing points to tie it in. Retension the kicking strap.

4 Sail now reefed

be led to the boom from the transom (aft sheeting) or from the centre-board casing (centre sheeting).

If the wind is too strong to carry full sails, most dinghies can be reefed. Aft sheeting enables you to reef the sail by rolling it around the boom, but the gooseneck fitting at the forward end must have a square shank to prevent the boom rotating when reefed.

To reef a dinghy sail when afloat, heave-to and lower the mainsail, then stow it securely so that it doesn't blow away. With one crew at the tack and one at the clew, first tuck 6 inches of the leech around the boom. Roll the boom, pulling the sail out tight with each roll.

Remove battens as you come to them. Usually, a reef to the first batten is sufficient, but in very strong winds you need small sails so don't hesitate to reef to the second

batten. If you want to use the boom vang, you should make up a webbing reefing strop, or use the sail bag. Roll it in with the last two complete reefs and attach the vang to the strop. Finally, secure the boom to the gooseneck and hoist the sail. The boom should never be lower than parallel to the water after a reef.

Slab reefing will be necessary if you have centre sheeting. In its simplest form, two sets of reef cringles (eyes) at the luff and leech will enable you to lash the sail to the boom in an emergency. Sophisticated systems attach to ram's-horns (hooks) at the gooseneck and have leech lines and jammers to control the leech.

Training dinghies such as the Wayfarer may use smaller mainsails and jibs in strong winds. The jibs require alternate or adjustable fair-leads to ensure the correct sheeting angle for the smaller sail.

USING THE CENTREBOARD & RUDDER

Together with the sails, the rudder and centreboard have a major influence on the speed and direction of the boat.

The purpose of the adjustable centreboard or daggerboard (and of the fixed keel of a yacht) is to counteract the boat's tendency to drift sideways as well as move forward when it's under sail.

A centreboard is a small, retractable keel that pivots up into a specially shaped trunking or box on the centreline of a dinghy or cruiser. Some cruisers have an outside stub ballast keel of iron which carries a pivoting plate of iron or steel. Others—lifting keel yachts—have internal ballast plates incorporating a trunking and centreboard.

The advantage of a centreboard over a daggerboard or a fixed keel is that it usually retracts of its own accord if the boat sails into shallow water. It can also be adjusted infinitely from fully down to fully up to match the exact point of sailing you chose.

The sideways drift of a sailboat (called leeway) decreases as the boat sails farther away from the wind. When you're sailing with the wind behind your dinghy there will be no leeway and thus no need for a centreboard, so you should retract it fully.

At the other extreme, when you're sailing close-hauled, the leeway will be at its maximum and so you should adjust the centreboard to its fully-down position. On a close reach, set the centreboard to three-quarters down, on a beam reach to half down, and on a broad reach to a quarter down.

In strong winds, reduce the values by a quarter for beam reach and above but leave a quarter down for the run to provide some lateral stability.

It is well worth laying your boat on its side to observe the positions of the centreboard and to mark the casing with 'down' values—down, threequarters, half, quarter and up. This will help you to set the centreboard quickly to the position you want.

Two areas to watch closely for damage are the gasket through which the centreboard extends—usually a nylon-based membrane—and the edges and bottom of the board.

The daggerboard has the same function as the centreboard, but is slid vertically up and down instead of being pivoted. Its main advantage is that it requires only a small opening in the bottom of the boat, thus eliminating the drag caused by a large centreboard slot.

Its drawbacks are that it jams if the boat sails in too-shallow water and can even damage the hull if the grounding is severe, and you have to take care not raise the board too high when gybing or it will foul the boom, causing an immediate capsize.

Lowering your centreboard or daggerboard will cause the boat to heel, because the board is resisting the sideways drift of the boat. To correct the heeling, you should move your weight farther outboard so as to bring the boat upright again.

Heeling, even if it's only slight, will cause the boat to turn, because the previously symmetrical shape of its waterplane (the area of the hull surface in contact with the water) is transformed into an asymmetrical shape when heeled. The rudder is often used to counteract such a heel-induced turn, as when, for example, a boat is hit by a gust and twists round into the wind.

You may also find that you have to use the rudder a lot to keep the boat on course when the centreboard is down. If you have to keep pulling the tiller towards you, raising the centreboard slightly should cure the problem; if you have to keep pushing the tiller away from you, lower the centreboard a little more.

Rudders come in a wide variety of shapes and sizes. Their principal task is to make large course alterations when tacking or gybing. Their secondary function, of great importance to the skilled sailor, is to act as a trim tab to correct the balance of the boat as it responds to wind and waves.

The simplest is the transom-hung fixed rudder of the Optimist, but

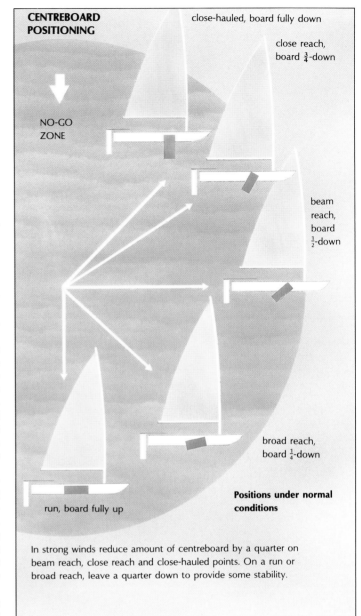

CENTREBOARD POSITIONING

NO-GO ZONE

close-hauled, board fully down

close reach, board ¾-down

beam reach, board ½-down

broad reach, board ¼-down

run, board fully up

Positions under normal conditions

In strong winds reduce amount of centreboard by a quarter on beam reach, close reach and close-hauled points. On a run or broad reach, leave a quarter down to provide some stability.

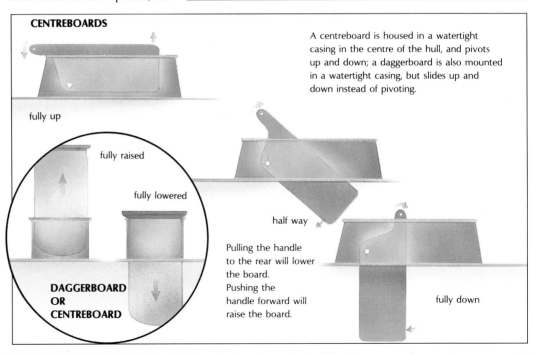

CENTREBOARDS

A centreboard is housed in a watertight casing in the centre of the hull, and pivots up and down; a daggerboard is also mounted in a watertight casing, but slides up and down instead of pivoting.

fully up

fully raised

fully lowered

DAGGERBOARD OR CENTREBOARD

half way

Pulling the handle to the rear will lower the board. Pushing the handle forward will raise the board.

fully down

most dinghies have an articulated lifting rudder which kicks up when striking an obstruction. The transom-bug rudder of the long-keeled ex-Olympic Dragon is protected by the keel itself.

The most vulnerable type is the modern spade rudder which protrudes through the bottom of the boat. To withstand the stresses and strains of sailing it must be strongly constructed of high-grade materials.

The rudder is operated by means of the tiller and works by swinging the stern of the boat around: the stern moves in the same direction as the tiller is moved.

When you move the tiller to the right (to starboard), the rudder moves to the left (to port) and swings the stern to starboard. This turns the bow to port. Similarly, moving the tiller to port causes the bow to turn to starboard.

The reverse happens when you are sailing backwards. Then, the stern moves in the opposite direction to the movement of the tiller, and the bow moves in the same direction as the tiller.

You and your crew should always sit on the windward side of the boat with your backs to the wind. So when you push the tiller away from you, the boat will turn into the wind, and when you pull it towards you, the boat will turn away from the wind. Handle the rudder sensitively, because any violent or excessive rudder movement will have a braking effect on the boat.

Most dinghies are fitted with a tiller extension, attached to the end of the tiller by means of a universal joint so that it can be swivelled both horizontally and vertically. This allows you to move around in the boat and to position your weight correctly while still retaining full control of the tiller.

You should sit with the tiller extension at the side of your body, holding it in your right hand when you're sitting on the port side and in your left hand when you're on the starboard side. Grip the extension as you would a dagger, so that you can move the tiller away from you by pushing the extension and towards you by pulling it.

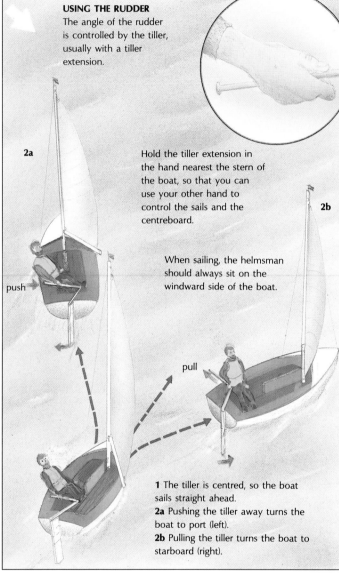

USING THE RUDDER
The angle of the rudder is controlled by the tiller, usually with a tiller extension.

Hold the tiller extension in the hand nearest the stern of the boat, so that you can use your other hand to control the sails and the centreboard.

When sailing, the helmsman should always sit on the windward side of the boat.

2a

push

2b

pull

1 The tiller is centred, so the boat sails straight ahead.
2a Pushing the tiller away turns the boat to port (left).
2b Pulling the tiller turns the boat to starboard (right).

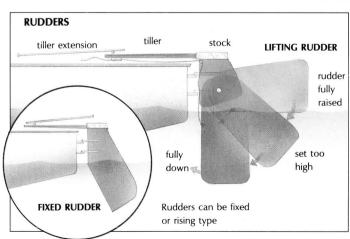

RUDDERS

tiller extension   tiller   stock   **LIFTING RUDDER**

rudder fully raised

FIXED RUDDER

fully down   set too high

Rudders can be fixed or rising type

DAGGER GRIP:
Dinghies fitted with centre mainsheets must be tacked and gybed with the skipper facing forward. The tiller extension is always held across the body at approximately 45 degrees to the vertical and the fore and aft lines. The most natural way to hold the extension is in the 'dagger grip' with the palm toward the body and the thumb extended toward the tip of the extension.

LAUNCH & RECOVERY

If you keep your boat at the water's edge, you have to learn how to launch and recover it in a wide range of wind and water conditions, and sailing on tidal waters adds the complication of tides, which determine the amount of slipway or beach exposed at launching or recovery time.

If you trailer your boat to different sailing venues (or carry it to them on the roof of your car), you face the additional problem of finding a suitable place to launch it and somewhere to leave your vehicle and trailer once you're afloat.

Trailers, by law in many countries, should not be immersed in water because of the inevitable disintegration of the wheel bearings and the seizing of the braking mechanisms.

For that reason, except when dealing with keelboats and very heavy dinghies, a launching trolley is the most commonly-used means of transporting the boat from car to water and back again. Car parking and launching charges are usually paid in advance.

Thorough pre-launch preparation is essential, whether your boat is kept near the water or trailered to the venue. As soon as you arrive at the sailing site you should check on the wind direction, the sea state and, where applicable, the times of high and low water. You should also check out the local weather forecast—listen for it on your car radio, or ask at the harbourmaster's office—and any other safety information applicable to the area.

Your planning should also take account of the fact that once the boat is afloat, someone must hold it while the launching trolley is returned to its allotted parking place. This is no problem if you're sailing two-handed, but if you're going out alone, you will need to arrange for someone to help you with the launch.

Sailing small craft requires considerable personal and boat preparation. Before you change into your sailing clothing, rig the boat to the point where all that is left is to hoist and set the sails, and leave the boat where it will not block the launching area while you change. This may be in the park, or on a wide slipway or beach, close to the water alongside other prepared boats.

Before launching, face the boat into the wind prior to hoisting the sails, and always launch with the bows pointing as near as possible into the wind if the sails are already hoisted.

When you are launching from a weather shore (where the wind is blowing from the land to the water),

Above Always launch with the bows pointing as near as possible into the wind. **Below far right** Unless you lower the mainsail first, you may arrive on a lee shore faster than you expected.

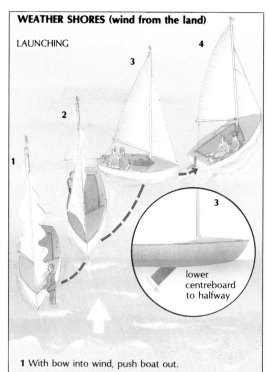

WEATHER SHORES (wind from the land)

LAUNCHING

lower centreboard to halfway

1 With bow into wind, push boat out.
2 When aboard, push jib gently into wind so that the boat drifts backward into deeper water, and push tiller away.
3 Lower centreboard to halfway position, release and sheet in jib.
4 Sheet in mainsail, steer away from the shore, setting sails correctly.

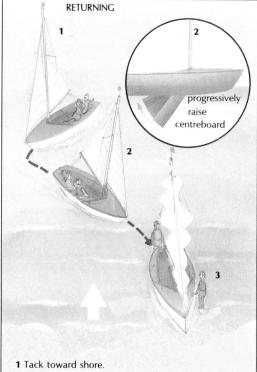

RETURNING

progressively raise centreboard

1 Tack toward shore.
2 Approach on a close reach course, raising the centreboard progressively as the boat sails into shallower water.
3 Point boat into wind, jump out and bring boat ashore.

LEE SHORES (wind from the water)

LAUNCHING

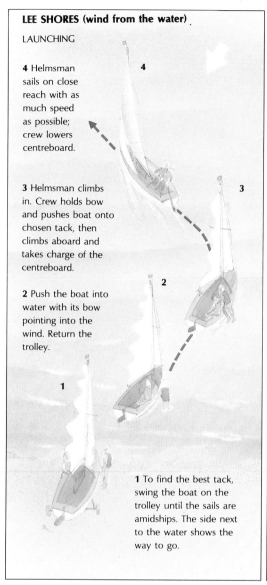

4 Helmsman sails on close reach with as much speed as possible; crew lowers centreboard.

3 Helmsman climbs in. Crew holds bow and pushes boat onto chosen tack, then climbs aboard and takes charge of the centreboard.

2 Push the boat into water with its bow pointing into the wind. Return the trolley.

1 To find the best tack, swing the boat on the trolley until the sails are amidships. The side next to the water shows the way to go.

RECOVERY

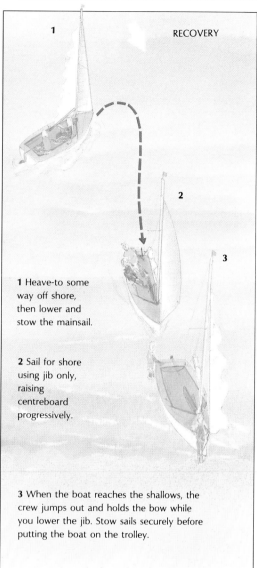

1 Heave-to some way off shore, then lower and stow the mainsail.

2 Sail for shore using jib only, raising centreboard progressively.

3 When the boat reaches the shallows, the crew jumps out and holds the bow while you lower the jib. Stow sails securely before putting the boat on the trolley.

site and jump out as the boat touches the bottom or comes alongside a landing stage.

You can take the boat out of the water with the sails still hoisted, if you wish, but take care to keep the bows pointing into the wind at all times while you do so.

When you are launching from a lee shore (where the wind is blowing from the water to the land), things look markedly different. The wind feels stronger, the waves are larger and break noisily on the shore. Exposed beaches can have waves up to $1\frac{1}{2}$ metres high, which pose a considerable hazard to all but the most experienced sailors.

Assuming the waves are reasonable, and that conditions are suitable for you to go sailing, you must first determine how you are going to get away from the launching area, because the wind and the waves will be pushing you back.

You can row, paddle or sail your boat away from the shore. If you sail, you have to choose the tack which gives you the best angle to the wind. Find this before you enter the water by raising the sails and swinging the trolley until the sails are amidships. Then, the side that is nearer the water indicates the way to go—if the right side is the nearer, sail right; if the left side is the nearer, sail left.

Push the trolley into the water until the boat floats, and have someone (your crew, or a helper) hold the bow while you return the trolley. When you've done that, climb aboard and check the rudder, centreboard and sail controls.

Next, the person holding the bow should pull the boat forward and to the chosen tack and, if he or she is your crew, climb aboard from the windward side and take immediate charge of the centreboard.

Boat speed is the key to getting away from a lee shore. Concentrate on sailing as fast as possible on a close reach, using the mainsail for power. As the depth increases, the crew should lower the centreboard until the boat can be sailed away. Negotiate the waves by pointing into them as they break and bearing away as soon as they have passed.

Returning to a lee shore requires skill and judgement. Very experienced sailors sail in at full speed, round up to 180 degrees in the shallows to face the wind, jump out and back their boat up on to the recovery area.

For the less experienced, though, it will be prudent to heave-to some way off shore, lower and stow the mainsail, and sail in under jib only until the boat reaches the shallows, enabling the crew to jump out and hold the bow while the jib is lowered.

launching is a relatively simple affair. The land affords some shelter and the waves are virtually non-existent. When you trundle the trolley into the water, the boat will float before the water reaches your knees, and it is then a simple matter to pull the trolley out and return it to the park while someone holds the boat to stop it drifting away.

When all is ready, climb aboard and back the jib (that is, push it gently into the wind) so that the boat drifts backward into deeper water. Then release the jib and sheet it on its correct side, lower the centreboard to its halfway position, and sheet in the mainsail to give additional power before bearing away to sail out from the shore.

Returning to a weather shore requires a tacking (zigzag) approach to bring the boat to one side of the launching area. Make the final approach on a close reach and pay particular attention to the centreboard, which should be raised progressively as the boat sails into shallower water.

The final manoeuvre is to point the boat into the wind at the landing

PONTOONS, HOISTS & MOORINGS

Most day sailing dinghies and many keelboats are kept ashore, and so even though many clubs have launching slipways, floating pontoons and finger jetties are increasingly used to ease the congestion at the end of the slipway on race days and at weekends. Many American and European clubs provide electric docking hoists which are operated by boat owners, while heavier boats and keelboats are often kept afloat on a permanent mooring, and the crew either row out in a tender or are ferried out by club launches.

Prior preparation is the key to all successful launching operations, so make sure your boat is fully prepared for sailing before you move it from its land base, floating dock or mooring. Then all you have to do once you are ready to sail off is to hoist whichever sail (or sails) is appropriate to the conditions, just as you would when launching from a beach.

If your boat is berthed on a pontoon, it will usually be chocked upright with padded 'knees' or wedge-shaped trestles. Remove these prior to sliding the boat into the water, and have one person holding the painter as the boat slides gently stern-first off the pontoon.

The wind direction determines your next move. On a weather shore (where the wind is blowing from the shore to the water) your boat's bow should be pointing to the shore. If the wind is strong, rig the jib only so that you can jump in, cast off your painter and, gaining speed, turn the boat onto a broad reach to gain enough sea room to round up and hoist your mainsail.

If the pontoon is parallel to the shore you can rig the sails prior to

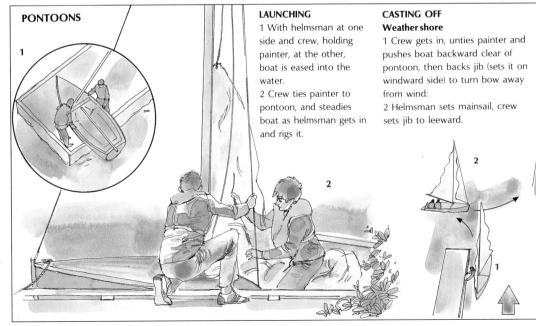

PONTOONS

1

LAUNCHING
1 With helmsman at one side and crew, holding painter, at the other, boat is eased into the water.
2 Crew ties painter to pontoon, and steadies boat as helmsman gets in and rigs it.

CASTING OFF
Weather shore
1 Crew gets in, unties painter and pushes boat backward clear of pontoon, then backs jib (sets it on windward side) to turn bow away from wind:
2 Helmsman sets mainsail, crew sets jib to leeward.

Lee shore
There is only one way for the boat to go.
1 Crew pushes off and jumps in.
2 The sails are set to take the boat on a close-hauled course.

launching. Once afloat, you and your crew both jump in, then you release the painter and the crew backs the jib while you push the tiller to leeward. When the boat is clear of the pontoon, the crew sheets the jib to the correct side and you pull the tiller to windward.

Returning to a pontoon or finger jetty on the windward shore requires a fine judgment, as you need to point the bow up into the wind to come alongside at a slow speed. When a pontoon is at right-angles to the wind, the crew must crawl along the foredeck and fend off as the boat stops head-on to it.

Alternatively, you can lower the sails and paddle alongside.

Launching from a lee shore (where the wind is blowing onshore) always brings additional problems caused by waves and the boat being pressed up against the pontoon, and the first thing to do is to ascertain the most beneficial tack to leave on.

On a finger pontoon you can lay the boat alongside, with sails hoisted and pointing into the wind. As you cast off, push the bow off and sail away on a close-hauled course.

On a shore pontoon it is best to leave the sails stowed ready for

hoisting. The crew pushes the bow off with the paddle and then paddles on the leeward side, while you fend off the back and help by pushing off and forward. Once under way, you apply gentle rudder pressure and the crew paddles against it. Once you have gained enough sea room, the crew hoists the mainsail and the boat is sailed farther offshore until the jib can be hoisted.

On returning to a lee shore pontoon or jetty, reduce sail by rounding up and lowering the main, then under jib alone sail back and round up with just enough room to stop and grab the pontoon.

As with all dinghy manoeuvres, you will need the correct amount of daggerboard or centreboard to enable you to turn correctly or to make headway off a lee shore. Returning to a lee shore you need half to threequarters down to keep the boat under control.

Electric hoists are especially useful on lakes and in areas of high tidal rise and fall. The low, short-armed hoist enables boats to be lifted off trailers and swung out over the dock wall to be lowered quickly into the water. Dinghies and keelboats can be fitted with lifting eyes or permanent strops to enable a team of operators to lift large numbers of boats in a short time.

Ready the boat for sailing before moving to the hoist, and ensure that the lifting strop, straps or wire are in place ready to attach to the hook of the hoist. Then move the boat to the hoist or free the boat from the trailer, and attach the hoist and bow and stern guiding lines. Operate the hoist and swing the boat out, and have someone keep the boat steady while you lower it. When your boat is safely in the water, either retract the hoist or, if another boat has to come out, hand over to the next operator. Once afloat, move away from the hoist area before the next boat comes in on top of you.

Launching and recovering by hoist is one of the simplest ways of handling a boat in and out of the water. Moorings, on the other hand, are about the most complicated and time-consuming option open to boat owners. The boat is kept afloat and so it must be anti-fouled, all the gear has to be transported in and out, and the mooring must be checked regularly for wear and kinking.

When leaving a mooring it is often best to hoist the mainsail, set it correctly, cast off the mooring and hoist the headsail. When returning, lower the headsail to free up the foredeck to enable the crew to handle the mooring.

Left *Prepare your boat for sailing before you cast off from a pontoon.*

Above *Moorings must be checked regularly for wear, and moored boats need antifouling.*

RETURNING

Weather shore

Boat approaches pontoon on a reach, and the sails are let out to slow it. The boat is turned into the wind to bring it alongside, and the crew grabs the pontoon and secures the boat.

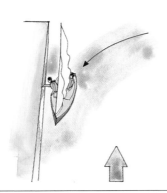

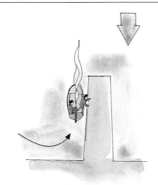

Lee shores

To return to a pontoon at right angles to the shore, sail in on a broad reach close to the shore. Round the boat up head-to-wind as it nears the pontoon, and drift to a stop alongside.

When the pontoon is parallel to the shore, first sail to a point upwind of it. Then turn the boat head-to-wind, lower the mainsail and sail in under jib alone on a broad reach. As the boat nears the pontoon, let the jib flap and drift sideways to come alongside the pontoon.

TACKING

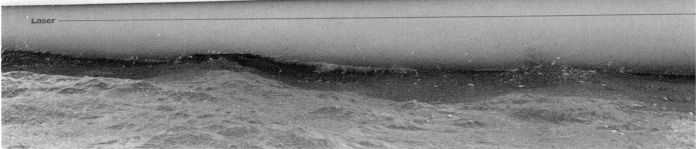

Changing direction into the wind is described as *tacking* or *going about*. The complete manouevre involves turning the boat through about 90 degrees from one close-hauled tack to another.

During the manoeuvre, the boat first turns toward the wind, a movement known as *luffing* because, when pointing directly into the wind, the sails are luffing (flapping) over the centreline of the boat. To move from being head to wind to sailing on the new tack, the boat turns away from the wind, and this is called *bearing away*.

Tacking is essentially the same for all boats, but there are differences between dinghy gear and cruiser gear; the procedures described here are for dinghy sailing.

Throughout the tacking procedure, the boom is the key reference point and its position dictates both the progress through the sequence and the actions and positions of yourself and your crew. Before tacking, you both sit opposite the mainsail, balancing the boat to keep it sailing upright.

You initiate the turn by pushing the tiller gently away from you. As the boat turns toward the wind, the sails will lose their driving and heeling forces, so you and your crew must move inboard toward the boom to keep the boat upright. When the boom crosses the centreline you should both be under it and

moving across to the other side, and as the sails fill with wind you both sit opposite them to counterbalance their heeling forces.

This sequence should be followed carefully because the order of events is important; the skipper and crew who find themselves sitting on the same side as the boom after tacking will get very wet.

How you handle the mainsheeting when tacking depends on your boat's mainsheeting arrangements. Most racing dinghies have centre mainsheets, while family or knockabout boats usually have aft mainsheets, and each type requires a different procedure.

With an aft mainsheet, the tail (end) of the mainsheet is led, via blocks, from the transom and over the tiller to the skipper. When tacking, the skipper faces aft when moving from one side of the boat to the other.

For beginners, the best way to practise tacking a two-sail, aft-sheeted boat is to tack from one reach across the wind to another. Tacking is usually a turn of about 90° from one close-hauled course to another, but the reach-to-reach tack, which involves turning through 180°, gives the novice extra time to think and to correct mistakes. It also gives additional time to watch the various changes occur.

To begin with, you and your crew sit opposite to and facing the

mainsail, with both sails set sufficiently to give the boat a reasonable speed. Before turning, you must check that you will not place your boat in the path of oncoming craft or crash into adjacent boats.

Having checked that all is clear, you call out 'Ready about!' Your crew does a similar check, especially under the sails to leeward, and if the way is clear replies 'OK!' or 'Yes!' and prepares to release the jib sheet. Meanwhile, you select a landmark over your rearward shoulder (the one nearest the back of the boat) to use as the new *goal point* toward which you will aim your new tack.

Before tacking, you should have been sailing with the tiller extension in your rearward hand with your thumb uppermost, and the mainsheet over the extension and held in your other hand. As you tack, quickly transfer the mainsheet to your tiller hand and grasp the extension with the other.

After another quick check that it is safe to turn, call 'Tacking!' or 'Lee ho!' and push the extension away slowly to a straight-arm position. As the boat begins to turn into the wind, move toward the centre of the boat with your front foot forward and tiller arm extended.

Your crew should react to the 'Tacking!' command by releasing the jib sheet and grasping the new jib sheet, and balancing the boat while moving toward the centre.

Above *When you're sailing singlehanded, face forward as you move across the boat when the boom swings over.*

You should by now be standing and facing aft. As the boom moves toward and across the centreline, you dip beneath it and turn toward the centre of the boat, pulling and twisting the extension to move the tiller toward the centreline to slow the turn.

As the mainsail fills and sets on the new tack, centralize the tiller and check that the boat is sailing approximately in the direction of your preselected goal point. Your crew should move to balance the boat as it turns onto the new tack, and sheet the jib as the tell-tales dictate.

The tacking procedure for a dinghy with a centre mainsheet is basically the same as that for an aft-sheeted boat, but there are two important differences. This first is that the skipper faces forward during the tack. The second is that, while sailing, he or she holds the tiller extension in the 'dagger' grip, and assumes the 'boxer' position in which both hands are held in front of the chest, like those of a boxer squaring up to his opponent.

Sitting on the side of the boat, hold the extension across your chest in the dagger grip, with your thumb beneath it and toward the upper end. The mainsheet, leading from

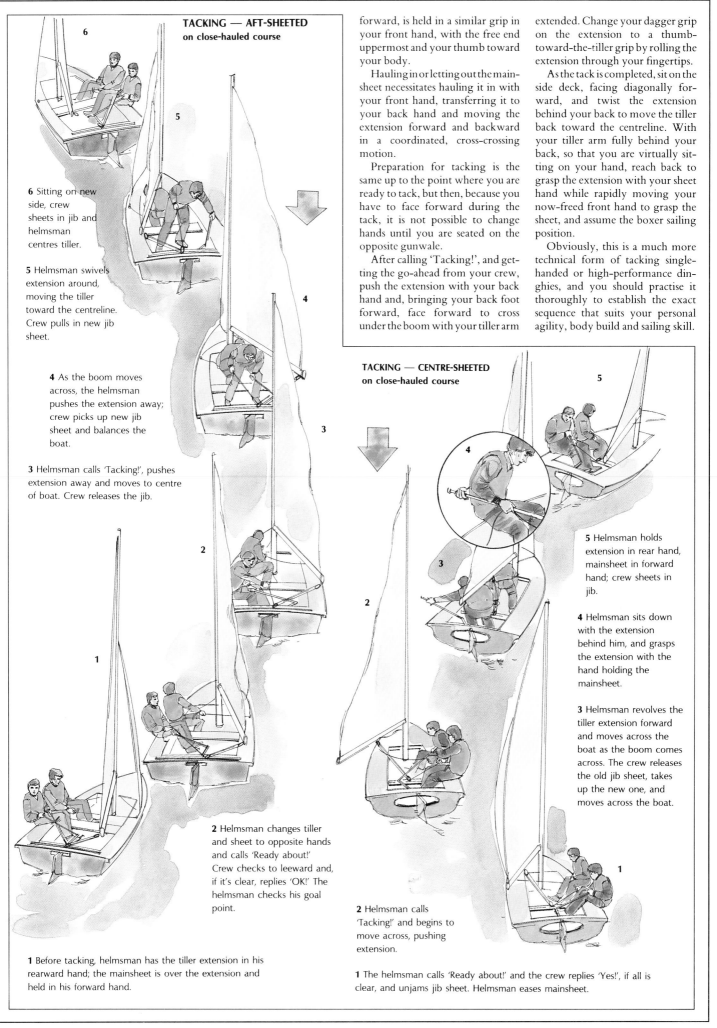

TACKING — AFT-SHEETED
on close-hauled course

6 Sitting on new side, crew sheets in jib and helmsman centres tiller.

5 Helmsman swivels extension around, moving the tiller toward the centreline. Crew pulls in new jib sheet.

4 As the boom moves across, the helmsman pushes the extension away; crew picks up new jib sheet and balances the boat.

3 Helmsman calls 'Tacking!', pushes extension away and moves to centre of boat. Crew releases the jib.

2 Helmsman changes tiller and sheet to opposite hands and calls 'Ready about!' Crew checks to leeward and, if it's clear, replies 'OK!' The helmsman checks his goal point.

1 Before tacking, helmsman has the tiller extension in his rearward hand; the mainsheet is over the extension and held in his forward hand.

forward, is held in a similar grip in your front hand, with the free end uppermost and your thumb toward your body.

Hauling in or letting out the mainsheet necessitates hauling it in with your front hand, transferring it to your back hand and moving the extension forward and backward in a coordinated, cross-crossing motion.

Preparation for tacking is the same up to the point where you are ready to tack, but then, because you have to face forward during the tack, it is not possible to change hands until you are seated on the opposite gunwale.

After calling 'Tacking!', and getting the go-ahead from your crew, push the extension with your back hand and, bringing your back foot forward, face forward to cross under the boom with your tiller arm

extended. Change your dagger grip on the extension to a thumb-toward-the-tiller grip by rolling the extension through your fingertips.

As the tack is completed, sit on the side deck, facing diagonally forward, and twist the extension behind your back to move the tiller back toward the centreline. With your tiller arm fully behind your back, so that you are virtually sitting on your hand, reach back to grasp the extension with your sheet hand while rapidly moving your now-freed front hand to grasp the sheet, and assume the boxer sailing position.

Obviously, this is a much more technical form of tacking single-handed or high-performance dinghies, and you should practise it thoroughly to establish the exact sequence that suits your personal agility, body build and sailing skill.

TACKING — CENTRE-SHEETED
on close-hauled course

5 Helmsman holds extension in rear hand, mainsheet in forward hand; crew sheets in jib.

4 Helmsman sits down with the extension behind him, and grasps the extension with the hand holding the mainsheet.

3 Helmsman revolves the tiller extension forward and moves across the boat as the boom comes across. The crew releases the old jib sheet, takes up the new one, and moves across the boat.

2 Helmsman calls 'Tacking!' and begins to move across, pushing extension.

1 The helmsman calls 'Ready about!' and the crew replies 'Yes!', if all is clear, and unjams jib sheet. Helmsman eases mainsheet.

GYBING

Changing direction *away* from the wind is called *gybing*. The manoeuvre differs from tacking in two ways: skipper and crew have to move the mainsail manually, and the wind fills it for all but a brief period during the manouevre.

Gybing calls for a certain amount of boat handling skill, and so, if a novice skipper is forced to gybe, he or she should do it by turning the boat quite quickly and keeping bodies and heads out of the way of the boom as it rattles overhead.

When a boat is running the sails are let out to their farthest extent. To change direction from one gybe to another requires the sail to be moved through about 160° from one side to the other. In light winds the crew can do this, but at all other times the full gybing sequence must be followed.

Until you are an expert, you need all the help you can get when gybing. Fortunately, there is a natural safe course, some 15° off the downwind course, which if held prior to the gybe will prevent an unexpected, accidental gybe.

From a reach, turn the boat away from the wind and adjust the sails and centreboard accordingly. At a point just before the dead run, the jib will collapse and move toward the centreline. Stop the turn at this point and, pushing the tiller away, turn back toward the wind until the jib just sets on the same side as the mainsail.

This point of sailing is the 'training run' used by sailing instructors to encourage students to identify the

As the boom moves across, the helmsman should be in the centre of the boat and facing aft.

correct downwind course from which to start a gybe.

It is essential to keep to this course before you turn, so choose a landmark to bow or stern to help you steer in a straight line while preparing to gybe.

When you're ready to gybe, turn the boat away from the wind by moving the tiller to windward. The wind will cross the stern, and your crew should then help the mainsail across to the other side. Both you and your crew should balance the boat throughout the gybe, especially when the sail crosses the boat and fills with wind.

No two gybes are the same, and the degree of control of the main by the crew increases with experience, particularly with a spinnaker set. Then, control of the boom by the skipper while the crew gybes the spinnaker is the key to successful gybing.

As with tacking, the procedure for gybing an aft-mainsheeted dinghy differs from that used for gybing a centre-mainsheeted boat.

By far the commonest problem with aft mainsheets is that the falls (loops) of the mainsheet catch on the corners of the transom as the boom swings across. If this happens regularly, you will need to incorporate a mainsheet 'flick' into the sequence as the boom moves toward the centre. This flick introduces an S-bend in the sheet which lifts it above the corner. Trial and error will teach you when to flick.

Preparing to gybe involves setting the boat up on a training run with a goal point to aim for. Sailing downwind, you and your crew will normally be sitting inboard to balance the boat, the crew perhaps sit-

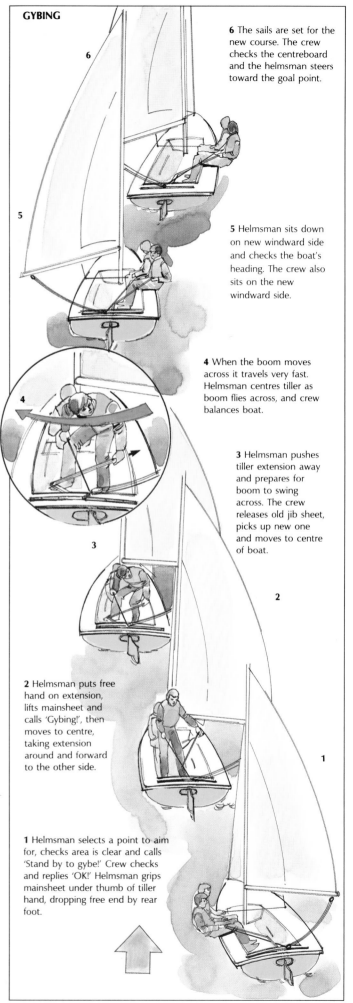

GYBING

6 The sails are set for the new course. The crew checks the centreboard and the helmsman steers toward the goal point.

5 Helmsman sits down on new windward side and checks the boat's heading. The crew also sits on the new windward side.

4 When the boom moves across it travels very fast. Helmsman centres tiller as boom flies across, and crew balances boat.

3 Helmsman pushes tiller extension away and prepares for boom to swing across. The crew releases old jib sheet, picks up new one and moves to centre of boat.

2 Helmsman puts free hand on extension, lifts mainsheet and calls 'Gybing!', then moves to centre, taking extension around and forward to the other side.

1 Helmsman selects a point to aim for, checks area is clear and calls 'Stand by to gybe!' Crew checks and replies 'OK!' Helmsman grips mainsheet under thumb of tiller hand, dropping free end by rear foot.

SLAM GYBE

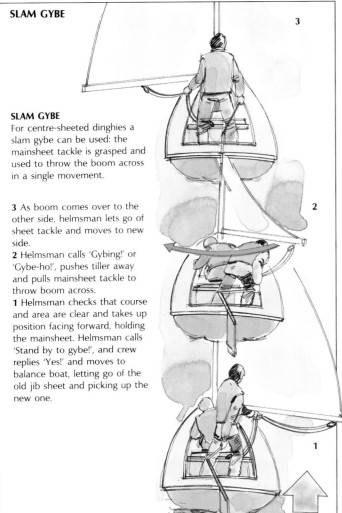

SLAM GYBE
For centre-sheeted dinghies a slam gybe can be used: the mainsheet tackle is grasped and used to throw the boom across in a single movement.

3 As boom comes over to the other side, helmsman lets go of sheet tackle and moves to new side.
2 Helmsman calls 'Gybing!' or 'Gybe-ho!', pushes tiller away and pulls mainsheet tackle to throw boom across.
1 Helmsman checks that course and area are clear and takes up position facing forward, holding the mainsheet. Helmsman calls 'Stand by to gybe!', and crew replies 'Yes!' and moves to balance boat, letting go of the old jib sheet and picking up the new one.

ting on the leeward side. The centre-board will have about 6 inches of its tip protruding through the slot.

When you are ready to gybe, check that you can turn without impeding other boats and call out 'Stand by to gybe!' Your crew should also check that it's safe to turn, and then reply 'OK!' or 'Yes!'

Change hands on the sheet and tiller extension, and move quickly to straddle the centreline with the extension swung 180° up and forward to point to the sail. As you do that, call out 'Gybing!' and push the tiller to windward.

As the boat turns, your crew should move to anticipate boat balance and grab the boom vang to assist the gybe. As the boom swings rapidly across the centreline, centralize the tiller to meet the sudden application of power as the sail fills on the new gybe

In strong winds, the sudden application of power against a centralized tiller will cause the boat to turn slightly away from the wind on the new course. You can correct this by gently easing the tiller to leeward and then centralizing it again.

Successful gybing depends on there being a narrow angle between the original and new courses, because if the boat is turned through a wide angle the sail will not catch any wind on the new course. This will encourage a capsize to windward, one of the commoner sights in a gybing fleet.

When gybing a centre-sheeted dinghy, the change of hands to resume control should be done as rapidly as possible.

It helps to remember that a heeled boat turns away from the angle of heel. This is aggravated by the fact that you may not have a lot of centreboard in the water to start with, and once the centreboard surfaces the boat will slide.

Some skippers advocate pulling in some mainsheet prior to the gybe to reduce the risk of catching the boom end in the water. Any such adjustment must be rapidly followed by the gybe itself.

When you're gybing a centre-mainsheeted dinghy, the most significant difference is that, as with tacking that type of boat, the change of hands occurs *after* the boom has crossed the boat.

Following the preparation and the call of 'Stand by to gybe!', change from the dagger grip to the underhand grip and move to the centre, lifting and rotating the extension toward the sail.

Then call 'Gybing!' and, without pause, push the extension to windward behind your back. As the boat turns, you or your crew should help the mainsail across by pulling on the mainsheet, vang, or boom. As the boom swings across, twist the extension and centralize the tiller while sitting on the side decks facing forward and inward.

TRAPEZING

The trapeze is a device that enables crews, and on some dinghies and catamarans, skippers, to stand on the side of the boat to use their weight to maximum advantage.

There is usually one trapeze on each side of the boat, and each is made up of a number of components. The trapeze wire is attached to the mast above the shrouds or swaged to the shrouds to reduce windage (deflection by the wind). It terminates in a grab handle that is used by the crew as a hand-hold when moving off or onto the boat. An adjustable ring, loop or 'dogbone' is attached to the handle.

This engages in a hook mounted on the front of an adjustable body harness worn by the crew, and is tensioned upward by a thin elasticated 'bungee' cord – the shock cord – which usually runs across the boat to the other trapeze.

Certain dinghies, including the Flying Dutchman, use continuous trapeze wires that enable the crew to remain clipped on while moving across the boat. The ring runs on a block that fits into the hook end of the trapeze wire when the crew is in position.

The trapeze permits crews to place all their weight outside the boat, and while some racing classes impose restrictions on the use of trapezes in competitions, others allow crews not only to use trapezes but also to wear water-filled jackets. These enable them to place even more weight outside the boat so as to give greater righting power

These 'weight jackets' have pockets that can be filled with water to provide more weight on upwind and reaching legs of a race, but which can be quickly emptied for downwind sailing when the extra weight would be a handicap.

Harnesses are usually padded, and strengthened with webbing. The crew's weight is taken by the hook, which is adjusted to a point between the pubic bone and the belly button. Its exact position is determined by the crew's centre of gravity: if the hook's too high, there is too much weight on the crew's legs; if it's too low, the crew risks hanging upside down.

Most harnesses have high-fitting

back supports and a tight-fitting, 'nappy'-type lower body support. Adjustable shoulder straps and front cross-belts ensure a snug fit that keeps the hook as near the body as possible.

If a boat is fitted with a trapeze, it indicates that it is a high-performance dinghy and if the skipper is unused to sailing such a boat he or she will find it difficult to handle in the early stages of ownership. Fortunately, while the skipper is learning to sail the boat the crew can use the trapeze system as a sitting-out aid without having to stand on the outside of the boat.

If you are a newcomer to trapezing, this limited use of the trapeze

system will enable you to establish the basic skills of hooking on, sitting out, coming in, unhooking and moving across the boat.

The first thing to practise is hooking on. The shock cord lifts the ring to a point above your trapeze hook when you are sitting on the side of the boat. To engage the hook, grasp the ring with your front hand and clip it onto the trapeze hook. The

Right On some of the larger, faster dinghies both skipper and crew can trapeze to keep the boat balanced. **Below** The crew of a 470 Class dinghy using a trapeze during the 1988 Olympics.

TRAPEZING — GOING OUT

1 Sitting well out, hook the trapeze onto the harness with your bow (forward) hand. Grab the handle and pull it outboard.

2 Slide out over the side deck, dropping down until your weight is on the wire. Rest your bow foot on the gunwale, next to the shroud.

3 Make sure your bow foot is secure, and push yourself out with your bow leg, keeping your body (as much as possible) at right angles to the boat.

4 Bring your stern (rearward) foot out to rest securely on the gunwale next to your bow foot. Then let go of the handle and straighten your legs.

tension of the shock cord will hold the ring in place.

The correct trapezing position is to have your body parallel to the water when the boat is sailing upright. This means that as you lower your backside over the edge of the boat, you will drop down to a position well outside the boat with your weight totally supported by the trapeze system.

This initial position is the one to use when first starting to trapeze. To get into it, sit on the side with your feet in the toestraps, then reach forward, grab the trapeze ring, and clip it onto the harness hook. (Always clip on from a sitting position, because it is dangerous to clip on while standing.)

Then grab the handle with your front hand and, pushing with your feet or free hand, drop your backside over the gunwale to sit on the outside of the boat, letting go the handle at the same time. Getting back in is a matter of reaching for the handle to pull yourself in again while leaning slightly aft.

In normal sailing trim, the ring of the trapeze will be about 1 to 2 inches above the side deck, but in the initial stages, to help you get back in, it can be raised to 3 to 4 inches above the deck.

To unclip the ring, put your hand inside the trapeze and push down with your palm. **This should be perfected, because in an emergency this method will enable you to release the ring even when your whole body weight is on it.**

To use the trapeze system correctly it is essential to commit your body weight to the wire at the earliest possible moment, as this makes every other movement so much easier. At an advanced level, you will have to handle the jib and spinnaker controls while trapezing.

When you are accustomed to sitting out on the trapeze, you can start going fully outboard on it. From the normal sitting-out position, grab the ring and clip it onto the hook. Then take the trapeze handle in your front hand and, while sitting out and down, swing your body slightly aft so that you can place your front foot against, or near, the shroud.

Now you can put your weight on your front leg and bring your back foot onto the gunwale. If the jib sheet is conveniently placed, you can use it to help you balance while you do this.

Place your feet about shoulder width apart, with your front leg braced to prevent you being thrown forward. From this crouching position, release the handle and adjust your weight, by pushing with your legs, to any point out to the fully-extended position.

COMING IN

5 With your feet at shoulders' width apart, lean back into the fully-extended position. Holding your bow arm behind your head gives more righting power.

6 To get back in, lean toward the stern, bend your knees and grab the handle. Take your weight on your bow leg and bring your stern leg onto the decking.

7 Keeping your body at a right angle, move into the boat, sit on the side decking and unhook the trapeze ring.

DINGHY SPINNAKER HANDLING

Most competitive dinghy classes permit the use of a spinnaker, which is set outside all other parts of the rig. It is usually a symmetrical triangular sail, with the head hoisted close to the mast and the clews controlled by sheets leading back to the skipper.

The windward clew is supported by a pole that clips to the mast. Its height is controlled by an uphaul/downhaul system, and its angle to the wind is controlled by the windward sheet (referred to as the *guy*). The spinnaker pole usually has simple spring-piston clips operated by a line joining the two. In use, the clips *always* face upwards.

Stowage and launching systems are either of the bow-mounted chute type or else use self-closing pouches mounted either side of the mast. With the pouch system, which is the more common of the two, the spinnaker is stowed securely in one or other of the two pouches, with both sheets and halyard attached. The halyard clips to the shroud or fastens under the reaching hook when not in use, and the sail is stowed with the head and clews at the top of the pouch.

If the spinnaker has been stowed in the leeward pouch, it can be hoisted directly from the pouch, but if it is in the windward pouch it must first be removed from it and then thrown to windward. The pole is usually clipped to the guy after the sail has been hoisted and just before it sets.

Close cooperation between you and your crew is essential when the spinnaker is being hoisted. You must be able to steer standing up, with the tiller gripped between your knees so that your hands are free to control the spinnaker. Whenever possible, sail on a broad reach when you want to raise or lower the spinnaker, as you will find it much easier to handle on that course than on others.

To hoist the spinnaker from the leeward pouch, steer onto a broad reach while your crew releases the halyard from the shroud or reaching hook, attaches the guy and the uphaul/downhaul to the spinnaker pole and then clips the pole to the mast. When the pole is in position, pull on the halyard to hoist the spinnaker and use the sheet and guy to set it.

Now your crew can sit on the windward side of the boat, cleat the guy and take control of the sheet, allowing you to sit down and steer the boat as normal.

To hoist the spinnaker from the windward side, you again sail on a broad reach and then stand in the boat, steering with your knees, and put the pole where the crew can pick it up easily when standing next to the mast.

The crew removes the spinnaker from the pouch, holding it in a tight bundle in his or her windward hand and taking the sheet in the other, while you take up the slack in the halyard. Then the crew throws the bundled sail up and forward to windward of the forestay, you pull rapidly on the halyard to hoist it, and the crew pulls the sheet to leeward.

Now you can take over the sheet to keep the sail set, freeing the crew to fix the guy and uphaul/downhaul to the pole and clip the pole to the mast. When the pole is in place, you both sit down to balance the boat and the crew takes control of the sheet.

To lower a spinnaker quickly, many crews ease the pole forward, unhook it from the mast and stow it. Then, while the skipper frees the halyard, they pull in the foot and the two leeches to windward of the jib.

Below *Good teamwork and close cooperation are essential when using a spinnaker.*

The sail is stuffed into the pouch during the process, and the halyard clipped to the shroud.

The chute system is semiautomatic, with a retrieval line attached to the centre of the sail, and when the line is pulled, the sail disappears into a below-decks sock or tube. This system is easier to use than the pouch type because it is mounted in the centre of the bow, rather than to windward or leeward.

To hoist it, the crew cleats the sheets, then you pull the halyard to raise the sail and keep it full, while the crew fits the uphaul/downhaul and guy to the pole, and then clips the pole to the mast.

To lower the sail, you pull on the retrieval line (spinnaker downhaul) to draw the sail down into the chute. The crew keeps the spinnaker foot against the jib luff as the sail descends, and releases the sheet and the guy and unclips the pole from the mast.

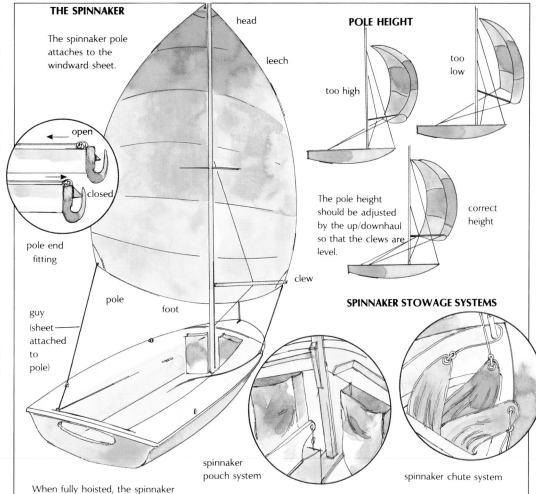

THE SPINNAKER

The spinnaker pole attaches to the windward sheet.

open

closed

pole end fitting

guy (sheet attached to pole)

pole

foot

head

leech

clew

POLE HEIGHT

too high

too low

correct height

The pole height should be adjusted by the up/downhaul so that the clews are level.

SPINNAKER STOWAGE SYSTEMS

spinnaker pouch system

spinnaker chute system

When fully hoisted, the spinnaker should be clear of the forestay and the jib, and of the mast shrouds and the trapezing wire.

In the pouch system, the spinnaker is stowed in one or other of two pouches, one at each side of the mast. In the chute system, the sail is stowed in a long tube below the foredeck, and emerges through an opening beside or in front of the forestay.

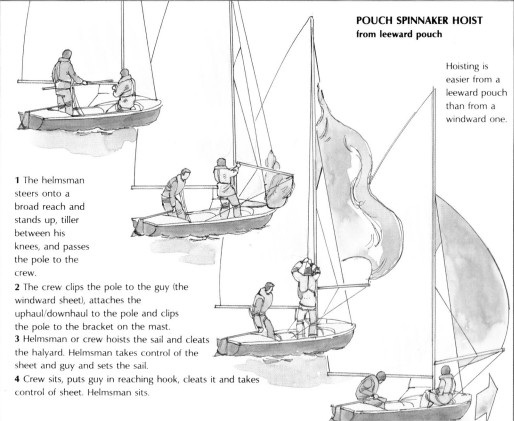

POUCH SPINNAKER HOIST
from leeward pouch

Hoisting is easier from a leeward pouch than from a windward one.

1 The helmsman steers onto a broad reach and stands up, tiller between his knees, and passes the pole to the crew.
2 The crew clips the pole to the guy (the windward sheet), attaches the uphaul/downhaul to the pole and clips the pole to the bracket on the mast.
3 Helmsman or crew hoists the sail and cleats the halyard. Helmsman takes control of the sheet and guy and sets the sail.
4 Crew sits, puts guy in reaching hook, cleats it and takes control of sheet. Helmsman sits.

CAPSIZING & MAN OVERBOARD

To be able to follow the correct emergency procedures when your boat capsizes, or someone falls overboard, you need a complete understanding of the boat, its equipment and the way it sails.

In training, both capsize recovery and man-overboard recovery are structured exercises designed to improve boat handling skills. Each is taught as a sequence, and each must be practised and perfected to the point of becoming a reflex action.

Sailing dinghies are actually quite difficult to capsize, especially in a training exercise. The simplest way is to sail close-hauled and tack violently without changing your position. Your weight and the force of the wind on the sails should be enough to cause the boat to lie sail-down on the water.

In real life, dinghies capsize because they are overpowered by a gust before the skipper has time to release the mainsheet, or they roll in while gybing or running in strong winds.

If your boat capsizes when you're sailing single-handed, the first thing to do is to step over the high side as the boat goes over. From a sitting-out position you place your forward leg over the gunwale and sit astride the side. As the sail hits the water, you lower yourself to the centreboard or daggerboard and right the boat by pulling on the gunwale. Then you can climb in and sail on.

The best way to right a two-man dinghy is to use the scoop method, which requires both of you to act

Right *Right a one-man dinghy by standing on the centreboard root and pulling on the gunwale.*

RIGHTING A TWO-MAN BOAT — SCOOP METHOD

1 Both helmsman and crew swim to the stern. The helmsman checks that the rudder is there and fitted properly, and holds it to prevent the boat inverting to the mast-down position. The crew finds the end of the mainsheet.

2 The helmsman takes the mainsheet to use as a lifeline and swims to the centreboard. The crew then swims inside and checks that the centreboard is fully down. The helmsman puts his weight on the centreboard to prevent inverting.

3 The crew finds the top jib sheet and throws it to the helmsman, who tells the crew when he has taken hold of it.

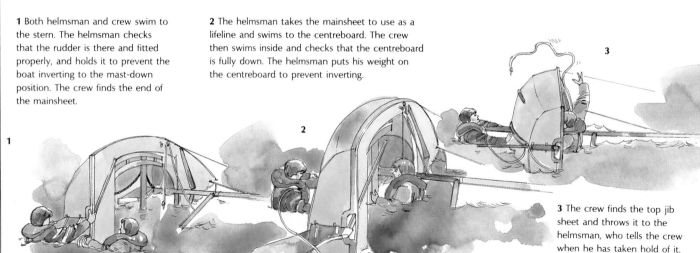

quickly the moment the boat capsizes. You don't need to lower the sails before righting the boat when using this method, but contact and cooperation between you and your crew is essential—so tell your companion exactly what you want to do so that he or she can help you.

The first task is to get your crew to move to the stern, to hold and twist the rudder so as to prevent the boat inverting to the mast-down position.

Then you can swim around the boat to grasp the centreboard or daggerboard protruding through the bottom of it. By pulling down on the board, or lying on top of it, you can prevent the boat inverting. In rough seas, take the mainsheet with you (or have it passed to you by the crew) for use as a safety line.

Once the boat is stable, the crew swims into the boat, finds the jib sheet which is on the high side, and throws it over to you. Having done that, the crew lies face down inside

the flooded boat, head facing forward and knees and arms resting on the lower side of the boat.

Now you can begin to right the boat. Climb onto the board, using the jib sheet as a climbing aid, then stand close to the root of the board (the part nearest the boat) and grasp the rope firmly. It's important to stand near the root of the board, because although you would get more leverage by standing near the tip of it, you would also risk breaking it.

Pull hard on the jib sheet while leaning well back with your knees slightly bent; a jerky motion will help to 'unstick' the sails from the water. As the boat rotates to an upright position the crew will be scooped up inside it.

If you judge the moment correctly, you can climb in as the boat reaches the vertical. If you end up back in the water, your crew can haul you in. When the boat is upright and both of you are safely

aboard, use a bucket to bail or sluice the water out of it.

A completely inverted boat can be brought back to the horizontal by both of you placing your feet on the same gunwale. One of you pulls on the centreboard while the other moves aft to sink the corner of the transom. The boat will slowly rotate to the horizontal, and then it can be righted by the scoop method.

'Man overboard!' is a cry that skippers dread to hear. In a two-person boat, the one remaining crew has to act quickly to bring the boat under control and swing immediately into a well-rehearsed sequence.

The standard dinghy pick-up sequence involves sailing away and returning on a reach, turning on to a broad reach just prior to turning toward the wind to stop alongside the casualty.

In practice, this manoeuvre can cause considerable difficulty to all but the most experienced sailor, so

concentrate on a number of key points.

Keep glancing back at the person in the water. Let the jib sheets go so that the jib flaps out to show where the wind is, and double check that you are sailing at 90 degrees to the wind. Control the boat speed with the main, and ensure that the centreboard is between threequarters down and fully down. Never go more than 50 metres from the casualty.

Tack firmly so that the boat turns through 180 degrees, and adjust your course to be about two boatlengths downwind at a point 45 degrees from the casualty. Round up slowly so that you can stop with the casualty amidships.

Slide forward, still holding the tiller extension and giving it a flick to windward as you make contact with the man overboard. Hold on with both hands until the boat finds its natural drift position and then haul the person back into the boat.

MAN-OVERBOARD DRILL

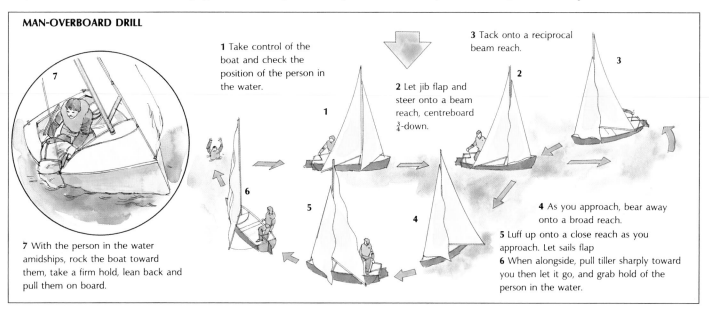

1 Take control of the boat and check the position of the person in the water.

2 Let jib flap and steer onto a beam reach, centreboard $\frac{3}{4}$-down.

3 Tack onto a reciprocal beam reach.

4 As you approach, bear away onto a broad reach.

5 Luff up onto a close reach as you approach. Let sails flap

6 When alongside, pull tiller sharply toward you then let it go, and grab hold of the person in the water.

7 With the person in the water amidships, rock the boat toward them, take a firm hold, lean back and pull them on board.

4 The crew lies in the boat, facing forward and floating above the submerged side deck, and tells the helmsman when he is in position.

5 The helmsman climbs onto the centreboard, using the jib sheet for support and keeping his weight near the hull. He rights the boat (which scoops up the crew) by leaning back and pulling hard on the jib sheet, jerking it to unstick the sails.

6 The helmsman climbs into the boat as it rights; he and the crew quickly bail out the water.

SAILING SMALL CATAMARANS

Catamarans derive their stability from the span of their slim hulls. On a 2-metre wide craft, the weight of trapezing crew can be 2.5 metres to windward of the immersed leeward hull, exerting a considerable righting movement to counteract the capsizing pull of the sails.

The typical catamaran has a pair of hulls joined by two aluminium beams that are firmly bolted or attached to each hull, and a sheet of sailcloth or a length of close-weave netting forms a 'trampoline' between the two beams and inside edges of the hull. To prevent damage and to simplify production, most hulls have integral keels to eliminate the need for daggerboards or centreboards.

Rudders are sophisticated assemblies designed to lock down while sailing but which spring up if in contact with an obstruction. A tiller bar joins the two rudders, so that both move when the bar is steered.

Hulls are usually made of GRP, but notable exceptions include the Catapult, which is an inflatable, and the French F1 Hurricane which, being made of moulded polyethylene, is a robust knockabout craft ideal for training and family sailing.

Masts and sails have been specially developed to withstand the heavy shock-loadings associated with the high speeds attained by multihulls. Masts are mounted on pivots for easy rotation, and most are fitted with a fixed set of diamond shrouds to ensure a rigid structure.

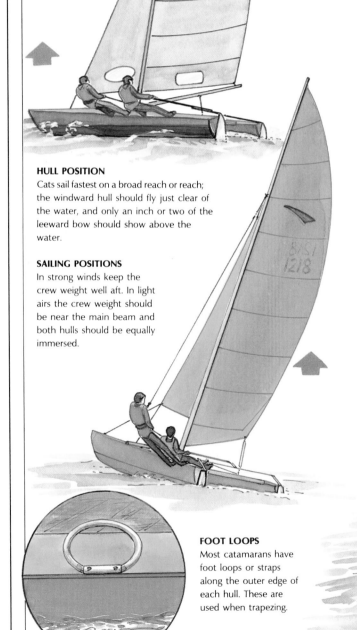

HULL POSITION
Cats sail fastest on a broad reach or reach; the windward hull should fly just clear of the water, and only an inch or two of the leeward bow should show above the water.

SAILING POSITIONS
In strong winds keep the crew weight well aft. In light airs the crew weight should be near the main beam and both hulls should be equally immersed.

FOOT LOOPS
Most catamarans have foot loops or straps along the outer edge of each hull. These are used when trapezing.

RIGHTING SMALL CATAMARANS
Push down on one end of the hull lying in the water to bring the uppermost hull down and swing the hulls into a vertical position. Then swim around to the mast side and push the boat over into its normal position.

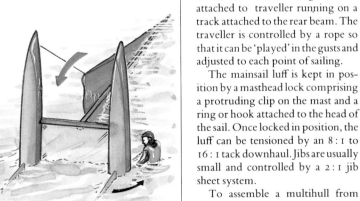

Sails are fully battened at about 1-metre intervals to give an almost rigid, preshaped aerofoil for the wind to act on. Booms, where fitted, are square-sectioned and strong. At the front end a mast 'spanner' determines the amount of overrotation of the mast.

The 8 : 1 to 16 : 1 mainsheet is, in effect, the boom vang, and is attached to traveller running on a track attached to the rear beam. The traveller is controlled by a rope so that it can be 'played' in the gusts and adjusted to each point of sailing.

The mainsail luff is kept in position by a masthead lock comprising a protruding clip on the mast and a ring or hook attached to the head of the sail. Once locked in position, the luff can be tensioned by an 8 : 1 to 16 : 1 tack downhaul. Jibs are usually small and controlled by a 2 : 1 jib sheet system.

To assemble a multihull from scratch you need a very good set of instructions or the assistance of someone who has done it before.

away, gradually tightening up the turn as the boat heads up into the wind. Flick the tiller extension into the water behind the mainsheet and move across the boat, picking the extension up on the other side and being sure to keep the rudders turned to their fullest travel. As soon as the mainsail sets on the new tack, centralize the rudders and sail off on the new tack.

If a jib is fitted, the crew should briefly let it out as the tack commences, then sheet it in again on the same side to back it and help the turn. As soon as the new tack is reached, the jib is released from its backed position and sheeted in on the new tack.

It should be noted that each different design has different handling characteristics when tacking. The position of the crew weight is often critical during the tack and you should start by moving weight after as the boat begins its turn.

Catamarans are noted for their high speed, and the correct attitude for high-speed sailing is to have the windward hull flying just clear of the water. Trim the leeward hull so that only about one or two inches of the bow are showing.

In very strong winds, especially when reaching in waves, there is a very real danger of driving the boat under, so keep the crew weight as far aft as possible. In very light airs, get the crew weight as near the main beam as possible, with both hulls immersed to the same degree.

If you have the misfortune to capsize, you need to act quickly to right the boat because catamarans will invert easily. A small catamaran, such as a Dart, can be righted by bringing the bows or sterns down until the boat is vertical.

To do this, you and your crew swim around to one end of the lower hull, and push down on it to bring the end of the uppermost hull down toward the water. As the end of the uppermost hull drops, grasp it and pull down on it with all your weight, while your crew pushes up midway along the lower hull. This will bring the boat to a vertical position in the water.

Now you both swim to the mast side of the boat, push it over into its normal sailing position and climb aboard immediately, before it sails off on its own.

To right a larger boat, pass a jib sheet over the uppermost hull while your crew steadies the lower one. Grab the jib sheet and stand on the keel of the lower hull, leaning back so that your weight pivots the uppermost hull around the lower one and down to the water.

When you've assembled and rigged it, put it on a padded, two-wheeled axle to trundle it into the water.

Hoist the mainsail without the mainsheet attached, and tension both jib and mainsail to suit the weather conditions. Once afloat, sail the boat into deeper water before attaching the mainsheet and fixing the rudders in their locked-down position. Baggy sails are bad news to beginners and experienced sailors alike, so always pull the sails in tight and adjust the boom angle with the traveller.

Acceleration and deceleration forces cause crews to be thrown backward and forward, so it's important that trapezing crews lock their feet into toestraps, where fitted, or use the skipper as an anchorage. Some catamarans are fitted with clip-on stern lines which prevent trapezing crews from being thrown forward.

The fastest points of sailing are the reach and broad reach. When sailing these points, keep the crew weight

Top The crew of a Tornado using a trapeze during the 1988 Olympics.
Above At high speeds the windward hull should just clear of the water.

well aft to prevent the leeward bow nosediving and initiating a barrel roll to leeward.

Catamarans are very manoeuverable, as you will find if you gybe to turn during the early stages of learning to sail one. The fully-battened sail allows you to turn downwind, slow down and gybe off onto a broad reach.

Tacking requires more finesse. From a close-hauled position, choose the right time to tack into the waves. Push the tiller bar gently

CRUISER RIGGING

of the waterline length of the boat. Headsails are large and powerful in contrast to the small mainsail, which acts as a secondary aerofoil.

The fractional rig places the mast farther forward in the boat. The mainsail is larger than that of a masthead rig and provides much of the drive. The rig is termed 'fractional' because the headsails emerge seven-eighths or three-quarters of the way from the base of the mast – hence 'seven-eighths rig' or 'three-quarter rig'.

Ketches and schooners have shorter masts and smaller sails in an attempt to make sail handling easier, but recent developments in self-stowing headsails and mainsails make for easy sail handling on other rigs and leave new multi-masted boats in a specialized custom market.

As with dinghies, the standing rigging of stainless steel wire keeps the masts in place. Cruisers are usually rigged with oversize wire to ensure long life and a large safety factor over the designed safe working load.

In older boats the shrouds and forestay will be attached with metal fittings called tangs, but new masts have captive T-bars or ball-and-socket arrangements which are inside the mast section. At the bottom ends of the shrouds and fore-

Left *Tensioning the boom vang, which with the mainsheet controls the shape of the mainsail.*
Below left *Tensioning the backstay.*
Below *A headsail furling system.*

The cruiser market is made up of a small percentage of wooden boats and a large percentage of glassfibre boats, some new but most second-hand and up to about twenty years old.

As with cars and motorcycles, cruising sailboats reflect the development of equipment in the racing sector. The potential buyer is, therefore, faced with a wide variety of rigs and hull shapes reflecting developments over past years.

If you buy a used boat (or if your existing boat is beginning to show its age) you can update the rigging to get better performance, but only to a point beyond which wholesale redesign work will be needed to produce any further improvement. However, there are many ways of improving the performance of an older design without resort to drastic surgery.

The basic rigs of modern cruisers are *masthead*, *fractional*, *ketch* and *schooner*. The masthead rig places the mast just forward of the middle

CRUISER RIGGING

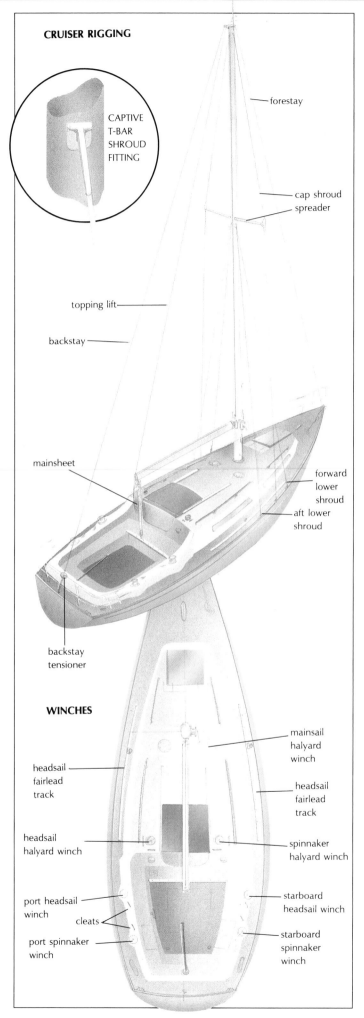

CAPTIVE T-BAR SHROUD FITTING

forestay

cap shroud

spreader

topping lift

backstay

mainsheet

forward lower shroud

aft lower shroud

backstay tensioner

WINCHES

headsail fairlead track

headsail halyard winch

port headsail winch

cleats

port spinnaker winch

mainsail halyard winch

headsail fairlead track

spinnaker halyard winch

starboard headsail winch

starboard spinnaker winch

---

stay, adjustable rigging screws are attached by clevis pins to toggles which act as universal joints to prevent metal fatigue.

In addition to the forestay, there is a backstay leading from the masthead to the stern and usually terminating in a mechanical or hydraulic backstay tensioner to control the forestay tension for upwind and downwind sailing.

All owners of cruising boats should be aware that many boatyards do not 'tune' the rig of cruising boats but usually step the mast and tighten the rigging on a 'that's about right' basis. Any mast which is not tuned will drastically affect the performance of the boat.

Basic tuning is not difficult, though, and even the least mechanically-minded owner can ensure that the mast is upright when viewed from the side and does not lean when viewed from ahead. A mast with more than one set of spreaders must be sighted up the after edge to ensure that no S-bends exist in it.

Most masts are raked aft a little, and you can check the rake by attaching a heavy weight to the main halyard. With the boat in normal trim, measure the distance from the back of the mast to the centre of the weight. Anything from 9 to 18 inches is normal. Raking the mast forward decreases weather helm (the boat's tendency to turn into the wind all the time), and raking it back increases it.

Also check that the mast does not lean to one side. If it does, adjust the rigging screw of each main or cap shroud (the ones that go to the highest point of the mast) until the mast is vertical. Any further adjustment of the screws to increase or decrease shroud tension must be equal on both sides, or else the mast will lean again.

To get the S-bends out of a multi-spreader rig, first ease the backstay and main shrouds. Then ease the intermediate shrouds, which lead to the base of the spreaders. Sighting up the back of the mast, adjust the lower set of spreader shrouds until they are just tight. Then adjust the next set to the same tension. Once the mast is straight all further tensioning must be done in pairs until all shrouds are very tight.

The shrouds should be tensioned enough to keep the mast secure in the boat when it is heeled to 20 degrees. At that angle, the leeward shrouds will just begin to show a little slackness but will not flap.

The principal cruising development in the last decade has been the development of effective, efficient and reliable headsail roller reefing systems. The principle has been around since the early 1900s, but has only recently been developed

for universal use.

A metal or plastic tube, grooved to accept the leading edge of the sail, is placed over the existing headstay, and when this tube is rotated the sail is wound around it and so reefed or furled (reefing is adjusting the amount of sail to suit the wind strength, and furling is rolling the sail up completely when you have finished sailing). At the tube's top end is a captive fitting containing a ball race which ensures that the tube rotates smoothly when the bottom fitting, consisting of another bearing and a rope or wire drum, is rotated by the control rope.

If buying a system from new, get one with two sail grooves to enable you to change sails without having to lower the sail in use before the other is set.

A parallel development is that of in-mast and in-boom mainsail furling systems, which simplify reefing the mainsail without too great a loss in performance. Self-tailing winches for the control lines make the use of sail furling and reefing systems even easier.

If your boat has the traditional hanked-on headsails, you can ease the task of headsail changing by replacing the standard cylindrical sailbag with a flat, zipped bag which accepts a folded headsail. This attaches to the lifelines or the toe rail for hoisting and packing.

It is *essential* for all cruisers to have netting or criss-crossed cord between the toe rail and lifelines from the pulpit to the mast to prevent sails being blown or washed overboard. In addition, permanent sail ties or elastic cords tied to the lower lifelines help control a sail as soon as it is lowered.

Running rigging is reasonably straightforward. Headsails are controlled by sheets which lead from the sail through adjustable fairleads to turning blocks and the winch. The position of the fairlead is critical to the performance of the sail, and this is especially so with roller reefing headsails. As a guide, the sheet should always be pulling equally on the foot and the leech of the sail.

This is achieved when a line drawn at right angles to the luff of the sail passes through the clew and continues along the pull of the sheet. If the sheet is too far back (a common fault), the leech is too loose and will flap. If it is too far forward, the leech is too tight and the sail will be too baggy.

The mainsheet, working in conjunction with the boom vang, controls the position of the sail relative to the wind. Many cruisers have mainsheet travellers which enable the mainsheet to be eased quickly in gusts or when running.

CRUISER SAIL HANDLING

Sail handling is greatly simplified if the sail stowage is properly organized. This involves ensuring that each sail has an easily accessible stowage point, that each sail bag is labelled with the type and number of the sail it contains (for example 'No. 2 Jib') and that the sail has been bagged correctly so that all corners are easily identified as soon as the bag is opened.

Many owners ensure that the tack, clew and head of each sail are tied in with the drawstring of its bag so that no amount of mishandling will dislodge them.

If you sail at night, tactile identification helps you to locate the sail you want. This can take the form of holes punched into a tag, or thick layers of tape around the drawcord or bottom strap of the bag.

Identification of the corners and sides of the sail often eases the job of newly-recruited crews and so speeds packing and hoisting. Many sailmakers stamp the corners and fix a coloured tape to the foot or leech, but if your sails lack these identification aids you can easily mark them yourself.

Roller headsails are often left on the headstay for long periods in the absence of the owner. The sail is then not covered by storm damage insurance, and the sailcloth is vulnerable to the damaging effects of the ultraviolet component of sunlight.

If your furling headsail can be removed easily it should be stowed away and not hoisted until you next sail. The headfoil should be secured with a triangular sailcloth which slots into the foil and which sheets down to the deck.

To rig a conventional mainsail from scratch, first feed the foot of the sail onto the boom by sliding the clew from front to back. Depending on the design, the foot will either fit into a groove on the top of the boom or run on plastic slugs or metal sliders over a metal track.

At the inboard end, the tack of the sail will be secured by a tack pin or shackle; at the outboard end it will either be lashed to the boom or, more probably, shackled to an adjustable clew outhaul which tensions the foot to match wind strengths.

During hoisting, check that the battens are securely fastened into their pockets. The usual arrangement uses offset batten pockets which ensure that the battens are securely anchored. If they have to be tied in, use a double reef knot.

Before hoisting the sail, first hoist the topping lift by about a foot to ensure that the weight of the boom does not interfere with the hoisting sequence, and then loosen the mainsheet.

Release the main halyard and attach it, usually by captive or snap shackle, to the headboard. What follows depends on whether your mast is fitted with an external metal track which takes metal sliders, an internal track which takes plastic slugs or sliders, or the conventional mast section which takes the bolt rope.

As you hoist the sail, check that the reefing lines are rove (inserted) in the correct order. Each reefing line should be a different colour – for instance green, orange and red – for increasing degrees of wind strength. Alternatively, if you have fewer reefing lines than reefs you should have thin 'messenger' line of elasticated cord rigged in a continuous loop through the top two leech reefing cringles.

Once the sail is hoisted, tension the halyard until a vertical crease appears in the luff. Then ease the topping lift until the boom tensions the sail, and tension the boom vang to give the leech a firm appearance.

Once you are sailing, you can tell when the sail is set correctly for the wind speed because at that point the vertical luff crease will disappear. If horizontal creases develop in the luff, re-tension the halyard or use the Cunningham tackle to remove the creases.

In strong winds, increase the backstay tension to pull the masthead to the rear. This will make the mast bend forward in the middle and so help to flatten the sail. Downwind, and in light airs, the backstay should be eased to allow the forestay to sag and the masthead to move forward. This will remove any tension on the sail and enable it to fill properly.

Headsails which have to be hanked on to the forestay require crew members to work in the most exposed and dangerous part of the boat. For this reason, even in the quietest conditions they should get into the habit of wearing safety harnesses that clip onto the wire or tape jackstays, rigged lines provided for that purpose.

Headsails should be folded and packed so that when the bag is opened, the three corners are at the top. On opening the bag, the crew first attach the tack to the tack fitting, which may be a shackle, pin or ram's horn. They then attach the sheets to the clew with as neat a bowline as possible. Preferably with the sail still in the bag the hanks, usually the piston type, are clipped to the forestay starting from the tack and working up to the head.

When the time comes to hoist the headsail, shackle the halyard to the head and pull the sail bag off the sail. Pull the leeward sheet to distribute the sail along the side deck prior to hoisting.

Once again, tension the halyard to create a vertical crease in the luff. When the sail is sheeted correctly with the sheet lead in the correct position, check that there are no creases in the luff. If horizontal creases develop, or the sail is scalloped between piston hanks, release the sheet and tighten the halyard until they disappear.

Changing sails while on the move should be done to suit the safety and working conditions of the foredeck crew, who should work out a plan of action with the skipper. If conditions are bad, the skipper should place the boat on a broad reach to ensure safer working conditions.

Firstly, the new sail should be set up on the windward (weather) rail so that the redundant sheet can be tied on and the sheet lead correctly positioned at its pre-marked point.

The old sail should be lowered and then stowed below through the fore or main hatch, lashed to the rail, or bagged by one crew member

Slugs or sliders ensure that the sail does not escape during hoisting or lowering.

The mainsail can be taken up by hand at first, and winched when it gets too heavy.

The mainsail should be tensioned until a vertical crease appears in the luff.

while the other hanks on the new sail. Tack the boat so that the new jib can be hoisted and set. The other sheet can then be attached.

Roller reefing headsails give crews a much safer ride, and this is especially important when family crews are sailing quite small boats over long distances. However, every skipper using a reefing headsail system must have a spare headsail which can be set if the system fails or the sail is blown out and cannot be lowered. An old No. 3 jib with a wire luff added is usually sufficient, as it will cover a wide range of windspeeds.

All flying headsails, such as spinnakers, should be set and lowered while a headsail is set on the forestay. This prevents the dreaded 'forestay wrap' – when the flying headsail wraps around the forestay – which can immobilize a boat. The headsail on the forestay is lowered once the flying headsail is set.

Cruising boats also use asymmetrical flying headsails such as cruising chutes and gennekars, often with handling devices designed to offer more control during hoisting and lowering.

The symmetrical spinnaker is a more effective sail because it operates through a greater range of angles to the wind. Its bad reputation stems from early unstable designs and aft sheeting positions which gave rise to wild broaches.

Sheeting systems have been simplified to single sheets, leading aft and running through a floating block controlled by a line running through a toe rail-mounted snatch block in the vicinity of the shrouds. This basic 'Barber hauler' system originated in dinghies, and enables the spinnaker to be pinned down forward of the beam for strong wind conditions, so preventing severe rolling.

Control of the spinnaker during hoisting is easily achieved by 'rubber banding' it: the sail is passed through a bottomless plastic bucket which has rubber bands stretched around it so that they can be slipped off the bucket and around the sail at intervals of 3 feet. The sail is packed in its bag or 'turtle' so that the head is at the front and the clews are on their correct sides.

The spinnaker is hoisted from the rail midway between mast and pulpit or from a pulpit-mounted turtle. To prepare for spinnaker hoisting on a cruiser, steer the boat onto a broad reach, rig the spinnaker bag or turtle, and then rig the spinnaker sheets securely to their appropriate clews.

Place the windward sheet in the spinnaker pole and attach the pole uphaul/downhaul, then hoist the pole so that it is parallel with the deck.

Lightly tension the sheet and guy before loading them onto the winches (preferably self-tailing) and cleating off. Hoist the sail quickly, being certain that it reaches the top by having a clear mark on the halyard.

Sheet the guy so that the sail is pulled to the pole end, and cleat the guy so that the pole is midway between the forestay and shroud. Haul in the sheet so that the rubber bands break and the sail fills. Once the spinnaker is under control, lower the forestay headsail to the deck but have it ready for instant hoisting. The spinnaker is correctly set when the pole is adjusted so that the two clews are level and the windward edge gently 'breathes' by collapsing rhythmically throughout its length.

To lower a spinnaker, first hoist the genoa and steer onto a broad reach. Place a rope over the leeward sheet to ensure that it can be reached to pull it in, and check that the halyard is free to run out without snagging. Ease the pole to the forestay, and release the windward clew from the guy using the tape tail fixed to the snap shackle.

Release the halyard and let it out rapidly. At the same time, pull the sail under the boom from the main cockpit hatch so that it goes into the saloon. Tidy up the sheets and halyard for the next session prior to packing the spinnaker away in rubber bands.

Above *Spinnakers should be set while a headsail is set on the forestay. Once the spinnaker is set, the headsail can be lowered.*
Below *When not in use, headsails can be stowed along the lifelines.*

HANDLING UNDER POWER

The majority of cruising boats are fitted with powerful, efficient diesel engines which, if regularly maintained, give good service. More engine problems occur because of lack of regular use than from abuse or heavy use.

User controls have been standardized to a single lever that selects forward (ahead), neutral and reverse (astern) gears and, when used in conjunction with forward and reverse gears, also controls the engine speed. This single lever has made handling under power a much more precise skill than it was in the days of individual gear and throttle levers.

The diesel is designed to be used in a robust manner and manufacturers take account of this when matching drive trains and propellers to specific engines. Cruiser propellers vary considerably in size, shape and format, from the three-bladed, fixed propeller through the streamlined, folding props of racing boats to the variable-pitch propeller of the heavy cruising yacht.

Whatever its size or shape, though, every propeller will produce a sideways turning force which affects the handling characteristics of a yacht. This effect is known as *prop walk* or the *paddle wheel effect*, as the blades bite into the water to produce forward (or reverse) thrust, they also create a sideways thrust.

If a propeller, when viewed from astern, is rotating clockwise, it will tend to swing the stern of the boat to the right. A skipper whose boat is fitted with a right-hand prop (one that turns clockwise when the boat is in forward gear) will know that the shortest turning circle in forward gear is to the left (port), because the back of the boat is kicked to the right by the prop, and this assists the action of the rudder. When going astern, the shortest turning circle will again be to the port side of the boat, because the prop will then be pulling the back to the left.

Knowing the direction of rotation or 'handing' of the prop enables you to use engine revs to advantage. If your boat has a right-hand prop, and you are turning it to port in a confined space, you can use sharp bursts of forward power to kick the stern to the right, interspersed by gentle use of reverse power to stop the boat in preparation for the next forward burst.

You continue this forward/reverse/forward sequence – keeping the tiller or wheel hard over throughout – until the turn is complete. To turn the boat to starboard, use sharp bursts of reverse power interspersed with gentle applica-

tions of forward power to achieve the best results.

If you keep forgetting which way your prop turns, put a little drawing near the controls showing its rotation in ahead (forward) with an arrow below to show the direction of prop walk.

As well as being affected by the rotation of the propeller, the direction of travel of the boat is influenced by the wind acting on the hull. All boats assume a specific *wind rode* angle to the wind, with the bow tending to drift downwind. Except when under sail, the wind acting on the hull and masts will work to push the boat to this angle.

Under power, the high sides and cabins of a cruiser will assist or hamper a turn depending on whether the boat is turning away from or toward the wind, so knowing how your boat drifts is important when you are considering a turn in strong winds. Any turn toward the wind will produce a wider, slower turn, and any turn away from the wind will produce a tighter, faster turn.

Above *An engine can be very useful in very light winds.*
Left *Engine controls have been simplified to single levers.*
Top right *Manoeuvring in crowded areas is better done under power than under sail.*

You can use these effects of the wind to help you manoeuvre, but if you are unsure of how your boat is affected by the wind, before handling it in a confined space practise turning it in open water.

Tidal movement is another variable affecting boat handling and it can also often be used to advantage. Once you have determined the tide's direction, you can face into it and match its speed so as to remain stationary.

Only in exceptional circumstances should you approach a stationary object by moving *with* the tide. This is because you will have to use reverse gear to stop or stay in position alongside the object, and in reverse most boats handle poorly and are notoriously difficult

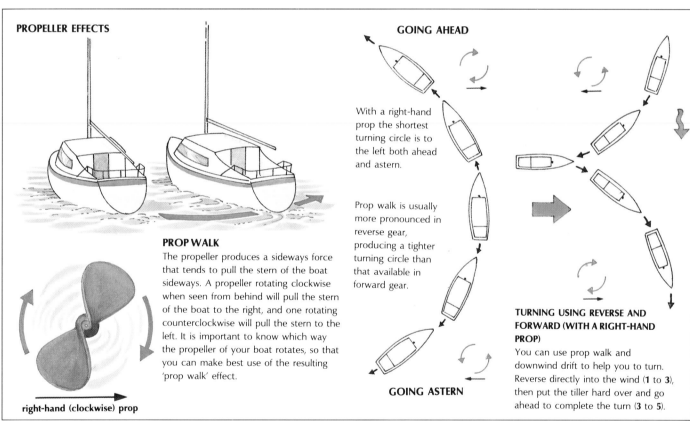

PROPELLER EFFECTS

PROP WALK

The propeller produces a sideways force that tends to pull the stern of the boat sideways. A propeller rotating clockwise when seen from behind will pull the stern of the boat to the right, and one rotating counterclockwise will pull the stern to the left. It is important to know which way the propeller of your boat rotates, so that you can make best use of the resulting 'prop walk' effect.

right-hand (clockwise) prop

GOING AHEAD

With a right-hand prop the shortest turning circle is to the left both ahead and astern.

Prop walk is usually more pronounced in reverse gear, producing a tighter turning circle than that available in forward gear.

GOING ASTERN

TURNING USING REVERSE AND FORWARD (WITH A RIGHT-HAND PROP)

You can use prop walk and downwind drift to help you to turn. Reverse directly into the wind (**1** to **3**), then put the tiller hard over and go ahead to complete the turn (**3** to **5**).

to steer accurately. Additionally, many engine/prop combinations do not produce sufficient power in reverse gear to combat a strong tide.

Your boat's speed should always be regulated to the minimum needed to complete the task in hand efficiently, but beware of being over-cautious and moving too slowly, because then you might not be able to counteract the effects of the wind or tide.

Picking up or releasing a mooring should be done carefully so that the crew member never has to take any weight on the mooring strop. Similarly, when coming alongside, the

whole boat should cover the last few feet moving sideways so that crew members can jump out and fix their mooring lines with the minimum of fuss and without having to fight the weight of the moving boat.

The momentum of a boat is enormous. It may weigh 3 to 4 tons or more, and even when moving at half a knot it can cause considerable damage if it hits a solid object. Large, well-secured fenders, set low for coming alongside pontoons or high for walls, should be generously arranged on the side which is expected to make contact. One or two large fenders, in the hands of

experienced crew members, should be kept in reserve for unexpected problems.

Gaining confidence in handling under power requires a period of concentrated practice, preferably under the guidance of a competent instructor or experienced boat handler. Without tuition, the average weekend sailor will probably continue to repeat mistakes rather than gain experience.

Whenever a boat is under power, it is the guy at the controls who determines what will happen, and proper management of the boat and its crew is vital for successful dock-

ing, mooring or anchoring. All ropes, warps and fenders must be prepared well in advance, and the crew must know their individual tasks, for instance to jump ashore with both warps and secure the one which will prevent the boat drifting away with the tide or wind.

Similarly the operational maintenance of the engine is the skipper's responsibility. Unlike an automobile engine, the marine diesel needs to be given a series of checks before, during and after use, to minimize the chances of something going wrong when the boat is away from shore.

LEAVING & BERTHING

The advent of marinas, with their finger berth pontoons placed at right angles to the main catwalks, has resulted in the need for some very close-quarter boat handling under power when leaving or entering them. In such situations, a proper understanding of the use of warps to assist in turning in confined spaces goes a long way toward preventing the wind or the tide taking control.

Every member of the crew must understand what is going to happen and what is expected of them. Leaving your permanent berth with a crew of non-sailing friends is the severest test of your ability to handle your boat in a confined space: either you know you can do it yourself with the minimum of help or you will have to brief your crew thoroughly.

The first thing they should learn is to look at you when they are speaking, so that you will hear clearly what disaster is about to happen. The second thing is that situations change quickly and they must always be listening for new instructions – you shouldn't have to shout at them to attract their attention before giving them instructions.

The majority of marina berths enable two boats to occupy each section. This gives a little manoeuvring space and enables you to use your neighbour to assist if the wind or the tide are pressing you onto your finger berth.

When leaving a berth, you should use warps to windward or uptide to check drift or assist your turn. You may have to send a crew member, with a warp, to a boat on the adjacent set of pontoons so that you can haul your boat astern, particularly if the wind is blowing strongly from astern. Aim to collect the crew member at a more accessible point on the marina, such as at the fuel berth.

The general plan is to reverse out of your berth, turn on to your desired exit course, change into forward gear and leave the marina.

Assume that you are moored with bow, stern and breast ropes, and bow and aft springs (a bow spring is a mooring rope led forward from the stern, an aft spring is one led aft from the bow). With the engine running and the boat prepared for sea, two of your crew members go ashore.

They first set up a warp which leads from the stern to the bollard/-cleat/ring on the end of the pontoon, and back to the stern. This is referred to as *singling-up* a warp, and it enables the warp to be retrieved by a crew member on board as soon as it has done its job. The on-shore crew then release the bow, stern and breast ropes, steadying the boat with their hands, and prepare to release the springs.

You should now be ready to leave as soon as the springs are cast off by the on-shore crew. After releasing the springs, they push the boat away from the pontoon and guide it astern as you engage astern. As they jump on, they push the boat away some more.

The stern warp is kept under control by a crew member under instructions from you. To use it to turn the boat, the crew takes a turn around the cleat and hauls it tight, easing out a bit at a time as the pull gets too great. The bow will be flicked out as the stern is held by the warp. During the turn, make sure that you always have sufficient space to manoeuvre in at both bow and stern.

As soon as the boat is facing in the new direction, you engage forward gear and the crew hauls in the rope as the strain decreases and the boat moves forward.

To kick the stern out prior to leaving the berth, a singled warp is attached from the bow to the end of the pontoon. You first push the tiller away from the pontoon and then, with short gentle bursts in forward gear, kick the stern out against the pull of the singled warp prior to cen-

Right Properly positioned fenders are essential, especially when boats are rafted up alongside others.

WARPS
All ropes used for mooring are known as warps, but when they are rigged in position they are given particular names:
(a) are bow and stern lines
(b) fore and aft breast ropes
(c) fore and aft springs.

PROTECTING WARPS
Warps are particularly prone to chafe where they go through fairleads or over the edges of quays. Threading a length of plastic tube on them gives good protection.

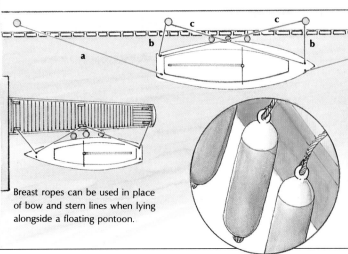

Breast ropes can be used in place of bow and stern lines when lying alongside a floating pontoon.

FENDERS
Fenders, which are made of plastic or sometimes of rope, are protective cushions hung over the side of a berthed boat from its grabrails or lifelines. They prevent the hull of the boat from making direct contact with the pontoon or quay or with another boat alongside.

Left *A typical yacht marina, with finger berth pontoons placed at right angles to the main catwalks.*

tering the tiller, engaging reverse and backing out prior to the turn. Then the warp is pulled aboard. Always use favourable winds or tide to assist your turns.

Returning to a marina berth has one advantage over leaving it, in that even a first-time crew now know a bit more about sailing and where everything goes.

As you approach, double-check that you are entering the section of the marina that contains your berth and that no-one else is in your space. Have all warps and fenders strategically placed, and brief the crew on what they have to do, especially those with 'wandering fenders' for unexpected contact with other users. Remember that it is often easier to go alongside your neighbour than the smaller finger pontoon, so have a few fenders ready on that side.

Your approach should 'test out' the wind and tide effects so that your final turn into the berth will take account of both. Place the boat well into your space so that a crew

member can jump ashore with the springs. Go astern to stop, being careful not to kick the stern out. Once the springs are secured, the breast ropes are attached followed by the usual berthing ropes. Often, owners have specially-protected permanent marina warps which are left attached to the pontoon. On return, these ropes are picked up and placed on their correct cleats or mooring posts.

When berthing at quaysides or long pontoons, you either have to raft up to previous arrivals or occupy a narrow space between them. First do a dummy run to assess wind and tide effects, usually by aiming straight at the quay or pontoon, then go around, prepare long bow and stern warps and plenty of fenders, and go alongside the chosen vessel or into the chosen space. Unless you are very experienced, never try mooring alongside with a strong following wind or tide unless you are certain that you can get a stern warp secured quickly.

Rafting alongside or mooring to a tidal quay requires a minimum of 50 metres of bow and stern warp to reach the shore and allow for rise and fall of tide.

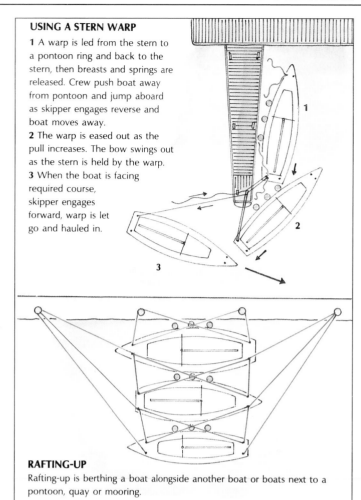

USING A STERN WARP

1 A warp is led from the stern to a pontoon ring and back to the stern, then breasts and springs are released. Crew push boat away from pontoon and jump aboard as skipper engages reverse and boat moves away.

2 The warp is eased out as the pull increases. The bow swings out as the stern is held by the warp.

3 When the boat is facing required course, skipper engages forward, warp is let go and hauled in.

RAFTING-UP

Rafting-up is berthing a boat alongside another boat or boats next to a pontoon, quay or mooring.

MOORING & ANCHORING

A mooring is a permanent anchorage where you keep your boat when it's not in use. It may be tidal, in which case the boat dries out twice a day, or deepwater, where the boat is afloat at all states of the tide. Anchoring is a temporary method of mooring your boat for reasons of safety or for convenience and comfort, such as for an overnight stop.

Mooring and anchoring involve the use of heavy gear, and you should handle this carefully to avoid permanent injury, especially to your back. The anchors and anchor chains on most cruising boats of up to 10 metres can be handled safely without winches, but on boats above 10 metres the weight of the anchors and chains makes the use of manual or electric anchor winches essential.

The working parts of a mooring are a large, spherical buoy that supports the weight of the heavy mooring chain, and a smaller buoy attached to the chain, wire or rope mooring strop that attaches the boat to the mooring.

When you moor your boat, lead the strop through the bow roller to a substantial cleat, bollard or sampson post, and cleat the lighter rope of the pick-up buoy over the strop to prevent it jumping off. Insert the bow roller pin to prevent the strop jumping out.

Before you leave a mooring, prepare your boat for the voyage. Choose the sails to suit the weather conditions, and run the engine to warm it up, even if you plan to leave under sail.

Ready the mooring by removing the pin from the bow fitting, uncleating the buoy line from the strop, and placing the buoy through the front of the pulpit and up over the guardrail so that it is free when the mooring is released.

In a tideway, check that the boat is wind rode and that hoisting the mainsail will not cause the boat to sail about wildly. Ready the headsail but keep it rolled, bagged and stowed on the rail.

Drop the mooring by uncleating the strop and then walking the boat forward by pulling on the mooring. Steer the boat away in an arc, sheet-ing in the main, and hoist the headsail when clear of obstructions. To back off under sail, push the boom into the wind.

To pick up the mooring under sail, first decide whether other moored boats are facing into the wind or tide, and then sail in – under mainsail, headsail or no sails – to position your boat to match those already moored. The secret of successful mooring is practice, plus a slow unhurried approach with a planned exit in case of emergencies. Have your engine running as a back-up.

Your boat should be equipped with two anchors which can be relied on to hold it securely in gale-force conditions. The main or 'bower' anchor should be the heavier of the two and should be matched to at least 50 metres of chain. Your second or 'kedge' anchor should have 6 metres of heavy chain and at least 100 metres of plaited or braided nylon anchor warp, preferably stored on a drum.

Chain must be carried for one anchor because it resists abrasion and its weight, combined with its catenary, acts as a spring in violent gale-force conditions. Stowing chain is a problem on modern boats, but a large plastic bin or box securely bolted inside a locker may be a good solution.

The end of the chain (the *bitter end*) must be secured to a strong eye-bolt with a rope lashing which can be cut in an emergency. Anchors must be securely stowed in their lockers to prevent structural damage in rough conditions.

When choosing an anchorage, check your tidal curves to ascertain the minimum depth at low tide. Make due allowances for boats already moored, especially if some are on rope and others on chain, because they will have vastly different swinging circles.

If anchoring with chain, flake about twice the depth onto the side decks, then lower the anchor to just above the surface and motor into the choosen position. Come to a stop facing into the wind and, as the bow blows off, lower the anchor to the seabed. Reverse away, letting out a

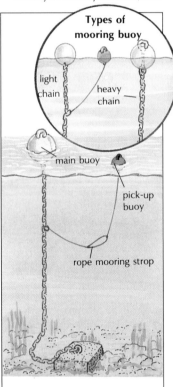

Types of mooring buoy

light chain

heavy chain

main buoy

pick-up buoy

rope mooring strop

MOORINGS

Moorings have three basic elements: a floating buoy, a chain and a sinker. They may simply have a ring on top to tie the boat to, or have a rope strop which can be secured to the boat. Some have a smaller pick-up buoy, attached to a ring on the chain to which the boat is tied.

TIDAL WATER

A moored boat will face either into the wind or into the tide, whichever is the stronger. A boat facing into the wind is said to be 'wind rode', and a boat facing into the tide is said to be 'tide rode'. When the effects of wind and tide are equal but opposite, a moored boat will line itself up at right angles to both, and is said to be 'across the wind'.

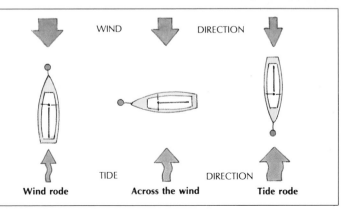

WIND DIRECTION

TIDE DIRECTION

Wind rode **Across the wind** **Tide rode**

length of chain about three times the high-tide depth of the water.

Check that the anchor has bitten and, when the boat has settled down, take anchor bearings to enable you to check for drift. Hoist a black ball in your forward rigging by day and replace it with an anchor light at night.

The kedge is used as a 'lunch hook' for short stays or as a second anchor when bad weather is expected from another direction. The classic example is during the passage of a cold front. In the Northern Hemisphere, when a cold front passes through, the wind veers from southwest through west to northwest, so the kedge should be motored, or laid by dinghy, in a northwesterly direction.

In the Southern Hemisphere, the wind backs from southeast through east to northeast during the passage of a cold front, so the kedge should be positioned to the northeast of the boat.

To retrieve two anchors, first pick up the kedge and then the main anchor.

ANCHORING

To find the minimum length (scope) of chain needed at an anchorage, multiply the depth at high water by three, and add extra length to allow for the distance from the windlass to the water. The weight of a chain causes it to hang down in a curve, known as a 'catenary'. Because rope isn't heavy enough to hang in a deep catenary, an anchor rope needs a longer scope (of at least five times the depth of water).

Once a boat is anchored, a black signal ball must be hoisted in the fore rigging, and at night this must be replaced by an anchor light.

The weight of an anchor alone is not enough to hold a boat: the anchor has to bite.

BITE

An anchor has bitten when it has dug into the bottom.

catenary

SCOPE

24 metres

8 metres

Above left *A typical mooring. The mooring strop runs from the bow of the boat to the underwater chain securing the mooring buoy.*

Above *Boats moored at buoys in a sheltered estuary. The boats are tide rode, facing into the incoming tide.*

BASIC CRUISER MANOEUVRES

The basic manoeuvres of tacking and gybing are essentially the same for cruisers as for dinghies, but the sail-handling gear is different and the manoeuvres take longer because a cruiser reacts more slowly than a dinghy.

Another difference is that winches have to be used to sheet in the headsail, because it is much larger than that of a dinghy. If your boat has self-tailing winches they can be operated by a single crew member, but if it has ordinary winches and you have sufficient crew, detail one to turn the winch and another to do the tailing. Tailing involves looping the sheet or halyard around the winch, and pulling on the end of it while the winch is being turned.

The procedures described here can be carried out by a skipper and one crew member, but if you have more than one crew you can divide the tasks among them, if you wish. For example, you could have one crew releasing the old headsail sheet and another handling the new one, or perhaps two handling the new one, with one of them tailing the winch and the other winding it if it isn't a self-tailer.

Before you begin to tack, your boat should be sailing fast and not too close to the wind, and you and your crew should double check that it is safe to tack and that you won't be obstructing other vessels when you do.

When you are ready to tack, call 'Ready about!' to inform the crew, who then uncleats the headsail sheet but does not ease it. Then call 'Lee-ho!' and push the tiller to leeward (or turn the wheel) to bring the bows round into the wind while the crew releases the headsail sheet.

As the sails move across to the other side of the boat, the crew should move across to take up the slack in the new headsail sheet and you should also change sides, keeping the tiller hard over. The crew now winches in the new headsail sheet to set it while you steer the boat onto its new course.

Gybing a cruiser is much simpler than gybing a small dinghy, because the larger boat is inherently more stable. Even so, you must maintain full control of the boat throughout the manoeuvre because the sails remain full and so they cross to the other side of the boat with some force. You must also, of course, check that it is safe for you to turn before you begin to manoeuvre.

With the boat on a broad reach, tell the crew you are about to gybe by calling 'Stand by to gybe!' The crew should ready the new headsail

sheet and take up the slack in it, and prepare to release the old one. Steer onto a dead run, and haul in the mainsheet to bring the end of the boom over the quarter (midway between the stern and the beam) so that it doesn't simply swing right across the boat.

Now call 'Gybe-ho!' and cross to the other side of the boat, changing hands on the tiller as you do. Let the boat turn until the sails begin to swing across to the other side, then stop the turn by centring the tiller and use the mainsheet to control the swing of the boom as it transfers to the other side.

The crew can now release the old headsail sheet and ease or winch in the new sheet to set the sail on the new side, while you steer the boat onto its new course and set the mainsail correctly.

The downwind performance of a cruiser can be improved by

Above At night, deck lights greatly assist foredeck work; otherwise, the simple mountaineer's head light can prove of great benefit to a crew member struggling in the dark.
Top Before you make any manoeuvre, check that it is safe to do so.

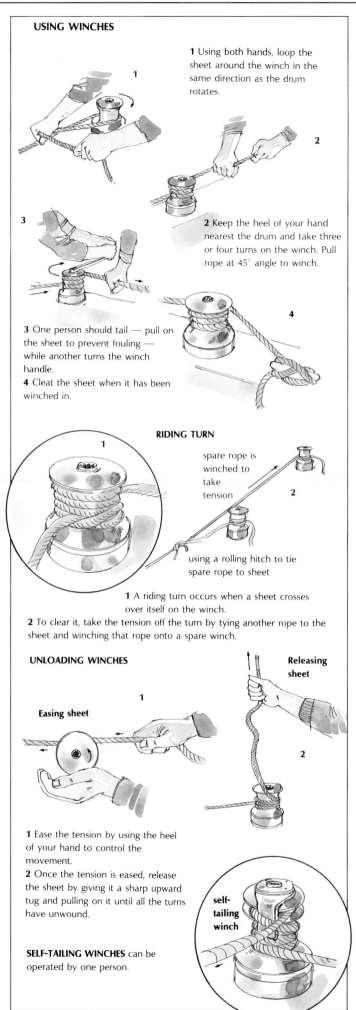

USING WINCHES

1 Using both hands, loop the sheet around the winch in the same direction as the drum rotates.

2 Keep the heel of your hand nearest the drum and take three or four turns on the winch. Pull rope at 45° angle to winch.

3 One person should tail — pull on the sheet to prevent fouling — while another turns the winch handle.
4 Cleat the sheet when it has been winched in.

RIDING TURN

spare rope is winched to take tension

using a rolling hitch to tie spare rope to sheet

1 A riding turn occurs when a sheet crosses over itself on the winch.
2 To clear it, take the tension off the turn by tying another rope to the sheet and winching that rope onto a spare winch.

UNLOADING WINCHES

Easing sheet

Releasing sheet

1 Ease the tension by using the heel of your hand to control the movement.
2 Once the tension is eased, release the sheet by giving it a sharp upward tug and pulling on it until all the turns have unwound.

SELF-TAILING WINCHES can be operated by one person.

self-tailing winch

using a cruising chute, a poled-out headsail or a spinnaker. Cruising chutes or poled-out headsails are usually preferable for family cruisers because they are much easier to handle than spinnakers.

You can gybe a cruising chute as you would a jib or genoa, if it has two sheets, but if it has only one then you will have to lower it before you gybe and reset it after. With a poled-out headsail, you remove the pole before the gybe and fit it on the new side after it.

To gybe the spinnaker, work on the principle of flying the sail without a pole so that it does not collapse. Ideally, only the mainsail should be swung across the boat to gybe, rather than the boat turned through a large arc.

Begin from a run, and with the pole set aft ease the uphaul/downhaul to enable the foredeck crew to move the pole. Prior to the gybe,

the foredeck crew should place the leeward genoa sheet over his or her shoulder to ensure that it ends up on top of the pole.

As the pole is eased forward the crew releases it from the guy, unclips the pole from the mast, clips the new guy to the pole and places the pole on the mast fitting.

This sequence is called *end-for-ending*. It's a complicated task, and the skipper and the crew handling the sheets and pole controls must give the foredeck crew plenty of time and space to complete it. Once the pole is secure, the sail is sheeted to the new course.

Racing crews use a *dip pole gybe* in which the pole remains attached to the mast. As the pole is eased forward and dipped to the deck, the foredeck crew releases the old guy and inserts the new one, then the pole is hoisted again. The mainsail is gybed during the manoeuvre.

CRUISER SAILING

Most sailboat skippers rely upon pilotage – the identification of landmarks and seamarks – while in familiar waters. This basic, easy-to-recall form of navigation frees them up to concentrate on their sailing and boathandling skills.

Except for the very few who use their boats for extended periods, the majority of owners are bound by schedules, even when taking a two- or three-week cruise. All too often, skippers opt for using the engine, not realizing that the boat will sail almost as fast if sailed properly. The term 'cruising boat' should not imply that it cannot sail well, given the right skipper.

Attention to the set of the sails on their spars, correct luff and foot tensions for the given wind conditions, and a basic concept of target speeds rather than closeness to the wind, go a long way to producing an efficient sailboat.

All displacement boats have a theoretical maximum hullspeed, which is related to the immersed waterline length. Designers incorporate hull features into their boats which increase waterline length when the boat is heeled, so as to increase the length of the wave created by the hull as it displaces the water.

Because the speed of a wave is governed by its length (the crest-to-crest distance), the length of the wave created by the hull dictates the speed of the yacht.

The formula for wave speed is 1.34 times the square root of the wavelength in feet. Therefore, the hullspeed of a 30-foot yacht with a static waterline of 25 feet will be 1.34 times the square root of $25 = 1.34 \times 5 = 6.7$ knots.

When the boat is heeled to about 20 degrees, the increased waterline length might give 7 knots as a maximum, and so the first fact which must be accepted is that no matter how much sail you put up, that boat will seldom exceed 7 knots.

Fit an inclinometer to show when you reach 20 degrees of heel; not only is this a reasonably comfortable working angle below, it also tells you that you have the correct amount of sail for the given windspeed. Obviously, in light airs the boat will be heeled less, but in such conditions the more upright the boat is the better, because you then need to reduce the wetted surface to reduce hydrodynamic drag on the hull.

To maintain maximum boat speed on all points of sailing you will need to either consult or construct a *speed polar* diagram for the principal points of sail – close-hauled, fetch (sailing close-hauled without tacking), close reach, beam reach, broad reach and run – for a given number of wind strengths, for example 6 knots, 10 kts, 16 kts, 21 kts, 27 kts and 33 kts. Sail combinations for each windspeed are shown on the left side of the diagram and are especially useful as a reminder of which sails are needed and how they should be reefed. It may take a season to complete the construction of a speed polar diagram for your boat, but it's a seamanlike exercise which will improve your sailing speed.

Another factor which seriously affects the speed of cruising boats is the sea state produced by the wind or the tide, or a combination of the two. Waves in coastal waters are usually short and steep and, remembering the formula used to find hull speed, a wave with a length of 4 feet will move at 2.68 knots. If you are sailing a 25-foot cruiser close-hauled you will be sailing against at least five of these oncoming waves at any one time.

To overcome the resistance of short, steep waves, change course to a fetch or a close reach to both increase the sail power and decrease the impact of the waves by meeting fewer crests at a greater angle.

The concept of having to reef the sails in strengthening winds is one readily accepted by racing crews, who appreciate that too much sail heels the boat excessively, slows it down, makes it difficult to steer, and is unnecessary.

Using 20 degrees of heel as a guide, start reefing if the boat repeatedly heels beyond 25 degrees and/or if the gusts turn the boat into the wind despite the application of opposite rudder.

With masthead rigs the headsails are the first to be changed or reefed. Fractional rigs start with a reduction in the area of the mainsail, while ketches douse their mizzens first.

The strategy for reefing any sailboat is four-fold: to maintain

Racing crews make good use of the extra hull speed that heeling can give them.

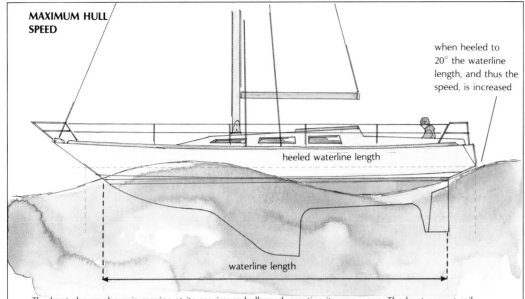

MAXIMUM HULL SPEED

when heeled to 20° the waterline length, and thus the speed, is increased

heeled waterline length

waterline length

The boat shown above is moving at its maximum hullspeed, creating its own wave. The boat cannot sail faster than the speed of this wave, and the wave's speed is governed by its length (crest-to-crest distance). In its turn, the wave's length depends on the waterline length of the boat's hull, and so this distance dictates the speed of the boat.

The formula for calculating the wave speed, and thus the maximum speed of the boat (in knots), is 1.34 times the square root of the boat's waterline length in feet. So for a 30-foot boat with a static waterline length of 25 feet, the maximum speed is $1.34 \times$ the square root of $25 = 1.34 \times 5 = 6.7$ knots.

Heeling the boat to about 20° might increase the waterline length enough to give a maximum speed of 7 knots.

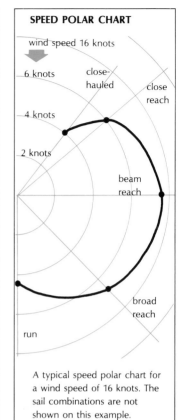

SPEED POLAR CHART

wind speed 16 knots

6 knots   close-hauled   close reach

4 knots

2 knots

beam reach

broad reach

run

A typical speed polar chart for a wind speed of 16 knots. The sail combinations are not shown on this example.

maximum hullspeed; to maintain an angle of heel; to retain the balance between headsails and mainsails so that the boat is not difficult to steer; and to keep the boat as comfortable and dry as possible below, given that circumstances may dictate a specific course of action.

In a progressively rising wind the degree of preparedness and organization of the boat begins to show through. For example, well-engineered furling and reefing systems continue to produce a headsail which is flat enough to drive the boat, and slab reefing systems pull down effective and secure reefs in the main without exposing the crew to unnecessary risks.

Fabric cockpit dodgers and main hatch pram hoods are substantial enough to prevent the ingress of water below. The cockpit is kept free of water by substantial cockpit drains which work even when the boat is well heeled, and bilge pumps operated from below and above deck have the capacity to clear large amounts of water. Down below, the stowage of all heavy items – batteries, anchors, chains, cans and so on – is such that nothing can be thrown out of its locker or stowage lashings even if the boat is knocked down flat.

All these considerations apply to every sailboat which cruises on exposed coastal or large inland

waters. Sudden squalls, often associated with thunderstorms or cold fronts, can produce wind and sea conditions bordering on storm force, often at very short notice.

The short-term answer to the sudden onset of very severe weather is to lower and lash all sails to 'lie a-hull' with the boat fully battened down – especially the main hatch

boards. Experienced skippers may want to keep a storm jib set and to sail off on a broad reach to keep the boat under control and to ride the waves as they rapidly increase in size. The main problem in such conditions is regulating boatspeed to a safe maximum due to the power of breaking crests and the steepness of the waves.

Heeling increases the waterline length of a boat and thus its maximum possible speed.

Heavy-weather strategy is a subject in its own right, and you should refer to some of the standard works on the subject just in case you ever get caught out in life-threatening conditions.

CRUISER EMERGENCY DRILLS

At sea, any potentially life-threatening situation must be treated as an emergency. Successful remedial action will downgrade it to an event, but unsuccessful action will result in the need for help.

The shock of the sudden onset of an emergency can be a mind-numbing experience. To deal with the emergency in a methodical, seamanlike manner, all crew members (and especially the skipper) must know where the emergency equipment is stowed and how to use it. A detailed stowage plan of all emergency equipment should be displayed in the saloon or pasted to the underside of a cockpit locker, and your responses to possible emergencies should have been thought out beforehand.

The VHF radio features prominently in emergency drills, because there are three internationally accepted states of emergency. 'Pan' and 'Securité' are advisory emergency calls, telling the outside world that you have a problem but not actually requesting help, while the third – 'Mayday' – is a call for immediate outside assistance.

It is far better to alert rescue agencies to a *possible* Mayday situation as the emergency develops, rather than to make a frantic Mayday call when the situation gets out

of control, and when you may be unable to give the essential information on who, where and what is involved. The emergencies you are most likely to encounter are man overboard, being holed or running aground, fire, and medical emergencies.

A man-overboard emergency can occur on any point of sail, or even at anchor, but it's always a real emergency and you must do everything and use everything – including daytime orange smoke, nighttime white flares or strobe (flashing) lights – to locate and rescue the person in the water.

The first essential is to mark the position of the man, woman or child overboard with a dan buoy with attached lifering, or orange smoke or strobe light, and assign a crew member to point at the man overboard.

The second is to stay as close as possible to that position while you get the boat under control to situate yourself for the pickup. The third is to make contact with the victim prior to rigging equipment to lift him or her from the water.

The reach-to-reach under sail man-overboard drill, which originated in the United States in the 1960s, assumes that the boat is not carrying spinnakers or boomed-out

headsails when the person falls overboard.

You first steer onto a beam reach for about ten boat-lengths, and then tack round onto a close reach to bring you back to the person in the water. Slow down by letting the headsail fly, and then heave-to to windward of the victim by letting the mainsail fly as well.

The worst-case situation is when you are sailing downwind with a spinnaker set. You then have either to ditch the spinnaker by letting the sheets and halyard run through their blocks, or to release the halyard for a 'float drop' and lash the spinnaker to the rail. Whichever option you choose, the person in the water will have a long wait before being picked up and so will need all the markers you can throw.

In all recovery situations you should lower and lash the headsail and pull all ropes inboard before using the engine to position the boat correctly for the pickup. You should try to make contact with the victim at the first attempt, preferably by throwing a rescue line with a buoy or weighted floating loop.

Thereafter the man overboard can be winched to the boat and hoisted aboard using the mainsheet or two halyards around two different winches. During the rescue,

Recovering a man overboard. The crew had to drop the spinnaker before turning the boat.

delegate a spare crew to issue a Securité call on Channel 16.

If at any time visual contact is lost for more than a minute, issue a Mayday call for outside assistance. It can always be cancelled if you locate the man overboard.

Floating debris such as drums or huge containers is an increasing passive hazard, while submarines and other vessels pose an active threat. A hole six inches across will sink a keelboat very quickly, giving the crew almost no time to issue a Mayday call, gather essential gear, don lifejackets and launch the liferaft.

If a boat suddenly starts letting in water, and it rises above the saloon floor, the first thought is to find the source. Unfortunately, most yachts' batteries are placed low down, and so while someone is looking for the site of the damage a Securité call must be made, alerting the coastguard to a possible emergency, *before* the batteries become immersed.

Your emergency equipment should include tapered softwood plugs with which to plug failed seacocks. Any hole in a GRP hull, however, will be a split or jagged fracture, and while it may be possible to plug it with bunk cushions, clothing or sails, the water usually rises so quickly that the crew will be working in deep water after a few minutes.

If the flow cannot be stemmed, and the pumps fail to prevent the level rising, it must be accepted that unless the boat can be beached, then sooner rather than later it will sink. A Mayday call giving *who*, *where* and *what* together with a description of the action taken will ensure that rescue services or local ships will come to your aid.

When you launch the liferaft or dinghy, try to keep everyone dry. Take the ship's flare pack and documents and any easily accessible high-energy food such as chocolate. As soon as the boat shows signs of instability, climb into the liferaft and cut the painter so that the raft is clear of the boat when it sinks.

If you are close inshore, let off smoke and a pattern of flares as soon as you abandon. If offshore, give rescue services time to reach you and space out the flares – red and white – at sensible intervals, saving the smoke for the final rescue.

If you go aground and are holed, the boat will not necessarily be lost. If the tide is ebbing, you may be able to make a temporary repair with a GRP repair kit, plywood screwed over the hole with self-tappers, or even plastic sheet and duct tape. Most damage occurs when the boat settles onto rocks as the tide recedes, so use fenders, bunk cushions, even bagged sails to protect the hull from damage. However, think carefully before inflating either the dinghy or liferaft to use as hull protection because you may need one or both of them if the situation develops into an emergency.

Use a Securité call to advise the coastguard of your problem, but **do not accept offers of professional assistance to tow you off unless you really need them and have agreed to insurance terms or on a specified fee**. Maritime laws concerning salvage, which is what this is, are quite clear as to how much of the yacht's value the salvage vessel can claim.

Just about every part of a yacht is combustible and gives off lethal fumes when it burns, and diesel fuel, bottled gas, engines and electrical systems can all trigger off a fire. Effective extinguishers and fire blankets must be easily accessible, preferably sited away from probable sources of fire. Always try to fight the fire in its confined space, without having to open the space up. As soon as you think that you are not winning, make a Mayday call before it becomes impossible to stay below. Once you decide to abandon, get out and away as quickly as you can, turning off gas or fuel cocks only if safe to do so.

Because of the risk of explosions, try to get at least 100 metres away. Anyone who is burned should have cold seawater poured over their burns to cool the flesh and prevent further injury.

A serious physical injury accompanied by broken bones or bleeding may need outside assistance. Once the casualty has been made comfortable a Pan Medico call should be made. This will result in on-the-spot treatment by the crew or evacuation of the casualty by rescue services. A well-stocked First Aid kit can be augmented by tea towels, sleeping bag liners, heavy-duty paper rolls and sailcloth.

Helicopter evacuation by static line transfer requires the yacht to be motored into the wind. The helicopter takes station on the port side and lowers a line to the cockpit which must be hand-held, *never* cleated. The helicopter crewman uses the line as a guide to transfer from helicopter to cockpit, and casualties are winched up from the cockpit.

Alternatively, the casualty, accompanied by a crew member, can be drifted astern in the dinghy on a long line. The helicopter crewman transfers down and lifts off the casualty.

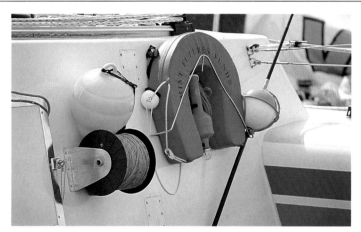

STOWING EMERGENCY EQUIPMENT

All the different items of emergency equipment on a cruiser should be stored securely but should be immediately accessible when they are needed. Lifebuoys and dan buoys, for example, should be kept on properly-designed brackets in the cockpit.

LAUNCHING A LIFERAFT

To launch the liferaft, secure the static line or painter to the boat, then pick up the valise or canister containing the raft and throw it overboard on the leeward side. Pull on the static line to activate the raft's inflation system, maintaining your pull on the line until the raft begins to inflate. When the raft has inflated fully, one person should climb on board and the others should pass down any gear, food, water or other items needed on board. Then the others can climb aboard, and the last one on should cut or untie the painter to free the raft from the boat.

DISTRESS SIGNALS

S O S
Morse code emergency signal, may be sent by radio or by flashing a light

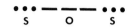

S O S

FLAGS
N flag over C flag:
'I am in distress. Help'

W flag:
'I require medical help'

V flag: 'I require assistance'

FLARES AND ROCKETS
Collision avoidance
All vessels sailing at night should carry at least four handheld white flares to use to attract the attention of larger craft when there is any danger of a collision

Inshore signals
When within 3 miles (5 km) of land or of potential rescuers, use handheld flares to attract attention and, when help is on its way, to pinpoint your position. Use handheld red flares in high winds, in poor visibility, and at night, and handheld orange smoke in clear daylight with light winds.

Coastal signals
When between 3 and 7 miles (5 and 11 km) from land, or when cloud is low, attract attention by firing rockets which discharge red stars. When help gets within sight, use handheld red flares or orange smoke to pinpoint your position.

Offshore signals
When more than 7 miles (11 km) from land, attract attention by using rockets which deploy parachute-suspended red flares. Pinpoint your position, when rescuers get within sight, by using red handheld flares (in poor visibility, darkness or high winds) or buoyant orange smoke (in clear daylight with light winds).

MAYDAY CALL (on radio)
1 Mayday (spoken 3 times)
2 This is [ship's name] spoken 3 times **3** Mayday **4** Ship's name
5 Position **6** Nature of emergency and assistance required
7 Any other relevant information

TENDERS & INFLATABLES

'Tenders' is the collective word for a wide variety of small craft used to service the needs of yachts. Originally, yacht tenders were of heavy clinker construction and were hoisted aboard in davits.

Today, two types are available. The first is the rigid GRP tender, which is usually used in conjunction with a swinging mooring. It is large enough to carry the crew and their equipment and strong enough to withstand robust use and storage ashore.

The second type is the inflatable dinghy, designed to be easily stowed on board when deflated. In use, it often gives its occupants a wet ride and is prone to windage (being swept off course by the wind). Nevertheless, it has found universal acceptance as being the best compromise for the many tasks it is called upon to perform.

When buying an inflatable, check that you can sit on a seat or inflated buoyancy compartment while you are rowing. If there's no seat, you will have to sit on the wet floor in an impossible rowing position. A plastic or plywood floor is an essential fitment on an inflatable. Not only does it give a more stable platform to work from, it also increases the craft's performance both when rowed and under engine.

Rowing both forms of tenders requires practice. The rigid tender is often heavy, and clumsy to manoeuvre, but it tracks well and carries large loads. The rowing action is long and measured. The inflatable needs a quick, dipping rowing action where the aim is to keep the oars in the water as much as possible to prevent the wind taking over. Captive oars can complicate the rowing action, however, especially in choppy seas.

A modern lightweight outboard engine is a must for all-weather operations, and a small 2-hp engine with self-contained tank will push most heavily-loaded inflatables against everything except a strong spring ebb.

The outboard attaches to a bracket on the transom of the inflatable, and a safety lanyard is permanently attached to the engine and clipped to the tender while in use. When not in use, the outboard is usually stowed on its own mounting board which is fixed to the back of the yacht's pushpit, and the safety lanyard is always clipped to the pushpit.

When transferring the outboard from its stowage to the dinghy it should always be clipped to something. While being handed down

Top Using a small outboard motor to drive an inflatable is easier and safer than rowing.
Above Inflatables can be towed, but only in calm conditions.

1 When getting into a tender, step carefully into the middle.

2 Release the painter, taking care not to lose your balance.

3 Carefully push the tender clear of the boat.

4 Fit the oars or start the engine and move off.

from the yacht, it is clipped to the crew member's wrist. As soon as it is in the tender it is clipped to the transom and then attached to its mounting.

Because of their light weight and considerable windage, inflatables do not tow well except in calm conditions. The principal danger to a towed inflatable is of being flipped upside down and creating so much drag that the painter breaks or, worse, pulls out its anchorage patches.

If your foredeck is large enough you can pull the inflatable aboard, invert it and lash it down. If it isn't, you have to deflate it and roll it up so that it can either be stowed on deck or placed into its bag and stowed in a locker.

Once ashore, it may be placed vertically in special shore stowage racks resembling toast racks, or placed on car roof bars and taken home, where it can be hoisted into the garage roof space using permanently-mounted hoisting strops.

When using the tender, each occupant should wear a life preserver. Statistics show that more people drown through accidents with tenders than through falling from cruising yachts.

In many cases, problems occur at night when crews return from an evening ashore. Skippers must accept that night work from an inflatable is both difficult and dangerous. The load should be kept within the maximum capacity and the driver should be skilled and capable of finding the mother ship.

The tender should be equipped with a torch, a pump, spare fuel, a toolkit and flares, and all items should be secured with line or placed in special sailcloth 'dinghy bags' fixed to the tender.

As well as its primary use for ferrying the crew to and from the yacht, the tender is a workboat which should be capable of carrying out the various traditional seamanship tasks, such as laying out an anchor.

Laying out a second anchor at an angle to the first is a task which calls for thought. Inflatables do not tow well because they skid across the surface when turned. They work best in reverse with the towed object attached to the bow painter. The engine, now at the front, can be aimed at your objective and everything else follows. If the anchor and chain are heavy, they should be placed in a box to prevent damaging the inflatable's fabric, and slung beneath the tender with a quick-release hitch.

If you have to use the tender to move your cruiser it is best to lash it firmly alongside using springs and bow and stern lines. The spring leading aft from the bow of the tender tows the boat forward, the stern spring tows it backward. The yacht is steered normally so that, in effect, the tender is being used as an auxiliary engine.

Cleaning the yacht's hull from the tender, especially the waterline, is often complicated because the tender tends to drift away. Place two large fenders along the sides of the dinghy and stern so that they leave a working space. You can then lash the dinghy tightly to the yacht to keep it in position.

Caring for and repairing tenders is usually on a 'permanent' first-aid basis. GRP dinghies can be fixed with the standard automobile repair packs and inflatables usually have a repair pack containing wooden plugs for emergencies and fabric patches for repairs.

Fortunately, the development of really tough laminated fabrics makes the inflatable a long-lived proposition requiring a visit to a servicing agent about once every three years. Sand, especially at the junction of floorboards and fabric, can be a threat to the fabric, though, and so regular washing and twice-a-season inspections are called for.

PILOTAGE

Pilotage is essentially navigating by using the landmarks and seamarks which are shown on charts. It relies upon the accurate identification of charted objects such as buoyage systems, lighthouses and prominent landmarks. Charts are contour maps of the seabed, drawn to show features and depths at the lowest low water (*lowest astronomical tide* or LAT) normally experienced in the area shown.

An experienced navigator will have the skills to interpret the depths shown on charts, but the newcomer would be wise to start out by sailing only in the areas which show sufficient charted depth, for example 2 metres, until the skills to fix the boat's position by using a handbearing compass have been mastered.

Fixing your approximate position by means of a handbearing compass, which is a special handheld compass incorporating a prism, is an essential skill which can be practised ashore in any open space.

To obtain an accurate magnetic bearing *from* your position *to* an identified charted feature, such as a lighthouse or a headland, you sight over the compass so that you can see both the feature and the bearing (0 to 360 degrees) in the prism. (The recently-developed electronic compasses record the bearing automatically if you press a button when pointing the compass at the feature.)

An accurate bearing gives you a line of position running from your position through the charted feature. You mark that line on your chart, and you then know that your boat's position is somewhere on that line.

To find out where on that line

you are, you need to take a second bearing – preferably at right angles to the line – and transfer that second line of position to the chart. The point on the chart where the two lines cross shows the position of your boat, and you should mark it on the chart as a *fix*, a dot within a circle. If the two features you took bearings of are close together, you should take a third bearing to improve the accuracy of your fix.

The difference between true (or charted) north and magnetic north is shown on the chart's compass rose as *variation* to the east or west of true north. The reason for the difference is that the earth's magnetic poles do not coincide with the geographic poles, and the earth's magnetic field is constantly changing at different rates in different parts of the world.

Each chart and each compass rose printed on it carries the variation which existed when the chart was drawn, and the annual increase or decrease in variation. At the start of each season, amend the variation on each compass rose to take account of the increase or decrease in variation since the chart was drawn, or since you last marked the variation on it. Each rose on the chart will show a true and a magnetic rose, printed concentrically.

Also printed on the chart are vertical lines representing longitude and horizontal lines representing latitude. Each is measured in degrees. There are 180 degrees of latitude, 90 degrees north and 90 degrees south of the equator, and there are 360 degrees of longitude, 180 degrees east and 180 degrees west of the *Greenwich Meridian*. Each degree is divided up into 60 minutes (') and

each minute into 60 seconds ("). So a point on the earth's surface described as being 53°.21'.24" N, 12°.42'.02" W would be at latitude 53.21.24 north (of the equator) and longitude 12.42.02 west (of Greenwich).

The reintroduction of latitude and longitude, in place of local chart references, has been brought about by the availability of electronic navigation equipment such as Loran and Decca systems, and it is important to understand it and to be able to chart it correctly.

If you are determined to go through the conversion of all bearings to true north you will have to learn, and remember, the conversion sequences. Various mnemonics such as C-A-D-E-T will help you to get it correct. C-A-D-E-T is used to

complete the conversion of a Compass bearing to a True bearing. However, the basis of the mnemonic – *C*ompass *A*dd *D*eviation *E*ast for *T*rue is only half the story. The full conversion sequence is *C*ompass course, *A*dd *D*eviation *E*ast (or subtract deviation west) to give magnetic course, add *E*ast variation (or subtract west) to give *T*rue course.

Using C-A-D-E-T to convert a true course to a magnetic one you change the 'add deviation east' to 'subtract deviation east'. You can probably understand why most weekend navigators prefer to work in magnetic only.

Charts are produced by national agencies, and each country has developed its own style of presentation and symbols for land and sea

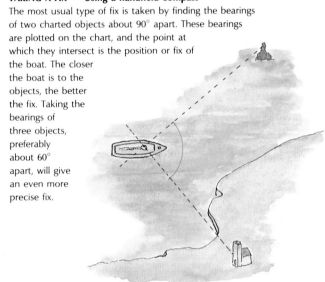

TAKING A FIX — Using a handheld compass
The most usual type of fix is taken by finding the bearings of two charted objects about 90° apart. These bearings are plotted on the chart, and the point at which they intersect is the position or fix of the boat. The closer the boat is to the objects, the better the fix. Taking the bearings of three objects, preferably about 60° apart, will give an even more precise fix.

NAVIGATIONAL TERMS
MAGNETIC VARIATION

This is the angle between the True (geographical) North Pole and the Magnetic North Pole as shown by magnetic compasses. This angle varies over the earth's surface, and changes from year to year.

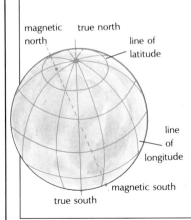

DIRECTION
Direction is measured clockwise from North

HEADING (COURSE)

The heading is the direction, relative to north, in which a boat is sailing
BEARING
The bearing is the angular direction relative to north of an object as seen from a boat

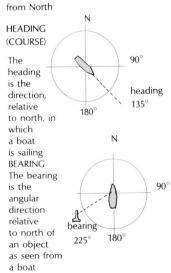

MEASUREMENTS
Knot The knot is the unit of speed used by boats and aircraft, and is equal to 1 nautical mile per hour.

Nautical mile The international nautical mile is a distance of 1.852 km (1.15 miles or 6067.12 feet). The international nautical mile has replaced previous units such as the British standard nautical mile of 6080 feet.

Metre The metre is a primary unit of measurement in the metric system, and is equivalent to 3.28084 feet (39.3701 inches).

Fathom The fathom, used for centuries to measure water depth, is being replaced by the metre. 1 fathom equals 6 feet.

SYMBOLS FOR USE ON CHARTS
Below are the symbols commonly used when plotting a course on charts. Using symbols is quicker than writing words and takes up less space on a chart

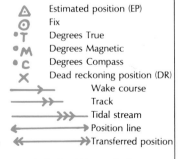

△	Estimated position (EP)
Ⓞ	Fix
●T	Degrees True
●M	Degrees Magnetic
●C	Degrees Compass
×	Dead reckoning position (DR)
→	Wake course
→→	Track
→→→	Tidal stream
←→	Position line
⇐⇒	Transferred position

Symbols should be marked on chart in plain or coloured pencil.

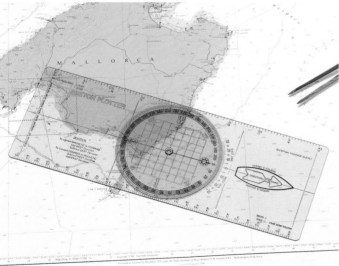

Top Using a parallel rule and dividers to plot a course on a chart.
Above A Breton Plotter, a very useful charting instrument devised by Captain Yvonnick Gueret. It has a rotatable plastic circle marked in compass degrees to allow easy conversion from magnetic to true bearings or vice versa.

features. It is necessary to obtain the relevant publication listing all the symbols on the charts you intend to use.

If you can already read a land map, it doesn't take too long to learn the most-used charted symbols. Start with those nearest the land, such as sandbanks which dry, and rocks which are awash or dry, then move on to shoreline types followed by charted depths and buoyage systems.

Charted features, especially those underwater (such as sandbanks) may change after the chart has been drawn. 'Notices to Mariners' are published at regular intervals to enable you, or a chart agent, to update your charts.

Charts are designed to be drawn on with a medium-grade pencil, and you can use a good-quality eraser to clean them after use. You should stow them in their numbered se-

quence, either folded flat in the chart table or stowed vertically in a specially-made easy-stowage rack.

When entering details on your chart, keep to a standard set of symbols. Use the 24-hour clock to show times, and mark your DR (dead reckoning) position with an 'X'. Show a fix as a circle with a dot in the centre, and an estimated position as dot inside a triangle. When constructing navigation *vectors* indicate their functions with arrowheads: one arrowhead on the course to steer, two on the track you wish to sail along, and three on the tidal stream. If you are using magnetic values as your norm, you must identify other values in your chartwork. Show degrees true as °T, and degrees compass as °C.

Accurate chartwork requires using whichever method best suits your capabilities, especially when under stress in adverse conditions.

PASSAGE MAKING

As soon as you leave the confines of an estuary and emerge into the open sea, pilotage becomes less useful and you must adopt a more demanding method of keeping track of or calculating your position.

On the open sea, your reliance upon your main steering compass requires you to know its *deviation values*, which are compass errors caused by factors external to the compass. All compasses are influenced by large masses of ferrous metal or electric fields built into the boat's structure, such as the keel, the engine, and the electrical system.

Deviation is found by checking (swinging) the vessel through 360 degrees by reference to shore marks, or by cross-checking the main compass readings with a handbearing compass, and built-in correcting magnets are adjusted to damp down large errors. (A professional compass adjuster should be employed when fitting new compasses.)

Deviation values are taken at 45-degree intervals and entered on a deviation card as 'east' and 'west' values. Display the card in the navigation space and enter the values in your Decca, satnav or Loran system. For most purposes, because it is not possible to steer within 5 degrees of a given course, errors of 2 to 3 degrees can be ignored on short passages.

Plotting your intended course requires proper passage planning before you set out. With the appropriate corrected charts you consult the almanac, tidal stream atlas and local sailing instructions to determine when you can sail and where you can sail; 'when' is determined by the tides, which govern depths and the speed and direction of the stream, and 'where' is determined by the wind.

When planning, you aim to take advantage of the wind and tide, and to negotiate tidal gates at slack water just before the stream turns in your direction, or to pass through the gates with the stream if sea state permits.

Your passage plan as drawn on the chart will be a series of vector calculations based on one-hourly units of tide. You can choose between letting the tide take you where it wishes while maintaining a steady course, or keeping to a predetermined track by allowing for the tide each hour. A coastwise plan would show as a series of waypoints.

The wind direction, and to a certain extent its speed, will determine whether you can follow those tracks. If you can't, you may have to tack to your waypoints. Calculating how long it will take to tack to an objective embodies the basic chartwork which must be understood before you venture offshore.

The vector triangle of calculation incorporates the leeway or drift of the boat caused by the wind, the tidal stream direction and speed, and the speed and direction of the vessel. The result of the calculation will be a course to steer when you are passage planning, or a dead reckoning (DR) position once you are out of sight of land and relying solely on published information and your instruments. Only the depth sounder will give you an observation, and you shouldn't forget its importance.

When you add an electronic or visual bearing to your DR it becomes an estimated position (EP), the change of name denoting that there is a greater degree of accuracy. Only a fix on identified charted features can be taken as an accurate position.

To construct your vector you draw a track, a line joining your point of depature to a waypoint destination. You then consult a tidal stream atlas, a tidal diamond or an almanac to determine the tide's speed and direction (which is always given in degrees true) for a given time. Using the true compass rose, mark in the tidal vector at the point of departure so that the arrows point in the direction of the stream. The vector's length is equal to one hour's worth of flow, so if, for example, the tide's speed is 5 knots, the length

If you plan your course before you sail, you will have less to do when under way.

COMPASS DEVIATION

A compass needle points north because it is attracted by the earth's magnetic field. However, it will also be attracted by large metal objects on board, such as the engine. These objects will make the compass needle point a little to either east or west of magnetic north, to a direction known as compass north.

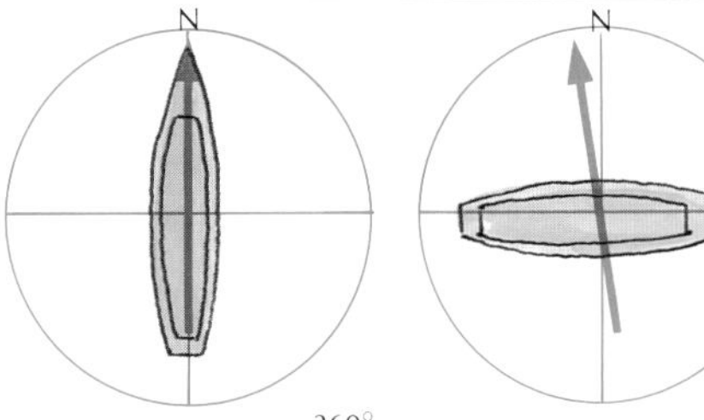

SWINGING THE COMPASS

When you instal a compass, find its deviation by 'swinging' it. On a calm day, with all gear in place, sail to a point where you can observe a transit between two charted objects. From your chart, find the transit's bearing and sail slowly past it on eight different headings. Each time you pass the transit, note your heading and the transit's bearing as shown by the compass. The difference between the actual transit bearing and the observed bearing on each heading will be the compass's deviation on that heading.

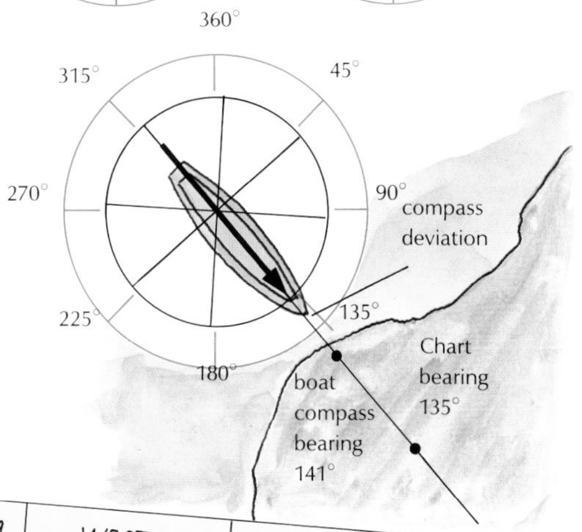

DEVIATION CARD

Use the information obtained from swinging your compass to draw up a deviation card. Mark each deviation on the card at the point where the vertical line representing its value crosses the line representing the heading on which the measurement was made. When you have marked all the values, draw a curve to connect them. Then you can use this curve to find the deviation on any heading.

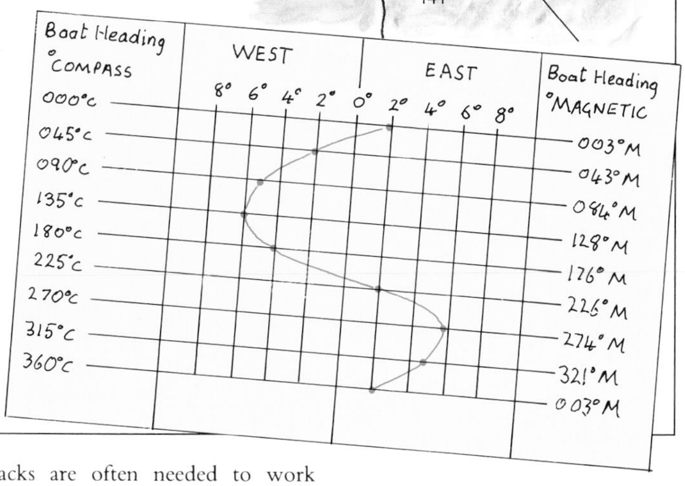

360°

315° · 45°

270° · 90° compass deviation

225° · 135°

180° Chart bearing 135°

boat compass bearing 141°

Deviation Card

Boat Heading °COMPASS	WEST 8° 6° 4° 2° 0°	EAST 2° 4° 6° 8°	Boat Heading °MAGNETIC
000°c			003°M
045°c			043°M
090°c			084°M
135°c			128°M
180°c			176°M
225°c			226°M
270°c			274°M
315°c			321°M
360°c			003°M

SHAPING AN HOURLY COURSE

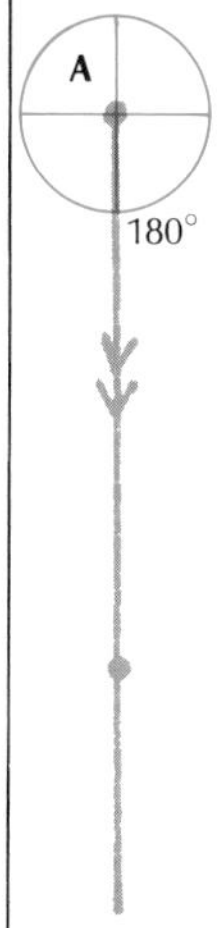

TRACK PLOTTING
Draw a line on the chart from the start (A) through the destination (B). If the tide was from directly behind and there was no leeway, the course shown here would be 180°M. As this rarely happens, allowance has to be made for the tide.

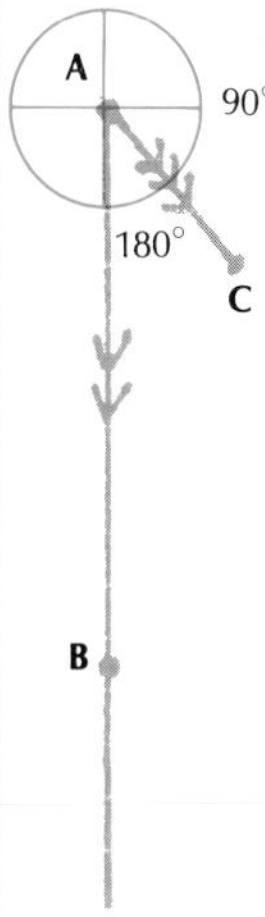

ALLOWING FOR TIDAL FLOW
Look up the tidal direction (°T) and speed (here 140°M at 1 knot) in your almanac. Using the latitude scale, draw a line (with three arrows) to point C to represent the tidal flow.

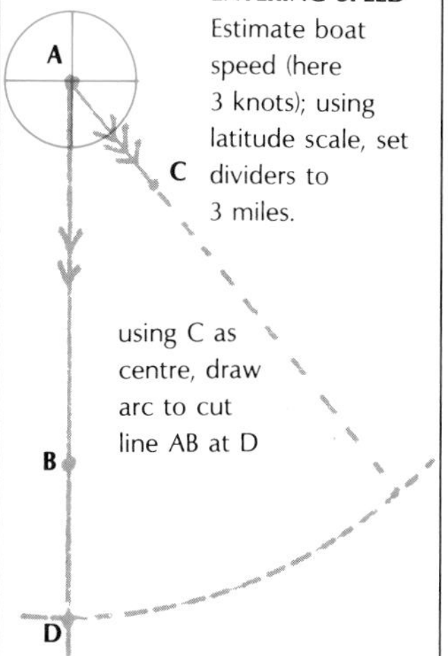

ENTERING SPEED
Estimate boat speed (here 3 knots); using latitude scale, set dividers to 3 miles.

using C as centre, draw arc to cut line AB at D

HEADING TO STEER
join points C and D

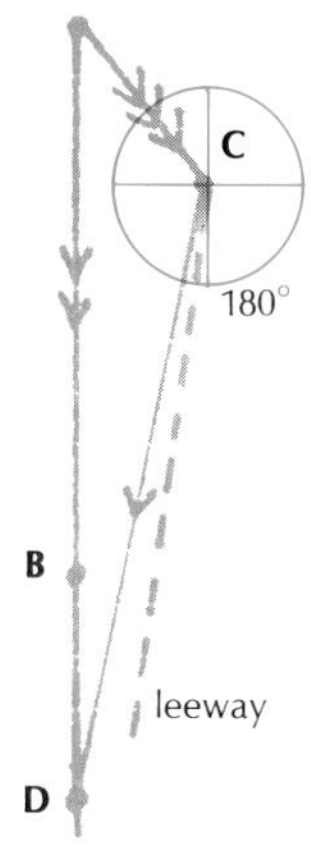

Read off the heading (here 185°M), and use deviation card to convert it to a compass heading (°C). Make allowance for leeway to find course to steer.

---

of the vector should represent 5 nautical miles.

The final construction is to draw in one hour's worth of estimated boatspeed from the end of the tidal vector and mark where it cuts the track. You now have the course to steer to move along your charted track. Before you measure its angle you can draw in your leeway angle to windward of the course to steer. Measure this angle to get a course to steer which will cancel out leeway and tidal drift. If you then add or subtract steering compass deviation, you will get a compass course to steer.

Once on your passage you are not theorizing. You have to take account of boatspeed, wind direction and tide for your DR position, and an estimate of the course steered by your helmsman.

If the wind direction makes it impossible to sail along your neat passage plan track, then the track becomes your rhumb line (the direct line to your destination) and you will zigzag along it.

You should update your chartwork hourly, and if you can also make one hour-tacks the updating will be simpler. However, half-hour tacks are often needed to work inshore of a foul tide, in which case you should note in the log the time of the tack, the average course steered during the preceding half hour and a note on leeway in degrees, especially when in short steep seas.

Your DR calculation will show a line, representing the course steered, starting at your last fix, EP or DR and ending at a point which coincides with your logged distance run in the preceding period. From this point the tidal vector (degrees T) is drawn in the direction of flow to a length with coincides with the time since your last DR. This time will usually be an hour, but if it isn't, beware of adding an hour's worth of tide. The end of the tidal vector is your DR position and you should mark it with an 'X'. If you wish to allow for leeway, apply it to windward of your course steered before you draw in the tidal vector.

Measuring from your previous fix, EP or DR to the new DR position will give your *speed over the ground* (SOG) and *course made good* (CMG). Of course, if you have Decca, satnav or Loran, you can get this information by simply pressing the appropriate button.

The key to successful manual navigation, on short passages out of sight of land, is to know that your steering compass is accurate to 3 degrees on all points of sailing at 20 degrees angle of heel; not to place steel cans or other large magnetizable or magnetic objects near the compass; have a reliable log to measure speed and distance; know how to find accurate tidal information related to local high water and springs and neaps; and to have vector triangles drawn into the front of your log book to show how to plot a course to steer and how to calculate a DR position.

Electronic navigation aids using ground- or space-based transmitters are rapidly replacing all other forms of aids such as radio direction finding and radio lighthouses. When using Decca, satnav or Loran systems it is essential to keep a traditional navigation system 'ticking over' in your ship's log. You should also plot an hourly electronic fix and compare it with a rough DR calculation. If there is a large discrepancy, suspect the electronic aid and immediately re-work your position from the ship's log data.

MARITIME BUOYAGE

If you intend to sail along coasts and in estuaries you will need to understand buoyage, the system of buoys and other markers used to identify features such as channels or obstructions. Two buoyage systems – Lateral A and Lateral B – were adopted in 1976 by IALA, the International Association of Lighthouse Authorities, for implementation worldwide by 1990. System A is used in the British Isles, Europe, Australia, New Zealand, Africa and most of Asia, including India. System B is operated in North, Central and South America, Japan, South Korea and the Philippines.

The need to mark the sides of shallow, winding channels was appreciated early on in the history of sailing. Originally, the markers were sticks, tree branches or floating barrels, but they became more sophisticated as larger vessels needed to gain access to inland ports.

A uniform colour coding of red for port (left) and green for starboard (right) markers was adopted, but the Europeans marked their channels from seaward while the Americans marked theirs from landward. Nonetheless, these *lateral systems* work well and confusion only arises when you sail from waters using one system into waters using the other, or into waters where neither system has yet been implemented.

The 'direction' of buoyage is determined by the direction in which the flood tide flows. Where two tides meet, such as in a narrow strip of water separating an island from the mainland, a change of buoyage direction is made at a specific point, which is marked on charts of that water.

The Lateral A system has red flat-topped cairns to port on entering, and green conical marks to starboard. With Lateral B, there are green flat-topped marks to port on entering and red conical marks are to starboard. In both systems, the marks may or may not have lights mounted on them.

The lateral systems are used in conjunction with the universally-adopted *Cardinal System* of buoys. This system marks the positions of hazards in relation to the four cardinal points of the compass (north, south, east and west), and the buoys are identified by shaped-top marks and colour coding. In principle, minor estuarial channels are marked with the lateral system and the approaches and major obstructions are marked with the cardinal system.

The identifying marks of cardinal buoys tell you their position in relation to the hazard they are marking, so a north cardinal will be placed to the north of the hazard, an east cardinal to the east of it, and so on.

The top marks of cardinal buoys consist of two black cones, mounted one above the other on the top of the structure and arranged as follows: both cones pointing up = north cardinal; both pointing down = south cardinal; one pointing up and the other down with their bases together = east cardinal; one pointing up and the other pointing down with their points together = west cardinal. If you get confused between east and west cardinals, think of the west as being waisted.

The colours used are black and yellow. North is a black pillar on a yellow buoy, and south is a yellow pillar on a black buoy. East is a black and yellow pillar on a black buoy, west a yellow and black pillar on a yellow buoy.

The colours are often quite confusing, especially when weed or bird fouling occurs, so always start with the colour of the buoy to identify north or west (yellow) and south or east (black), and then positively identify the top mark, making sure that no resting birds are confusing the issue.

Three additional types of mark in the IALA systems are the isolated danger mark, the safe water mark and the special mark. An isolated danger is one, such as a rock, that has navigable water all around it, and the marker for this has horizontal black and red bands and has two black spheres on top.

The safe water mark is a spherical buoy, or a pillar or spar, with vertical red and white stripes and with a red ball on top, and is used to mark landfalls and as a mid-channel marker.

Any special marks to zone off recreational areas, for instance for water skiers, are yellow and may have an X-shaped top mark. They may be any shape, as long as they cannot be confused with a navigational mark.

At night, shapes and colours are of no use to the mariner and so an equally organized system of top lights is used to identify lateral and cardinal systems.

When entering a channel from seaward at night you should have a prepared list of all lights which may be visible during the approach. Your chart of the channel will tell you the characteristics of the lights you will see, and you will find detailed descriptions of the lights used on buoys in any good nautical almanac.

INTERNATIONAL BUOYAGE
Used in conjunction with lateral buoyage, regions A and B.

CARDINAL SYSTEM

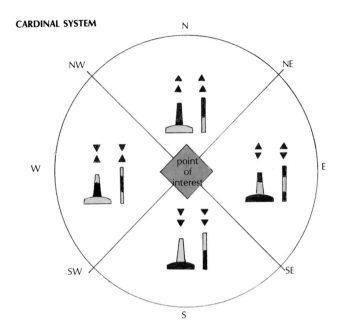

Cardinal buoys warn of hazards, and their identifying marks tell you their position in relation to the hazard they are marking. A north cardinal, for example, is placed to the north of the hazard.

SAFE WATER MARKS
A safe water mark (placed, for instance, in the middle of a channel) indicates that there is navigable water all around it.

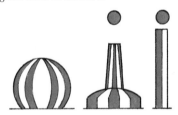

ISOLATED DANGER MARKS
These mark a danger spot that has navigable water all around it.

SPECIAL MARKS
Special marks are not intended primarily to assist navigation but are used to indicate features or areas that may be referred to in nautical almanacs or local sailing directions. A special mark may be any shape, provided that it cannot be mistaken for a navigational mark.

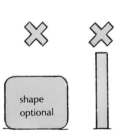

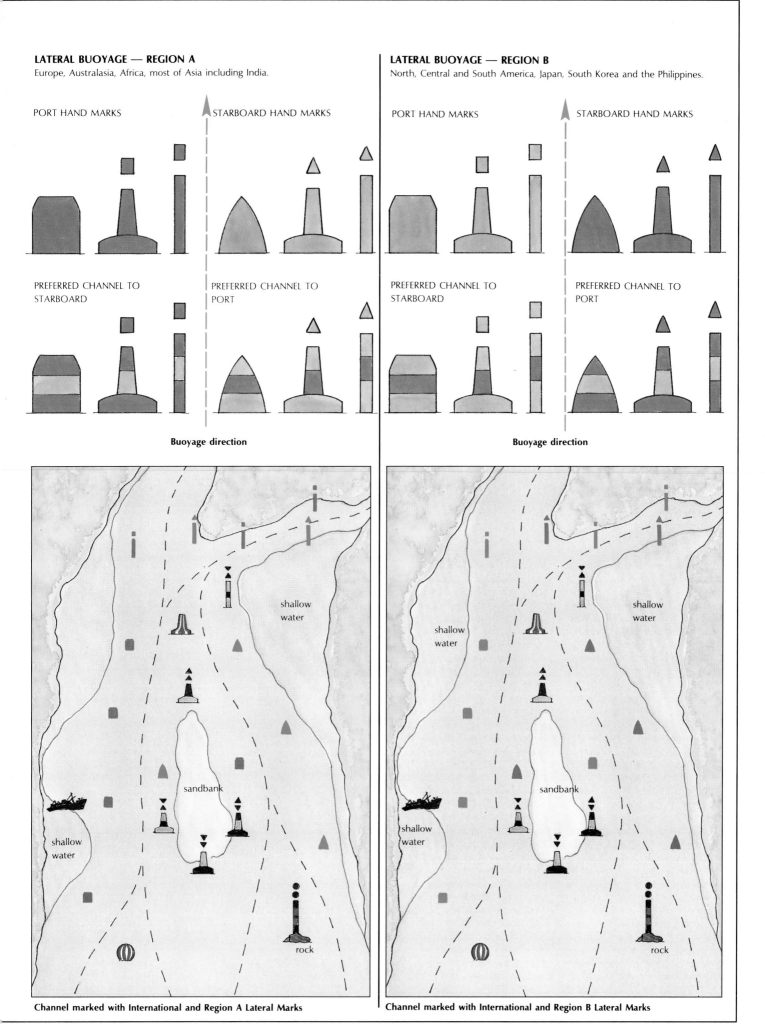

LATERAL BUOYAGE — REGION A

Europe, Australasia, Africa, most of Asia including India.

PORT HAND MARKS

STARBOARD HAND MARKS

PREFERRED CHANNEL TO STARBOARD

PREFERRED CHANNEL TO PORT

Buoyage direction

Channel marked with International and Region A Lateral Marks

LATERAL BUOYAGE — REGION B

North, Central and South America, Japan, South Korea and the Philippines.

PORT HAND MARKS

STARBOARD HAND MARKS

PREFERRED CHANNEL TO STARBOARD

PREFERRED CHANNEL TO PORT

Buoyage direction

Channel marked with International and Region B Lateral Marks

shallow water

sandbank

shallow water

rock

ROPES & KNOTS

Being able to tie secure, reliable knots is an essential skill for all sailors, and it's important to use knots that are suitable for their intended purposes, such as attaching halyards or sheets to a sail.

The introduction of Kevlar and prestretched polyester ropes has enabled owners of all but the hottest racing machines to revert to using ropes for halyards. Racing boats continue to use the wire halyard/rope tail because it is the least affected by stretch.

Kevlar-based polyester braids offer the next least stretch, but Kevlar does not take kindly to repeated kinking in the same spot, as for example over a halyard sheave. It is used primarily in dinghies, keelboats and cruiser racers of up to 15 metres.

Traditionally-laid, 3-strand, super-stretched polyester is popular with cruiser racer owners who prefer to dispense with wire. Its sheave abrasion characteristics are good and it can be spliced easily. Sixteen plait multibraid over a 3-strand core is the ideal combination for spinnaker and genoa halyards. Although you can splice it yourself, it is often better to get a rigging specialist to splice multiplait, especially if it is joined to Kevlar or wire tails.

To prevent a halyard running back up the mast, use the double thumb knot, which is easy to tie and easily untied again after years of use. For attaching halyards directly to the head of a sail, and possibly a sheet to a headsail if the bulk of a bowline is not acceptable, the figure-of-eight overhand hitch is a very useful knot to use.

One of the prime requirements of ropes used as sheets is a high resistance to the abrasion caused by running through blocks and around winches and being dragged around shrouds. In use, sheets develop a slightly 'furry' finish which helps them to resist abrasion and improves their grip on winches and rope jamming devices.

Because sheets have to be handled by crew members, it is essential that they are of sufficient diameter to give a comfortable grip when under severe load. For this reason, many dinghy sailors use a thin Kevlar sheet to run through the blocks and splice on a 10- to 12-mm diameter braided tail leading back to the helmsman or crew.

Cruising boats usually cover more ocean than racers and are at sea for longer periods. This adds up to considerably more wear on all ropes and gear, and for these boats' sheets 16-plait matt finish polyester over a 3-strand core gives the required strength and longevity. Dayboats and dinghies can often use 8-plait polyester and lightweight multifilament polypropylene for all running lines.

Sheets are attached to sails by a bowline, which is the one general purpose knot that all sailors need to be able to tie in any situation. The sheet bend is the traditional method of attaching a sheet to a strop spliced to the clew, and is also used for joining ropes of different diameters. Note that the two short ends of rope must be on the same side of the finished 'bend'. It can be doubled for extra security or slipped if an easy getaway is required.

The rolling hitch is an essential emergency hitch when a sheet fouls and jams on a winch when an inexperienced tailer pulls down instead of up at an angle of 45 degrees. To free a sheet jammed under load, attach a spare rope or sheet to it with a rolling hitch. Then take the tail of that rope or sheet to a spare winch and winch it in until the load on the jammed rope is eased and you can free off the riding turn.

The rolling hitch works on the principle of tightening its grip as the pull increases, so remember to construct the early parts in the same direction as the intended final pull.

To cleat a rope, lead it to the back of the cleat, and secure it with a round turn and at least one figure-of-eight around both horns of the cleat. Small cleats require a half-hitch to finish.

Ropes suitable for mooring and anchoring have good stretch characteristics derived both from their fibres (nylon) and from their loose construction. The introduction of nylon to replace chain has made short-stay anchoring a far less cumbersome prospect, but chain is still preferable for serious cruising and for anchoring in heavy weather. Warps used to moor alongside need to be chafe-resistant.

There is a wealth of knots, bends and hitches with which to attach your vessel and its tender to rings, bollards, poles and other ropes, but if your mind goes blank you can revert to the bowline to create a loop in the shore end. Once your vessel is safely attached, you can think about the alternative knots at your leisure. These include the round turn and two half-hitches, which is quick and simple.

To tie a rope to an anchor ring, use a fisherman's bend with two half-hitches to finish; it may need seizing (trying back) for extra security. The figure-of-eight overhand hitch is useful for anchoring or attaching dinghies to the shore.

PARTS OF A KNOT

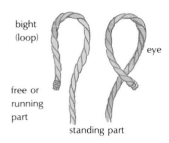

bight (loop)

eye

free or running part

standing part

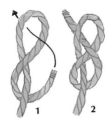

Stop knot — figure-of-eight knot

simple stop knot to prevent rope slipping through blocks or fairleads

1   2

Half-hitch — simplest form of knot, basis for many others

Slipped half-hitch — quick release knot, used where speed of untying is needed

Reef knot — originally used to tie reefing lines. Can be used to join equal thicknesses of rope but will spill if one end is pulled sharply. Good flat knot

1   2   3

Round turn and two half-hitches — for tying rope to standing objects

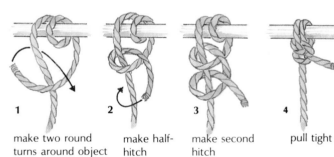

1   2   3   4

make two round turns around object

make half-hitch

make second hitch

pull tight

Belaying a cleat

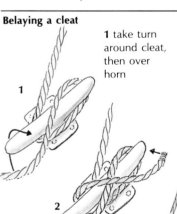

1 take turn around cleat, then over horn

1

2

2 wind around horn in a figure-of-eight

3 several figure-eights can be wound on. Finish with another turn around cleat or tie a slipped hitch

Securing spare rope

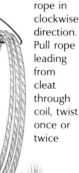

1 Coil rope in clockwise direction. Pull rope leading from cleat through coil, twist once or twice

2 hang the loop on top of the horn of the cleat

1

2

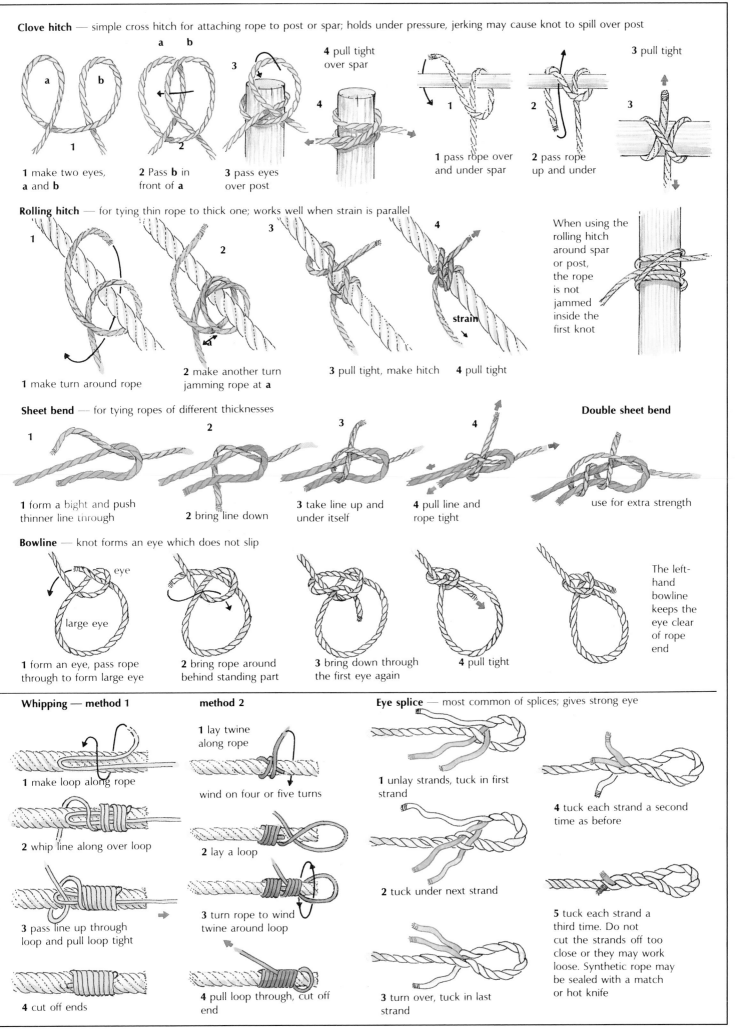

Clove hitch — simple cross hitch for attaching rope to post or spar; holds under pressure, jerking may cause knot to spill over post

1 make two eyes, **a** and **b**

2 Pass **b** in front of **a**

3 pass eyes over post

4 pull tight over spar

1 pass rope over and under spar

2 pass rope up and under

3 pull tight

Rolling hitch — for tying thin rope to thick one; works well when strain is parallel

1 make turn around rope

2 make another turn jamming rope at **a**

3 pull tight, make hitch

4 pull tight

When using the rolling hitch around spar or post, the rope is not jammed inside the first knot

Sheet bend — for tying ropes of different thicknesses

1 form a bight and push thinner line through

2 bring line down

3 take line up and under itself

4 pull line and rope tight

Double sheet bend

use for extra strength

Bowline — knot forms an eye which does not slip

1 form an eye, pass rope through to form large eye

2 bring rope around behind standing part

3 bring down through the first eye again

4 pull tight

The left-hand bowline keeps the eye clear of rope end

Whipping — method 1

1 make loop along rope

2 whip line along over loop

3 pass line up through loop and pull loop tight

4 cut off ends

method 2

1 lay twine along rope

wind on four or five turns

2 lay a loop

3 turn rope to wind twine around loop

4 pull loop through, cut off end

Eye splice — most common of splices; gives strong eye

1 unlay strands, tuck in first strand

2 tuck under next strand

3 turn over, tuck in last strand

4 tuck each strand a second time as before

5 tuck each strand a third time. Do not cut the strands off too close or they may work loose. Synthetic rope may be sealed with a match or hot knife

COMPETITIVE
SAILING

If you analyze it in terms of skill levels, sailing is a relatively simple physical exercise. If, however, you analyze the *sport* of sailing, you will find that it is one of the most complex of sports to master because of the huge range of skills and activities involved in it.

The majority of dinghy and open keelboat sailors spend at least part of their sailing careers in the competitive side of the sport. This requires them to develop more advanced close-quarter boat handling skills than are needed for leisure sailing, plus an ability to understand and interpret the often-complicated racing rules while involved in tactical and strategic sailing. These skills spill over into the big-boat racing arena, where the degree of sophistication of the craft is matched by the racing pedigree of the crews and the sophistication of the electronic navigation equipment.

Sailboat racing can be as exciting and demanding as any other sport which relies upon complicated racing machines. At world championship and Olympic levels, you need not only the fitness and strength of an athlete but also the mental power of a chess player, so that you can interpret wind, waves and strategies to produce a winning combination.

Fortunately, however, racing is conducted at many levels, not just at international or Olympic level. These range from casual weekday evening races through regular club series to cut-throat one-design class meets and championships, and so there is ample opportunity for any competent sailor to enjoy competitive sailing at a level that suits his or her abilities.

As with all other sports, coaching, physical fitness and practice are all essential to success at higher levels of competition. The casual racer will often gain immense benefit by asking an experienced, successful skipper or crew aboard so that they can sort out the systems and tune the rig. The serious aspiring competitor will need to participate in a structured, land-based physical training schedule in addition to on-the-water sail, boatspeed and technique evaluation sessions either with another boat or with a coach in attendance.

The basis of all sailboat racing is a universal set of rules administered by national sailing authorities on behalf of the International Yacht Racing Union (IYRU). These rules, based on the International Rules for the Prevention of Collisions at Sea (IRPCS), have been developed over a century of racing and are extremely complex. Fortunately, you don't have to learn them all at once. They progress from a few simple, basic rules which everyone *must* know and are easy to learn, through rules which everyone *should* know to rules which you have to look up in a book because they are so obscure.

Rules for the conduct of racing require a proper course to be set, a period of preparation before the start, and a recognized starting signal to be given when all the boats are in position behind the starting line. The race finishes when boats which have correctly sailed the course without infringing any of the rules cross the designated finishing line in the correct direction. Because the rules are usually enforced by the competitors, in most races any infringements are resolved as the race continues. If this is not possible, the aggrieved boat signals a protest, which is then resolved by a jury or protest committee after the race has finished.

The great majority of dinghy owners participate in handicap racing against boats of different designs, and in one-design racing against boats of the same design. Handicap racing thrives in small dinghy clubs and among cruiser racer owners who wish to race against each other in inshore and offshore events. One-design or 'boat-for-boat' racing gives the closest racing and places a premium on boat-handling skills. It also enables the owner to trail to other venues as part of the class points and ranking system.

Boat-for-boat competitions are typified by the various match racing-series held throughout the world. These may involve two boats being matched against each other, as in the America's Cup, or be aggregate competitions such as the Congressional Cup, where a group of selected skippers and crews race against each other in a round-robin series to determine the finalists, or the outright winners.

Yacht racing did not become a media sport until the involvement of certain politicians and pop stars, and the publicity caused by the 1979 Fastnet storm, brought it to the attention of the general public. Since then, in countries such as the United States, France, Australia and New Zealand, racing yachtsmen and women have been elevated to the status of national heroes because of their ability to win prestigious events. In the wake of this public awareness has come an increasing commercial interest from companies wishing to use the not-inconsiderable expanses of hulls and sails as billboards in exchange for sponsorship money.

In many ways, the commercialization of the sport has been a good thing because it has enabled sailors to choose between being amateur or professional, and allowed organizers to run sponsored events with a clear conscience. Sponsorship has already secured the future of many exciting competitions, and has encouraged the design and construction of new breeds of monohulled and multihulled racers that otherwise would never have seen the light of day.

INDIVIDUAL DINGHY RACING

The encouraging aspect of competitive dinghy sailing is that success often comes to those who apply themselves wholeheartedly to the sport. For example, many skilled and enthusiastic young sailors have been selected by top sailing coaches for specialist squad training and have gone on to win Olympic medals.

Less spectacular, but nonetheless rapid, progress can be made by newcomers to racing who take the trouble to practise and to understand the rules. Very little advanced coaching will be available at club level, and you will need to learn by observation, experience and by reading the many excellent books available covering all aspects of competition.

As an example, suppose you have bought a two-man, 14-foot dinghy of international status, suitable for both racing and family use, and you want to take up racing. During the first year of ownership, you and your crew will be primarily engaged in learning to sail the boat in a wide variety of wind conditions at your club.

Racing will usually be a fairly haphazard affair to start with because of your lack of sailing skill. You should concentrate on successfully negotiating the race course and learning the fairly complicated procedures of starting and the basic racing rules. Most of your activity will be confined to the club waters, with the occasional excursion to the coast or other sailing venue to gain experience in towing, launching, and navigating in unfamiliar waters.

At the end of the first year, you and your crew will have become able to handle the boat with confidence in medium winds. You will both have a reasonable understanding of what racing entails and an idea of whether your boat has the potential to be tuned to a competitive level.

The second year usually determines whether you will be 'average' club racers or have the potential to become very good racing sailors. Much depends on your degree of organization and whether you are working to a proper 'game plan'.

Before the second season starts, draw up a rough itinerary to show the pattern of competition, which may well include an excursion to the Class Association's 'Nationals' to gain experience in big-fleet sailing and to meet up with other enthusiastic owners.

Spend the early part of the season perfecting starts and sailing good windward courses. Later in the season it should be possible to engage in boat-for-boat tactical racing and to develop an overall strategy for each race dependent upon the prevailing weather conditions. Average finishing positions somewhere above the bottom third of the fleet will indicate good progress.

If a handicap series is available, sail it to improve your ability to overtake or to block an overtaking boat. Your results will often serve to encourage rather than discourage you. Sail in local regattas at other clubs, prior to attending the National Championships if they are being held in a reasonably sheltered area. The experience of attending a National for the first time is worth all the frustrations of big-fleet racing when your sailing and racing skills may not match your ambitions. Finish the season with a short series and only sail the 'frostbite' (winter series) if it provides relaxation.

During the third year you can expect to see a few first places coming your way in some of the less competitive series. Boathandling and racing skills, especially in the area of boat-to-boat tactics, will develop quite quickly as confidence builds and you are prepared to contest starts, initiate tacking duels and fight off challenges at rounding marks. The racing rules will begin to make sense to you by then, and you should begin to use the rules to advantage and to protest about those who infringe them.

If you have decided to develop your racing skills further, you will now have to make a decision about the competitiveness of your boat. By attending a series of class open meetings at different venues you can assess its overall performance. It may be that new foils and/or sails will suffice, or that the boat needs a complete overhaul during the winter.

The Nationals will be less of an unknown quantity and you should seek a finishing position somewhere near the middle of the fleet, given reasonably good sailing conditions. Near the end of the year your club rating should be within the top third of your class, with a number of top placings in some of the races.

At the start of the fourth year, you will appreciate that application and attention to detail are the keys to success, and if you have a new boat it will have to be race-tuned. The best way to tune your boat is to find another good skipper and crew to tune up with, so that each of you can benefit from a set of on-water tune-up exercises.

Much will depend on the strength of the class in your area or country; if the Nationals are attended by upwards of a hundred boats, the class is healthy. Sailing at the club will be confined to known popular and closely-contested events and a spring or autumn series which will provide the opportunity to win a trophy. Otherwise, open meetings and championships will form the basis of your summer programme, culminating in a serious attempt to put together a good set of results at the Nationals.

Jaap Zeelhuis (Holland) fights off Roger Schultz (Germany) in the 1988 Laser Worlds.

Tornado catamarans at the start of the 1987 World Championships. Close fleet racing in fast boats is exciting for both competitors and spectators.

TEAM DINGHY RACING

Team racing in dinghies is perhaps one of the most tactically demanding forms of sailing, as sailors are able to make great use of the rules to prevent their team from losing. For example, certain moves intended to slow the opposition down are permitted by the rules, and slowing the opposition down is very much a feature of team racing. Only rarely are the tactical skills inherent in this used in other forms of racing, such as championship racing.

Typically, team racing will be between two teams of three boats per team, all of the boats being from the same class, but two-boat and four-boat team racing are common variants.

Scoring in team racing is under the place points system, with 3/4 point for the first place (except in two-boat team racing) and the number of points for each other place being numerically equivalent to the boat's position in the finishing order, for example 2 points for second place, 3 points for third, and so on. The team with the lowest aggregate points score will be the winners.

It is essential that, in a tight team race, close attention is paid to the team's overall score, so that winning combinations of finishing places can be sought. Tactical considerations must be aimed at getting the team into a winning position.

For instance, one boat a long way out in the lead will not always ensure a win for its team, and 2-3-4 is one of the classic winning team race patterns as the leading boat is isolated from the rest of its team and is ineffective in the tactical battle for the remaining places.

The highest points total with which it is possible to win in three-boat team racing is 10 points compiled from placings of 2, 3 and 5, not immediately obvious as a winning total. As has already been suggested, two boat team racing is scored slightly differently in that the scoring system is modified so that the team with the last boat over the line loses.

While team racing takes place throughout the world, in many ways the United Kingdom and the United States are the leading centres of the sport because of their flourishing university and college racing circuits. The British Universities Sailing Association (BUSA) runs a team racing league and hosts an annual championship, and there is a similar league and championship for polytechnic colleges.

In the United States, university and college racing is organized by the Intercollegiate Yacht Racing Association (IYRA), whose annual events include the IYRA Team-Racing Championship and the National Women's Intercollegiate Championship. The United States Yacht Racing Union (USYRU) also organizes team races, including the US team-racing championship (the Hinman Cup).

The British National Team Racing Championship, sponsored by the Royal Yachting Association (RYA), seems to have fallen a little by the wayside and has been replaced by the World Team Racing Championship (the Wilson Trophy) which is hosted by West Kirby SC. This is sailed in Firefly dinghies supplied by the club and sponsored by local companies, and each team is given boats and sails of a particular colour so that the spectators can easily see how the race is developing.

The boats used for team racing range from the 12-foot Firefly dinghy up to 36-foot yachts which are used for the British-American Cup team racing series, and include dinghies such as the International 14 and the 505 which are raced using trapezes and spinnaker. The use of trapezes and spinnakers adds to the excitement, but it does rather detract from the tactical aspect of team racing as boatspeed may

Any type of dinghy can be used in team racing. Here, six Lasers vie for a winning combination.

become a more significant factor in deciding the race winners.

In general, team racing is best suited to two-man racing dinghies raced without trapeze or spinnaker, and on the college circuit in the UK the most popular classes are the Lark and Laser II. Both boats are very simple to sail and accelerate and decelerate quickly, which is a key feature for good team racing.

Good acceleration and deceleration are important in team racing because of the techniques employed to slow down the opposition. There are a number of such techniques,

which involve a skipper slowing an opposing boat so that his or her team-mates can overtake it, and most are used on the upwind legs.

One of the main techniques is to cover a boat so as to get between it and the wind, thus placing it in a wind shadow. This needs careful positioning of the boat, and a very close cover is most effective.

The leebow tack is another very effective way to slow a boat down. By sailing to leeward of a rival, and staying just ahead of its wind shadow, a boat can get close enough for its sails to bend the wind onto the

leeward side of its rival's sails.

Away from the beat, the most common site for team-racing place changes is at marks, where intelligent placing such as stopping in the two-boat-length circle to force an opponent's boat wide can have its role.

On a reach, the most common tactic to allow place changing is to luff so as to force an opposing boat way above the rhumb line (the direct line to the next mark). Alternatively, if an opposing boat tries to go to leeward it can be blanketed by the wind shadow of a windward

boat, and the windward boat can exacerbate the slowing effect by overtrimming its mainsail.

The tactics and techniques of team racing are many and various, and a free-thinking approach is needed so that tactics can be matched to the prevailing conditions. Usually, a team will race two races in matched flights of boats, swapping boats between races. In this way, the effect of any differences in boatspeed between the flights of boats can be offset, and this is important if a fair race is to result.

BOAT CLUB RACING

Organized racing within boat clubs is the foundation on which all the higher levels of sailing competition are based, and clubs come in all shapes and sizes. The Royal Yacht Squadron at Cowes was originally constituted as an arm of the British Navy, and its members still fly the Royal Navy Ensign. The New York Yacht Club, famous for its long custody of the America's Cup, created a chain of clubs along the Eastern Seaboard so that its members could benefit from the services of the club when they visited popular ports such as Newport, Rhode Island. In contrast to these large, prestigious clubs, hundreds of clubs throughout Europe and the Americas sail on small lakes and reservoirs, some as small as a few acres in size.

A common theme running through these clubs is the quasi-naval hierarchy of club officials, which includes such ranks as Admirals, Commodores, Flag Officers, Sailing Masters, Officers of the Day, Gunners, Cadets and Bosuns. Many clubs, especially those 'senior clubs' with large memberships and a tradition of social activities, also have their own club dress uniforms and codes of conduct.

If you wish to join a club, membership is usually by election by the club committee. What type of club you join will depend largely on the area in which you live or sail, and the type of sailboating in which you wish to participate.

The majority of newcomers to dinghy sailing will join a local club so that they can participate in local activities midweek as well as at weekends. Cruiser racer owners living some distance from the sea will have to join a coast-based club, or a Class Association which organizes races through a club or group of clubs.

Another factor which influences the type of racing you will become involved in is the availability of one-design or handicap racing. In the United States, one-design racing is the order of the day and there is comparatively little dinghy handicap racing. In the UK, the majority of dinghy clubs organize racing for both one-designs and handicap fleets. The cruiser racer scene was originally based on handicap fleets, but the popularity of one-design fleet racing increased during the last decade as owners became dissatisfied with local and international handicapping systems.

Perhaps the best option is to join a club which offers one-design and handicap racing to all boat owners. One-designs race on equal terms, and first home is always the winner as long as all the racing rules have been complied with.

There are many different handicapping systems. The Royal Yachting Association's 'Portsmouth Yardstick' system allocates a particular number to each of 114 different classes of dinghy and keelboat. The number is based on annual reports, supplied by clubs, suggesting changes based on their handicap race results. The objective is to enable the slowest boats to compete on equal terms with faster boats by allowing them additional time on

Right *The International Canoe class provides exciting racing worldwide in a craft which is sailed from a sliding seat and is very difficult to control.*
Below *A typical mixed bag of dinghies competing in a club handicap race.*

the course. The amount of extra time is calculated from a set of tables which relate to the boat's number and the time taken to sail the race course.

Cruiser racer handicap systems, such as the Channel Handicap System, operate to a secret formula. Owners must supply accurate details and measurements of their boats to the measurement office. They then receive a CHS number or rating which is applied to all races run to the CHS system. It goes without saying that the historical path of yacht racing is littered with discarded handicap and rating systems, abandoned as owners became disgruntled with them and demanded new ones.

Your choice of boat for racing will depend on the designs adopted by the club you want to join – it's no use buying a Dragon if the club doesn't allow keelboats. Conversely, if you already have a boat, or you have decided on the type of boat you want to race, you will have to find a club that races that type.

Once you have joined a club and bought your boat you will be pitched into racing at the deep end. Most racing sailors learned that way, so you should seek all the advice you can get beforehand from fellow club members, especially about the basics of the immensely complex International Yacht Racing Rules. Ideally, you should attend a series of courses in racing procedures and the racing rules during the early part of your racing career.

The pattern of club racing has become standardized around the world into seasonal series. For instance, in northern latitudes 'frostbite' or winter sailing takes place from November to March or April or until the waters freeze over and sailing is impossible.

A spring series encourages sailors onto the water in sufficient time to compete in the summer series, which lasts until the main holiday season of late July and August when many crews will take their boats away to national or regional championships and to local regattas staged at nearby clubs. An autumn series gives those who missed out on the earlier series the opportunity to win something before the frostbite season comes around again.

Prizes usually centre on a principal cup or plate donated by an ex-club member or passed down from earlier competitions, and prizewinning can extend down to 10th place in a well-attended series. Most clubs have so many individual class and handicap trophies for the numerous series and individual championships that the annual prize-giving can last for up to two hours as the silverware is distributed.

The majority of clubs encourage family membership, and many incorporate junior fleets and have extensive summer programs. In the United States, the larger clubs are prominent social centres and stage summer-long junior programs staffed by professionals. In the UK, junior programs tend to be ongoing with the emphasis on spring and fall training courses, leaving the summer free for racing.

The wide choice of venue – inland lake or reservoir, river, estuary or open sea location – combined with the great number of clubs, means that most sailors can find a club that suits them.

Above *Racing in Optimist dinghies provides children with an excellent introduction to competitive racing.*
Right *The Salcombe Yawl, originating in Salcombe, Devon, is one of the many flourishing local one-design classes.*

PERFORMANCE CRUISER RACING

The performance cruiser offers the comfort of a cruising yacht plus enough speed and manoeuvrability to ensure that its owner need not feel outclassed in local racing. Cruiser racing, whether handicap racing where all yachts are different, or class racing between identical yachts, is organized through clubs at weekends and, usually, one or two evenings a week.

Racing is relaxed and informal with little of the cut-and-thrust of offshore racing. Courses are shorter – perhaps over a maximum of 20 miles – and the racing is an ideal way for an owner to compare the performance of his yacht with that of others of a similar size.

Racing at this level is a good way to hone skills that will, inevitably, come in useful during cruising. For example, it offers a chance to use the spinnaker and to indulge in a little close-quarters tacking. Apart from that, most modern cruisers owe much of their design to their racing cousins, and this type of racing gives their owners the opportunity to put their speed and manoeuvrability to good use.

Cruiser racing takes place at all levels and owners find their own level quickly, most being content to leave the offshore racing to those who enjoy the discomfort, and occasional thrills, of long passages out of sight of land. The average owner of a modern cruising yacht usually prefers to combine a day's sailing with a little not-too-strenu-ous racing, improving his or her skills and sharpening up the crew.

Some classes enjoy close racing. Fleets build up, owners get together and soon the top yachts are beginning to consider entering class championships. Here the line between offshore racing and cruiser racing starts to blur. If an owner decides to take racing seriously there is no reason why he should not enter some of the longer, offshore races, especially if his family or regular crew have caught the bug sufficiently to make up the numbers.

Unless the class is one-design, the owner will then need to have the boat measured according to whichever rule is in force where he wants to race. This could be the International Offshore Rule (IOR), the International Measurement System (IMS), the Channel Handicap System (CHS) or one of a number of others, all designed to equalize the performances of widely differing yachts and their rigs.

With such a rating the yacht can now be entered in major regattas like Cowes or Burnham Week, where the owner will meet owners of similar, or identical, yachts and through enjoyable racing compare performance and different gear and thus improve both his yacht and his racing.

Many areas have associations that organize racing among clubs. For instance, on the East Coast of England there is the East Anglia Off-shore Racing Association, in Ireland

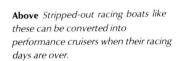

Above *Stripped-out racing boats like these can be converted into performance cruisers when their racing days are over.*

Left *One-design cruiser racers, such as these Ranger class yachts, are often used for international match racing.*

the Irish Sea Offshore Racing Association, and in Poole the Poole Yacht Racing Association. There are many equivalents elsewhere in Britian and throughout America.

Performance cruiser racers make up the vast bulk of yachts both in England and America. The success-ful compromise between the two roles which the yacht is designed to

play depends on many factors, most important of which is the need for good accommodation without the boat becoming too much like a cara-van. The owners of small cruiser racers usually have to put up with limited headroom but when design-ing yachts of over 30 feet, naval architects have perfected clever ways to keep the profile sleek without cutting down on comfort.

Modern out-and-out racing yachts are, by and large, useless for cruising. In the effort to keep weight to a minimum all superfluous inter-ior furniture is left out, leaving an almost-bare hull that is only toler-ated by dedicated crews in their quest for victory. The performance

cruiser, on the other hand, provides comfortable accommodation and will have a sparkling windward performance – vital in racing – without the complexities of a racing rig that requires maximum con-centration and tuning to get the best out of the sails.

Performance cruisers are, in effect, de-tuned racing boats with easily-handled rigs. They are the marine equivalent of sporty family cars, built and styled to appeal to those who like comfort but dislike being overtaken. Their construc-tion is sturdier than that of their rac-ing counterparts, and they are nowhere near as exotic.

For, perhaps, half the price of a

dedicated racer, the cruiser racer offers far more than half the per-formance and twice the comfort. Not dissimilar in profile, with deep keels and adequate rig, its life ex-pectancy and usefulness far outstrips that of a racing yacht.

That high performance is not wasted when it comes to cruising because, in many respects, speed is of greater importance in a cruising yacht than in a racer. Racing depends on closely-matched yachts, whose crews are expected to get the best out of whatever they sail, whether it be a high-performance yacht or a sailing barge. The skipper of the barge may be sailing slowly, but as long as he is sailing the boat as

fast and efficiently as it can go, he will beat the other barges and win the race. The race can take all day; winning is the important thing, not speed.

The cruising skipper, on the other hand, may have a hungry, tired family aboard, longing to reach the nearest port. It is essential that he gets there before the tide turns, and for that he needs a yacht that is not only comfortable, but swift. The cruising skipper races every time he goes sailing. A little cruiser-racing practice will allow him to polish the skills needed to bring his yacht safely home to port before the pubs close or the family lose their tempers completely.

OFFSHORE RACING

The origins of offshore racing can be traced back to 1866, when two wealthy New York yachtsmen were stung by a newspaper article criticizing their timidity for venturing no farther than the sheltered waters of the Hudson River and Long Island Sound. In response, they decided to race across the Atlantic, in the dead of winter, for a wager of $30,000. Three yachts took part in that race, and the winner was J Gordon Bennett Jr's *Henrietta*.

Nearly 40 years later, Kaiser Wilhelm of Germany proposed another transatlantic race. This attracted eleven entries and was won by the magnificent three-masted, 187-foot schooner *Atlantic* whose record of 12 days and 4 hours stood until a few years ago.

A year earlier, however, Thomas Fleming Day had organized a 300-mile race from New York to Marblehead for much smaller yachts and it is to this race, and subsequent races, that modern offshore racing owes the greatest debt. No longer, in the words of the American yachtsman Sherman Hoyt, was 'going to sea in moderately small craft, with attendant discomfort' a 'mild form of insanity', but an accepted part of yacht racing.

By 1925, thanks to the efforts of British yachtsman Weston Martyn, one of the greatest offshore races of all, the Fastnet, had been established. By 1938 the Royal Ocean Racing Club was organizing ten annual offshore races. That same year there were 49 starters in the Bermuda Race and in 1939 37 yachts set out to race from San Francisco to Honolulu.

John Illingworth was another of the pioneers, having developed a passion for offshore racing while serving as an engineer officer in the Royal Navy. Thanks to his enthusiasm, offshore racing spread throughout the world, and one of his greatest achievements was the setting up of the first Sydney to Hobart Race, in 1946.

By 1957 the sport had acquired its centrepiece, the Admiral's Cup. This competition is open to three-boat teams from all countries and is a mixture of inshore and long-distance races, culminating in the classic Fastnet.

The sport flourishes today, under various handicapping rules, from Australia to Argentina. The balance is now shifting away from the International Offshore Rule (IOR), which attempts to equate the performance of widely differing sizes of yachts, toward simpler rules like the International Measurement System (IMS) and Channel Handicap System (CHS). The difficulty of organizing fair races between different boats inevitably leads to criticism, and since 1970 the IOR has been modified several times.

Nevertheless, wherever there are owners keen to pit their individual boats against each other offshore, the rule makers are on hand to devise a handicapping system and the designers soon find ways to circumvent it.

Offshore racing yachts range in size from about 30 feet to over 80 feet, but not all are built to conform to a rule. The most popular offshore racing takes place in identical one-design yachts with no handicapping, such as the Sigma 33 and Contessa 32.

In the United States, there is a thriving class of 50-footers which race under IOR but with no time allowance. This form of racing, or level rating competition, puts a premium on boat handling, although the races seldom venture truly offshore.

Offshore racing is perhaps the most taxing of all competitive sailing. Teamwork, seamanship and stamina are required to get the best out of a yacht over 200-mile courses far out to sea, and the ability to drive the yacht at its fastest through all conditions from gale to calm is vital. During the tragic 1979 Fastnet Race, for example, while the rescue services were coping with hundreds of Mayday calls, many of the Admiral's Cup teams were racing at top speed under storm sail in appalling conditions, breaking records in the process.

At its highest level, offshore racing is a sport for the expert, and today the crews of the top yachts are likely to be professionals, hired by owners to drive and handle their expensive investments. At its basic level, most yacht clubs include at least a couple of offshore races in their calendar, ranging from 40-mile coastal events to longer cross-Channel or inter-island races.

In England, the Junior Offshore Group organizes a full season of racing for a mixed bag of small yachts, both cruisers and cruiser racers. For the yachtsman newly graduated from dinghies, this provides an early taste of the rigours to come, although many are content to stick to offshore racing at this level.

A more recent development has been the growing popularity of organized transocean races, which are something between a rally and a cruise in company.

The late Jack Knights summed up the joys and skills of offshore racing better than anyone: 'Ocean racing calls for better teamwork and a more comprehensive range of talents than any other type of yacht racing. Navigation, tactics, strategy, helmsmanship, sail trimming and weatherlore are all critical factors, and so is sheer luck. It is not for everybody. If you are prone to motion sickness, you had better put it out of your mind. Nevertheless, there are people, owners mostly, who have raced regularly for years and been seasick regularly for years.

'You need to be at home on the high seas, in good weather and bad; you need to be able to suffer physical discomfort happily; you need to be able to make do with a minimum of sleep; and you need the will to operate at close-to-peak efficiency for a continuous two or three days.

'Frankly, only a very few really enjoy bad weather at sea; the others endure it for the sake of the real pleasure that offshore racing brings. It is, after all, the most testing, most profound form of yacht racing. Some will say it is the only true yacht racing.'

Left *'Outsider' gets a lift as she rounds the leeward mark in the first inshore race of the 1985 One Ton Worlds.*
Top *This One Ton division fleet includes 'Centurion', 'Xeryus', 'Jamarella' and 'I-Punkt'.*
Above *Offshore events demand precise navigation and weather interpretation. The seas, as here between Cuba and Jamaica, are often quite large.*

MULTIHULL RACING

Despite the fact that the multi-hulled craft of the Pacific and Indian Oceans were documented by the early European explorers, very few attempts were made to develop these fast, lightweight, easily-driven craft known as 'Feejee' boats.

One of the first recorded designs for a 'double boat' was by H Melling of Liverpool who, in 1873, had what he called a 'safety yacht' constructed on the double-hull principle. A few years later, in 1876, the legendary American designer and builder, Nathaniel Herreshoff, produced the 32-foot catamaran *John Gilpin*, which proved to be very fast and incorporated a number of ingenious features, such as toed-in tillers to

take account of the fact that, when turning, the outside hull had to travel farther than the inside hull.

On both sides of the Atlantic, attempts were made to race catamarans against 'metre rule' boats, but in each case the designs were banned from racing the monohulls because of their greater speed. This effectively killed off the development of multihulls until the late 1950s and early 1960s, when designers again began to experiment with small day sailing catamarans and trimarans.

The multihull configuration provides stability from the beam rather than from a weighted keel. Catamarans have two identical hulls placed

wide apart with the mast carried centrally either on a metal beam or, in the case of cruising and racing catamarans, on the bridgedeck superstructure. Trimarans have a larger central hull flanked by two thinner outriggers supported by arched beams. When sailing, only two of the three hulls are in the water at any one time.

In Europe, the multiplicity of dinghy designs was echoed by the development of day racing catamarans such as the Shearwater class which dominated early one-design racing. In America, however, the emphasis was on beach boats such as the Hobie range of catamarans designed specifically to ride the surf

of the Californian beaches.

There has been a gradual amalgamation of design concepts, culminating in the Dart class which combines the symmetrical rounded hull shapes of European development with the smooth hulls resulting from the lack of centreboards.

Small day racing catamarans of up to 25 feet received their greatest boost when the International Yacht Racing Union (IYRU) designated four international catamaran classes in 1962. These were 'A' Class, for singlehanded boats 18′ × 7′6″ carrying 150 square feet of sail; 'B' Class, two-man boats 20′ × 10′ carrying 278 square feet of sail; 'C' Class, two-man boats 25′ × 14′ carrying

300 square feet of sail; and 'D' Class, three-man carrying 500 square feet of sail.

The IYRU move was to encourage further the catamaran development which had been in evidence in America at the Miami 'one-of-a-kind regattas' and the International Catamaran Challenge Trophy – the 'Little America's Cup' – which had been competed for by teams from the UK and the United States.

For a while, 'C' class development grabbed the headlines as Australia joined in with superbly built double-enders, but in 1967 the IYRU held trials to select 'A' and 'B' class catamarans to go forward for Olympic selection. The Rod March-designed and Reg White-built Tornado swept the board, and in 1976 Reg White won the first Olympic gold medal for multi-

Left The French trimaran 'CDK/Media de la Mer' powers to windward in a Formula 40 Grand Prix event.
Below The Olympic gold medallist Randy Smyth reaches downwind in his catamaran 'The Smyth Team' during a Grand Prix event.

hulled craft.

The advantages of beamy, unballasted cruising craft did not go unnoticed. Early examples were cold-moulded with thin veneers of wood and then, as GRP technology advanced, the new material was found to be especially suited to the smooth shapes of hulls and bridge decking.

In America, hulls were deep and V-shaped and often asymmetric, but in the UK the hulls continued to have rounded lower sections. The first commercially-available trimarans had deep V-shaped sections and were designed by an American, Arthur Piver, while James Wharram introduced a whole range of build-it-yourself designs based on the deep-V hull, and thousands of cheap, seaworthy catamarans have been built to his designs.

Perhaps multihull development would have stagnated but for the introduction of the Singlehanded Transatlantic Race in 1964. Dominated by monohulls in its early years, this quadrennial race is now largely the preserve of exotic sponsored multihulls, most of them

French. France has, in fact, been the main driving force behind the massive interest in multihull development and racing, and was largely responsible for the introduction of the Formula 40 class which is run on the same sort of basis as Formula 1 motor racing.

Although initially highly successful, the Formula 40 class has been showing signs of strain. Technical development has been rapid and so the boats are now very expensive, while the circuit itself has suffered from some of the race meetings being poorly organized.

However, at its best, Formula 40 racing is absolutely spectacular thanks to the incredible speed and agility of the boats. It may prove to have been a short-term gimmick, soon forgotten, or it may become a permanent part of the international racing calendar.

It has always been accepted that multihulls capsize, especially in extreme conditions. Nevertheless, long-distance races continue to attract large multihull entries, and day racing catamarans have their own long-distance events, often

raced around islands. The Rond am Texel is typical of such races, attracting entries from all over the world to race around the island of Texel, one of the West Frisian Islands off the coast of Holland.

In the United States there is the Worrell 1000, a stage-by-stage race for specially-adapted catamarans. Starting in Florida, it runs north for a thousand miles up the East Coast. It gives crews the opportunity to race long distances by day and rest up overnight, and in many ways echoes the Tour de France à la Voile race in concept.

Racing a multihull is very similar to racing fast vehicles on land. The object is to go for speed on all points of sailing by keeping the boat as level as possible. The key tactic is to tack downwind, retracing the same tracks covered in upwind tacking. The reason for this manoeuvre is that the greater speeds attained on a series of broad reaches results in a higher aggregate *speed made good* downwind than does a directly-sailed downwind course.

OLYMPIC RACING

First seen at the Games in 1900, but not an official Olympic sport until 1908, Olympic sailing is for many the ultimate in sporting endeavour. Since the Olympics come around only once every four years, a chance to compete in them is a rare prize to be seized by anyone of sufficient ability to qualify.

Eight different types of sailing boat now take part in the Olympics. Of these, one class is for women alone, while two classes feature racing for both men and women. Thus there are ten events in total, with racing being held over a seven-race series.

The Olympic course consists of a windward leg, two reaching legs, another windward leg, a run and then a final leg to a windward finish. A good balance of sailing skills is tested over a course of this type, but the long legs of the course put a premium on good speed and clear tactical planning.

Olympic-class sailing is not confined to the Olympics themselves, as each four-year cycle sees prospective Olympians engaged in a series of Olympic Class regattas which may take them to all parts of the world. Of these regattas Kiel Week, held in northern Germany in late

June, is among the largest, with racing for all Olympic classes and many others besides.

Across Europe, a formal linking of the Olympic Class regattas has been put together to create the Eurolymp series, which allows a ranking to be developed of all participating competitors. Nine regattas are involved, with entry lists restricted to competitors sponsored by their national authorities. Outside this series there remains a number of well-established regattas for sailors to enjoy.

The largest of the Olympic boats is the Soling, a three-man keelboat with a weight of 1035 kg (2282 pounds) and an overall length of 8.2 metres (27 feet). The class has been in the Olympics since 1972 and the crew weights are typically 265 to 280 kg (585 to 620 pounds).

Hiking-out using harness is very much the order of the day in the Soling, which is a strict one-design hull whose principal builders are to be found in Canada, Denmark and Germany.

Next down the range is the Star, a classic keelboat design first seen at the Olympics in 1932 and one of the most demanding of sailboats. With a weight of 672 kg (1482 pounds)

and a length of 6.93 metres (23 feet), the Star has a two-man crew weighing in at between 175 and 200 kg (385 to 440 pounds).

The most distinctive feature of the Star is its massive mainsail, which powers the boat along in very light breezes. In strong breezes a flatter mainsail is required, and this must be created by using the rig controls. These are highly sophisticated on this boat, with running backstays and checkstays supporting the mast.

The Star is one of the most-sailed keelboats in the world, and it is said that a Star Class world championship is among the highest of honours in the sport.

The catamaran classes are represented at the Olympics by the Tornado, which first appeared in 1976. This fast, two-sailed boat provides an exciting ride and even at the speeds achieved the racing is intensely tactical. Hull shapes in this class are essentially one-design, with few differences between builders' products.

There are two principal rig options available for the Tornado. One uses a straight mast, and a full mainsail controlled by a powerful downhaul that is pulled on hard to depower the rig. The other rig

option uses a pre-bent mast and a flatter mainsail, and mast rotation is a more important control with this rig.

Two two-man trapeze boats – the Flying Dutchman and the 470 – are used at the Olympics. The Flying Dutchman is very much the powerboat of dinghy classes. First seen at the Olympics in 1960, the boat provides the highest of performance for those who enjoy tuning a rig which is fully controllable.

Mast rake is very much the name of the game in the FD class, and the massive overlapping genoa is fitted with several clew eyes up its leech. These extra clew eyes are used to keep the genoa leech firm as the mast is raked aft. No-one knows precisely why aft mast rake is fast in a breeze, but it is and so it is used by all sailors. The main builders of the Flying Dutchman are to be found in Germany and the United States, and crew weights are of the order of 150 to 165 kg (330 to 365 pounds).

The 470 is for much lighter crews, 125 to 135 kg (275 to 300 pounds) being typical. The class was first seen at the 1976 Olympics, and it provides very tight racing with only very small speed differences between boats. The rig is essentially

underpowered, and is not easy to set up as class rules preclude many of the rig controls seen on the Flying Dutchman. At the Olympics the 470 is used for both men's and women's classes.

The Finn singlehander, designed for the 1952 Olympics and present ever since, is a real test of sailing skill since boats are provided by the race committee. Helmsmen usually weigh in at 85 to 95 kg (187 to 210 pounds) and are intensely self-motivated.

The unstayed mast and una rig must have an exact match between the mainsail luff curve and mast, and a very soft cloth is used for the mainsail to allow this to depower in a breeze.

From 1992 the Finn is joined by a second singlehander, the Europe, which in Olympic racing is a women's class. This 3.35-metre (11-foot) boat is perfectly suited to its task and, like the Finn, features a una rig on an unstayed mast.

The final Olympic class is the Sailboard, raced in separate men's and women's classes. The 3.9-metre (12.75-foot) Division II board is used, and both boards and rigs are supplied at the event by the race committee.

The three-man Olympic Soling keelboat class after the start of the third race in the 1988 event, held off Pusan, South Korea. The Solings revelled in the boisterous wind and sea conditions.

Top *Marit Soderström and Birgitta Bengtsson of Sweden winning their silver medal in the Women's 470 Class event, 1988.*
Above *1988 Star Class gold medallists Bryn Vail and Mike McIntyre.*

SINGLEHANDED RACING

The earliest known singlehanded ocean crossing took place in 1786, when Josiah Shackford sailed a 15-ton gaff sloop east to west across the Atlantic from Bordeaux, France, to Dutch Guiana (now Surinam). The first west to east singlehanded Atlantic crossing did not come until 1876, when Alfred Johnson, a Grand Banks fisherman, made the journey in a 20-foot dory called *Centennial*. The problems he encountered, of damage, gales and fatigue, are well known to all those who have attempted to sail the oceans of the world alone.

The motivations behind these voyages are many. Some have done it for spiritual enlightenment, others to prove themselves in competition, or out of philanthropy, and even as a result of mutiny. In 1877 Richard McMullen set off from Greenhithe, Kent, for Cherbourg with two crew. A week after arrival they became so reluctant to obey orders that he sacked them, returning alone.

Ten years earlier Rob Roy Mac-Gregor, a Cambridge graduate with a taste for adventure of all kind, and a gift for self-publicity, had made many voyages in his small canoe. In 1867, he decided to sail alone, from London via Boulogne to Paris, to deliver a cargo of Protestant tracts to the 'godless' French Roman Catholics. His accounts of his adventures captured a wide readership at the time.

Captain Cleveland of Massachusetts claimed to have crossed the Indian and Pacific Oceans in a 15-foot boat in 1800, but the first substantiated claim to a singlehanded Pacific crossing was that of Bernard Gilboy, from Buffalo, New York. He achieved this incredible voyage in 1882-3, in his 18-foot boat *Pacific*.

However, the true father of singlehanded sailing was undoubtedly Captain Joshua Slocum. In 1895, at the age of 51, he set off from Newport, Rhode Island in his 36 ft 9 in gaff yawl *Spray* to become the first to circumnavigate the world alone. The 46,000-mile voyage, via the Magellan Straits, took three years.

Slocum, a professional seaman but a non-swimmer, was lost during a subsequent voyage, but after him came a string of pioneering sailors, including Harry Pidgeon, whose four-year round-the-world voyage ended in Los Angeles in 1925, and Fred Rebel and Edward Miles, who both crossed the Pacific from west to east in 1932.

Most of the early pioneers were American, but by the 1950s the list of singlehanded sailors had become more cosmopolitan with Australians, Norwegians, Argentinians, French and Germans joining it. These included Alain Bombard, of France, who sailed the Atlantic in an inflatable.

The great era of competitive singlehanded sailing dawned in 1960. The following decade saw the first singlehanded one-stop circumnavigation, and the interest shown by British newspapers such as the *Observer*, *Sunday Times* and *Financial Times* drove singlehanded sailors farther and faster than ever.

In 1964, Francis Chichester won the first Observer Singlehanded Transatlantic Race (OSTAR), and in 1966 in *Gypsy Moth IV* (now preserved at Greenwich) he became the first man to sail solo, with one stop only, around the world. Other well-known boats of the time include *Lively Lady* – Alec Rose's 36-foot yawl – *Suhaili*, in which Robin Knox-Johnson became the first man ever to sail non-stop around the world, Bernard Moitessier's *Joshua*, Nigel Tetley's *Victress* and Chay

Top *'Jester', the boat that started it all when Blondie Hasler issued the first transatlantic challenge. She was abandoned to the Atlantic in the 1988 race.*
Right *Philippe Poupon, in 'Fleury Michon', won the 1984 OSTAR.*

Blyth's *British Steel*. These boats and their skippers laid the foundations for modern singlehanded sailing.

Among the many women who have made their mark on singlehanded sailing are Gladys Gradeley, the first woman to cross the Atlantic alone (in 1903); Ann Davison, who in 1952-3 made the first east-west Atlantic crossing by a woman; and Sharon Sites Adams, the first woman to sail solo across the Pacific (in 1969). Nicolette Milnes-Walker, Naomi James, Anna Woolf and Clare Francis also set transatlantic records in their time.

The sport today is dominated by the French. Transatlantic solo races have proliferated since the early Observer races and crossing times have fallen dramatically, and long-distance racing also has a number of solo events.

Both the 1981 and the 1986 three-stop BOC Round the World Races were won by Frenchman Philippe Jeantot, who holds the record in a time of 134 days 5 hours and 23 minutes. The outright record for a one-stop singlehanded circum-navigation is held by another Frenchman, Olivier de Kersauson, who complete the voyage in a trimaran faster than many fully-crewed yachts. However, the American,

Dodge Morgan, holds the non-stop record, a time of 150 days 1 hour and 6 minutes, which he achieved in his boat *American Promise* at an average speed of 7.16 knots.

Despite fears about the safety of sailing multihulls singlehanded there is a hard core of sailors willing to push themselves to the limits, people like Philippe Poupon, one of the OSTAR winners. No longer are these races like cruising voyages; singlehanded multihull racers are among the most highly paid, professional sportsmen in the world. But the price they pay is often their lives.

The list of singlehanded sailors

who have died at sea, although not necessarily while sailing alone, includes Alain Colas, who sailed his trimaran to a new circumnavigation record of 168 days in 1974, Loic Caradec, lost in the Atlantic in 1987, Daniel Gilard from his catamaran *Jet Services*, and Jacques de Roux. Most of the great solo sailors, including Eric Tabarly, winner of the 1964 and 1976 OSTARs, Chay Blyth and Philippe Jeantot have survived capsize and disaster. Despite modern position-plotting and efficient rescue services, solo sailors are as vulnerable as ever to the power of the sea, and yet there are always those willing to take the risk.

TRANSATLANTIC RACING

Transatlantic racing and the history of singlehanded racing are inextricably mixed. Some of the greatest contemporary sailors have cut their teeth on the storms and bitter seas that lie between the coasts of the great seafaring nations of America and Europe. Although there are now longer races, and perhaps harder ones, the unpredictability of the Atlantic always presents a challenge to even the best-found boats.

The idea of racing across ocean was frowned upon until relatively recently. Yachts were predominantly for day racing and, although manned by professional crews, it was not thought seamanlike to race out of sight of land and especially not at night.

The first yachts to race across the Atlantic took part for a wager between their wealthy New York owners. Unable to settle an argument which took place on 26 October 1866 at the Union Club in New York, Pierre Lorillard and the Osgood brothers, George and Frank, decided to race across the Atlantic in their respective yachts. They were later joined by J Gordon Bennett Jr, the only one to actually sail on the vessels.

At the appointed time, one o'clock on 11 December 1866, the three 200-ton schooners, *Henrietta*,

Vesta and *Fleetwing*, set sail for Cowes. The stake was $90,000. The race was hard fought and the yachts encountered the worst of the winter gales. On the ninth night out *Fleetwing* was struck by a mighty wave, and eight men on watch were swept overboard. Two of them were recovered, but six were lost. Eventually, J Gordon Bennett's 105-foot schooner *Henrietta* sighted land to win the race on Christmas Day, in a time of just under 14 days.

The race was more a stunt than a competition, and it was some time before the feat was emulated. In 1905, however, the three-masted schooner *Atlantic* knocked two days off that record, cutting it to 12 days 4 hours and 1 minute. The boat's skipper was the redoubtable Charlie Barr, and the new record was to remain unbroken for 75 years.

The race was for a cup, presented by the German Kaiser. *Atlantic*, *Endymion*, *Hamburg* and *Ailsa* were the four starters, but under Barr's inspired command the great schooner soon left her rivals far behind. Her owner, Wilson Marshall, pleaded with his skipper to reduce sail, but to no avail. *Atlantic* raced on through icebergs and gales, averaging over 14 knots, reaching the Bishop's Rock in 11 days 16

Above *Tony Bullimore drives the trimaran 'Apricot' over the Plymouth start of a two-handed race.*
Left *'Chica Boba II', seen here off Rame Head at the start of the 1972 singlehanded race, was typical of the early monohulls.*

hours, and Cowes 12 hours later, beating *Hamburg* by over a day.

Between 1851 and the end of that race, only 45 yachts had made the crossing. From then on, though, the trickle of crossings became a flood, and the Atlantic became the ultimate proving ground for ocean racing yachts.

Today, there is a plethora of transatlantic racing, singlehanded, two-handed and fully-crewed. The greatest race of all these is the Singlehanded Transatlantic Race, originally funded by the *Observer* news-

paper. It was then called the Observer Singlehanded Transatlantic Race (OSTAR), but is now sponsored by Carlsberg and known as the CSTAR. The French run their own version to the Caribbean called the Route du Rhum and there is now a cruising race, the Atlantic Race for Cruisers (ARC), sponsored by a British yachting magazine.

Atlantic's record was first smashed in 1980 by the famous French sailor Eric Tabarly in a time of 10 days 5 hours and 1 minute. Since then Tabarly's record has been broken four times, all by French multihulls. In 1987 it was cut to an astonishing 7 days 12 hours and 50 minutes, by Frenchman Philippe Poupon in the 75-foot trimaran *Fleury Michon VIII.* His average speed for the whole voyage was over 17

knots, and at one point the boat made a 24-hour run of 520 nautical miles, or 21.67 knots. It is interesting to compare this with *Virgin Atlantic Challenger's* powered record (itself broken in 1989 by Tom Gentry) of 3 days 8 hours and 31 minutes.

The advent of the two-handed transatlantic races has allowed trimarans, dangerous to sail alone, to be pushed at full speed. Chay Blyth and Rob James together won the first of these events in 1981, in the trimaran *Brittany Ferries*, and there have been several such races since. James was tragically lost a few years later from another trimaran, off Salcombe, Devon; ironically, there was a full crew aboard.

Another Two-Handed Transatlantic Race was won by the French catamaran *Royale*, skippered by Loic Caradec, later to lose his life in

mid-Atlantic on a record attempt.

Conventional races, like those organized by the Royal Ocean Racing Club (RORC), achieve nowhere near these record speeds, or the level of danger. Monohull racing across the Atlantic is often no more than cruising in company, with yachts taking the Trade Wind route via the Canaries. Normal crossing times are around 27-21 days.

One of these monohull events is the ARC race, which draws cruising boats from all over Europe and has become the most popular transatlantic race of the calendar. The race takes the yachts in a gentle southward sweep across the ocean to the Caribbean, and it gives crews a chance to extend their normal cruising, with an element of competition to spice the experience.

THE WHITBREAD RACE

The Whitbread Round the World Race, held every four years, was the first fully-crewed circumnavigational event to be established in the yachting calendar. No-one who saw that first fleet set off from Portsmouth in 1973 could have imagined how much the technology of round-the-world sailing yachts would change over the next decade or so.

For years it was common to dismiss the first race as no more than a jaunt. It is true that the elapsed times dropped steadily over the first four races, from the 144 days 11 hours set by the 77-foot ketch *Great Britain II* under Chay Blyth in 1973/4, to the 117 days 14 hours of Pierre Fehlmann's two feet larger, but five tons lighter, fractional sloop *UBS Switzerland* in 1985/6.

But don't try suggesting that the 1973/4 event was just a 'cruise in company' to the friends of Bernie Hosking, washed overboard from *GB II*, or the friends of Corporal Paul Waterhouse, sailing aboard the Italian yacht *Tauranga*, who was thrown into the water while trying to retrieve a broken spinnaker halyard one night in the Southern Ocean, or to the family of Dominique Guillet, ill-fated co-skipper of *33 Export*.

The first race was the inspired idea of Anthony Churchill, a magazine publisher, and his friend Guy Pearse. They later handed over their files to the Royal Naval Sailing Association, which has run the event ever since, with sponsorship from the UK brewing company Whitbread.

The winner of the first race was *Sayula II*, a standard Swan 65 ketch skippered by Ramon Carlin of Mexico. Fourteen yachts finished that race and much that befell them on their 27,000-mile voyage has become part of the 'Whitbread Experience'. *Sayula* suffered perhaps the severest knockdown ever recorded, limping back to Portsmouth triumphant but battered. The Nicholson 55 *Adventure*, placed second on handicap, was similarly savaged by the elements and the tale of destruction did not end there.

Eric Tabarly's *Pen Duick* lost her mast, Les Williams' aluminium ketch *Burton Cutter* split her hull, and most of the survivors of the race came back awed by the strength of the ocean and what it can do to even a well-found cruising yacht.

In the second Whitbread, in 1977, there were fifteen finishers and ten days were knocked off the recorded. Again it was *Great Britain II*, the

Alan Gurney-designed foam sandwich ketch, skippered this time by Rob James, that achieved the fastest time. Each of the crew paid £4000 for the privilege of beating Blyth's paratroopers' four-year-old record for line honours, which was as much a tribute to James' leadership as the yacht's design.

The winner on handicap, however, was Cornelis van Rietschoten's *Flyer*. Van Rietschoten's careful preparation for the race proved spectacularly right. He had hired Sparkman & Stephens to draw him a ketch-rigged improved Swan 65, to be built in aluminium by Huismans in Holland, and the boat was in the water long enough before the event to have completed two transatlantics and ironed out most of the problems that every new boat has.

Flyer's handicap win was a narrow one. Just over two hours separated her from Nick Ratcliff's modified sloop-rigged Swan 65 *King's Legend* at Portsmouth after a race that had kept both crews stretched for the entire voyage. Two hours was also the margin that split the two at Cape Town on the first leg, and at times the two yachts had swapped tacks in mid-ocean. Van Rietschoten had learned the

Top *'Philips Innovator' running before the enormous swells of the Southern Ocean. Sustained surfing speeds in excess of twenty knots place considerable strains on crews and equipment.*

Above *The Whitbread trophy symbolizes the essential elements of the race. The winners of this maritime marathon are a very select band.*

Right *Relentless driving in the worst conditions imaginable is the key to gaining a good result.*

lessons of the first race and applied them correctly, setting an example in preparation that no skipper can afford to ignore.

He repeated his victory four years later in another aluminium *Flyer*, this time a sloop designed by German Frers. For the first time, a yacht was to win the race both on handicap and elapsed time.

This was no compromise boat, whose skipper had chosen between extremes of handicap and line honours, but a gamble that paid off handsomely for the first, and possibly only, time. Although her corrected time was almost identical, she sailed the course just under 16 days faster than the old *Flyer*, pipping Alain Gabbay's French sloop *Charles Heidsieck* on corrected time by under a day and taking over $14\frac{1}{2}$ days off *Great Britain II's* record.

The race was a third disappointment for New Zealander Peter Blake, who had been on board the ill-fated *Burton Cutter* in the first race, and on *Heaths' Condor* when she lost her mast in the second. This time, Blake's 68-foot, Bruce Farr-designed *Ceramco New Zealand* broke her mast on the first leg. Rather than replace her mast after a gruelling season working up for the race, he had kept the old one, and paid the price.

The 1985/6 Whitbread was dominated by the battle between Blake's strong, but outclassed, 78.5-foot Ron Holland-design *Lion New Zealand* and Pierre Fehlmann's strong but highly competitive *UBS Switzerland*. Challenges from the other Kiwi yacht, Digby Taylor's *NZI Enterprise* – near sister-ship to *UBS* – and Padda Kuttel's *Atlantic Privateer*, which lost her rig on the first leg, faded.

After that, some of the edge went off the excitement when it became clear that Blake could only win if *UBS* hit trouble. *UBS* took only a couple of days off the old *Flyer's* time and Lionel Pean's much smaller *L'Esprit d'Equipe* took the handicap prize.

The Whitbread is now *the* classic ocean race. The first four races were run over a 27,000-mile route, but for the 1989/90 race the distance was increased to 33,000 miles. The first leg of the race was from the Solent to Punta del Este in Uruguay, instead of to Cape Town as in previous races. From there, the route was east through the Southern Ocean to Fremantle, Auckland and Cape Horn, then north to Punta del Este once more and on to Fort Lauderdale, Florida, before returning to Portsmouth.

THE ADMIRAL'S CUP

The Admiral's Cup series, a biennial event held in the Solent off Cowes and in Christchurch Bay further west, has benefited enormously from supporting sponsorship, first from Dunhill, the tobacco company, and in recent years from French champagne producers G H Mumm et Cie.

Organized by the Royal Ocean Racing Club (RORC), the Admiral's Cup racing series was the brainchild of five senior members of the club. The idea was to encourage overseas competitors, particularly Americans, to come to British waters every two years to contest the cup – a silver gilt trophy named after Sir Myles Wyatt, then Admiral of the Royal Ocean Racing Club.

The first series was held in 1957, off Cowes, and since then the event has grown to become one of the most prestigious and important yacht racing regattas for offshore sailing yachts in the world. In the series sailed in the 1970s, particularly those of 1977 and 1979, fifty-seven yachts from nineteen nations took part, a far cry from the two-team competition held twenty-two years previously.

Each nation is invited to send a team of three yachts to take part in the six-race series. The races are an around-the-buoys race in the Solent, two races over an Olympic-type course in Christchurch Bay, the 220-mile (345-km) Channel Race, a long inshore race and the world's toughest ocean race, the 605-mile (975-km) Fastnet. The Fastnet starts from the Royal Yacht Squadron line off Cowes, and from there the boats sail west to round the Fastnet Light, perched on a rock off the southern tip of Ireland, and return to the finish at Plymouth.

To avoid the many other yachts competing during the annual Cowes Week regatta, Admiral's Cuppers are given their own inshore courses and, except for the two long offshore races, are started away from the Squadron line to the east or the west of Cowes. Since 1977, the first of the inshore races has begun a few days prior to Cowes week.

Following the example set by the British, the various national teams are picked by a selection committee from fleets of yachts competing for places in the selection trials. These trials invariably take the form of normal offshore races on the yachting calendar organized by the equivalent of the RORC in each country.

In the formative years of the event, only four countries participated. They were Britain, who won the first and second matches, the United States, who took the cup in 1961, and France and Holland. Australia joined the fray in 1965, but went home empty handed after a strong British team retrieved the cup from the Americans. But the Australians returned in 1967, along with Denmark, France, West Germany, Holland, Ireland, Sweden and the United States.

In keeping with the economic

Top *Just after the start of the 1985 Fastnet, Swedish team member 'Indispensible Too' storms through the Solent chop.*
Below *The Admiral's Cup is yachting's premier trophy for offshore racing boats.*
Right *The gybe mark is fiercely contested by Spain (E), Australia (KA), France (F), Sweden (S) and the UK (K) during a 1987 inshore race.*

state of the host country, the British team did not do well in 1967 and it was clear from the outset of the series that the Australians were determined to take the cup down under. By the time the Channel Race and the two inshore races had been run, Australia was ahead by 40 points with Britain struggling to hold second place ahead of the United States and France. In the Fastnet that followed, the Australians scored a devastating success and walked away with a 104-point lead.

It took the British four years to recover their composure, despite many new yachts being launched for the selection trials. Among their owners was one of the great names in contemporary ocean racing: Arthur Slater. Crippled in a motor racing accident some years previously, he was determined to see the cup return to England. His Sparkman & Stephens-designed *Prospect of Whitby* joined *Phantom* and David Jonson's *Casse Tete III*. The United States was back again with a powerful team which included the two large yachts *Carina* and *Palawan*, and a design by a relative newcomer to the field of superyacht design, Dick Carter's *Red Rooster*.

The lifting keel *Red Rooster*

scored the highest individual points of any yacht in the eleven-team series and romped home in that year's Fastnet Race. The United States moved from third place to first ahead of the Australians and the British.

In 1971, two things happened which set the course of the Admiral's Cup on the road to a secure and popular future and simultaneously but indirectly enhanced the popularity of yachting worldwide. The Dunhill company injected sponsorship money into the Admiral's Cup, enabling proper press facilities to be set up in Cowes so that reporters and photographers could cover the event as never before.

Coincidentally, the British Prime Minister at the time, Edward Heath, who had progressed from dinghy sailing to winning the Sydney to Hobart Race in 1969, captained the British team in his yacht *Morning Cloud*. Its beautiful varnished wooden hull was one of the 27 designed and built that year as potential Admiral's Cup winners.

There can be little doubt that the Prime Minister's involvement and success in his various *Morning Cloud* yachts did much to publicize yachting in general and the Admi-

ral's cup in particular. He was to lead the British team again in 1979.

In the 1980s, the series moved into top gear and became a slick and colourful event, grabbing prime-time coverage on television worldwide. West Germany's first win in 1973 persuaded other countries from farther afield to get into the fray. Japan, Hong Kong, Singapore, Poland, Canada and New Zealand have regularly sent teams to compete, and there have even been competitors from Papua New Guinea.

The Admiral's Cup was the world's first inshore/offshore event, and since its inception many other yacht racing organizations around the world have copied its successful formula. These include the Southern Cross series in Australia, which culminates in the Sydney to Hobart Race, the Rio Circuit in Brazil, the Sardinia Cup, and the Pacific Clipper Cup which is sailed in the sparkling blue waters off Hawaii.

However, among all these events the Admiral's Cup continues to attract the largest number of competing nations, providing a colourful sight for spectators and perhaps the greatest variety of sailing conditions for competitors.

THE SYDNEY TO HOBART RACE

The instigator of the Sydney to Hobart Race – now one of the world's classic offshore races – was a visiting sailor on attachment to the Royal Australian Navy at the end of the Second World War. The sailor was John Illingworth, who, with his Laurent Giles-designed *Maid of Malham*, had already done much to promote the racing of well-found craft back in his native England.

Illingworth, hearing that Sydney's newly-formed Cruising Yacht Club was organizing a cruise to Hobart, Tasmania, signed up for it and persuaded the other eight participants to make a race of it. During the race a gale blew up (as has happened in many subsequent Sydney to Hobart races) and Illingworth, in his recently-acquired, double-ended 34-foot cutter *Rani* pressed on through the gale while the others sought shelter. He crossed the finishing line, well up the Derwent river, some seventeen hours ahead of his nearest rival.

Since Illingworth's win in the 1945/46 race, the Sydney to Hobart has been held every year, starting on Boxing Day and, for some of the later finishers, continuing into the New Year. In 1967, after winning the Admiral's Cup, the Cruising Yacht Club of Australia introduced its own international team series, the Southern Cross, comprising three inshore races plus the Sydney to Hobart.

One thing which sets the Sydney to Hobart apart from all other long-distance races is the intensive media coverage coupled to a genuine and knowledgeable public interest throughout Australia. A contributory factor to the continuing interest in the race has been the mandatory position updates that all competitors have to supply every eight hours. These positions are broadcast as overall line-honour and corrected positions, so that the public knows what is going on and the competitors know what is expected of them. Australians are among the best sailors in the world, and the public

Left *At the first turning mark off Sydney Harbour, 'Police Car' holds on to her spinnaker while 'Highland Fling' drops hers.*
Above *The fleet gathers for the start of the Sydney to Hobart Race.*

interest generated by the Sydney to Hobart races fuelled the near hysteria when Alan Bond won the America's Cup in 1983.

In common with those of other long-distance races, the Sydney to Hobart course can be divided into a number of sections, each with their own characteristics. The race begins at a starting line inside Sydney Harbour during the Christmas holidays when, in Australia, it's midsummer and even if there were no Sydney to Hobart Race the harbour would be alive with pleasure craft.

Surrounding the harbour, and especially on the headlands around the entrance, tens of thousands of spectators line every vantage point to watch the spectacle and see the fleet away on its 500-mile (800-km) trek south to Hobart. The start is always well policed, and the thousands of spectator craft usually keep well out of the way of the competitors as they make their way out of the harbour to the turning mark off the heads, before beginning the long haul down the New South Wales coastline.

Having completed the first phase of the race, the competitors' next objective is to make best possible speed along the coast, with the prospect of picking up a southerly set (tidal current) of some 2 knots which is generated by the seasonal northwesterlies. Those going in search of the drift may have to go fifty to sixty miles (80 to 100 km) east of the rhumb line (direct course) to benefit from it.

Once clear of the New South Wales coastline, the fleet then has to face up to the gales and storms that frequently occur in the Bass Strait, which separates Tasmania from the mainland, and to the strong southeasterlies that may be encountered on the approaches to the Tasmanian coastline.

The entrance to the Derwent river is the aptly-named Storm Bay, which is often reached after a hard beat up the Tasmanian shore. The last phase of the race, inside the Derwent, is usually conducted in light, flukey conditions which can see an apparent win fade away to a lowly place as a new breeze carries the back markers up the river.

After John Illingworth's win in the first race, he donated a trophy –

The Illingworth Cup – to be awarded to the first boat to cross the finishing line. The boat that wins the line honours is often accorded more hospitality than the boat that wins on corrected time, and is the boat that the spectators come to see.

One notable exception to this occurred in 1969, when the boat that took the line honours was overshadowed by the winner on corrected time, a boat called *Morning Cloud* which was skippered by the then British Prime Minister, Edward Heath.

It is not often that a serving prime minister or head of state wins a major sporting event, and the attention of the world's media placed Australian sailing and the Sydney to Hobart Race squarely on the sporting map.

Morning Cloud was designed by the legendary Olin Stephens and was an almost-standard Sparkman & Stephens 34 production yacht. Heath was the first Englishman since Illingworth to win the Sydney to Hobart, and his account of the race in his sailing autobiography *A Course of my Life* gives an insight into the nature and characteristics of the race as seen through the eyes of a first-time entrant and eventual winner.

THE AMERICA'S CUP

The America's Cup is the oldest international sporting trophy of any kind, dating back to the middle of the 19th century. The Royal Yacht Squadron had planned a series of races off Cowes to celebrate the Great Exhibition of 1851, and at the invitation of the then Commodore, the Earl of Wilton, the New York Yacht Club sent the schooner *America* across the Atlantic to race in English waters.

Because *America* was owned by a syndicate of businessmen, the host yacht club at Cowes refused to allow the Americans to compete in their races, citing a 'gentlemen's rule' that disallowed competition by yachts owned by more than one person.

The Royal Yacht Squadron relented, however, and proposed that *America* be allowed to sail in the 53-mile (85km) Round the Island Race on August 22. The sole American entry was up against seventeen of Britain's crack racing yachts, ranging in size from the 47-ton *Aurora*, the favourite, to the 392-ton, three-masted schooner *Brilliant*. The prize was not to be the pot of a wager, but a rather ornate and, some thought, ugly silver ewer made specially for the occasion by Garrards, the Crown Jewellers. The cup contained 134 ounces of fine silver and was named 'The Hundred Guinea Cup' because that was what it had cost.

At the finish, *America* was ahead of *Aurora* by 18 minutes, although that figure has been in dispute ever since the eventful day. The Hundred Guinea Cup was hers, and became known from then onward as the America's Cup.

Six years after the race around the Isle of Wight, the surviving members of *America*'s owners' syndicate gave their prized Cup to the New York Yacht Club on the understanding, written into the Deed of Gift, that any foreign yacht club be allowed to challenge for it. Between then and the early 1980s, the NYYC was challenged twenty-five times for the Cup, and won every time.

The longest winning streak in the history of sporting events finally came to an end in 1983, when Australian businessman Alan Bond and his yacht *Australia II*, skippered by John Bertrand, took the Cup away from the Americans in the greatest sailing match race ever seen, on the waters off Newport, Rhode Island.

Bond's designer, Ben Lexen, had developed a secret weapon in the shape of a winged keel on *Australia II* that made the Australian boat more manoeuvrable than Dennis Conner's sluggish-looking *Liberty*, the American defender. For the first time in the history of 12-metre America's Cup matches, the series went to seven races. Australia won, thus ending 132 years of American domination.

Subsequently, the man who lost the Cup was to become the only man to to have lost it and to have won it back. During a gruelling four-and-a-half-month campaign of elimination races off Fremantle, Western Australia, Dennis Conner won the right to challenge for the Cup after defeating twelve other syndicate yachts in some of the most testing conditions that 12-metres had ever sailed in.

In reality, Conner's only serious adversary was the young Chris Dickson sailing *New Zealand*, or *Kiwi Magic* as the 12-metre became known. In the end, it was the sheer wealth of Conner's match racing experience and the fact that he had the faster boat that won the day.

Of the defenders, Alan Bond's *Australia III* and *Australia IV* were eliminated from the trials along with *Steak 'n' Kidney* and *South Australia*. Kevin Parry's Taskforce '87 syndicate, owners of the *Kookaburra* yachts, were chosen to defend the cup with Iain Murray and Peter Gilmour as skipper and tactician.

After the first race on Gage Roads, *Kookaburra III* was given little hope by veteran observers of Cup racing. She was simply too slow and nothing that her skipper Iain Murray could do in that or subsequent races could save the day. Conner had made his mark in yachting history, and the next match would be held off San Diego, California.

A match did take place off San Diego, but it wasn't the kind of 'match' race that everyone had assumed it would be. The first challenge after Fremantle came from New Zealander Michael Fay's Mercury Bay Boating Club. Fay's challenger turned out to be a monster yacht more than twice the size of a 12-metre, nearly 130 feet overall.

San Diego Yacht Club and the Sail America Foundation, under whose auspices the next match race was to be run, were irritated by Fay's attitude and got an injunction to prevent *New Zealand* from participating. Michael Fay went to court, and after many weeks of deliberation in the New York State Supreme Court, Judge Carmen B Ciparick ordered that the challenge be allowed to stand and that there should be a race.

San Diego had, in Dennis Conner, a man whose greatest pleasure was to sail and who disliked losing. Sail America called in the best technicians and aerospace designers that money could buy and came up with a 60-foot catamaran, *Stars & Stripes*, with which to defend the Cup. The New Zealanders objected, but the Americans insisted that their craft met all the requirements laid down in the original America's Cup Deed of Gift, handed down to the New York Yacht Club by the remaining members of *America*'s owners' syndicate in 1857.

In September 1988, the two craft came together for the first time on the waters off San Diego. Dennis Conner and his crew were able to wind up the catamaran so that it could accelerate like a sports car or stop dead in the water. The New Zealanders put up a brave show; they knew that unless Conner's craft was dismasted or broke up, there was little they could do except sit and watch the Americans zip around the course to win.

Six months later, having listened to Fay's lawyers, studied the Deed of Gift and listened to the arguments put forward by the San Diego Yacht Club, Judge Ciparick ordered that San Diego be disqualified and the Cup forfeit to New Zealand, a decision that was later reversed by another court.

As a result of the row over *Stars & Stripes*, it has been decided that future Cup matches will be sailed in a new 75-foot class of yacht. These yachts will be more in keeping with modern IOR designs, and will not be restricted by the complicated formula that hounded progress with the earlier 12-metre yachts.

Left *1987 America's Cup challenger Dennis Conner sailing 'Stars & Stripes' to victory over Iain Murray and 'Kookaburra'.*
Above *In the semifinals of the 1987 elimination trials, 'French Kiss' holds off 'America II' in an exciting spinnaker chase to the downwind mark.*

RULES OF THE ROAD

When you go afloat, even in a small inflatable, you immediately become a 'Master' of a vessel subject to the International Regulations for the Prevention of Collisions at Sea (IRPCS). You can buy copies of these regulations, which are also reprinted in almanacs, and you should take the trouble to learn the most important of them because every Master is liable for their proper application, especially in relation to other water users.

Sailors talk about the 'rules of the road' which are, in effect, the rules they are most familiar with and which apply to their everyday use of the highways of the sea, usually when in confined channels where they have to apply the rules when they meet other vessels.

Other responsibilities include keeping a proper lookout at all times, proceeding at a safe speed, and taking into account the state of the sea and strength of the wind when close to navigational hazards.

The owner of a sailing vessel fitted with a motor has to be aware of the different rules which apply when sailing and when motoring, while for racing yachtsmen there are additional rules which are based on the IRPCS.

The main purpose of the rules is to prevent vessels crashing into each other, given that at most times ships are free to move in any direction they choose. Large ships don't, in practice, move in just any direction, because they follow well-charted sea routes, but smaller sailing vessels have greater freedom and do criss-cross these routes.

The risk of collision exists when two boats are in sight of each other. If another boat appears to be on a converging course to your own, take a series of compass bearings on it. If the angle remains constant, you are on a collision course and should prepare to take avoiding action.

As an alternative to taking compass bearings, you can use a part of your boat, such as a stanchion, as a reference point. If the other vessel stays in line with it, you are on a collision course; if it moves forward of the stanchion it will pass ahead of you, if it falls back you will pass ahead of it.

Because the rules are quite specific there are duties that each vessel much observe. The rules describe situations in which two vessels are approaching each other, and designate one as the *give-way* vessel, which must take avoiding action, and the other as the *stand-on* vessel, which has the right of way. To avoid a collision, the give-way vessel must take positive action in plenty of time and the course alteration or change in speed must be obvious to the other vessel. The master of each vessel is entitled to expect the other to act according to the rules, but must be prepared to take action himself if necessary.

When in narrow navigable channels, it may not be possible to make large changes of course without going aground. Yachts should keep to the periphery of channels when commercial vessels, which are constrained by their draft, are in the channels.

The main 'rule of the road' is that traffic keeps to the right (starboard) while navigating channels. Another rule, especially applicable in a channel with blind bends, is that the appropriate sound signals should be made prior to carrying out specific manoeuvres.

Sound signals are short blasts of 1 second duration and prolonged blasts of from 4 seconds to 6 seconds. A vessel approaching a blind bend should sound one prolonged blast. If another vessel approaches the bend from the opposite direction it should sound a prolonged blast in reply.

When in sight of each other, vessels (mostly those in excess of 12 metres) sound one short blast to indicate an alteration to starboard, and two short blasts to indicate an

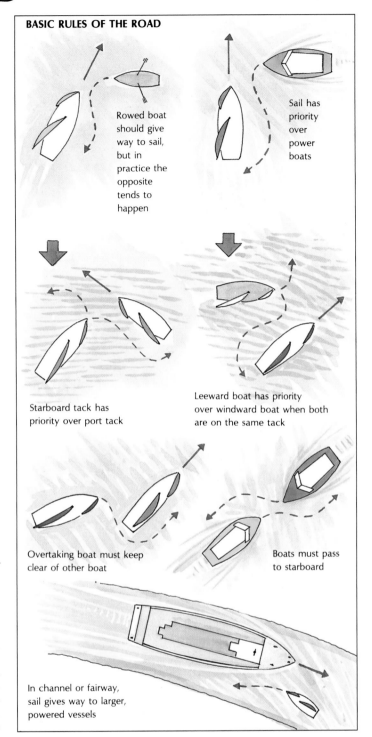

BASIC RULES OF THE ROAD

Rowed boat should give way to sail, but in practice the opposite tends to happen

Sail has priority over power boats

Starboard tack has priority over port tack

Leeward boat has priority over windward boat when both are on the same tack

Overtaking boat must keep clear of other boat

Boats must pass to starboard

In channel or fairway, sail gives way to larger, powered vessels

alteration to port; three short blasts tell other craft that the sounding vessel's engines are going astern. Five short and rapid blasts can mean anything very rude you can think of; this signal shows that the sounding vessel has no idea what you are doing and wants you to get your act together to avoid a collision.

In a narrow channel, if a vessel coming up behind you gives two prolonged blasts followed by a short one, it means 'I intend to overtake on your starboard side.' Two of each means 'I intend to overtake on your port side.' To learn these signals, think of the first two prolonged

SAIL SYMBOLS

Sails may carry a number of symbols, the most important being the registration number which, if the boat is racing internationally, will be prefixed by the letter denoting the country for which the boat is racing. The boat's class symbol (if any) is shown above the number, and numbers and symbols are placed higher on the starboard side of the sail than on the port side.

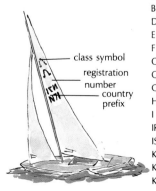

class symbol
registration number
country prefix

B	Belgium	KZ	New Zealand
BL	Brazil	L	Finland
D	Denmark	M	Hungary
E	Spain	N	Norway
F	France	OE	Austria
G	West Germany	PZ	Poland
GO	East Germany	S	Sweden
GR	Greece	SR	USSR
H	Holland	US	United States
I	Italy	Y	Yugoslavia
IR	Ireland	Z	Switzerland
IS	Israel		
K	Great Britain		
KA	Australia		
KC	Canada		

blasts as meaning 'Wake up!' in each case; then you only have to remember that one short following blast means 'starboard', and two mean 'port'.

The signal is acknowledged by four blasts – one prolonged, one short, one prolonged and one short – meaning 'I agree and will keep my course.'

In restricted visibility there are numerous signals which must be understood. The principal rules governing a motor sailing vessel are: when sailing, one prolonged and two short blasts at not more than two-minute intervals; when motoring, one prolonged blast at not more than two-minute intervals. If you are at anchor in an area where a risk of collision exists, ring a bell or strike a gong (even a saucepan, if you've nothing else available) for five seconds once a minute.

In clear visibility the rules are

designed to get vessels to take positive early action. For the yachtsman there are three categories of vessel to watch out for. The first category is fishing vessels, which are a 'law unto themselves' because they move in all directions. The rules acknowlege this and advise everyone to keep clear of vessels identified, by the appropriate lights or shapes, as fishing vessels.

The second category is commercial shipping, and these vessels should be treated with great caution. In theory they should give way to sailing vessels, but in practice they are on autopilot in open waters and restricted in narrow channels, so you should plan accordingly to make your intentions clear. Don't insist on your right of way over commerical shipping; it's as unwise as arguing with trucks on the highway.

The third category is other sailing

vessels, which will expect you to know and obey the sailing rules.

When two powered vessels meet, the following rules apply. When they are approaching each other head-on, each should alter course to starboard, so that they pass each other port-to-port. When crossing each other's path, the vessel which has the other vessel on her starboard side should keep out of the way, preferably without crossing ahead of the other vessel. The rule can be remembered by 'If I am on the right, I am in the right.' Lastly, an overtaking vessel, which will usually be approaching from about 22 degrees either side of dead astern, must keep well clear of the overtaken vessel.

The rules relating to sailing vessels form the basis of the racing rules. When two boats are on different tacks, the vessel on a port tack (with the wind blowing over its port

The rules of racing are based on the IRPCS rules for sailboats.

side) must keep out of the way of one on a starboard tack (with the wind over its starboard side).

When two boats are on the same tack, the windward boat (the one closest to wind) must keep out of the way of the vessel to leeward. Any vessel on a port tack and unsure of what tack another vessel is on must keep out of its way. In the racing rules, the windward side is determined as being the opposite side to that on which the mainsail is carried.

Overtaking rules are the same as for powered vessels and are designed to keep the overtaking vessel away from the vessel being overtaken.

Generally, a commonsense approach to the rules will stand you in good stead as long as you do what is expected of you, either as a stand-on vessel or a give-way vessel.

LIGHTS, FLAGS & SIGNALS

The standard patterns of lights for both vessels and buoyage systems ensure their identification at night, and while most signalling is now confined to the VHF radio, shapes, flags and Morse still have a role to play in communications.

When entering a channel from seaward at night you should have a prepared list of all buoyage or other fixed lights which may be visible during the approach and when within the channel. These should include distant lighthouses which, even though not directly visible, can be identified by their *loom* as the light sweeps the night sky below the horizon.

Your list should also include inland features such as radio and television transmitter masts, which are very good navigational features because of their height and distinctive aircraft warning lights.

The correct details of each light visible in or from the channel will be contained in the *Admiralty List of Lights*, which is often reproduced in nautical almanacs, and this list, rather than your chart (which will also give details of the lights), should form the basis for your own list. As you identify each light, mark it on the chart with a tick, and as you sail past it and leave it abeam, change the tick to a cross.

The description or characteristic of a particular light, as given in a published list or on a chart, tells you its colour and period and, for some types, its elevation and range.

The lights that are to be carried by different types of vessels is a complex subject, but one that is usually well-covered by most almanacs. In essence, most vessels must show a red light to port and a green light to starboard, plus one or more white or other coloured lights depending on the vessel's size, type and use.

Yachts under power display port, starboard and stern lights low down, with a single white 'steaming' light higher up. When under sail a yacht may show the three lowers or, more commonly, a masthead tricolour (which uses less electricity). Very small sailboats may simply show a single all-round white to avoid collisions.

Signalling by flags and lights has largely been superseded by spoken messages over VHF radio. Nevertheless, the international code of flag signals and the Morse code are still in daily use, and should be learned because they may be used by larger vessels or shore stations to send a message to you.

You should also learn the international phonetic alphabet, in which each letter of the alphabet is assigned a word, such as 'Alpha' for 'A' and 'Delta' for 'D'. By using this phonetic alphabet, names and other words can be spelled out over the radio without confusion between, say, 'F' and 'S', or between 'B', 'P' and 'D'.

FLAGS, PHONETIC AND MORSE ALPHABETS

SINGLE-LETTER MEANINGS

The single-letter signals are the most important of all the code signals, and you should try to learn them by heart so that you can act upon them immediately. They may be made by any method of signalling, but if they are made by sound they must be made in accordance with the relevant rules (34 and 35) contained in the International Regulations for the Prevention of Collisons at Sea (IRPCS).

THE THREE SUBSTITUTES

Flags used to repeat other flags

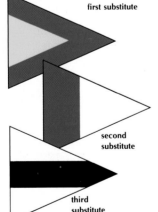

first substitute

second substitute

third substitute

A .− ALPHA

I have a diver down; keep clear and pass at low speed

B −... BRAVO
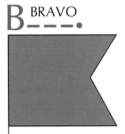
I am loading, unloading or carrying dangerous goods

C −.−. CHARLIE

Yes; confirmation of preceding signal

D −.. DELTA

Keep clear, I am manoeuvring with difficulty

J .−−− JULIET

I am on fire and have dangerous cargo on board; keep clear

K −.− KILO

I wish to communicate with you

L .−.. LIMA
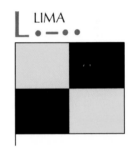
You should stop your vessel immediately

M −− MIKE

My vessel is stopped and making no way through the water

S ... SIERRA

I am going astern under power

T − TANGO
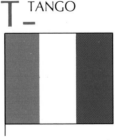
Keep clear, I am engaged in pair trawling

U ..− UNIFORM

You are running into danger

V ...− VICTOR

I require assistance

1 .−−−−
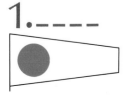

2 ..−−−
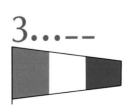

3 ...−−

4 ....−

5 .....

LIGHTS

A. Masthead (steering light) white with unbroken arc of 225°

B. Side lights green starboard red port unbroken arc of 112.5°

C. All-round light unbroken arc of 360°

D. Stern light white unbroken arc of 135° placed as near stern as possible

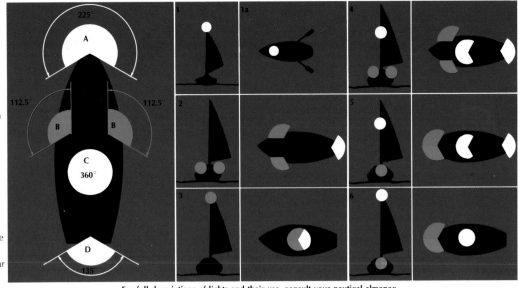

Boats under 7 m
1, 1a All-round white light

Boats 7 to 20 m
Under sail
2 Side and stern lights or **3** combined tricolour light on masthead

Under power
4 Side, stern and steaming lights or **5** combined side lights, stern and steaming light

Under 12 m
Side lights and all-round masthead light

For full descriptions of lights and their use, consult your nautical almanac.

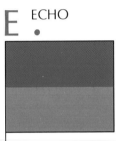
E ECHO • —
I am altering course to starboard

F FOXTROT • • — •
I am disabled, communicate with me

G GOLF — — •
I require a pilot or (on a fishing vessel) I am hauling in nets

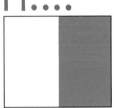
H HOTEL • • • •
I have a pilot on board

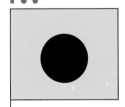
I INDIA • •
I am altering course to port

N NOVEMBER — •
No; the preceding signal should be read in the negative

O OSCAR — — —
Man overboard

P PAPA • — — •
I am about to put to sea

Q QUEBEC — — • —
My vessel is healthy and I request clearance to come ashore

R ROMEO • — •
Single letter code R has no allocated meaning; see the IRPCS

W WHISKY • — —
I require medical assistance

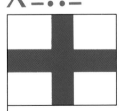
X X-RAY — • • —
Stop carrying out your intentions and watch for my signals

Y YANKEE — • — —
I am dragging my anchor

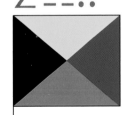
Z ZULU — — • •
I require a tug or (on a fishing vessel) I am shooting nets

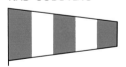
ANSWERING PENNANT AND CODE FLAG

The code flag is flown to show that the International Code is being used, and to acknowledge a message.

6 — • • • •

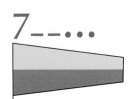
7 — — • • •

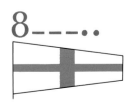
8 — — — • •

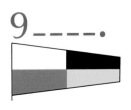
9 — — — — •

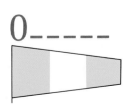
0 — — — — —

SAILING TERMS

A

Aback A sail is said to be aback when its clew is to windward and the wind is pressing it against the mast, for instance when the boat is hove-to, or as a result of a sudden change in the wind.

Abaft Toward the stern.

Abeam At right angles to the centreline of a boat.

About To go about is to change tack.

Adrift Free-floating, without power or control.

Aft At, toward, near or behind the stern.

Afterpart The part of a boat aft of the beam.

A-hull A boat is lying a-hull when hove-to with all sails furled (see also **Lie**).

Aloft Overhead.

Amidships Midway between the stem and the stern of a boat.

Anabatic wind A wind created by air blowing up a slope. It is the result of the air at the bottom of the slope being warmer than the air at the top, and rising by convection (see also **Katabatic wind**).

Anchor light An all-round white light displayed at night (usually on the forestay) by an anchored vessel. Also called a riding light.

Antifouling A protective compound (usually a paint) applied to a hull to inhibit the growth of marine life, such as barnacles, on it.

Apparent wind The perceived wind flowing over a moving boat. It is the resultant of the speed and direction of the true wind and the speed and direction of the boat (see also **True wind**).

Aspect ratio The ratio of the length of the foot of a sail to the length of its luff. A tall, narrow sail has a high aspect ratio, and a low, broad sail has a low aspect ratio.

Astern Behind a boat. To go astern means to reverse.

Athwart from side to side across the centreline of a boat.

Avast 'Stop!' (see also **Belay**).

Aweigh An anchor is said to be aweigh when it has come free of the ground.

B

Back To push a sail out so that the wind fills it from the other side.

Backstay A stay leading aft from the masthead.

Ballast Weight (usually metal) placed in the bottom of a boat or fitted to the keel to increase stability.

Bar An offshore ridge of sand, mud or shingle, parallel to the shore and across the mouth of a river or bay or the approach to a harbour.

Barber hauler A line or tackle attached to a sheet, at a point between the clew and the fairlead, which is used to adjust the angle of sheeting.

Battens Thin strips of wood or plastic inserted into pockets in a sail to preserve its shape.

Beam The maximum width of a boat.

Bear away To change course away from the wind.

Bear down To approach from upwind.

Bearing The direction of an object expressed in compass notation.

Beating To sail to windward by repeated tacking.

Becket A small loop or eye in the end of a rope or on a block.

Belay To secure a rope to a cleat or a belaying pin; an instruction meaning 'Stop!' (see also **Avast**).

Bend One of various types of knot; to knot two ropes together; to attach a sail to a spar.

Bermudan rig A rig with a triangular mainsail. Also known as a Marconi rig.

Bight Any part of a rope between its ends; a curve or loop in a rope; a wide indentation in a coastline, or the water bounded by that indentation.

Bilge The part of a vessel's hull where the side curves in to form the bottom; the part of a vessel between the lowermost floorboards and the bottom, where water often collects.

Bitter end The end of a line or chain, especially the end secured in the chain locker or to the bitts.

Bitts A pair of small posts on the deck of a vessel for securing mooring lines.

Block A casing containing one or more freely-rotating pulley wheels (sheaves).

Bollard A sturdy wood or metal post, fixed to a quay or wharf, to which mooring lines are attached.

Bolt rope A strong rope sewn around the edge of a sail to reinforce it.

Boom A spar used to extend the foot of a fore-and-aft sail, such as a mainsail, and to control its position relative to the wind.

Boom preventer A line or tackle that prevents unwanted movement of a boom, such as an accidental gybe.

Boom vang A line or tackle that prevents the boom from riding up when the mainsail is set. Also called a kicking strap.

Bosun's chair A canvas bucket seat on which a person can be hoisted up a mast.

Bow The forward end or part of a vessel.

Bower A main anchor carried at the bow of a vessel.

Bowsprit On some boats, a heavy spar projecting ahead from the bow, enabling headsails to be set farther forward.

Breast line (breast rope) A rope, used for tying up to a jetty, which is led from forward or aft at right angles to the side of the vessel.

Bring up To stop or come to anchor.

Broach to To swerve sharply and dangerously in a following sea, slewing broadside-on to the waves.

Bulkhead An upright, wall-like partition within a boat.

Bulwarks A solid, fencelike parapet along the outer sides of a deck.

Burgee A small, triangular or swallow-tailed flag, flown from the mast of a yacht to indicate the owner's membership of a particular yacht club, or to act as an indicator of the apparent wind direction.

By the head Having greater draught forward than aft (see also **By the stern**).

By the lee Sailing on a run with the wind over the same side as the mainsail (over the lee side). This can result in an accidental gybe.

By the stern Having greater draught aft than forward (see also **By the head**).

C

Cable An anchor chain or rope; one tenth of a nautical mile.

Camber The curve of a set sail; the slight upward curve from the side to the centre of a deck.

Capstan A vertical drum for hauling in or letting out the anchor chain.

Careen To heel a vessel onto one side so as to be able to work on her bottom.

Carvel-built Having a wooden hull whose planks are made flush at the seams (see also **Clinker-built**).

Cast off To release the lines securing a boat to a dock or mooring.

Caulking Waterproof material packed into the seams between planks to make the structure watertight.

Centreboard A pivoting wooden board let down through the bottom of a sailboat to provide lateral stability and reduce leeway (see also **Daggerboard, Keel, Leeboards, Leeway**).

Centreline The fore-and-aft line through the centre of a boat.

Chain plates The metal fittings at the sides of a boat to which the shrouds are attached.

Chart datum The water level — usually the level of the lowest astronomical tide — from which all depths shown on a chart are measured.

Chine A sharp angle between the side and the bottom of a boat.

Chord An imaginary straight line, parallel to the foot, joining the leading edge (luff) and trailing edge (leech) of a sail.

Claw ring A C-shaped fitting, slipped over the boom when the sail has been roller-reefed, that allows the kicking strap (vang) to be re-attached.

Cleat A two-armed metal or wooden fitting to which ropes can be secured.

Clew The lower aft corner of a fore-and-aft sail, where the leech meets the foot.

Clinker-built Having a wooden hull whose planks overlap at the seams (see also **Carvel-built**).

Close-hauled Sailing as close to the wind as possible.

Cockpit The well at the stern of a sailboat, where the helmsman stands or puts his feet.

Coffee grinder A large, pedestal-mounted sheet winch with two handles on a horizontal spindle.

Committee boat In racing, the boat carrying the race officials.

Companionway A stairway or ladder leading from the deck to the cabin or saloon.

Cringle An eye or loop set in the bolt rope of a sail.

Cross-trees Struts on each side of a mast to increase the spread and holding power of the main shrouds. Also called spreaders.

Cunningham hole An eye in the luff of a sail, just above the tack, to which a tackle (Cunningham tackle) is attached to adjust the luff tension.

Cutter A single-masted boat rigged with a staysail and jib. It may be Bermudan-rigged or gaff-rigged.

D

Daggerboard A sliding wooden board let down through the bottom of a sailboat to provide lateral stability and reduce leeway (see also **Centreboard, Keel, Leeboards, Leeway**).

Day mark An indicator, usually a white-painted shape, which marks a shore feature by day.

Dead reckoning Navigating by using the measured speed, elapsed time and course steered from a known position to calculate the boat's present position (see also **Fix, Observed position**).

Deck The structure completely or partially covering the interior of a boat.

Deckhead The underside of a deck; the roof of a boat's cabin or saloon.

Displacement The weight of the water displaced by a floating boat; the displacement is equal to the actual weight of the boat.

Dodger A canvas strip fitted between the guardrail and the gunwale of a yacht to protect the crew from spray.

Dolphin A pile, post or buoy for mooring a vessel in a harbour.

Double-ender A boat which has a hull that is pointed at bow and stern.

Downhaul A rope or tackle used to haul down a sail (such as a spinnaker) or to tension the luff of a sail by pulling down the tack (see also **Uphaul**).

Draught The depth of water occupied by a vessel, meaured as the vertical distance from the waterline to the lowest point of the hull or keel.

Drogue An object, such as a canvas sea anchor, towed behind a boat to reduce its speed.

Drying features Features, such as sandbanks, which are covered at high water but exposed as the tide drops.

E

Ease To let out a line, sheet or anchor chain gradually.

Ebb tide The flowing back of the tide from high to low water (see also **Flood tide**).

Ensign A flag flown by a vessel to indicate its nationality.

F

Fairlead A channel, ring, eye, loop or bolt for guiding a rope in the required direction.

Fairway The main shipping channel in restricted waters.

Fall The part of the rope, leading from a tackle, that is hauled on.

Fathom A unit of measurement of water depth, equal to 6 feet (1.83 metres).

Fetch To sail close-hauled without tacking.

Fin keel A single, centrally-placed and ballasted keel (see also **Keel**).

Fix A vessel's position, as obtained by taking accurate bearings (see also **Dead reckoning, Observed position**).

Flood tide A rising or flow tide (see also **Ebb tide**).

Flukes The pointed parts of an anchor that dig into the ground.

Following sea A sea travelling in the same direction as the boat (see also **Head sea**).

Foot The bottom edge of a sail.

Fore At, toward or near the bow.

Fore-and-aft Along or parallel to the centreline.

Foresail A triangular sail, such as a jib, set ahead of the main mast (see also **Headsail**).

Forestay A stay leading from the masthead to the bow.

Forward Toward the bow.

Freeboard The distance between the deck and the waterline.

Furl To roll a sail and fasten it to its boom when it is not in use (see also **Reef**).

G

Gaff The spar that supports the head of a gaffsail.

Gaff-rigged Having one or more gaffsails.

Gaffsail A four-sided, fore-and-aft sail.

Galley The kitchen of a yacht.

Gaskets The small cords used to tie up a furled sail. Also called ties or furling lines.

Genoa A large foresail that extends aft beyond the mainmast.

Gimbals A pair of pivoted, concentric rings used to hold a compass or stove horizontal, regardless of the motion of the boat.

Gnomonic projection A type of map or chart projection with straight longitude lines and curved latitude lines (see also **Mercator projection**).
Go about To turn a boat head-to-wind to change tack.
Gooseneck A pivoted fitting that secures a boom to a mast.
Goosewing To sail downwind with the mainsail set on one side and the foresail on the other.
GRP Glass-reinforced plastic, made by impregnating glassfibre matting with resins such as polyesters.
Gunter rig A rig in which gaff is used as an extension of the main mast.
Gunwale (or **gunnel**) The top edge of the side of the hull.
Guy A rope or wire used to steady a spar.
Gybe To move a fore-and-aft sail from one side of the boat to the other when changing course on a run.

H

Halyards Ropes or wires used to hoist sails.
Hanks Clips or rings that attach sails to stays.
Harden up To sail closer to the wind.
Hawse pipes Bow pipes through which the anchor cables pass.
Hawser A heavy rope used for towing, mooring or warping.
Heading The compass direction in which a boat is pointing.
Headsail A sail, such as a spinnaker, set forward of the main mast (see also **Foresail**).
Head sea A sea travelling in the opposite direction to that of the boat (see also **Following sea**).
Heads The toilets on a boat.
Head-to-wind With the bow pointing into the wind.
Heave-to To stop a boat, for instance by backing the foresail or by letting the sails flap on a beam reach.
Heaving line A light rope thrown ashore when berthing and used to haul a heavier mooring line ashore.
Heel To lean over or list; the bottom of a mast; the aft end of a keel.
Helm The tiller or wheel.
Helmsman The person steering a boat.
Hitch To tie a rope to a spar or stay; a knot that can be undone by pulling against the direction of the strain that holds it tight.
Holding ground Ground that an anchor can dig into.
Hounds The part of the mast to which the shrouds and stays are attached.

I

Inboard Situated within the hull; toward the centreline.
Inshore Close to the shore; toward the shore from the water.
Irons A boat is said to be 'in irons' when it is pointing directly into the wind and unable to move forward.
Isobars Lines on a weather map joining points of equal barometric pressure.
IYRU The International Yacht Racing Union, which is the controlling body for international yacht racing.

J

Jamming cleat A cleat into which a rope may be jammed to secure it.
Jib A triangular sail attached to the forestay.
Jury rig A temporary replacement for damaged rigging.

K

Katabatic wind A wind created by air flowing down a slope. It usually occurs at night, when the air at the top of a slope cools quicker, and so becomes heavier, than the air at the bottom (see also **Anabatic wind**).
Kedge A small anchor used in conjunction with the main anchor; to move a boat by deploying the kedge and pulling on it.
Keel The underwater extension of the hull of a sailing boat that provides lateral stability and reduces leeway. It is usually fixed, but on some boats can be raised and lowered (see also **Centreboard, Daggerboard, Leeboards, Leeway**).
Ketch A two-masted boat, rigged fore-and-aft. The forward mast is the main mast, the aft mast is called the mizzen.
Kicking strap A line or tackle that prevents the boom from riding up when the mainsail is set. Also called a boom vang.
Knot A speed of one nautical mile per hour (see also **Nautical mile**).

L

Land breeze A breeze blowing from the land. It occurs mainly at night and in the early morning, when the land is cooler than the sea because it has lost more heat after sunset (see also **Sea breeze**).
Landfall To sight or arrive at land.
Lanyard A short length of rope or cord for attaching one thing to another.
Lash To tie something in place by binding it tightly with light rope.
Latitude The angular distance of a position in degrees north or south of the equator (see also **Longitude**).
Launch To slide or lower a vessel into the water; a small motor-driven tender.
Lay up To take a boat out of use, for example during the winter.
Lee The area downwind (to leeward) of a boat or other object (see also **Weather**).
Leeboards Boards fixed vertically to the sides of a boat's hull to provide lateral stability and reduce leeway (see also **Centreboard, Daggerboard, Keel, Leeway**).
Leech The rear edge of a fore-and-aft sail.
Lee side The downwind (leeward) side of a boat or other object (see also **Weather side**).
Lee tide A tide running with the wind (see also **Weather tide**).
Leeward (Loo'ard) Toward the lee side; the direction to which the wind is blowing (see also **Windward**).
Leeway The sideways drift of a vessel, to leeward, caused by the wind; the distance between the course steered and the course actually run.
Let fly To let go a sheet so as to spill the wind from the sail it controls.
Lie To keep a boat stationary; to keep a boat as steady as possible during a gale, for instance by lying a-hull (see also **A-hull**).
Lifeline A safety line for the crew to hang onto, fitted fore-and-aft or around the deck.
Lift A rope or wire supporting a spar (see also **Topping lift**).
Line squall A usually violent squall accompanying the cold front of a depression. Its low black cloud forms a distinct line or arch.
Log An instrument used to measure a boat's speed through the water; a book (logbook) in which the details of a boat's voyages are recorded.

Longitude The angular distance of a position in degrees east or west of the Greenwich Meridian (0°) (see also **Latitude, Meridian**).
Loom The reflection on the clouds of the light from a lighthouse or lightship, when the light itself is still below the horizon.
Loose To let go of a rope; to unfurl or set a sail.
Loose-footed A loose-footed sail is one whose foot is not laced to a boom.
Low water Low tide.
Lubber line The line marked on a compass to indicate the fore-and-aft axis of the vessel.
Luff The forward edge of a sail; to bring a boat closer to the wind.
Luff up To turn a boat directly into the wind.
Lug (lugsail) A four-sided, fore-and-aft sail.
Lugger A boat rigged with a lugsail.

M

Make fast To secure a rope.
Marconi A rig with a triangular mainsail. Also known as a Bermudan rig.
Mark A fixed onshore or offshore feature used as a guide when navigating.
Marlin(e) spike A pointed metal or wooden spike used for separating the strands of a rope to splice it.
Mast A vertical pole or set of poles for supporting a sail or sails.
Mast gate The fixture that secures the mast of a dinghy where it passes through the foredeck.
Masthead The top section of a mast.
Masthead sloop A sloop on which the forestay (which carries the foresail) extends from the bow to the masthead.
Mast step A fixture into which the foot of the mast is fitted, either on the deck (for a deck-stepped mast) or on top of the keel (for a keel-stepped mast).
Mercator projection A type of map or chart projection with straight longitude and latitude lines crossing at right angles (see also **Gnomonic projection**)
Meridian An imaginary circle drawn around the earth and passing through both poles. All lines of longitude are meridians (see also **Longitude**).
Millibar A unit of barometric pressure, used on weather maps. 1000 millibars (1 bar) is equal to 29.53 inches of mercury. From the earth's surface, atmospheric pressure decreases by about one millibar for every 28 feet (8.5 metres) of increase in altitude.
Miss stays When tacking, a boat is said to miss stays when it fails to go about and so remains on its original tack.
Mizzen The aftermost mast of a two-masted vesel; on a vessel with three or more masts, the third mast from the bow; the sail set on a mizzen mast.
Moulded hull A hull made of GRP or built up by bonding layers of marine ply.

N

Narrows A narrow channel.
Nautical almanac A book, published annually, containing navigational, tidal, astronomical and other data of use to sailors and navigators.
Nautical mile A unit of length, used in navigation, equal to 1852 metres or 6076.103 feet (see also **Knot**).
Navigation lights The identifying lights that vessels must show at night.
Neap tides The tides that occur at around the first and last quarters of the moon, and have a relatively small range (see also **Spring tides**).

No-go zone The area, about 45° to either side of the wind, into which a sailboat cannot sail without tacking.

O

Observed position A vessel's position as obtained by direct observation of charted features (see also **Dead reckoning, Fix**).
Offshore Away from the shore.
Offwind Any point of sailing away from the wind.
One-design A boat built and equipped to conform to strict rules, so that it is identical to all the other boats in its particular class.
Onshore On or toward the land.
On the quarter Something is said to be on the quarter when its bearing is 45° abaft of the beam of the boat (see also **Quarter**).
Outhaul A rope used to tighten the foot of a sail by hauling the clew along the boom.
Overfall A turbulent stretch of water resulting from currents flowing over an underwater ridge.

P

Painter A line attached to the bow of a small boat for tying it up.
Pay out To ease a line or chain.
Pennant A tapering or triangular flag.
Pilot Someone authorized to navigate vessels in and out of a port, or through a channel; a book of sailing directions.
Pitch The downward motion of a boat's bows as it plunges into the trough of a wave (see also **Yaw**).
Pitchpole To tumble stern-over-bow when upended by a wave.
Plane A boat is said to plane when it lifts onto its bow wave and skims over the water rather than moving through it.
Plot To mark a chart with bearings, directions and courses.
Points of sailing The main angles to the wind on which a boat may sail.
Pontoon A floating platform or walkway to which boats may be secured; a float supporting such a platform.
Port The left-hand side of a boat as seen when facing the bow.
Port tack A boat is said to be on a port tack when the wind is blowing over its port side (see also **Starboard tack**).
Position line A line on a chart along which a vessel's position lies.
Preventer A line, tackle or stay that prevents unwanted movement of a mast or boom (see also **Boom preventer**).
Prop walk The tendency of a propellor to pull the stern of a vessel to one side.
Prow The fore part of a vessel, including the bows.
Pulpit A guard rail set around the bow or stern of a boat. That at the stern is also called the pushpit.
Purchase A tackle or lever mechanism used for raising, moving or tightening things (see also **Tackle**).
Pushpit A guard rail set around the stern of a boat (see also **Pulpit**).

Q

Quarter The part of a boat between the beam and the stern (see also **On the quarter**).
Quarter berth A bunk under the side of the cockpit.
Quartering With the wind or waves on the quarter of the boat.

R

Race A rapid current, especially through a narrow channel.

Rake The rearward slope of a mast.

Range The difference in water level between low and high tide.

Rating A way of classifying boats of different types and sizes so that they can race on a handicap basis.

Ratlines small lines fixed between adjacent shrouds to form steps.

Reach To sail with the wind blowing approximately abeam; the stretch of water between two bends in a river.

Reefing Folding or rolling a sail to reduce its area.

Reef points Short pieces of rope used to tie up the reefed part of a sail.

Ride To lie at anchor; to ride out a storm when at sea is to wait for it to pass (see also **A-hull, Lie**).

Riding light An all-round white light displayed at night (usually on the forestay) by an anchored vessel. Also called an anchor light.

Rig The arrangement of masts, spars and sails carried by a vessel.

Rigging The ropes and wires on a boat that keep the mast or masts in place and work the sails (see also **Running rigging, Standing rigging**).

Roach The curved part of a fore-and-aft sail, bounded by the leech, that projects behind an imaginary straight line from the clew to the head.

Rudder A movable underwater vane at the stern of a vessel, used for steering.

Rudderpost The aftermost timber of a boat.

Run To sail with the wind aft or nearly aft.

Running rigging The sheets and halyards that raise, lower and control the sails (see also **Standing rigging**).

S

Safety harness A harness attached to a line secured to the boat, and worn by crew in bad weather.

Sam(p)son post A vertical wooden or metal post to which warps or cables may be secured.

Schooner A vessel with two or more masts (the aftermost of which is the main mast) and all lower sails rigged fore-and-aft.

Scupper An opening let into the bulwarks of a vessel to allow deck water to drain away; to sink one's own vessel deliberately.

Sea anchor A drogue deployed as a floating anchor to help a vessel ride out a gale or storm.

Sea breeze A breeze blowing from the sea. It occurs mainly during the day, when the land is warmer than the sea (see also **Land breeze**).

Seacock A valve in the hull of a vessel, below the waterline, for admitting seawater or pumping out bilge water.

Shackle A U-shaped link, closed by a bolt or pin.

Shackle key A metal tool for unscrewing shackle pins.

Shake To loosen or cast off.

Shank The main shaft of an anchor.

Sheave A pulley wheel (see also **Block**).

Sheer The deck line of a vessel, as seen from the side.

Sheet The rope attached to the clew of a sail, with which the sail may be trimmed or tensioned.

Shock cord A strong, elasticated rope.

Shrouds Wires fixed at each side of a mast to support it (see also **Standing rigging, Stays**).

Side lights The red (port) and green (starboard) lights that a vessel must show at night.

Slack tide The short period at high or low tide when there is no tidal flow. Also called slack water.

Slip To release or let go, for instance to slip anchor.

Sloop A single-masted boat, Bermudan-rigged or gaff-rigged, with a single headsail.

Snatch block A block into which a rope can be inserted quickly from the side instead of being threaded through.

Sound To measure the depth of the water; a relatively narrow stretch of water linking two larger areas; an inlet or deep bay.

Spars A general term for the various pole-like pieces of gear on a boat, including masts, booms and gaffs.

Spinnaker A large, light, three-cornered headsail.

Spit A thin strip of sand or shingle projecting from the shore.

Splicing Joining two ropes by intertwining their strands.

Spreaders Struts on each side of a mast to increase the spread and holding power of the main shrouds. Also called cross-trees.

Spring A mooring line led forward from the stern or aft from the bow.

Spring tides The tides that occur at or near full and new moon, and are the lowest low tides and the highest high tides (see also **Neap tides**).

Sprit A spar extending from the mast to the peak of a four-cornered sail.

Square-rigger A ship rigged with four-sided sails hung on yards athwart (across) the ship.

Stanchions The upright posts that support the guardrails and lifelines.

Standing rigging The shrouds and stays that support the mast or masts (see also **Running rigging**).

Stand on To maintain course.

Starboard The right-hand side of a boat as seen when facing the bow.

Starboard tack A boat is said to be on a starboard tack when the wind is blowing over its starboard side (see also **Port tack**).

Stays Wires fixed fore and aft of a mast to support it (see also **Shrouds, Standing rigging**).

Staysail An auxiliary sail, usually triangular, attached to a forestay.

Steerageway A boat is said to have steerageway when it is moving fast enough to allow it to be steered.

Stem The main timber or structure at the bow of a boat; the foremost end of a boat, as in the phrase 'from stem to stern' (see also **Stern post**).

Step The fixture into which the heel of a mast is fitted.

Stern The after (rear) part of a vessel.

Stern post The main timber or structure at the stern of a boat (see also **Stem**).

Stiff A vessel is said to be stiff if it is relatively resistant to heeling or rolling, and returns quickly to the vertical (see also **Tender**).

Stock The part of a rudder to which the tiller is fitted.

T

Tack The forward lower corner of a fore-and-aft sail; to turn the bows of a boat through the wind; to sail a zigzag upwind course by repeated tacking; to sail with the wind blowing from forward of the beam (see also **Port tack, Starboard tack**).

Tackle A rope and block purchase system (see also **Block, Purchase**).

Take up To tighten.

Tangs The metal fittings that secure the shrouds and stays to the mast.

Tell-tales Small lengths of wool sewn to each side of a sail to indicate the airflow over it.

Tender A small boat towed or carried by a larger vessel and used to ferry people and stores between the larger vessel and the shore; a boat is said to be tender if it is easily heeled over by the wind (see also **Stiff**).

Thwart A seat running across a dinghy or other small boat.

Tide The regular rise and fall of sea level caused by the gravitational pull of the sun and the moon; the horizontal flow of water resulting from these changes in sea level.

Tide rode A moored or anchored boat is said to be tide rode when it has swung round so that its bows are facing into the incoming or outgoing tide (see also **Wind rode**).

Tiller A wooden or metal handle attached to the top of a rudder and used to control it.

Toe straps Loops into which dinghy crews can put their feet to keep them secure when sitting out.

Topping lift A rope or tackle that supports the end of a boom.

Track The intended course of a vessel.

Transit Two objects are said to be in transit when, from the point of view of an observer, they are directly in line with each other.

Transom The stern surface of a vessel.

Trapeze A support used by the crew (and sometimes the helmsman) of a racing dinghy to place his or her weight outside the boat.

Traveller A sliding fixture, travelling on a track, to which a sheet is attached so that its angle can be altered.

Trim The fore-and-aft inclination of a boat; to change or adust the set of a sail.

True wind The actual speed and direction of the wind, rather than the apparent wind as perceived on a moving boat (see also **Apparent wind**).

Trysail A loose-footed, triangular sail used in place of the mainsail in heavy weather.

U

Under way On the move.

Uphaul A rope or tackle used to haul up a sail (such as a spinnaker) (see also **Downhaul**).

V

Vang A rope used to support a gaff or sprit (see also **Boom vang**).

W

Wake course The course actually travelled by a vessel.

Warp A rope used to secure or move a vessel; to move a vessel by hauling it with ropes.

Weather The area upwind (to windward) of a boat or other object (see also **Lee**).

Weather side The upwind (windward) side of a boat or other object (see also **Lee side**).

Weather tide A tide running against the wind (see also **Lee tide**).

Weigh anchor To lift the anchor off the bottom.

Whipping Binding the end of a rope to stop it fraying.

Whisker pole A pole used as a boom for the jib when sailing goosewinged (see also **Goosewinged**)

Winch A hand-operated or powered machine for hauling in sheets or halyards.

Wind rode A moored or anchored boat is said to be wind rode when it has swung round so that its bows are facing into the wind (see also **Tide rode**).

Windward Upwind; toward the weather side; the direction from which the wind is blowing (see also **Leeward**).

Y

Yard A spar suspended from a mast to spread a sail.

Yaw The sideways motion of a boat's bows as it plunges through waves (see also **Pitch**).

Yawl A two-masted vessel, rigged fore-and-aft, with a large main mast and a small mizzen (rear) mast stepped just aft of the rudderpost.

SAILING ORGANIZATIONS

BOATLINE
British Marine Industries Federation
Boating Industry House
Vale Road
Oatlands Park
Weybridge
Surrey KT13 9NS
(BOATLINE is a free information service on all aspects of
sailing. Telephone 0932 845890.)

Cruising Association
Ivory House
St Katharine's Dock
World Trade Centre
London E1 9AT

Dinghy Cruising Association
4 Medlars Mead
Hatfield Broadoak
Bishops Stortford
Herts CM22 7JB

Inland Waterways Association
114 Regents Park Road
London NW1 8UQ

International Yacht Racing Union
60 Knightsbridge
London SW1X 7JX

Royal Institute of Navigation
1 Kensington Gore
London SW7 2AT

Jubilee Sailing Trust Ltd
Test Road
Eastern Docks
Southampton
Hants SO1 1GG
(Provides sailing for able-bodied and disabled people aboard its
square-rigged barque *Lord Nelson*.)

Ocean Youth Club
The Bus Station
South Street
Gosport
Hants PO12 1EP
(Provides berths at sea, on eleven large sailing vessels, for
young people aged 12 to 24.)

Royal Ocean Racing Club
20 St James's Place
London SW1A 1NN

Royal Yachting Association
Victoria Way
Woking
Surrey GU21 1EQ

Sail Training Association
2A The Hard
Portsmouth
PO1 3PT

Yacht Charter Association Ltd
60 Silverdale
New Milton
Hants BH25 7DE

BIBLIOGRAPHY

Asher, Dr Harry *The Alternative Knot Book* (1989)

Bond, Bob *The Handbook of Sailing* (1980, repr 1987)

Bond, Bob and Sleight, Steve *Cruiser Handling* (1983)

Bond, Bob and Sleight, Steve *Dinghy Sailing* (1983, repr 1988)

Caig, John and Davison, Tim *Racing: A Beginner's Manual*
(1988)

Calder, Nigel *Repairs at Sea* (1989)

Childers, Erskine *The Riddle of the Sands* (1903, regularly
reprinted)

Cunliffe, Tom *Celestial Navigation* (1989)

Denk, Roland *The Complete Sailing Guide* (1983)

Howard-Williams, Jeremy *Canvas Work* (1989)

Johnson, Peter *The* Yachting World *Encyclopedia of Yachting*
(1989)

Macmillan & Silk Cut Nautical Almanac (published annually)

Mason, Charles (ed) *The Best of* Sail Trim (1989)

Mellor, John *The Sailing Cruiser Manual* (1989)

Merry, Barbara *The Splicing Handbook* (1989)

Myatt, John *The Shorebased Sailor* (1988)

Nicolson, Ian and Nicolson, Richard *Race Winner!* (1989)

O'Connell, Geoffrey *The Boatbuilding Book* (1989)

O'Connell, Geoffrey *The Boat Owner's Maintenance Book*
(1989)

Pelly, David *Faster, Faster!* (1984)

Pelly, David *The Illustrated Encyclopedia of World Sailing*
(1989)

Pera, M *Yacht Racing Rules 1989–1992* (1989)

Reed's Nautical Almanac (published annually)

Sanderson, Ray *Meteorology at Sea*

Sanderson, Ray *Weather for Sailing* (1986)

Snyder, Paul and Snyder, Arthur *Handling Ropes and Lines
Afloat* (1989)

Streiffert, Bo and Johnston, Turlough (eds) *Glassfibre Boat
Manual* (1989)

Ward, Douglas *Berlitz Complete Handbook to Cruising* (1989)

Houseby, Trevor, Oglesby, Arthur and Wilson, John *The
Complete Book of Fishing* (1987)

INDEX

Page numbers in bold type (eg **134**) indicate main entries, and those in italics (eg *74*) indicate photographs or diagrams.

CREDITS

AUTHORS:
Bob Bond
Jonathan Clark
Brian Grant
Adrian Morgan
David Pelly

EDITORIAL:
US Consultant Editor
Madelyn Larsen
UK Consultant Editor Bob
Bond
Editor Ian Wood
Art Director Steve Leaning

ARTISTS:
Boats section Tony Gibbons
Technical artwork Rod
Sutterby, Tony Garrett, Ian
Heard, SB Design

PHOTOGRAPHY:
Studio photography Theo
Bergström
*Additional equipment
photography* Mike Millman

Location photography Mike
Millman, Bill Jenner, John
Darling, Theo Bergström
Additional photography
Jonathan Eastland of Ajax
News and Features Service;
Colin Jarman of Eyeline
Photos; Roger Lean-Vercoe
of Yachting Photographics;
Pickthall Picture Library

ACKNOWLEDGEMENTS

*Our special thanks to the
following for supplying
materials and providing
assistance:*

Simon of
Captain O M Watts Ltd
45 Albemarle Street
Piccadilly
London W1X 4BJ

*The Secretary and Members
of*
Grafham Water Sailing Club
Perry
Huntingdon

Navico Ltd
Star Lane
Margate
Kent CT9 4NB

Ian Proctor Metal Masts Ltd
Duncan Road
Swanwick
Southampton
Hampshire SO3 7ZQ

International Paint
Yacht Division
24–30 Canute Road
Southampton
Hampshire SO9 3AS

North Sails (UK) Ltd
Newgate Lane
Fareham
Hampshire PO14 1BP

Volvo Penta UK Ltd
Otterspool Way
Watford
Hertfordshire WD2 8HW

Retreat Boatyard
Topsham
Devon

DETAILED CREDITS

Page 6: *photo* Lean-Vercoe
8: *photo* Jarman
10–11: *illustration* Garrett
12: *photos* Eastland (top), North
Sails/Michael Richelson (bottom
left), Jenner (bottom right)
13: *illustrations* Garrett
14: *photo* Lean-Vercoe
15: *photos* Bergström (top left),
Proctor Masts (bottom left),
Darling (top right), Millman
(middle and bottom right)
16–17: *photo* Bergström, *supplier*
Captain O M Watts Ltd
18–19: *photo* Bergström, *supplier*
Captain O M Watts Ltd
20–21: *photo* Bergström, *supplier*
Captain O M Watts Ltd, *insert
photo* Millman, *illustration* SB
Design
22–23: *photos* Millman
24: *photo* Bergström, *supplier*
Captain O M Watts Ltd
25: *photos* Millman except
bottom left Navico Ltd
26–27: *photos* Millman except
middle left Navico Ltd
28: *photo* Navico Ltd
29: *photos* Millman (top left),
Darling (top centre), Navico Ltd
(top right and centre), Millman
(bottom left and right)
30–31: *photos* Millman
32–33: *photos* Millman
34: *photos* Millman
35: *photos* Volva Penta (top),
Millman (bottom)
36–37: *main photo* Bergström,
supplier Captain O M Watts Ltd,
insert photo Millman
38–39: *photos* Bergström,

supplier Captain O M Watts Ltd
40: *photo* Lean-Vercoe
42–43: *photos* Millman,
illustrations Sutterby
44: *photo* Bergström, *illustration*
SB Design
45: *illustration* Garrett
46: *photo* Eastland, *illustration*
Heard
48–49: *photo* Millman
50–51: *photo* Eastland

52: *photo* Jenner
54: *photos* Jenner
55: *photos* Millman (top), Lean-
Vercoe (bottom)
56: *photos* Millman (top), Jenner
(bottom)
57: *photo* Darling, *illustration*
Garrett

58–97: *all illustrations* Tony
Gibbons

98: *photos* Lean-Vercoe
100–101: *photo* Darling,
illustrations Sutterby
102–103: *photo* Eastland,
illustrations Heard
104–105: *photos* Bergström
106: *photo* Bergström
106–107: *illustrations* Sutterby
107: *photo* Millman
108–109: *photo* Millman,
illustrations Sutterby
110–111: *photo* Jarman,
illustrations Garrett
112: *photo* Bergström,
illustrations Garrett
113: *photo* Darling

114: *photo* Lean-Vercoe,
illustrations Heard
115: *photo* Bergström
116–117: *photo* Bergström,
illustrations Heard
118: *photo* Millman
118–119: *illustrations* Heard
119: *photo* Jarman
120: *photo* Eastland
120–121: *illustrations* Heard
121: *photo* Lean-Vercoe
122–123: photo Jarman,
illustrations Heard
124–125: *photo* Pickthall Picture
Library, *illustrations* Heard
126–127: *photos* Lean-Vercoe
(top), Bergström (bottom),
illustrations Sutterby
128: *photos* Darling (top, bottom
left), Millman (bottom right)
129: *illustration* Garrett
130: *photos* Darling
131: *photos* Lean Vercoe (top),
Pickthall Picture Library
(bottom)
132: *photos* Millman (top),
Darling (bottom)
133: *photos* Darling, *illustration*
Sutterby
134–135: *photos* Millman,
illustrations Sutterby
136–137: *photos* Millman,
illustrations Sutterby
138–139: *photos* Lean-Vercoe,
illustrations Heard
140: *photo* Eastland
141: *photo* Pickthall Picture
Library, *illustrations* Heard (left),
SB Design (right)
142: *photo* Jarman
143: *photos* Millman, *illustrations*
SB Design
144: *photos* Eastland (top),

Millman (bottom)
145: *photos* Darling
146: *illustrations* SB Design
147: *photos* Navico Ltd (top),
Bergström (bottom)
148–149: *photo* Darling,
illustrations SB Design
150–151: *illustrations* Sutterby
152–153: *illustrations* Sutterby

154: *photo* Jarman
156–157: *photos* Jarman
158–159: *photo* Jarman
160–161: *photos* Lean-Vercoe
(top; bottom 160), Jenner
(bottom left 161), Millman
(bottom right 161)
162–163: *photos* Lean-Vercoe
(top), Eastland (bottom)
164: *photo* Eastland
165: *photo* Lean-Vercoe
166: *photo* Eastland
167: *photo* Jarman
168: *photos* Eastland
169: *photos* Lean-vercoe (top),
Eastland (bottom)
170: *photo* Lean-Vercoe
170–171: *photo* Jarman
172–173: *photos* Eastland (top),
Lean-Vercoe bottom)
174: *photos* Lean-Vercoe (top),
Eastland (bottom)
175: *photo* Lean-Vercoe
176–177: *photos* Lean-Vercoe
178–179: *photos* Jarman
180: *photos* Jarman
181: *photo* Eastland

182: *illustrations* Sutterby (top),
SB Design (bottom)
183: *photo* Lean-Vercoe
184–185: *illustrations* Sutterby,
SB Design (top 185)